History of Salem County
New Jersey

BEING THE STORY OF JOHN FENWICK'S COLONY,
THE OLDEST ENGLISH SPEAKING SETTLEMENT
ON THE DELAWARE RIVER

Joseph S. Sickler

HERITAGE BOOKS
2009

HERITAGE BOOKS
AN IMPRINT OF HERITAGE BOOKS, INC.

Books, CDs, and more—Worldwide

For our listing of thousands of titles see our website
at
www.HeritageBooks.com

A Facsimile Reprint
Published 2009 by
HERITAGE BOOKS, INC.
Publishing Division
100 Railroad Ave. #104
Westminster, Maryland 21157

Originally published 1937

— Publisher's Notice —
In reprints such as this, it is often not possible to remove blemishes from the original. We feel the contents of this book warrant its reissue despite these blemishes and hope you will agree and read it with pleasure.

International Standard Book Numbers
Paperbound: 978-1-58549-476-7
Clothbound: 978-0-7884-8154-3

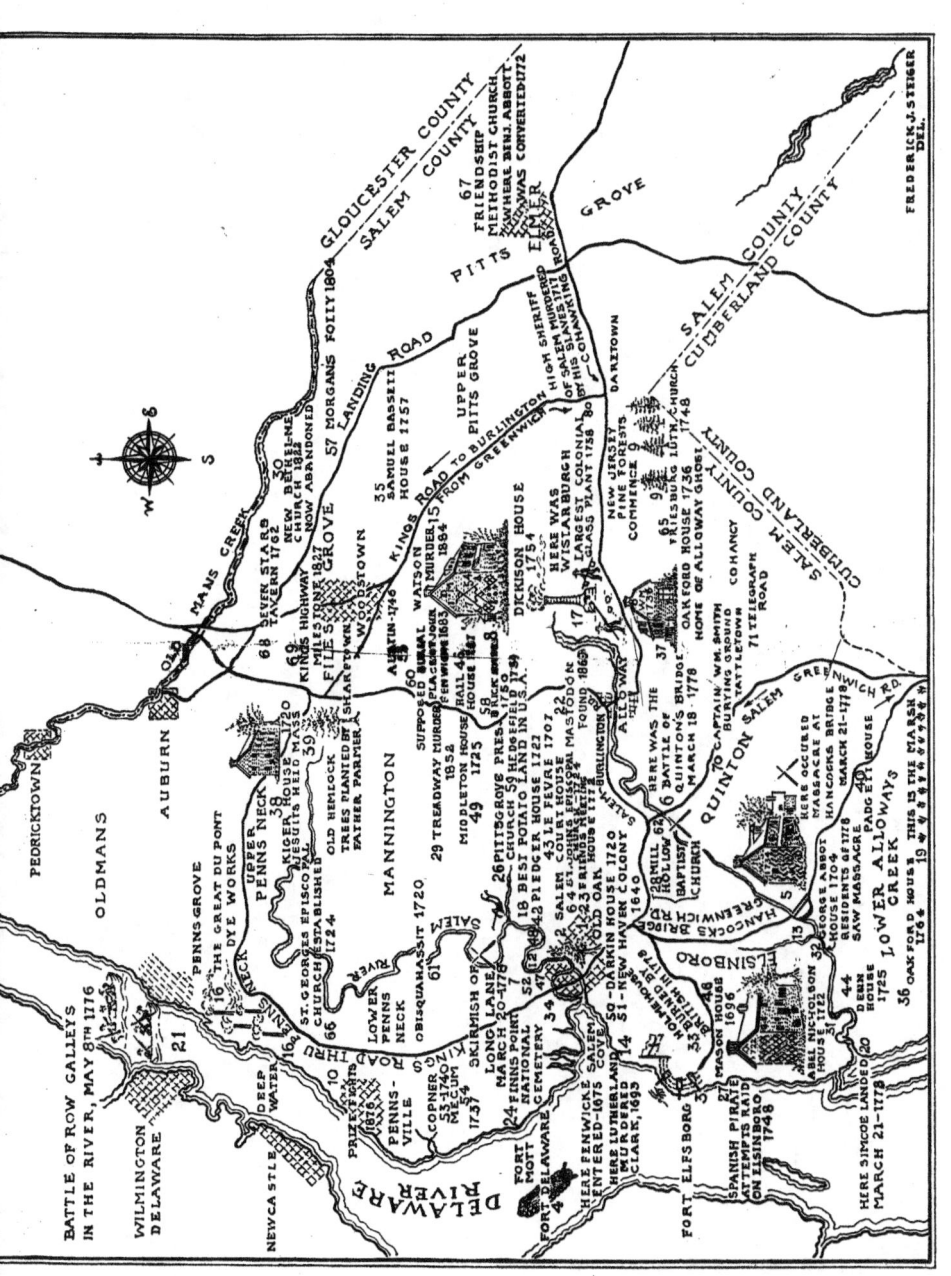

Dedication

This book is affectionately dedicated by the author to the memory of his mother, Ruth Sheppard Sickler, and his cousin, Ellen Bradway Smith, M. D., two women who did their part toward making Salem what it is; to whom the author owes his inspiration and who are now "part of the planet 'till the planet ends."

CONTENTS

CHAPTER		PAGE
I	Indians, A Mastodon and an Old Oak Tree	1
II	The Dutch, The Swedes, The New Haven Colony, The Knights of New Albion and How They All Led to the British Conquest of the Hudson and the Delaware	7
III	Constructive Trusts, Mortgages and the Arrival of Major John Fenwick in Salem	17
IV	The First Settlers and Fenwick's Troubles in Salem	25
V	Of Fenwick's Forced Appearance Before Sir Edmond Andross, Governor of New York and New Jersey, and of Fenwick's Many Troubles	33
VI	The Last Days of Fenwick	43
VII	The Years Between Death of Fenwick and the Dawn of a New Century	52
VIII	The Story of the Organization of the Earliest Religious Societies in Fenwick's Colony	65
IX	An Early Politician, and of the Murder of the High Sheriff of Salem County	71
X	Of Many Things Which Happened in the First Fifty Years of the Eighteenth Century	80
XI	Casper Wistar's Glass Works at Wistarburg	92
XII	The New Religious Congregations Up to 1800	101
XIII	Benjamin Abbott Whose History was the Story of the Methodist Church in Salem County	115
XIV	Of Divers Happenings Between 1750 and the War of the Revolution	122
XV	The Revolution and How It Came to Salem County	138
XVI	The American Defense of the Alloways Creek	146
XVII	The Massacre at Hancock's Bridge	154
XVIII	Events After the Massacre, The British Withdrawal from Salem County, the Long Court, and the End of the Revolution	164
XIX	From the Close of the Revolution to 1820	177
XX	The 1820's	198
XXI	The 1830's	215
XXII	The 1840's	229
XXIII	The 1850's	257
XXIV	Salem in the Civil War and the 1860's	273
XXV	The 1870's	301
XXVI	The 1880's	323
XXVII	The 1890's	338
XXVIII	Salem County Since the Turn of the Century	352
INDEX		377

PROLOGUE

The setting determines the drama. Geography predetermines the course of history. So it was with Salem. Unobtrusively located on an inland river flowing into the Delaware River from the east it became a source of empire chiefly for its own peoples. Its geography determined that it would be a port of local prominence but never become a great metropolis. Lying as it does, it missed the great flow of the nation's commerce and travel. Both geography and history combined to keep it still quiet; out of the way of the great press of American affairs.

Its very slowness in development brought one immeasurable gain to those of us who love and appreciate history today. The gain was this: Here, quietly sequestered, Salem has kept in its old houses and its old traditions the full memory of the past. True by this position and by these causes and effects, the business of the county was retarded until the World War put a new impetus upon the lower Delaware River Valley. But, the mementoes of posterity have been worth the preserving and the historian is grateful for the fact that the magic touch of progress did not change Salem too rapidly.

The setting determined the drama. The geographical location of Salem determined that the people of this community should be in some degree dependent upon themselves for their existence and the future of their children. It is also true that in the 300 years of our existence almost every conceivable event known to man has happened within the confines of this county. Situated where the roads end, it has nevertheless played a dominent part from within itself, in the great drama of American history.

ACKNOWLEDGMENTS

It has been no easy task to write the history of a people and a county which covers the space of three hundred years and yet the task of recording, even briefly, this narration has been one of utmost pleasure to me. In it I have tried to show the social life, the economic changes and the causes and effects which have motivated this community. Besides the many references I have studied and abstracted, there have been a number of devoted people to whom I gratefully acknowledge my indebtedness.

George C. Bowen, business manager of the *Salem Sunbeam* and Thomas H. Bowen, editor, receive from me heartfelt thanks, not only for their invaluable aid in preparing this book for publication but also my gratitude for having been the instrumentality by which these historical effusions have seen the light. Likewise I wish to thank Louis E. Ballenger of the *Salem Sunbeam* staff for his loyal help in editing the manuscript.

Not all the information contained herein came from printed authorities. In fact, despite the seemingly large bibliography, the authorities are decidedly sketchy. In order to obtain the best results it was necessary to interview a large number of people. To Frank H. Stewart, of Woodbury, whose library and services were ever available, the writer is greatly indebted. Encouragement is always a feature of the life of a "budding" historian and Mr. Stewart by words and deeds has well furnished that necessary ingredient. In the same category, I am grateful for help from the late Charles S. Boyer, the late William J. Casper and the late George Ward Price. To these men who have passed on, I render my homage.

I also pay my respects to the memory of the two men who have preceeded me in this work and whose contributions to Salem County History are so monumental that they can not be adequately acknowledged. It is needless to say I refer to Colonel Robert Gibbon Johnson and Thomas Shourds. The last named, the writer is proud to say, was his great, great uncle.

Others to whom I cheerfully and gratefully acknowledge help of a historical nature are Mrs. M. A. Pettit, Mrs. Mary R. C. Clayton, William S. Calcott, George Abbott, George J. Miller, Lewis T. Stevens, Charles Sheppard and William H. Harris.

Lastly, I am under obligations to a number of devoted persons who have helped in one way or another in the details of typing and arranging this volume. They are Mrs. Elizabeth Treen Mullen, Mrs. Charlotte C. Harris, Mrs. Catharine I. Hagood, Mrs. Ann List, Miss Hannah Whitesell, Miss Matilda Flitcraft, Mrs. Dorothy G. Cummings, Mrs. Emma Seibert and, with a final bow, my wife.

JOSEPH S. SICKLER.

Salem, New Jersey, November 1, 1937.

CHAPTER I

OF INDIANS, MASTODONS AND AN OLD OAK TREE

The history of the Indians of Southern Jersey, like most of its history, has been neglected. In this instance however, it may have been because the Indians of this locality, in the days of their possession, attracted little attention. Unlike Massachusetts Bay, Colony and Central New York, there were no Indian wars within the borders of Fenwick's Colony. It is quite to the honor of the Swedes, the Dutch and the English that, as far as this colony was concerned, the Indians were fully paid for their lands. How much "fully" means, depends on the point of view. The Indian probably had no conception of the permanent possession of the land implied in the white man's deed but supposed he was selling the right to hunt, fish and camp in accordance with his own customs. But at any rate, there are many certificates, signed with the marks of Indian chiefs acknowledging full payment for their lands. In exchange for their lands the Indians received hard liquor, combs, scissors, pipes and knives, shoes, looking glasses, beads, balls, etc. They also, in some cases, received a few guns, coats, a few handfuls of gunpowder and some bars of lead.

Despite this, within twenty-five years after the English occupation the red man was well elbowed out of Salem county, Dating this from Fenwick's occupation in 1675, by 1710 at the latest, except for a few Indian servants in the homes of the early colonists, the great bulk of the red men had started on their northern and western trek.

Instances of these servants are as follows: John Smith of Amwellbury, Salem county, whose estate was inventoried in 1716, owned an Indian slave; Thomas Hill of Salem advertised for a runaway Indian who had smallpox, in 1721, and Joseph Brown of Salem county, who died in 1711 had an Indian boy whom he valued at forty pounds.

The Indian tribes which occupied Salem county were known as the Lenni Lenape. These Indians extended as far north as the Delaware Water Gap. The sub-division of the Lenapes which held dominion over this particular territory were known as the Unalachtigo. Other Indian tribal names in this territory were the Kagkikani-Sakins, the Narraticons, the Siconeeses and others.

They have left behind them two sets of historical reminders. The first, a large number of Indian relics, tomahawks, arrowheads, etc., which have been found in practically every part of this county, the second a number of names of localities deriving their title from Indian names. A few of these are now in everyday use.

Two Salem County townships, Alloway and Mannington, are named after the chiefs who occupied those localities when the white man arrived, Chiefs Alloway and Manito. Alloways or Aloes seems to have been kindly disposed towards the colonists and is said to have furnished grain and supplies to the famine-stricken settlers in one of the first winters. Both Alloway and Mannington creeks, considerable water courses in the county, have the same derivatives, while Nicomus Creek near Woodstown, crossed by State highway route 45, is named after another chief, one who signed the second purchase deed to Fenwick. Other water courses with Indian names in the bounds of Fenwick's Colony are the Conahockink, now the Cohansey; the Manimuska, the Mackinippuck and the Menantico. These last mentioned are all in Cumberland county. Other Indian names, unfortunately now in little or no use, are the very melodious Obisquahassit, for the territory that is now Lower Penns Neck and Wootsessingsing for Elsinboro. Salem creek was once the Assamhocking, Oldmans the Forcus, and Salem also the Mosacksa. This last name as late as fifty years ago was adopted by a Salem baseball team.

* * * *

A second survivor of prehistoric times is a mastodon, a genus of elephant now extinct, which was found by workmen in a marl pit at Swedes Bridge, Mannington township, on the farm of Joseph Hackett in August, 1869. The discovery of this monster at a day when biological evolution was being warmly discussed, caused a great sensation among the scientists of this country.

The head of the mastodon was five feet long and weighed 400 pounds. The under jaw, detached from the upper, weighed 120 pounds. The monster had eye sockets of seven-inch diameter and a cavity of five-inch diameter where a tusk is supposed to have been. The rest of the body was in fragments, but several complete parts were located. A bone, believed to be a rib, measured four feet in length. Several other large bones, unclassified, measured anywhere from 14 to 15 feet.

Cook, the state geologist, came to Salem and identified the creature as a "mastodon gigantious," tentatively placing its period as the Pleistocene Age or that of a time period four to forty million years ago. There were some reports that Dr. Joseph Leidy, world famous Philadelphia scientist and head of the Museum of National Sciences, was coming to see the mastodon also. But the newspapers do not report either his visit or his opinion.

Mr. Hackett exhibited his discovery at the Fair or agricultural exhibit held at Salem a few days later. From here the mastodon was taken to the museum of Rutgers University at New Brunswick.

As far as is known this was the first discovery in either West or South Jersey of a mastodon. The discovery was of a great importance to scientists and geologists of the state. It decidedly aided geologists in determining the age of this section of the state and in proving the great antiquity of the Atlantic coastal plain.

* * * *

With reverence we speak of the third and living survivor of early Salem county, the "venerable oak," the estimated age of which runs up and over five hundred years. Some authorities maintain the age is four hundred years, but it is indeed a moot question. The dead of two hundred and fifty years are buried beneath it while tradition says the Indians used it as a burying ground before the white man came. A great part of its silent history is wrapped in the forgotten stretches of the years. It saw the white men come and the Indians leave and it is said that under its branches the bargain between the Indians and the English was consummated.

On the less romantic side, its statistics are as follows: its height, seventy-three feet; its trunk, thirty feet, five inches at the widest part; and its coverage ten thousand square feet or .23 of an acre. Its name is the Quercus Alba or white oak and it is one of the few survivors of its species in Eastern North America.

Its venerability, its age and its history is epitomized beautifully by one of Salem's local sons, the late Jacob M. Lippincott:

Venerable Oak! thou grand, majestic tree!
Thou sole survivor of the primal woods,
Whose arches echo'd the wild revelry,
Or through whose deep, unbroken solitudes
Tumultuous rang the din of Indian feuds;
Or settler's axe, with loud resounding stroke;
Whose sturdy arms dispersed the savage broods;
Thy comrades fell'd, the virgin fallow broke,
And founded Salem Town, where stood the groves of oak.
May thy green branches wave! thy heart of oak
Through long decades endure as firm as now;
Or blight or tempest shock or lightning stroke
Shiver thy trunk, or blast a single bough
Forever branded be the caitiff's brow.
Palsied his arm who smites thee with a blow,
Or injury or insult will allow,
Till through thy veins the sap shall cease to flow.
And slow decay and death have laid thy honors low.

A small boy sat in the auditorium of the Salem High School and listened with rapt attention to a gentleman who was telling his audience that the stirring events which had occurred here almost three hundred years before had caused his Majesty Charles II, King of England, to send his warships across the ocean to strike forever from the valleys of the Delaware and Hudson the flag of the Dutch Republic, his chief competitor in the quest for colonial empire.

It was a fascinating story the speaker told his auditors that March day a good many years ago. It conjured up to the boyish imagination a swiftly-moving spectacle of three nations fighting for supremacy in the marshes of Elsinboro, for the control of a river that meant life or death to their plans; of midnight marches from New Amsterdam through the gloomy pine forests, of fights and alarms and fugitives; of cannonades with musket blunderbusses: of political machinations before Cromwell; of the same intrigues before Charles II; and at last, the appearance of the red-coated fleet in New Amsterdam harbor and the submission of the intrepid peg-legged Dutch governor of the town.

The speaker above referred to was one Edward C. Van Helfenstein, of Philadelphia, who spoke under the auspices of the Salem Historical Society. His actual address has been mislaid and to notes furnished by Mrs. M. Augusta Pettit, the writer, who still remembers this thrilling talk, is indebted. Mr. Helfenstein had made researches which took him not only to the state archives at Trenton but to Hartford and Albany as well. From Governor Winthrop's memoirs at Boston also comes data concerning the New Haven expedition. It is quite likely that in London may also be found some fragments of these necessary records.

It is a long step from the mosquito-infested point at Elfsborg on the Delaware river to the court of St. James where "old Rowley" decided upon the conquest that was to make this section English and not Dutch or Swedish. There was, however, in spite of the loss of records and the haze of tradition, some direct connection between the early attempts to colonize Salem, thirty-five years before Fenwick, and the final intervention of the English fleet in 1664\ There is no doubt whatever that the colonists who did try to settle here moved heaven and earth, to influence the court to intercede and rout the Dutch so that the English might have a free hand in their colonization of the Delaware.

In recounting the history of the pre-Fenwick settlements the writer will depart somewhat from the Helfenstein notes and give as fully as possible what has been found of these early attempts at colonization and show some cause for the intervention of England twenty years later. It will be shown that this locality was far more important in motivating the powers across the water than historians, mostly from New England, have acknowledged. Elsinboro Point deserves renown in our national history for this was the focal point which controlled the Delaware. Here the Swedes, the Dutch and the English fought for supremacy. Three nations and two factions of one nation contested in a prolonged struggle on this marshy shore of the Delaware. Eventually, all three were to lose to a combination of the descendants of them all. Symbolically, the American flag floating over the battery at Fort Mott, is the survivor of that struggle on the opposite marsh nearly three hundred years ago.

CHAPTER II

OF THE DUTCH, THE SWEDES, THE NEW HAVEN COLONY AND THE KNIGHTS OF NEW ALBION AND HOW THEY ALL LED TO THE BRITISH CONQUEST OF THE HUDSON AND THE DELAWARE

It is no part of this history to recount in minute detail the various grants emanating from their respective royal highnesses of England which confuse and perplex the historian and which cover a period of over a hundred years. But for the purpose of local history, one early charter was tremendously important and that was the one granted by Charles I to Lord Edmund Ployden on July 24th, 1634. With truly royal disregard of his patent to Lord Baltimore only a month previous, Charles I merrily granted to Ployden and his associated Knights of New Albion a great piece of land, running from Long Island to Cape May and from there inland the same distance which partially overlapped the realm of the Marylanders. It of course took in William Penn's land of Pennsylvania but that was of little moment then. Ployden and his followers were good royalists. Even in 1634 he probably foresaw the storm which a few years later engulfed England in a civil war. It is exceedingly strange that Ployden has not received more attention historically than he has, because this attempt to form a royal colony in the wilds of West Jersey has many picturesque and political aspects. It must be remembered also that the Knights of New Albion penetrated the forests about the same time as the New Haven colonists. They were the other British faction in the struggle for the supremacy of the Delaware to which a previous reference has been made.

In addition to the royalist impulse Lord Edmund had grandiloquent ideas of government and of the spread of salvation among the savages which infested his land. He spent no less than eight years in preparing on paper his county palatinate which was to be, in the wilds of the New Jersey forests, a principality of no mean parts. It is this feature of quasi royal imagination which has been totally disregarded by Salem historians. I say, quasi royal, because Ployden was an earl and his domain created as a palatinate, and one of his agents was named Plantagenet and as such deemed himself to be a blood brother of England's earlier line of kings. For eight years, laboring in the comfort of "cosy" castles and living on the fat of the land that was England, Ployden and his Knights drew up a gigantic framework of government, which three hundred years later makes one wonder what place this would have been had the paper principality come to pass.

The capital of this new political state was the manor house of Watcessit, fairly determined as being in Elsinboro, Salem county, which Lord Edmund, by careful study of his maps had determined to be central and which "plenteous lands" he had reserved as his own and also had made it the shire town of his principality. Lord Edmund was the "big shot," speaking in the jargon of today. Below him were deputy governors, a secretary of state, a supreme council, a court of chancery, sheriffs, clerks, courts and so on.

It was a lot of fun making high-sounding names to impress the savages over whom the Knights would rule and Edmund was no "piker" in the matter of titles. Just listen to this one: "Edmund by Divine Providence, Lord Proprietor, Earl Palatine, Governour, and Captain General of the Province of New Albion."

Tradition has it that Lord Edmund was the proud papa of seventeen children and the eldest of these, Barbara, he created Baroness of Richneck which adjoined Watcessit and was a broad land twenty-four miles long, so that Elsinboro might have contained the manor house but could have hardly extended for fifty miles, in modern geography. The proximity of these lands to Varchens Kill or Salem creek is about the only thing which certifies the Salem location. Lady Barbara being taken care of, the other sixteen were also made baronets and great ladies but where their domains were, history has failed to tell us.

But the titles of which Lord Edmund was so fond took another turn and in the name of the enterprise we may read the story of the proselyting zeal which made Lord Edmund yearn for the spiritual wants of the poor savages who inhabited his land. This was "The Albion Knights for the Conversion of the Twenty-three Kings." Some one might stop and ask why try to convert kings when the proposed scheme of Knightly enterprise embraces only earls and knights. The answer was easy. The twenty-three kings were Indians who were spread from Long Island to Cape May throughout New Albion and these twenty-three kings were to feel the missionary zeal of Lord Edmund until they should, like the Knights, become fervent Christian citizens. If the Indians failed to appreciate his missionary endeavors there was always another way. That was the ever trusty sword, which through the ages, had been of so much use to the respective Christian Crusaders. Heraldry was called in to aid in this matter. The decoration of the order showed a medal on a riband and on the medal an open book, the Word. A hand grasped a dagger and in a surrounding circle was a crowd of Indians, supposedly the twenty-three kings, all of whom had their heads cut off, except one, the inference being that one king had accepted Salvation.

But the Indian kings lived on, blissfully ignorant of the medal, the riband and the plans for their conversion in the mind of Lord Edmund. Perhaps they fell victims to some other enlightening force, but the Knights of New Albion were never destined to do much converting in the wilds of Salem and Gloucester counties.

It is necessary to jump from the paper schemes of the Knights back to reality and see just what had happened on the shore of the river in what is now known as Elsinboro. This account cannot be even a partial one of all that went on in the Delaware river valley for it is concerned only with what happened to the Salem side of the Delaware.

The Dutch had built Fort Nassau near what is now Gloucester in 1623. The English had also been on the river and in 1635 some Virginians "captured" the empty and abandoned Fort Nassau, only to be gobbled up by the Dutch governor and sent home to England. In 1638 the Swedes made their first attempt at colonization and settled at the mouth of Christiana creek, close to the modern Wilmington.

It is important to realize that from the 1630's on, the eyes of three nations and of two factions of one nation were on the fertile valley of the Delaware. The royalist Knights of New Albion have already been discussed. The other faction was the Puritans, the forerunners of the Roundheads in the English Civil War, then starting. They came from England to New Haven and thence to Varchens Kill. Here was the first English settlement within the bounds of Salem county. No stone or marker commemorates the efforts of the New Haven colonists in their ill-starred adventure but by all rights of historical remembrance there should be one. Neither has their story been told in Salem except for the Von Helfenstein lecture and a few scattered fragments. Johnson is quite silent on this earliest of all Salem settlements, thirty-five years before John Fenwick.

In 1641, when William Kieff was the Dutch governor of New Amsterdam, (and one year before the "man mountain," Johann Printz of the Swedes made his appearance in the Delaware valley,) a ship bearing fifty families from England who had stopped at New Haven, Connecticut, appeared at New Amsterdam (New York) and apprised the Dutch governor of their errand.

Previous to the New Haven boatload, one Captain Nathaniel Turner with a force of men had penetrated the forests and had emerged at Varchens Kill to prospect the land for the expected settlers. They had purchased land from the Indians, unmindful that it had been sold to the Dutch and that Charles I had given it away to Lord Edmund Ployden. The company of New Haven colonists sailed in a boat belonging to one Lamberton and commanded by Robert Coggesall. As before mentioned, they apprised the Dutch governor Kieff at New Amsterdam of their errand. In a statement now extant, Kieff issued a testy and lofty warning not to settle upon land belonging to the Dutch West India Company nor at the mouth of "our rivers, sealed with our blood," unless the settlers would swear allegiance to the lord general and the Dutch West India Company. If they failed to do that, the good governor would, like a modern railroad regarding its pass holders, accept no liability. Coggesall told the governor that it was not his company's intention to settle upon land of the West India Company but if they did, they would swear allegiance to the Dutch government.

The New Havenists came on to Varchens Kill, now Salem creek, sometimes known as Assemhocking, as was the country around it, and somewhere, in all probability, Elsinboro, erected a blockhouse, trading post and small homes for the shelter of the colonists. There were supposed to be about fifty families in the New Haven colony whose intentions were to plant the lands, engage in trade and establish churches in "gospel order and purity." Very little remains of their history, no relics at all of their settlement and only by inference can their subsequent actions be gleaned. The main thing is that here only twenty years after Plymouth Rock, was the first English settlement on the Delaware and the first known settlement in Salem county.

It was destined to a short existence as shall soon be seen. The least of their trouble was the swearing of allegiance to the nations who claimed the river. It has been shown that they promised the Dutch they would be their citizens if they settled on Dutch territory. In the absence of certain geographic boundaries the colonists were probably ignorant of the actual bounds of the Dutch domain. If they were not, they probably figured they were too far from New Amsterdam to be bothered anyhow. But sometime between 1640 and 1643, the dates are very hard to ascertain, the Swedes at Wilmington came across the river and forced the English at Varchen's Kill to swear allegiance to them. As to the matter of swearing allegiance (which was about all the English did, except die of pleurisy) there appeared one more plaintiff.

This was none other than the high and mighty Lord Edmund Ployden, Earl Palatine, Captain General and missionary de luxe, who after eight years of "roll-top desk work" had heard, far off in merry England, that this band of dissenting ingrates had actually possessed the temerity to settle upon his land at Watcessit. By this intelligence the mighty lord was moved to action. Shipping via Virginia, the earl of Watcessit, Elsinboro, and the second Oak, etc., landed with full panoply of glory at Varchen's Kill and demanded of the English, "how come?" He had with him not only his own righteous indignation at the affront handed him by these outlaws, but also a royal letter from Charles I, who in seven years would issue no more royal letters but would be conducted to execution by a squad of cavalry including one Major John Fenwick. This letter declared that Lord Edmund was the "big boss" by royal grant and that Coggeshall, Turner etc., were royal and public enemies. This was in 1642 and it is more than a shame that no artist or writer has preserved this picture or account of the Earl Palatine landing in all his glory on the mosquito-infested shore of Elsinboro and demanding another show of allegiance from the much-harassed English at that place.

Nothing daunted, the English swore allegiance again, for swearing allegiance was easier than not, to every earl, Dutch governor and Swedish overlord who asked for it. Perhaps the mosquitoes chased Lord Edmund. Possibly Virginia or England looked far better to him because he seems to have left immediately after the ceremony and returned to Virginia. And although he never appears at Salem again we are far from being done with Lord Edmund.

The English, fighting the insects and pleurisy, remained at Varchen's Kill, but not for long. In either 1642 or 1643, the eagle eye of the Dutch commandant at Fort Nassau fastened on them and reported to Governor Kieff at New York that here was trouble and that the English had after all settled upon lands belonging to their lords of mightiness the West India Company. Kieff wasted no time nor did he bother about allegiance swearing. He sent two ships to the Delaware with the order to clean out the English and this his henchmen did with neatness and dispatch. The Dutch swooped down upon the unsuspecting English and although no blood seems to have been shed, they burned the blockhouse and the trading post and evicted the English without allowing them a "just inventory of their goods." What really happened is lost in conjecture. Accounts declare that their numbers were depleted by an attack of pleurisy. From still conflicting stories it is quite possible that the remainder of the colony returned to New Haven because in 1643 we find one of the original leaders, Coggesall, at his home in New Haven, Connecticut.

It has often been believed that some isolated families of the English New Haven Colony stayed on their small farms in the Salem county section. Shourds in the History of Fenwick's Colony states that one Robert or Roger Windham remained on his Tillbury farm in Elsinboro and was there when Fenwick landed. Shourds also gives Windham's family tree, setting out that his daughter married an early settler of Fenwick's colony named Richard Darkin. The majority of the Salem historians say that this is another of Shourds' mistakes and that Windham was only the name of a landing in Elsinboro and not a family name; and that no trace at all of the colony remained in the county.

With Lord Edmund back in England and the New Havenists gone from the scene, a new figure sweeps majestically across the stage to blaze his hour of glory and then like the rest be gone. This was John Printz, the new royal governor of Sweden. He arrived on the river in 1643, took up his quarters near the modern Wilmington and, during his ten-year administration, controlled the river in the name of Sweden. Printz was "a fine figure of a man weighing four hundred pounds" but was never exhibited in a side show. In all seriousness he was an empire builder of no mean proportions and it was he who played a new pawn in the game of conquest by building a fort whose name should be written large upon American history books and whose erection was to cause the advancement of the Swedish interests to no mean extent. This was Helsingborough, known to every Salemite today as Fort Elfsborg. The reason for its construction was this. Near Gloucester the Dutch had Fort Nassau, at the mouth of the Christiana the Swedes had the fort of the same name but the Delaware river was wide there and there were no means to exclude the ships of the Dutch.

So Printz, exercising splendid judgment, constructed Fort Elfsborg on the point of that name, facing the river, and mounted it with sufficient ordnance so that every ship, Dutch or English, was forced to strike its colors before ascending the river. It was a master piece of strategy because by one fell stroke it gave the Swedes the command of the river and allowed them to say who could and who could not ascend the stream to trade or colonize.

Like every other historical fact of importance which is far back in the shadow of the years, the story of Fort Elfsborg is subject to dispute. There are three great points of variance in the stories. The first of these is the date. Johnson and Smith both (probably the first copied from the second) declared that the fort was built in 1631. This is without foundation and can be easily overthrown. The Swedes did not come to the river until 1638 nor did any one else erect a fort there until 1643 when Printz built Elfsborg. The English might have had a blockhouse there in 1640 but, like most of the New Haven history, it is a matter of conjecture. Sufficient to say it was not like Printz's fort in any detail. The positive proof of the fact that it was at least twelve years after 1631 when the Swedes built the fort comes from a report of the doings of Governor Printz in the archives of Colonial History of the state of New York as follows:

"What regards the garrisons of the Swedes on the South River of New Netherland is as follows: At the entrance of this river three leagues up from its mouth, on the east shore, is a fort named Elsenborough, usually garrisoned by twelve men and one lieutenant, 4 guns, iron and brass of 12 pounds, iron balls, 1 mortar (potshooft.) The fort is an earthwork and was ordered to be erected there by the aforesaid John Printz, shortly after his arrival in the river. (This arrival is definitely determined as February 15th, 1643.) By means of this fort, the above mentioned Printz, holds the river locked for himself, so that all vessels, no matter to whom they belong, or whence they come, are compelled to anchor there."

The second point of contention is the location. Quite a few local historians have argued that the fort was placed on the Salem creek side of Elsinboro point and not on the river side. Just where it was has not been determined. But in view of the fact that the Swedes meant to hold the river and that cannon of that day were not long-range affairs, it is contrary to good reason to presume any location except somewhere between Mill creek and Elsinboro point.

The third point deals with one of the most delightful legends of Salem history—a legend comparable with Rip Van Winkle or the Headless Horseman of Sleepy Hollow—the story of the Swedes and the mosquitoes at Elsinboro. Frank Stockton, in his stories of New Jersey, and Washington Irving, in his Diedrich Knickerbocker history of New York, have left the story of more legend than fact regarding the mosquito invasion of the Swedes at Elsinboro. I do not wish to say that it is legend that there are mosquitoes at Fort Elfsborg. A commission *de lunatico inquieriendo* would be held for any one who said so, for there is certainly no reason to believe that there were less mosquitoes in 1643 than there are in 1937. It is quite probable that the distinquished ancestors of the same mosquitoes which playfully bit the populace of Salem early and often last summer tormented the Swedes in 1643.

The legend which contradicts the fact is that Stockton alleges that the Swedes, having built the fort in the fall, were routed in the summer by the invincible insect which resisted all counter attacks. Knickerbocker pictures Printz as "moving in a cloud, with mosquito music in his ears and mosquito stings to the very end of his nose" and how the mosquitoes "absolutely drove him out of the country."

But the Swedes did not surrender to the mosquitoes as Stockton tells in his delightful tradition, nor did they pursue Printz out of the country. Printz never stayed there but the Swedes did, bites or no bites, for what must have been ten summers of torture, until approximately 1652. Then, by the force of other circumstances, Printz was caused to abandon the fort. The Swedes have a name for the fort they built and in which they suffered. It was "Myggenborg" or "gnat fort".

The descriptions of the fort vary. The best account comes from DeVries, a Dutch explorer and colonizer who had planted an ill-fated colony near Lewes, Delaware, in 1630. DeVries returned in October, 1643, and after being stopped by the Swedish artillery, went up the river to call on Printz. He said in his memoirs that "it was an earthwork fort, laid after the English plan and was unfinished. There were lying there six or eight pieces, twelve pounders."

After Fort Elfsborg was evacuated by the Swedes in 1652, or thereabouts, it was allowed to fall into decay as testified by several eye witnesses who touched there or voyaged up the river.

In September 1655, it figures again in the news; this time as the rallying place of the one-legged Dutch governor, Peter Stuyvesant, of New Amsterdam. Stuyvesant landed there with his Dutch army to prepare for the attacks on Fort Casimir, New Castle, and Fort Christiana, Wilmington, in his drive to force the Swedish flag from the Delaware. He had sailed with his fleet around Cape May from New Amsterdam and on the night of August 30th, 1655, anchored off Fort Elfsborg. In the morning he brought his army ashore for rest and organization.

Stuyvesant, determined to clean out the Swedes, thus held his dress parade before battle on Salem county soil and prepared for the struggle he believed was ahead of him with the forts up the river. He reviewed the martial array on Elsinboro point and divided his force of about three hundred men into five companies. The plan of attack had included surprise but the Swedes undoubtedly saw them at Elsinboro from New Castle. So the Dutch, having the evening on their hands and perhaps thinking they would frighten the mosquitoes away, "volleyed and thundered" their cannon all night.

An early historian, Ferris, states in his history of the affair that when Stuyvesant landed at Fort Elfsborg, he found some persons in or near the fort and made them his prisoners. Unfortunately, Ferris does not state whether they were English or

Swedes but by inference it might easily be believed that they were remnants of the English New Haven colony cleaned out by the Dutch under Keiff in 1643.

Although the adventures of Stuyvesant on the west bank of the Delaware do not concern this history, it is necessary to add that the Dutch subdued the Swedes at New Castle, Wilmington and Tinicum and that from then until 1664 the flag of Holland waved in triumph over the river.

* * * *

While the Swedes held undisputed sway of the river and before Stuyvesant descended upon them in 1655, we must return to our old friend, Edmund, Lord Ployden, who after receiving the allegiance of the New Havenists at Varchens Kill, had returned disgusted to England. I say disgusted because, after leaving Elsinboro, his crew mutinied and marooned him on a Maryland island from whence he was finally rescued. Ployden now carried on the warfare with the English, Dutch and Swedish intruders with his favorite weapon: paper.

About 1648, there was published in England a book entitled, "A description of the Province of New Albion and a direction for adventurers with small means to get two for one and good land freely." It was as "classy" a piece of real estate writing as was ever issued. The promoters of the next Florida boom might take lessons from it. It was the first real estate prospectus ever issued covering this area.

It told, glowingly, how any adventurer could get five thousand acres if he settled fifty men upon it. Or if he desired, he could settle one man. It set forth that "Lord Ployden hath a pattern of the same" and that the Swedes are planted there and have a great trade of furs. The full account of the New Albion land boom, printed in Smith's history of New Jersey, is well worth reading, clearly indicating that the gentlemen who wrote the thirty-eight-page pamphlet were no mean dispensers of the King's English.

The pamphlet is important in that it presents a fair picture of the Indian tribes and, allowing for exaggeration, of the natural wealth of the present state of New Jersey. It was written by Beauchamp Plantagenet, who claimed the royal blood of England and who was Ployden's chief lieutenant in the New Albion enterprise. Some authorities claim that Plantagenet came to New Jersy and lived among the Indians for seven years but the exact movements of both him and Ployden are lost in the maze of language in the book and in the uncertainty of antique narration.

The bargain sale of properties seems to have gone unheeded in England, except that in 1650 Ployden granted a pass to several families to go to New Albion. But there is no record of their sailing. Ployden is frequently represented as saying that some time he would go to the river and deal with Governor Printz and the Swedes for their haughty action towards him. But, like everything else, nothing seems to have been done about it. In short the best thing Ployden did was to protest and these oft-repeated protests against the Swedes and the Dutch laid the earliest framework of the eventual decision of Charles II to drive out the Dutch.

Nor was Ployden's the only voice of protest. England had passed, by 1651, into a republic and Cromwell's friends among the "roundheads" undoubtedly included the friends and relatives of the New Haven "Puritan" colony who also had something to complain about. That the New Havenists made protest against the treatment they received from the Dutch seems highly probable because their own party was in power. Men do not forget the indignity of being dispossessed from lands they believe they have rightfully purchased. The New Haven protest certainly received more attention than the royalist faction under Ployden. In fact, during this period, Ployden died, it is alleged, in a debtor's prison.

Cromwell however, disliked trouble with the Dutch. He had inherited a war with the Dutch but because he viewed Holland as one of the staunchest of Protestant powers, refused to make any more trouble for them over the contentions of American colonization.

England drifted on from a republic to a restored monarchy under Charles II while Elsinboro remained peacefully under no one's heel, but the mosquitoes'. The Dutch had not bothered to refortify it, although they held undisputed sway of the Delaware.

The new line-up under the Stuarts took up with a vengeance the restoration of England's policy towards the New Netherlands and the valley of the Delaware. Ployden was dead but some of his stockholders still lived and saw in the Stuarts their chances to recover their land. The New Havenists, puritans as they were, were yet subjects of Charles II and it cost him nothing to listen to their grievances of twenty years' standing.

Charles' brother, James, the Duke of York, was openly adverse to Holland. There were personal reasons and there was also the vast amount of trade including that in slaves that James saw was going to the pesky Dutch in New Netherlands. Also James was an admiral. He had a fleet of ships and he wanted a fight. Moreover he had assembled around him several malcontents from America who could speak for themselves as well as the New Haven colonists and all other colonists whom the Dutch had mistreated. James saw a vast possession of rich lands coming to him as the heir presumptive of his brother, Charles. The pressure was kept up and in 1664 Nichols and Carr appeared at New York to demand the end of Dutch rule in America.

Every school boy knows of Stuyvesant's surrender. With that surrender came the end of Holland's domination of the Delaware and Salem, Assamhocking, Varchens Kill, call it what you like, passed under the English flag with the stage set for British settlement eleven years later. The Dutch came back however for one year from 1673 to 1674 when, by machinations of certain treaties, their provinces were restored, only to go back to England by another treaty the next year. It was in 1674, when the English regained the New Netherlands territory, that another man's plan for a colonization in the lower Delaware River valley started and came to full fruition with the settlement of New Salem in November, 1675. The man's name was John Fenwick.

CHAPTER III

OF CONSTRUCTIVE TRUSTS, MORTGAGES AND HOW MAJOR JOHN FENWICK
CAME TO SALEM

It was a pleasant day, that twenty-third of November, 1675, when the good ship *Griffin* cast anchor opposite the old Swede's fort at the mouth of Salem river. Likewise, it was pleasant weather the following day when the ship ascended the river about three miles and came to final anchorage. The weather was not only pleasant but the point of land near which they were moored was, in their language, "pleasantly located." Determining upon this spot as the final destination John Fenwick, late major in Cromwell's cavalry and the commanding spirit of the little expedition, gave orders to disembark. This was the beginning of the settlement of Salem, the first permanent English speaking settlement on the Delaware river.

Thirty-five years before Fenwick landed, the New Haven Colony and the Knights of New Albion had both attempted to settle upon the banks of the Assamhocking or Salem river. The Dutch and the Swedes likewise had colonized this same location. But ten years before the *Griffin* sailed into Salem river, history had decided that Great Britian was to rule the Delaware valley and that the colonial enterprises of Sweden and Holland were at an end.

Fenwick and his band of colonists were pawns in England's great rush for colonial empire. They were to decide that the laws, the manners and the customs of the English-speaking race would be established in this part of the world.

But in order to understand the background of who John Fenwick was and why he came, it is necessary to recall the history of England at that time.

It must be remembered that Charles II, restored to the throne of his fathers in 1660, had conveyed to John Lord Berkley and Sir George Cartaret a tract of land in America that is now New Jersey. Both of these gentlemen were royal favorites of Charles II and to them His Majesty clung tenaciously in spite of the patent fact that both were guilty of bribery and corruption. But a little thing like bribery and corruption and abuse of office meant little to Charles II or to his brother the Duke of York, who actually conveyed the land. Berkley and Carteret had both been friends of the House of Stuart and they were to be remunerated in one way or another.

Nine years after this grant John, Lord Berkley, Baron of Stratton, Lord Lieutenant of Ireland, Ambassador to France, and faithful henchman of Charles II, conveyed to Major John Fenwick his undivided moiety of New Jersey for the sum of one thousand pounds and an annual royalty of forty beaver skins.

On the surface, this transaction looked like a general warranty deed with all indications of good faith. But it was not. Edward Byllynge, a brewer of London, whose financial affairs had become involved to such an extent that he had seen the interior of New Gate prison for a time, to avoid the payments of his debts had procured the deed to be made to John Fenwick for the purpose of defrauding creditors. After many suspicions and recriminations, Byllynge faded into oblivion, and although he was to become a thorn in the side of John Fenwick, he was not destined to become the Lord Proprietor of Salem.

Fenwick, who now becomes the chief figure in this rapidly-moving picture of land deals, trusts, and mortgages was born in the year 1618 in England. He was a member of a prominent noble family of Great Britain. Some authorities state that at the age of eighteen he received the title of Knight and Baronet. His father was Sir William Fenwick, Baronet, who sat in Parliament for the county of Northumberland in 1659. This was the last Parliament under the Commonwealth. John was one of four brothers, Edward, John, Roger and Ralph. Whether Edward pre-deceased his father and whether John became the Baronet on the death of Sir William is an undecided question. Suffice it to say that he never used the title in America. Fenwick studied law at Grey's Inn, London, in 1640, but whether he ever became a practicing lawyer is also debatable, albeit in the last ten years of his life he had ample need for lawyers to escort him from the maze of legal intricacies in which he became involved.

With the coming of England's civil war Fenwick, like his father, took the side of Parliament and became an active soldier under Cromwell. He was commissioned as major at Carlisle by Cromwell in October, 1648. At the close of the war, and after the trial and conviction of Charles I, Fenwick was detailed as a commander of horse to guard the streets of London on January 30, 1649, date of the beheading of the monarch.

The order is well worth repeating here: "These are therefore to will and require you to see the said sentence executed in the open streets before Whitehall, upon the morrow, being the thirtieth of this instant month of January, between the hours of ten in the morning and five in the afternoon of the same day, with full effect. And these are to require all officers and soldiers and others the good people of this nation of England to be assisting unto you in this service." The order is signed by the judges who condemned Charles I to death.

Fenwick's religious views are worth some attention here because it is likely that his association with the Society of Friends led him into contact with Edward Byllynge and furnished one of the motivating causes in leading a band of Quakers to the new world. It appears in a document in the possession of the New Jersey Historical Society that, in 1649, Fenwick belonged to a sect known as the Independent Congregation. Subsequently he withdrew from the Independent Congregation, better known as the "Fifth Monarchy Men", and joined the Society of Friends. Records do not reveal how and when Fenwick joined this latter society but interest in his membership is heightened by the fact that the men he met and knew in its bonds were to occupy the stage with him as long as he lived. These men, Nicholas Lucas, Edward Byllynge, William Penn, Gawen Laurie, Edmund Warner and John Eldridge were to be uppermost in his mind and the target of his enmity early and often in the eight hectic years from 1675 to 1683. They were active principals in the two legal transactions which annoyed and harrassed Fenwick to the time of his death.

The first of these was the transaction which involved the original purchase from Lord Berkeley of West Jersey in 1673. As stated previously Edward Byllynge, involved in debt, obtained the conveyance to Fenwick with funds furnished by himself, largely for the purpose of defrauding creditors.

The quarrel involving the Quaker membership entirely, the dispute between Fenwick and the creditors of Byllynge was submitted to arbitration and a young Quaker, son of a British admiral, was selected as arbitrator. His name was William Penn.

The creditors of Byllynge claimed that he owed them fifteen hundred pounds and claimed that this amount was included in the funds given Fenwick by Byllynge to purchase West Jersey. This Fenwick denied, asserting that his deed should not be questioned and that he had an absolute title to all the territory conveyed.

Penn heard the testimony and decided in favor of Byllynge and his creditors, and against Fenwick. Byllynge had meanwhile admitted the truth of the charges, making it easier for Penn to decide.

The decision was that Fenwick did not own more than one-tenth of the whole of West Jersey, and that the other nine-tenths went to the hitherto defrauded creditors and to Byllynge. The nine-tenths it was decided should pay the creditors and Byllynge, accommodating the creditors and pursuant to the award, conveyed the rights of the remaining territory away from Fenwick to his new trustees, Penn, Nicolas Lucas and Gawen Laurie.

Fenwick was greatly annoyed when the award was made, and wrote his refusal of concurrence in the decision. He wrote to Penn, who although not a creditor of Byllynge, had been named as a grantee in the trust deed for the nine-tenths taken from Fenwick's domain.

His letter has not been preserved, but Penn replied:

"John Fenwick:—The present difference betwixt thee and Edward Billinge fills the hearts of Friends with grief, and with a resolution to take it, in two days, into their consideration to make a public denial of the person that offers violence to the award made, or that will not end it without bringing it upon the public stage. God, the righteous judge, will visit him that stands off. Edward Billinge will refer the matter to us again; if thou wilt do the like, send me word, and oppressed as I am with business I will find an afternoon tomorrow or next day to determine and so prevent the mischief that will certainly follow divulging it in Westminster Hall. Let me know by the bearer thy mind. O John! let truth and the honor of this day prevail. Woe to him that causeth offenses! I am an impartial man.
WILLIAM PENN."

But Major Fenwick, nothing daunted, replied to the umpire, reiterating that improper motives had prompted award and arbitrators alike and again refused to abide thereby.

It called for a second letter from Penn.

"John Fenwick:—I have upon serious consideration of the present difference (to end it with benefit to you both, and as much quiet as may be) thought my council's opinion very reasonable—indeed thy own desire to have the eight parts added was not so pleasant to the other party that it should now be shrunk from by thee as injurious—and when thou hast once thought a proposal reasonable and given power to another to fix it, 'tis not in thy power, nor indeed a discreet or civil thing, to alter or warp from it and call it a being forced. O John! I am sorry that a toy, a trifle, should thus rob men of their time, quiet and more profitable employ.

I have had a good conscience in what I have done in this affair, and if thou reposest confidence in me and believest me to be a good and just man, as thou hast said, thou shouldst not be upon such nicety and uncertainty. Away with vain fancies, I beseech thee, and fall closely to thy business. Thy days speed on, and make the best of what thou hast. Thy grandchildren may be in the other world before the land thou hast allotted will be employed. My council, I will answer for it, shall do thee all right and service in the affair that becomes him, who, I told thee at first, should draw it up as for myself. If this cannot scatter thy fears thou art unhappy, and I am sorry.

Thy friend,
WILLIAM PENN."

Fenwick wrote no more and at least tacitly accepted the award, but he never hesitated to reiterate his innocence of all claims that he cheated the creditors of Byllynge. To that end the last recorded act of his life, his will, contains in the preface the following clause—"I, John Fenwick, late of Binfield, in the County of Berks, within the kingdom of England, Esq., late absolute lord and chief proprietor, by law and survivorship, of the Province of New Caesarea, or New Jersey, and now of Fenwick Colony, who doth hereby, as I have in the hazarding of my life, appeal to the Almighty God, and do now appeal to Him who is my witness, that I never cheated any man nor went about to cheat, circumvent or defraud Edward Byllynge. But he, Gawen Laurie, and others his creditors, and others his factors hath most covetously and most un-x-tianly dealt with me as I have often declared, and particularly in my just claims and remounstrance. Whom I do freely forgive and heartily desire God, the searcher of all hearts, to make them sensible of it."

The deed to Penn, Laurie and Lucas on February 9, 1674, put an end to the trouble, at least temporarily. Fenwick still had a tenth of the original West Jersey, and there was still ample room to construct the little principality of which he had dreamed ever since he had become a land owner.

The whole hundred parts of West Jersey were divided into lots and at a meeting of the trustees held in London on Third month, seventh, 1675, not long before Fenwick sailed, he drew ten lots which were to be his division of the whole. The lots were numbered irregularly and there seems to have been no map among the trustees to determine the actual location of them.

But to all modern intents and purposes it is sufficient to say that Fenwick's ten lots embraced the east bank of the Delaware from Oldmans creek, which Fenwick named Berkeley river in honor of his grantor, down to or near the present West creek; in short, the present confines of Salem and Cumberland counties.

Fenwick began in earnest to fulfill his plans of colonial empire. He was not the first Englishman to engage in real estate development in this part of America. That honor belonged to the late Edmund, Lord Ployden, but whereas Ployden did most of his principality work on paper, Fenwick actually achieved his goal and left an English-speaking settlement behind him.

Fenwick, for all his action, also resorted to the printed word in addition to personal appeals to his friends for support. He published this paper, circulated not only among Friends, but the general public as well: "An Address. Friends:—These are to satisfy you or any other who are sober and are any wise minded to go along with me and plant within my colony, that we shall no doubt find but that New Caesarea, or New Jersey, which is the place which I did purchase, together with the government thereof, is a healthy, pleasant and plentiful country, according to the report of many honest Friends and others, who have been there, and the character given thereof, by John Ogilby, in his 'America', which I herewith send. The method I intend for the planting of all or so much thereof as I shall reserve to myself, my heirs and assigns forever" . . .

The paper continues:

"We shall conclude our Discourse of this Country with a notable character given thereof by a late writer, as to the great advantage of happy living in all respects, for whosoever shall be pleased to betake himself thither to live.

"If there be any terrestrial happiness (saith he) to be had by any People, especially if of any inferior rank, it must certainly be here. Here any one may furnish himself with Land, and live Rent-free, yea with such a quantity of Land, that he may weary himself with walking over his Fields of Corn, and all sorts of Grain, and let his Stock amount to some hundreds; he need not fear their want of Pasture in the Summer, or Fodder in the Winter, the Woods affording sufficient supply, where you have Grass, as high as a Man's knees, nay, as high as his waist, interlaced with Pea-vines and other Weeds that Cattel much delight in, as much as Man can pass through; and these Woods also every Mile and Half Mile are furnished with fresh Ponds, Brooks or Rivers, where all sorts of Cattel, during the heat of the day, do quench their thirst, and cool themselves. These Brooks and Rivers being inviron'd of each side with several sorts of Trees and Grape-Vines, Arbor-like interchanging places, and crossing these Rivers, do shade and shelter them from the scorching beams of the Sun. Such as by their utmost Labors can scarcely get a living, may here procure Inheritance of Lands and Possessions, stock themselves with all sorts of Cattel, enjoy the benefit of them whilst they live, and leave them to their Children when they die. Here you need not trouble the Shambles for Meat, nor Bakers and Brewers for Beer and Bread, nor run to a Linnen-Draper for a supply, every one making their own Linnen, and a great part of their Woollen Cloth for their ordinary wearing. And how prodigal (if I may say) hath Nature been to furnish this country with all sorts of Wild Beasts and Fowl, which every one hath an interest in, and May Hunt at his pleasure; where besides the pleasure in Hunting, he may furnish his House with excellent fat Venison, Turkies, Geese, Heath-hens, Cranes, Swans, Ducks, Pigeons and the like; and wearied with that, he may go a Fishing, where the Rivers are so furnish'd, that he may supply himself with Fish before he can leave off the Recreation. Here one may Travel by Land upon the same Continent hundreds of miles, and pass through Towns and Villages and never hear the least complaint for want, nor hear any ask him for a farthing. Here one may lodge in the Fields and Woods, travel from one end of the Country to another, with as much security as if he were lock'd within his own Chamber. And if one chance to meet with an 'Indian' Town, they shall give him the best Entertainment they have, and upon his desire direct him on his Way. But that which adds happiness to all the rest, is the healthfulness of the Place, where many People in twenty years time never know what Sickness is; where they look upon it as a great Mortality, if two or three die out of a Town in a years time. Besides the sweetness of the air, the Country itself sends forth such a fragrant smell, that it may be perceiv'd at sea before they can make the Land. No evil Fog or Vapor doth any sooner appear, but a North-West or Westerly Wind immediately dissolves it, and drives it away. Moreover, you shall scarce see a House but the South-Side is begirt with Hives of Bees, which increase after an incredible manner. So that if there be any terrestrial 'Canaan' 'tis surely here, where the Land floweth with Milk and Honey."

The book by Ogilby was a ponderous tome of 700 pages and, as seen above, a bit rosy in its description of the New World. The Friends in England, disturbed by the address and by its reference to Ogilby, issued a testimony warning the prospective buyer that it all was a scheme to sell the land rather than to benefit the purchaser. But it enhanced rather than hindered the plans of Fenwick for by giving notoriety to it, the American scheme attracted far more notice than it might have otherwise.

Now arises the second of the legal transactions which troubled Fenwick to the end of his days. In his anxiety to formulate plans for his new colony and worried by the first legal battle over his trusteeship with Byllynge and other matters, he had neglected to pay his bills. It seems from the schedule that he owed everybody in London; the linen draper, the attorneys, his wife's relatives, the "biskett maker," the "caik baker" and more.

Knowing he was planning to soon leave the country and realizing that if he did, it would probably mean an end of all chance for collection, his creditors—personal ones now, not those of Edward Byllynge—came down upon him in full force.

Imprisonment for debt was still very much in vogue in England in 1675, and incarceration in a debtors' prison would probably have meant a sad end to all his plans for an empire beyond the seas. But two Quakers, personal friends of Fenwick's—John Eldridge, a tanner, and Edmund Warner, a poultryman—appeared on the scene and not only advanced cash for his debts but additional funds which he badly needed to carry on his plans of emigration.

Messrs. Eldridge and Warner were the immediate means of freeing Fenwick from the shadow of the debtors' prison, but in the ensuing years they caused the worthy major of Cromwell's Cavalry plenty of trouble and much vexation of spirit. On July 17, 1675, just before Fenwick sailed, they took a deed in the nature of a mortgage for Fenwick's one-tenth part of New Jersey to secure the payment of one hundred and ten pounds, fifteen shillings, advanced by them to secure the discharge of Fenwick's debts. In this deed the grantee-mortgagees, Eldridge and Warner, had the right to sell and convey land in the ten parts; to account to the grantor-mortgagor for the purchase money and apply it to the satisfaction of the debt. They assumed the obligation of paying some of Fenwick's creditors named in the schedule, and were to account for monies received from the land sold and paid to persons so mentioned.

So, with the mortgage given and delivered, with his pressing debts paid and some ready money available, John Fenwick with his small party of adventurers set sail for the New World in a boat called the *Griffin* and commanded by a Captain Griffith.

In the summer of 1675, he left his wife, relatives and friends in a land he was never to see again and set his face resolutely toward the west and the new land of his promise which was to be his own principality.

But behind him in the rolls of the Chancery Office in London, he left an innocent-looking cylindrical document, classed upon the rolls as C-54-4433-27 Car. II Patent, 6-No. 28, the mortgage given by him to John Eldridge and Edmund Warner, which was later to be used to attack the validity of his legal and equitable rights in the Salem colony, take him twice a prisoner in irons to New York, embarrass and annoy him with his fellow adventurers and finally cause him to lose his gallantly assumed title of "Lord and Chief Proprietor of the Province of Nova Caesaria or New Jersey and Governor of Fenwick's Colony" and worry him into a premature grave.

CHAPTER IV

OF THE FIRST SETTLERS AND FENWICK'S TROUBLES IN SALEM

The passenger list of the *Mayflower* is celebrated in American history and a society has been formed to perpetuate the memory of those who immigrated upon this ship. Equally famous should be the passenger list of the *Griffin*, whose members colonized the first permanent English-speaking settlement in the Delaware valley.

The list is as follows:
Major John Fenwick and his three daughters Elizabeth, Anna and Priscilla; John Adams, husband of Elizabeth, and their three children, Elizabeth, Fenwick and Mary; Edward Chamneys, husband of Priscilla, and their two children, John and Mary; Fenwick's ten servants, Robert Turner, Gervas Bywater, William Wilkinson, Joseph Worth, Michael Eaton, Eleanor Geere, Ruth Geere, Zachariah Geere, Sarah Hutchens and Ann Parsons; the servants of Edward Chamneys, Mark Reeve, Edward Webb and Elizabeth Waites; Mary White, nurse, who later shared in Fenwick's will; Samuel Nicholson, his wife Ann, their children, Parobel, Elizabeth, Samuel, Joseph and Abel; John Smith, his wife Martha, their children Daniel, Samuel, David and Sarah; James Nevill, Edward, Robert and Samuel Wade; Richard Hancock; Samuel Hedge, who on arrival married Fenwick's daughter Anna; Isaac Smart, Richard Whitacar and William Malster.

There is much contention over the immigration of John Pledger and Hippolite Lefever, later large land owners of Salem county, who it is said came over in March of 1674, antedating Fenwick's arrival by a year and a half. Johnson, who is descended from Pledger, claims they did. Others dispute it. The mix-up is probably due to the uncertain manner, at that time, of recording the English calendar.

These were the pioneers, the first settlers of Salem. Their numbers were augmented in the next seven years by several boatloads of new emigrants.

The *Griffin* returned to England and arrived again at Salem with emigrants within the next year.

In November, 1677, arrived at Elsinborough the ship *Willing Mind*, Capt. John Newcomb, with emigrants.

On 12th of twelfth month, 1677, arrived the ship *Mary* with emigrants, commanded by Capt. John Wall. The *Mary* made a second voyage from Ireland, with emigrants, and landed them at Elsinborough the same year.

In 1677 arrived the ship *Kent*, Capt. Gregory, with emigrants, to Salem.

In 1677 arrived the ship *Success*, commander Stephen Nicholson, from Virginia, with emigrants, to Salem.

In 1679 arrived the ship *Success*, Nicholson, commander, with emigrants.

In 1679 arrived the ship *Willing Mind*, Capt. Newcomb, with emigrants.

In 9th month, 1681, arrived the ship *New Adventure*, commander John Dagger, with emigrants, to Elsinborough.

In 1681 arrived from London the ship *Henry and Ann*, with emigrants.

In November, 1682, arrived the ship *Pink*, commander John Dagger.

Among other passengers in this last ship was Mark Newby, celebrated in our histories as the first financier that New Jersey produced, and whose Assembly conferred upon him the high honor of issuing half pence, to be called Patrick's half pence.

On 8th month, 1685, arrived the ship *Dorothea*, with emigrants, commander Bridgeman.

In 1685 arrived the ship *Charles*, commander Edward Payne, with emigrants.

In 1686 arrived at New Castle the ship *Shield of Stockton*, in the 5th month. Many passengers came and settled near to Salem.

In 1705 many more emigrants arrived at Salem, but the name of the ship is unknown, the remaining leaves of the record being lost.

One of Fenwick's first acts seems to have been an immediate negotiation with the Indian chiefs of the territory for a purchase of their lands. In all there were three separate purchases, the first of which was of the land lying between Salem and Oldmans creeks, which the Indians called Mosacksa and Forcus. The chiefs who granted this land were named Tospaninkey and Henaminkey. The second purchase, which included an area between Salem creek and Cohansey creek, was bought from Chiefs Mahoppony, Necomis, Myhoppony, Shuccotery and Alloways. Alloways' creek was so named in honor of the latter. The third and last purchase extended from the Canahockink to the Wahatquenack, now the Cohansey creek and Maurice river. The grantors of this purchase were Mahawskey, Mohut, who styles himself king; Newsego, Chechenaham, Torucho and Shacanum.

In the aggregate the payment to the Indians for the land which now constitutes Salem and Cumberland counties was four guns, powder and lead; ten and one-half ankers of rum, equal to about 336 gallons; some shirts, shoes, and stockings; four blankets; sixteen match coats; one piece of match coating, and other English goods. Meagre as this sum seems, based on present-day value, it apparently was entirely satisfactory to the Indian grantors.

It is to the everlasting glory and credit of Fenwick that during these negotiations and in subsequent relations with the Indians, no trouble or warfare ever took place between red man and white in Fenwick's colony. It is a fact which has unfortunately received but little attention from historians who have traced relationships between the Indian and the white man.

* * * *

Fenwick exercised excellent judgment in laying out his town of Salem, which he called New Salem, denoting the peaceful aspect of the place. Leading from what is now the "Major's Wharf" away from the creek, in an easterly direction, he constructed a wide street, known to them as Wharf street, which later became West Broadway. In the approximate center of the town he constructed another street leading north to the other branch of Salem creek, which is known today as Fenwick creek. This second or cross street was known first as Bridge street. Later, because of the fact that markets for the sale of goods and produce were held upon it, it became Market street. For some reason the lord proprietor did not continue Market street beyond its intersection with Broadway, but made it a dead end in the center of the town. It was not until 1912 that the street was extended south of Broadway.

Fenwick also had in mind several other settlements, but his attention at first was focused on New Salem, the capital of his colony, and his proposed town of Cohanzick, the present Greenwich. He directed his surveyor general, Richard Noble, to lay off town lots in Salem and Cohanzick.

But the infant colony, which had been started so auspiciously, soon ran into the fogs of trouble. The earliest document extant published in Salem is dated the twenty-fifth day of the fourth month, 1676. It shows two things very clearly; the doubts which assailed the new settlers arising out of the mortgage to Eldridge and Warner left behind in England, and the community ideas for the settlement and laying out of their new capital town. Because of its great importance and the light it shed on subsequent events, it is reproduced here in full:

THE FIRST AND GENERAL ORDER, AS AGREED UPON BY FENWICK AND THE FIRST PURCHASERS.

We whose names are here subscribed, do first declare, as hereby is declared, that we have been exposed to great hazards, straits, dangers and cruelties whilst at sea. John Lord Berkeley's deed being declared to be left in England, was the cause of our troubles we met with there, and at our arrival, when our sorrows were multiplied, our miseries increased through cruelties and oppression; so that, as it appeared, John Eldridge and Edmund Warner labored to send us away with the shadow, whilst they detained from us the substance, that should every where preserve us and our interest from ruin, even the ruin under which we hitherto groaned, and like to be ruined, having received no relief from England, neither can we hear when to expect any; but wholly left as a people forsaken, even forsaken of them that pretended to take care of us; and many of those that embarked with us in the same undertaking did also desert us, and disperse themselves into other countries; so that now, if we can live, we may—if we cannot, we may die, for the care that has been and is taken by those men, as if their own interests were our destruction. But, blessed be the God of heaven and of earth, who hath showed us mercy, (to the amazement of our enemies here, and so it will be also to others in due time,) praised be his name forever, he hath also by his Spirit stirred in the hearts of many good people to pity us, and made them willing to come and join with us, sitting down together in this tract of land, which John Fenwick, the chief proprietor, purchased of the natives for his colony, and to satisfy every one of his purchasers by setting out their tracts of land therein accordingly. To the end, therefore, that the Lord's requirings may be answered, the desires of strangers satisfied, the said colony planted, we and our families preserved from ruin, every purchaser having his land set out, the natives neither provoked nor tempted, but all our lives preserved by setting out and planting the land as people come to take it up, and so sitting down together as in other countries—We, after many meetings and serious consultations, do unanimously agree and conclude upon the method following, which we, the chief purchasers of Fenwick's colony, and other the purchasers and freeholders residing within the same, do approve of and judge to be most just, reasonable and equal; and do therefore declare and order, that every purchaser that is resident shall forthwith have his tract of land set out—the one-half in the liberty of Cohanzick, the other in the liberty of Alloways, or as the chief proprietor shall order the same there or elsewhere; the said purchasers casting lots only, who shall begin and succeed till their tracts be surveyed and set out; and after their tracts of land are set forth and surveyed, then in order according to the lots as aforesaid, shall the tracts of which they are entrusted with be set out and surveyed also, as they come to sit down upon and improve the same, making it first appear to the chief proprietor and council that they really intend the same.

2d. That there shall be a neck or two of land set out for a town at Cohanzick, and divided into two parts—the one for the chief proprietor, the other to be set out in town lots for the purchasers, which lots are to be reckoned as part of their purchases. The chief proprietor is to settle upon the town, gratis, a common of marsh, and to dispose of his part for the encouraging of trade. That the said lots shall be sixteen acres a-piece, and that every purchaser shall take their lots in the town as they come to take them up and plant them.

And as for the settling of the town of New Salem, it is likewise ordered that the town be divided by a street; that the south-east side be for the purchasers, who are to take their lots of sixteen acres as they come to take them

THE FIRST SETTLERS

up and plant them, as they happen to join to the lots of the purchasers resident, who are to hold their present plantations, and all of them to be accounted as part of their purchases; and the other part, on the north and by east and by south, is to be disposed of by the chief proprietor for the encouragement of trade; he also giving for the good of the town in general, the field of marsh that lieth between the town and Goodchild's plantation;—and,

Lastly, we do leave all other things concerning the setting forth and surveying the said purchases, unto the chief proprietor, to order as he sees fit.

Signed accordingly, the twenty-fifth day of the Fourth month, 1676.

FENWICK.

EDWARD WADE, JOHN SMITH, RICHARD NOBLE, SAML. NICHOLSON, JOHN ADAMS, HYPOLITE LEFEVRE, EDWARD CHAMPNES, RICHARD WHITACAR, WILLIAM MALSTER, ROBERT WADE.

It is a moving document and the language of it pathetic; they say "John Eldridge and Edmund Warner laboured to send us away with the shadow whilst they detained from us the substance". And the settlers were right. The two mortgages had indeed deprived them of the substance. The time period for the mortgage was two years. It had not expired and would not for some time to come.

Stripped of its legal verbiage, the mortgage on record in London meant that Eldridge and Warner would pay the debts of Fenwick, take out the money for them, and make allowance and satisfaction for the surplus. They seemed to have done nothing about it except possibly to take out the money. They certainly never paid the debts. And they certainly never made allowance for the surplus. But they did, with a great deal of ability, spread the story throughout England and the new plantations of West Jersey that, since Fenwick was no longer the owner of the land, they had a right to dispose of the property; and that Fenwick could not give clear title to the lands he had sold both in London and upon his residence in West Jersey.

This doubt and suspicion cast upon the clarity of Fenwick's title permeated even to Salem and caused consternation in the hearts of those who had emigrated with him. They naturally thought that if Fenwick's original title had been bad and they had paid good money for their lands based upon his title, then their own sacrifices were of no avail and they could not pass clear title to their children or successors.

Instances of this flit through the first letters written back by Fenwick's colonists to their relatives in England. As early as fourth month, 1676, Robert Wade writes to London:

"For John Fenwick is now about to save the land for those that have purchased of him, now he sees that he cannot bring us to subscribe to him for his aim was altogether for his own exultation and not for the Publick good."

And Rodger Pedrick, founder of the modern Pedricktown, wrote in 1676 to friends in England:

"But John Fenwick would not set us out land except those that were concerned would set their hands to such papers as he drew up which would have been to ensnare us."

Martha Smith, writing to her brother Richard Craven in Limehouse, London, on the twenty-second of ninth month, 1676, says, "and dear brother, it would be the joy of my heart to see thee and thy wife and children here. I have more comfort in one day here than I had in many days in England which is great joy to my soul and I do desire if the Lord be pleased that we may end our days together, and you may believe me it is a brave country but the Lord Proprietor doeth not what our friends say he should."

Meanwhile, in England, William Penn, Nicholas Lucas and Gawen Laurie, the trustees for Byllynge, had joined forces with Eldridge and Warner and had made their first overt act against Fenwick's supremacy in West Jersey. In a most unusual document dated August, 1676, they empowered Richard Hartshorne, through James Wasse and Richard Guy, to deal with Fenwick. This document is also given in full because it shows how this coalition of trustees and mortgagees beyond the seas had combined to deprive Fenwick of his right to West Jersey. The salient portions of the document are:

1st. We desire you to get a meeting with John Fenwicke, and the people that went with him, but we would not have you tell your business until you get them together; then show and read the deed of partition with George Carteret; also the transactions between William Penn, Nicholas Lucas, Gawen Laurie, John Eldridge and Edmond Warner, and then read our letter to John Fenwicke and the rest, and show John Fenwicke he hath no power to sell any land there without the consent of John Eldridge and Edmond Warner.

2nd. Know of John Fenwicke, if he be willing peaceably to let the land he hath taken up of the natives be divided into one hundred parts, according to our and his agreement in England, as casting lots for the same—we being willing that those who being settled and have cultivated ground now with him, shall enjoy the same, without being turned out, altho' they fall into our lots: Always provided, that we be reimbursed the like value and quantity in goodness out of John Fenwicke's lots.

4th. They direct that they "lay out four or five thousand acres for a town," but if not, then let there "be two thousand acres, and let him divide it in a hundred parts; and when it is done, let John Fenwicke, if he please, be there; however, let him have notice; But, however, let some of you be there, to see the lots cast fairly by one person that is not concerned."

5th. If John Fenwicke, and those concerned with him, be willing to join with you in those things as above, which is just and fair, then he or any of them may go along with you in your business; and let them pay their proportion of what is paid to the natives, with other charges; And so he and they may dispose of their lots with consent of John Eldridge and Edmond Warner.

THE FIRST SETTLERS

6th. If John Fenwicke and his people refuse to let the land they have taken up of the natives to be divided, and refuse to join with you; you may let the country know in what capacity John Fenwicke stands, that he hath no power over the persons or estates of any man or woman more than any other person.

7th. What land you take of the natives, let it be taken, vis:—Ninety parts for the use of William Penn, Gawen Lawrie and Nicholas Lucas, and ten parts for John Eldridge and Edmond Warner.

12th. Then direct them to get a certain man, by name Augustine, but if he cannot be obtained, then "send for William Elliot, who had offered himself to Gawen Lawrie to be surveyor. He had a good character in Virginia, but was not able to keep it; he is a fair conditioned, sober man."

13th. If John Fenwicke be willing to go on jointly with you there, his surveyor may go along and help ours, and the charges shall be brought in for both proportionably on all. Mind this, and speak to Richard Guy or Richard Hartshorne, and leave orders with them to let William Elliot have provisions for himself till spring.

In studying this document it seems very difficult to reconcile the instructions given these commissioners without being decidedly suspicious of their motives. In the first section they were told to get Fenwick and his colonists together and tell them that they had no power to sell land without the permission of Eldridge and Warner. It was obvious to many of the colonists that Fenwick had a clear title to one-tenth of West Jersey; that the mortgage to which he had given his hand and seal was only for the purpose of paying a certain schedule of debts; that the mortgage had not been foreclosed; that Eldridge and Warner were selling lands in excess of the mortgage debt and that no accounting at all was given Fenwick.

In the fourth section of the instructions they even went so far as to lay out a town of their own, with or without the consent of Fenwick. If he wished to be present, it was all right with them. If not, it was all right also. But before these extraordinary messages reached America the town of New Salem had been surveyed and laid out, and the coalition's plan for a new government in this regard, at least, was frustrated.

The fifth section is even more bald in its orders. If Fenwick wanted to join them and pay the Indians it was satisfactory to these gentlemen across the seas; but still Warner and Eldridge must be consulted. The question arises, why all this interest on the part of the mortgagees if they were amply secured in the mortgage from Fenwick?

As the instructions progress, the coalition becomes more high-handed. If Fenwick and his people should refuse to comply with their instructions, the worthy gentlemen, Hartshorne, Wasse and Guy, would summon the whole influence of the country against him and deprive him of his authority. And if the commissioners should purchase any additional land from the

Indians in the whole area of West Jersey, ninety parts thereof were to be taken for the use of William Penn, Nicholas Lucas and Gawen Laurie and ten parts for John Eldridge and Edmond Warner. In other words, Fenwick's interest was voided.

To any new settlement, a surveyor was most important. Fenwick had truble with his own surveyors. Before his death he had three. The coalition in England ordered the commissioners to obtain a surveyor by the name of Augustine; they condescended to say that if John Fenwick "is willing", his surveyor may help their surveyor and the charges would be in proportion.

Fenwick had discharged Richard Noble and later Richard Hancock as surveyors because they combined with his enemies. It was not until he employed Richard Tindall that he found a man whom he could trust.

This document from Messrs Penn, Lucas, Laurie, Eldridge and Warner speaks for itself. In rebuttal thereof and in an attempt to show clearly that Fenwick's fellow Quakers in London were linked against him, the words of the first historian of Fenwick's colony, Col. Robt. Gibbon Johnson, are quoted:

I am inclined to believe those six Proprietors acted not with the caution, prudence and Christian spirit becoming meek, quiet and unoffending Quakers. I believe them all, as well as Fenwicke, to have been men possessing high and honorable feelings, but I cannot regard those instructions in any other light, than as evincing great envy and jealousy—and more especially censurable for the indirect and aggravated suspicion cast upon the character of Fenwicke for the want of honor and honesty.

On looking back, however, to the days when these Proprietors were on the stage of life, we shall find that they were, every one of them, speculators in these western lands, and that their sole object was to accumulate fortunes; and although they were all men of high character and distinction, yet it must be apparent to every observer that self-interest was at the bottom of all their schemes and manoeuvres; hence the scheme which had a tendency to deprive Fenwicke of his fair name, to alienate the confidence of his friends from him, and compel him to surrender his rights in the tract which he had purchased from Lord Berkley and the Indians, that they might derive the benefit of his Salem proprietary, to the great damage of himself, his relations, and friends. It illy became those Proprietors to give utterance and countenance to such disrespectful and uncharitable sentiments respecting one of their own faith and order; especially as two of their number were public friends or preachers. They appear to have forgotten to practice, what we may presume they frequently inculcated from their pulpits, the injunctions recorded in the scriptures—such as "to speak evil of no man;" "Speak not evil one of another, brethern; he that speaketh evil of a brother, speaketh out of the law, and judgeth the law."

CHAPTER V

OF FENWICK'S FORCED APPEARANCE BEFORE SIR EDMOND ANDROSS, GOVERNOR OF NEW YORK AND NEW JERSEY, AND OF HIS MANY TROUBLES

A new shadow and a new antagonist soon crossed Fenwick's path. This latest entrant into the field of his adversaries was Sir Edmond Andross, the royal governor of the provinces of New York and New Jersey. For a brief time, Fenwick's struggle with his fellow Quakers back in London were forgotten while this new antagonist proceeded to harass and annoy the Lord Proprietor of Salem as much and as often as the six Quakers across the seas.

Almost as soon as Fenwick had landed, the commander at New Castle had acquainted Andross in New York with the fact. The commander had received notice to keep strict watch over both banks of the Delaware river and, to report any happenings of moment at once to the governor.

The authorities at New Castle undoubtedly secured the services of a fleet-footed Indian, who took their message by land and water to Andross in New York. On the fifth of December, 1675, Andross received the message that an intruder claiming the rights of royal proprietorship, of court leets, court barons and the like had landed in his dominion.

Human envy and jealousy did the rest. In addition, a few instructions from the Duke of York materially aided the royal governor of New Jersey in issuing his demands. Andross received instructions that the title to the soil of New Jersey and particularly the right of government, which was claimed by the grant from the Duke of York to Berkeley and Carteret, under which Fenwick held proprietorship, was totally inoperative and void by the Dutch treaty of 1673-1674; that the second patent of King Charles to the Duke of York restored the original elements of title and government held by him in the first patent: that similar grants must come from His Royal Highness to make any rights good to the eastern shore of the Delaware River; that the government by Andross and his council administered from the city of New York was the only legitimate one within the boundaries given by his commission; that he should expect all persons living therein, including Major John Fenwick, to submit to the laws or suffer the penalty thereof.

Thus did a new thorn pierce Fenwick's side. Now he was concerned not only with a constructive trust and a faulty mortgage but also with a direct challenge to his authority as governor of the colony at Salem. It was now a question of who was to be "boss" and the struggle was plainly between Fenwick and Andross.

Soon after his arrival at New Salem, Fenwick had conducted a town meeting and an election, at which time he had been elected governor of Fenwick's Colony. Following is his oath:

"I, John Fenwick, one of the Lords or Chiefe Proprietor of the Province of New Cesaria or New Jersey in America being chosen by the Proprietors, purchasors and freeholders now Resident in Fenwick's Coloney within the said Province to be their Governor for this present year 1676 doe hereby Declare and promise That I will heartily endeavor to promoate the honour of Allmightie God in all my undertakings who is the King of Kings And hath shewed me that he requires of All men to doe Justly, Love mercy, and to walke humbly with their God. And accordingly I further declare and promise, that I will beare true allegence to the King of England his heires, and Successore. And in my place and Imploymt Shall by the power received from both faithfully endeavour to discharge the Trust Reposed in me by the people, not only in being faithful to their sevrall Interests, but alsoe endeavour the peace (&) wellfayre of them and the said Coloney by doeing equall Justice to them and all men according to my best skill and Judgment without corrupcon, favour, or affection. In witnes whereof I have here Unto subscribed my name this one and Twentyth day of the fourth Month comonly called June In the Yeare one thousand six hundred seaventie and Sixe.

FENWICKE.

One Samuel Leete was the complainant against Fenwick for the usurpation of His Majesty's authority in West Jersey. This presentment may still be seen in the archives of the state of New York at Albany. Governor Andross, anxious to test his power and to block the authority of this intruder who had the audacity to call himself governor, acted with promptness and dispatch. To Captain Edmond Cantwell, sheriff at New Castle, he issued this warrant:

Whereas I am credibly informed, That Major John Fenwick, now living at the East side of Delaware River doth pretend and give himselfe out to bee Proprietor of that side of the River and hath presumed to act accordingly, graunted Land extravagantly, dispossessed persons in those parts, sold their land, arrogating to himselfe a power of Judicature, and hath given out Lycences for distilling contrary to the order settled in the River; By which means hee hath inveigled some persons from other parts, and distracts the mindes of the Inhabitants, thorow out the whole River and Bay, not having any Lawfull Power or Authority. You are therefore without delay, to repaire over the River, to the said Major Fenwick, and all other places on that side, to informe yourself of the truth of the above Particulars, and to forewarn any such of the danger and premuniry they incurre; And if the said Major Fenwicke hath acted as alleged, That you summon him in his

Maties name to appeare without delay, to answer the same before mee and myselfe Councill in this place, in default at his utmost perill; and yo to make a due returne of this Warrant; and in case of any opposicon by doing yor duty, by going from place to place, on the said Accompt, All his Maties subjects are required to be Aiding and Assisting to you; for which this shall bee to you and every of them, a sufficient warrant;

Given under my hand and seale in New Yorke, this 25th day of Sept. Anno 1676.

E. ANDROSS

But Fenwick, who believed himself as much a governor as Andross, paid no attention to the summons. Neither threats, nor persuasions, nor veiled invitations from the commander at New Castle accomplished any results. Andross, fretting in New York over the gall of this intruder who paid no attention to him, finally issued a warrant on September 25, 1676, summoning John Fenwick to appear before him at New York. This time Captain John Collier, who had succeeded Captain Cantwell as commander at New Castle, wrote a polite letter to Fenwick informing him that Andross had issued orders and requesting him to come to the fort. Fenwick refused in polite but decided language. The worthy captain finally came to Salem with others and renewed his request in person. Fenwick bolted the doors of his residence and refused him admittance. He spoke to Collier through a small window at the end of the dwelling house and told him that he would have nothing to do with him. Collier returned empty handed to New Castle and communicated his failure to the justices of that place. Torn between a wish to be friendly with Fenwick on the one hand and a desire to avoid the censure of Andross on the other, they ordered one Lieutenant De Haes, two sheriffs and twelve soldiers to Salem, to seize Fenwick at any cost.

On the eighth of December, 1676, De Haes with his men proceeded to Salem and marched directly to Fenwick's residence at Ivy Point (determined now as near the foot of the present Ward street, Salem, facing Fenwick Creek) and demanded his surrender. Again Fenwick bolted the doors and refused to acknowledge service of the summons. The officers, spurred on by the fear of what their chiefs would say at New Castle, broke the door down, fired at him without injury, and finally captured him.

This was probably an exciting night in the infant Quaker community. The settlers saw their governor carried off in irons by strange soldiers. Many of them no doubt wondered what the end would be.

Fenwick was taken to New Castle that night, sent at once by sea to New York, where he arrived on December 16th. On January 5th, 1677, he was given a trial. Over that trial Governor Andross presided, the mayor and the alderman of New York City formed the court and Samuel Leete, the informer, made the charges. These charges said: "He hath with force and arms ryoteously and routeously, with other persons, taken possession of large tracts of land on the east side of the river, which same were within the bounds of His Royal Highness' patent, from his majesty. . . . . that he, with other persons, hath driven settlers away and torn down their houses; . . . . that he hath issued license to distill . . . ."

The jury was summoned and the trial proceeded. The King's Council offered the King's Patent to the Duke of York and the Duke of York's instructions to Governor Andross. The early studies of Fenwick at Gray's Inn, London, stood him in good stead now, for he pleaded his own case, making a long discourse in his own favor. He showed that his title was derived from the fountain of all British justice, the King himself, and under the English laws was good and sufficient for him and those who held under him. He was, however, much handicapped by the fact that he had left his deeds in England and it would take several months to obtain them. He had the courage to proclaim to the court that he denied the authority of Governor Andross under the second patent of the Duke of York over the territory of New Jersey and that the whole proceedings against him were contrary to law and precedent.

It is a shame that no historian bent on immortalizing great moments of American history has portrayed this picture of the one-time major in Cromwell's cavalry, who had the fortitude, the bravery and the audacity to beard Andross in his den. For bravery of a high order was needed here. He put himself on a par with the Royal Governor before whom he was being tried and refused to make any concessions whatever.

It was but natural that Andross, beholding this stubborn man before him who claimed to be of equal rank with him, should charge the jury both upon the law and facts and direct a verdict for the King, which the jury very quickly returned. After some private consultation of the court, the jury's verdict was approved and Fenwick was sentenced to pay a fine of forty pounds and costs; to give security of five hundred pounds for good behavior and a promise not to act in public capacity until this court should authorize him; and to remain in custody until all these requirements were satisfied. They were kind enough to grant him the right to appeal if he pledged to pay an additional five hundred pounds.

The defendant refused. He was still stubborn and determined that he would not yield his authority. Over his refusal the court was in a quandary. They had no means of collecting the fine and they had not as yet exacted a promise from him that he would stop exerting his authority in Fenwick's Colony. So until August of that year they kept him in the fort at New York, uncertain as to what disposition should be made of their contentious prisoner.

In August of 1677, however, while Fenwick was still a guest-prisoner at the fort at New York, the ship *Kent* arrived with more English Quaker colonists bound for West Jersey. They had with them copies of the King's Patent to the Duke of York, under which Fenwick claimed proprietorship, and all subsequent grants of New Jersey which would help Fenwick in his claim. Andross, seeing for the first time the defendant's claim in black and white, became obstinate. He clung to the second patent of the Duke of York, made after the English restoration of 1675, and to his instructions which, he argued, prevented him from recognizing the rights and authority of Fenwick.

After some controversy and probably with the thought that he might at last get rid of his competing governor, Andross released Fenwick on parole, to return to New York on the sixth of October of the same year. Probably in order to check Fenwick's authority, Andross named several of the new Quaker settlers enroute to West Jersey as his magistrates on the eastern bank of the Delaware.

This seemed for the time being the best way out. At least it was to Andross. Fenwick departed on the *Kent* with the colonists and arrived in Salem some days later. Thus far he had won his fight. Although he had been a prisoner in New York for several months, he had not paid the fine imposed upon him by the court, nor had he yielded one iota of his authority as Lord Proprietor and Governor of Fenwick's Colony.

Faithful to his parole he returned to New York on the sixth of October and was this time immediately told by Andross to return to Salem and "to go about his lawful occasions". His faithfulness in returning injured him with Andross not at all. It has been said that Andross was much surprised when this man appeared before him on the day and date set. It is probably true that Andross had a secret admiration for the courage and faith of this man who was true to his pledge. In addition, Andross had not received further instructions from England on this vexing case and he was probably very willing to leave the matter where it was for the present.

Fenwick returned to Salem once more. He was still the governor and he attended to his duties as such with much zeal and energy until April, 1678, when the storm clouds gathered over Fenwick and his colony once more. By this time the authorities at New Castle had reported to the governor at New

York that Fenwick was again exercising gubernatorial authority over the east bank of the Delaware. This grew out of an election held at Salem April 30, 1678. At that time there were present in Salem, Edmond Cantwell, Foppe Outhout, a Justice of the Peace; Michael Baron and Raynier Van Hirst, who took these depositions:

Edmond Cantwell declared in R: Salem (alias) Swamptowne, of Aprill 1678; where Major John Fenwicke ordered a meeting of ye east syde of This River, hee the sd Fenwicke did then apoint suitable officers vist Samuell Hedge Surveyor Generll, James Nevell to bee secretary, Samuell Winder Register, and declared that hee would nominate and appoint other officers att his Leasure and caused his sd Secretary to read severall papers, as his Magties Pattent to his Royll highnesse, and his Royll highnesse to ye Lord Berckley, and a Coppy (as he said) of ye Lord Berckleys, to him the sd Fenwicke wth severall other papers wch ye attestant did not minde, and after ye Reading of all these papers hee the sd Fenwicke, demanded in his magtis name the Suppreority and the submission of ye People there as his Right and propriety, after his demand he brought a Paper upon the Table in the forme of an oath or some such thing, wch severall of his People or officers sighned, after they had don, I tould him that the most parte of the People that was there, did not know what was read, hee answered mee that they could know well a noff to take away his Land, I alsoe tould him that there was a small Levy Laid by the Cort upon ye People on that syde he said ye Cort had no power to Lay no Levy on that syde & said whoe soever did pay any Levy should forfeit their Lands & priviledges. I asked him if hee would beare them out & hold them harmlesse. Hee said hee would give them his hand to answer itt before the ....and sayed that the People should stand on their owne defence if any boddy came to demand it, and alsoe did forbid Fop Outhout not to act any thing in behalfe of ye Cort of New Castle upon the forfeiture of his Estate. I told him yt his honor ye Governor had Commissionated him the sd Mr. Outhout, and was stiff pleased for to Continue him, hee said the Governor had nothing to doe on that Syde, and that hee meaning himselfe was Subject to no man but God and the King, hee alsoe said that hee would doe nor act nothing wth out the advyse of his Counsill wch hee would nominate verry suddenly, wth severall more Speeches wch ye attestant doth not now Remember. . . . Major John Fenwicke came to the house & demanded why ye deponant & ye rest yt were there did not come att New Salem as others did to acknowledge him (meaning himselfe to bee Lord & proprietor of ye place). Upon which they answered him saying how they could owne him, so Long as they paid Levy to will 12½ gilders pr head att New Castle Cort—Whereupon hee the sd Fenwicke Replyed saying that all those whoe paid ye same should never Injoy a foot of Land on the Eastern Shore, and further sayeth not.

Despite the fact that these statements led to Fenwick's arrest again and another trip to New York, it seems that at this election a pleasant time was had by all. The commander at New Castle, Cantwell, and his friends who sent these statements to Andross, seem to have been very friendly with Fenwick for all their rivalry. After the election was over a banquet was held, military uniforms mingled with plain Quaker garb, speeches were made and it seems that, for a time at least, ill feelings were banished.

The statement, however, went forward to New York and the authorities there again ordered Fenwick to desist from exercising authority. He was ordered to New York to answer the same set of charges as before. This time he said he would not go to New York alive, but the commanders at New Castle finally persuaded him to go on his own initiative to face the council in New York. Fenwick went by land, taking with him a retinue of guides and servants, no doubt to give strength to his position and to convince his rival governor of New York that he, too, had a following.

Andross had been in England. He returned a few days before the court convened on August 22nd, 1678. It was really the story of the first trial over again. At this time, however, it was charged that Fenwick had disregarded his parole and had harassed the settlers who did not recognize his title under the grant of Lord Berkeley. As in the first trial he was again convicted. He filed appeal with an intention to go to England and lay the case before the king, which was never done. Fenwick was again kept in custody in New York for some time but finally, seeing that nothing could be done with him, Andross again let him go home.

He returned to Salem and proceeded again to be governor in name and fact of his little colony. From New York, Andross again sought to cramp him. He named as commissioners William Penton, Richard Guy, James Nevell, Edward Bradway, William Malster and Edward Ward, and gave them authority to settle disputes over land with a concurrence of Foppe Outhout, who had been one of the signers against Fenwick in the statement sent to New York after the meeting of April 30, 1678. They were authorized to hold court at Elsinboro in or near the site of the old Swedish fort. From this court an appeal might be taken to the court at New Castle. One reason for this court, irrespective of Andross' desire to limit Fenwick's authority, was that some of the Dutch, Swedes and Finns had commenced suit against Fenwick in the court at New Castle over their lands. These individuals undoubtedly had remained over from the early colonial occupation of the Delaware by their respective nations.

Fenwick's answer to these people was that he had been obstructed in the settling of his colony, that he had suffered great loss by men who had tried to cheat him of his land and money, and that the chaotic conditions of his colony, which affected these people, was due solely to the acts of his enemies. But in order to give fair treatment to his protesting foreigners, and to hear their case again, he summoned "Fopp-hout-out, Michael Barrowne, Lucas Picturs, John Erickson, and all other the Dutch, Finns, Swedes, and all other foreigners who are inhabitants within my manor of East Fenwick, (now the township of Lower Penns Neck, Salem county) in my said colony; and in his majesty's name to charge and command them, and every of them, to come and appear before me, at my house near New Salem, upon Monday, by nine of the clock in the forenoon, being the 26th day of this instant, Fourth month, to the end that they may enter their several claims, and make known their several titles to the lands they plant, so that they may be settled according to the said concessions, so far as law and equity will warrant the same."

This appeal was successful, and the meeting ended in an agreement to pay a yearly quit-rent to the governor, which, though very small, recognized his right to convey the land and their title to it. These lists of quit-rents may be found in the New Jersey Archives, showing that their obligors paid these rents for some years after Fenwick's death.

* * * *

While Fenwick was spending his time answering warrants at New York and seeking to pacify the Dutch and the Swedes, who claimed he had not given them good titles, the coalition in England had not been idle. Eldridge himself came to North America, visiting Fenwick at Salem and demanding his money. Fenwick's answer was to punch Eldridge in the face and knock him down. Eldridge fled to New Castle after the brief pugilistic battle in which he came off second best. Fenwick sent after him with a posse of men and a warrant seeking his arrest. The authorities at New Castle, however, would not allow Eldridge to be arrested, knowing that if they sent him back to Salem it would go very hard with him. They shipped him off to England and advised him to stay away from Salem in general and Fenwick in particular. He did so and did not trouble Fenwick thereafter, although he made life miserable for Mrs. Fenwick in England.

Fenwick was married twice. His first wife was Elizabeth Covert, daughter of a Sussex knight, Sir Walter Covert. She was the mother of the three daughters who came with him to America. After her death he married Mary Burdett, a blood relation of his own. By this marriage there were no children. She did not come to America with him and he never saw here again after he left for his colony in the new world. She seems to have had little affection for him, but at least enough to help him in his times of trouble. Her letters, apparently published only in Johnson's *History of Salem*, shed a great deal of light upon Fenwick's tangled affairs both in England and America. In them she tells how, in 1678, she and her friends interceded with Sir Edmond Andross on his behalf. She wrote to her husband, "I should have told thee first that I received thine sent by Sir Edmond Andross, and I came to London in January purposely to wait on him about giving thee liberty, as thou didst desire me; and the Earl of Carlisle, who is since going to be Governor of Jamaica, spoke to him in my behalf, by my cousin Edward Burdet's means; and thy cousin Edward Burdet went to him himself, but his answer was that it was not in his power to release thee, but the court of assize must do it, or else the king, or Buckham; and I was advised not to petition them, because Sir Edmond Andross in his discourse did so against thy offence in increasing more authority there than was belonging to any subject, and presumed to believe all the story that had been brought against thee, that it might have been rather a hurt to thee than any kindness, to have made in thy behalf whilst he was here, who in all probability would have opposed it in his own justification, and he has great power and friendship, as I hear, more than ever. For thou must be careful to give him no offence, by work or deed, hence-forwards; he sayd that thou hadst liberty, and might have staid at home, and needst not have returned to New York when thou didst."

In addition Mrs. Fenwick enlisted the aid of Mrs. Hippolite Lefevre, who was a friend of Sir Edmond Andross, to the end that Fenwick might have his liberty.

Relative to the legal intricacies, she wrote that "the business is so confused and out of my element to understand it, that I am exceedingly too sick to know what to do in it, besides that I have no money to disburse." She discloses by her letters that Edmond Warner seemed to have had some doubts about the whole case and expressed the hope that he might be free from the whole business. Warner seems to have been half decent about the whole matter, but Eldridge was not. Eldridge bothered her often, importuning her for money, and complaining bitterly to her that her husband had struck him in the face. She chided him briefly for not keeping his temper when he met Eldridge, and she advised him not to come to England because "I verrily believe that thou wouldst not enjoy liberty to do thyself any good, and that I have will scarce maintain me; for that I cannot supply thee at all."

On another occasion she wrote: "Eldridge and Warner have been with me. Eldridge says there was designs laid for his life, and that it was thy fault that you did not agree, and that thou wouldst not choose any but thy son Hedge (Samuel Hedge, who married Fenwick's daughter). They both say they would have their money. I told them they must have it raised out of the land there; but they say thou hast sold more than thy share already; but Warner says he would be willing to take land there for the money due him, and would fain be at liberty. Eldridge said thou didst refuse to set out his land, and told him he should not have one foot; they said they would come again to me to try if there can be any way found out to compose their differences. But I know not yet who I can get to help me, or do anything for me therein. When my nephew Ward hears what they offer, we shall consider of it, and send thee word by the next ship."

She gave him good advice, as she thought, judged from the information she had received, "I insist thou wouldst forbear to act as a Lord Proprietor, and to make orders and summon the people, 'til thou hast thy deed, and authority to do it."

She concluded her last letter on a high plane of advice: "I am uncertain where thou art now, for till I hear from thee I think not convenient to send anything to thee, but by hearty well wishes, that thou wouldst consider the time thou or I or any one in this life is short—that we ought to seek peace and ensue it, and to bear injury patiently, and to deny ourselves, to become fools that we may be wise, to learn of him that was meek and lowly in heart, our great master, that we may find rest, to whose peace I commend thee and all thine."

She added a postcript: "Eldridge told me that thy purchasers here intend to sue him and me for their bargains, but all he says is not to be believed, as soon as the weather is a little warmer, I intend to go to some of them myself."

CHAPTER VI

OF THE LAST DAYS OF FENWICK

No one may say that Fenwick yielded to his many enemies without a struggle. One of the most remarkable documents in American colonial history is that in which the sorely beleaguered Governor answered his enemies one by one, and gave them blow for blow:

THE REMONSTRANCE AND DECLARATION BY JOHN FENWICKE ESQUIRE, ONE OF THE LORDS OR CHIEF PROPRIETORS OF THE SAID PROPRIETARY, AND PARTICULARLY OF FENWICKE'S COLONY, LYING WITHIN THE SAME, SENDETH, GREETING:—

Whereas, it cannot be denied, but owned and acknowledged by all that have been and are concerned with me, both in England and here in America, that I bought, with my own money, (besides my great expenses and care,) of John, Lord Berkley, one of the late and absolute Lord Proprietors of the said province, all his royalities in as full and ample manner as James, Duke of York, had granted unto him, as by his deed of the 18th day of March 1673-4, upon record both in England and within the said colony, appeareth.

That afterwards, to wit, for the sake of God's own blessed truth, and for my own outward peace, more than for any other obligation which either law or equity could compel me to, I was persuaded by William Penn, to reserve the tenth part of my said justly purchased interest to me, my heirs and assigns for ever, (in hopes to have peaceable and quietly enjoyed the same for a colony,) and to sell the other nine parts to him, the said William Penn, Gawen Lawrie and Nicholas Lucas, their heirs and assigns, for £900, as by the deed triparte thereof, likewise upon record appeareth.

Notwithstanding many illegal practices and designs (which are too many now to mention, because at this time I design brevity) have been perpetrated, and most ruinously carried on against me and my said interest, by these men and their abettors, in order to the ruining of me, my family, and all those that, in simplicity, embarked with me, and claimed lands under me, within said colony.

That by means of such unchristian perplexities, my person has been several times assaulted, my life often and greatly endangered by forcing a gun, laden with many swan shot, within four yards of my breast, and a pistol discharged, with two bullets, within two or three feet of my neck; after, my house was beset, my door broken open, and my person seized on in the night-time by armed men sent to execute a paper order of the Governor of New York, to whom I was sent prisoner, in the depth of winter, by sea—his order being to bring me dead or alive;—where he tried me, himself being judge, keeping me imprisoned for the space of two years and about three months,—albeit that it was not, nor could not be proved that I had broken any of the King's laws.

During which time, John Eldridge, Edmund Warner, William Penn, Gawen Lawrie, Nicholas Lucas, Edward Billinge, and Richard Langhorne, of the Temple, Councellor at law, (who lately was executed for treason,) combined together to cheat me of my whole estate, as by the said Langhorne's letter, under his hand, which I have ready to be produced, having therein, as it were, buried me alive; so that my name was never to be used in theirs, nor my own concerns aforesaid.

That Gawen Lawrie sent or delivered the aforesaid letter to James Wasse, who being in my colony, caused it to be read to all the inhabitants, and it was published afterwards by Richard Guy, throughout the said provinces; in and by which their notorious treacheries and deceit was proclaimed, as well as I was considered naked (for having no estate or interest either in land or goods,) as an oak leaf. Upon the reading and publishing of the said most shameful letter, James Wasse and Richard Guy began vigorously to seize upon my said colony, causing the same to be surveyed by Richard Hancock, (my sworn surveyor-general) without my knowledge, albeit they knew, or might have known, that I purchased the Indian interest thereof, at my own just charge, of all or most parts of the land which lieth between a creek beyond Cohanzick, to Oldman's Creek, called by the natives Masucksey.

And further, to the end that they might enjoy this their unparalleled fraud, the said confederates, or some of them, wrote many letters to Richard Guy, and other three agents at Burlington, to use all their care and industry to keep and improve this their illgotten interest in my said colony, and so dispose thereof as by their orders.

And in pursuance thereof, Richard Guy, Edward Wade, Edward Bradway, and James Nevell have done what they could to promote the same (under the pretext of the said Governor's commission, which was for one year, or until further order, and since the expiration thereof, which was in the eighth month last,) by hindering me from disposing of my land and governing the people according to my legal authority, and government established within this province, which can no wise be legally altered but by the Lords or Chief Proprietors, their council and assembly, summoned by their authority; and thus all that are concerned will, in time, be forced to acknowledge and submit to, before the confusion which is now among us can be appeased, and those great and many enormities which it hath produced be swept away, for thereby the name and blessed truth of God has been and is blasphemed. And all that owns and professeth the same is become a scorn and hissing to the common people (nay even the natives) who are more righteous in their dealings and love to one another, than those who know and professeth the truth; but by their deeds, (which are not warrantable neither by the laws of God nor the king,) do wilfully rebel against, which is a grief and burden to my soul, and the souls of those who groan within, in, and under the sense to instigate the people of Burlington to stand up and oppose the power that has hitherto obstructed the settlement of this part of the said province, upon the true basis of the said power and government which is and ought to be within the whole province, and its entire right, and they have met, as I am given to understand, and appointed the 25th month, in order to their settlement; nevertheless they seem to be in pursuit of those unwarrantable and illegal conspirators of justice, (which was to rob me of my just right and property, in which the people are concerned also,) having, as it were, to attend them at the trial and place appointed, as if my said colony and people therein were to be subjected under them, and led by the concessions of their own controversies, which is contrary to law, royalty and good conscience, the customs of all foreign plantations, and the said government established within this province, and so has been all the said former proceedings against me, as will be proved to the shame of all that have had a hand therein.

LAST DAYS OF FENWICK   45

For proof of which, I desire all sober men further to consider what the known and established laws of England saith—I mean Magna Charta—which has been confirmed by above thirty-two Parliaments, and the 29th chapter runs thus: "No man shall be taken or imprisoned or disseized of his freehold, or titles or free customs, or be outlawed or exiled, or merchandize destroyed, nor shall the King pass or send upon him nor condemn him but by lawful judges, or by his equals, or by the laws of the land—we shall set to no man's nod, shall deny or defer to no man either justice or right."

This law is the rule of every just judge; his line, his measure, his weight, his yard, his balance; it is called right itself, and common law because it judgeth common right by a right, which is the judge of itself.

Now where is the judgement, where is the sentence, or decree by virtue of this law that has condemned me to die, or to have no society among these men, in this affair, nor to enjoy my own property? Where is the sentence, by this law, that has taken from me my property, justly purchased, right, title and interest, and divested me of all my freeholds, liberty and free enjoyments? Where is the decree to be found, grounded upon the said law, that doth declare that my whole estate pretence whereof the said John Eldridge and Edmund Warner wished to secure themselves £170 15s, and pay me other debts as by the deed of mortgage and trust is Eldridge's credit, Warner's and not mine, which neither law or equity mentioned in the deed was not stated by them, as they promised me before I executed the said deed, that I might sign the same to them, and they likewise to me. Secondly, That the debts which they undertook to pay out of the said sum, remaining in their hands for that purpose, they never yet made it appear that they paid the same, nor did they ever pay me the said sum of £100 15s, any otherwise. Thirdly, They sold not one foot of my land to pay any of my debts mentioned in the said security by John Eldridge in his confessions before many witnesses; but made a fraudulent deed of my temporalities (those 140,000 acres were excepted out of the security given William Penn, as aforesaid,) to William Penn, Gawen Lawrie and Nicholas Lucas, in consideration of twenty shillings, to cheat me. Besides, they have received (by virtue of a letter of attorney, which I gave them for their further security) £119 out of £451, which they should have received for me, and as yet never gave me any account of. Oath is made therof, in chancery, where they refuse to answer and give me a just account (that so it might have been, or now, determined for me or for them,) because they pretend they cannot swear, while their consciences have been and are so large as to endeavour all along to cheat, circumvent and go beyond me; and that with open-face, thinking to weary me and all that any wise assist me, and so to ruin me and mine out of all we have, by boasting of their great purses, and multitudes of their confederates with them, in these their hellish designs. But I doubt not of their being disappointed and frustrated in their hopes, as that their grand jesuitical Councillor Langhorne was. For the righteous God, whose wrath has been revealed from heaven in all ages, against all ungodliness and unrighteousness of men, neither slumbers nor sleeps—neither doth the aforesaid law, for the breakers or alterers thereof have been generally punished, by the execution of forty-four unjust judges, under one king, and many more since, under others. And for any to alter the established laws, in any part, by force, is judged by Parliament to be high treason, as also, if any go about to subvert them, is likewise noted high treason.

Foreasmuch, therefore, as law, equity and good conscience, the same government and customs of this and other provinces, every way plead for my just right, title, interest and present possession of this my colony, I do henceforth resolve, and do hereby declare, that I will assume my said lawful and absolute power and authority, desiring all the King's loving, peaceable and obedient subjects, and in his majesty's name, do hereby will and require them, and every of them inhabiting within my said colony, to take notice therefore, and to yield obedience hereunto. For it is invested in me, by virtue of his majesty's letters patent, here exemplified, and the great seal of England, granted at my request, according to law, to justify my said interest; which I derive from the said Duke of York, granted to John, Lord Berkley, and the said Lord Berkley's grant to me. So that no man can claim any right to any part of the said Lord Berkley's late interest, but what they claim under me, as aforesaid.

And accordingly, I will put my said power and authority in execution, in settling the grievances within my said colony, according to that government which has been and is observed and settled within the said province, and to govern his majesty's subjects according to the concessions and laws established by the said John, Lord Berkley, and Sir George Carteret. And I shall and will forthwith choose a council, and issue forth my precept, (with their advice) to call an assembly, to sit within my colony, that it may be settled, and the peoples' rights and properties preserved, together with the public peace. And thereby suppress or prevent all mutinies, insurrections and confusion. That so we may be in a capacity to associate with other of his majesty's plantations, our neighbour provinces and colonies, against his majesty's and our public enemies, whenever they attempt to disturb our peace. Given under my hand at Fenwicke's Ivy, the Twelfth day of the first month, commonly called March, in the 31st year of the reign of the King, and the year 1678-9.

FENWICKE.

There is more than heroism in this man who, speaking from the depths of an American forest, called upon Magna Carta and the inalienable rights of Englishmen to sustain him in his position.

A survey of the deeds and manuscripts in the case must convince an impartial observer that the coalition in England had, as he said, sought to leave him "naked as an oak leaf." Particularly apt is his reference to the consciences of his adversaries, espcially Eldridge and Warner, who claimed they could not swear to the account existing between them and Fenwick in the chancery suit then pending. His reference to the "jesuitical Langhorne" was also apt. Langhorne had become involved in the Titus Oates plot and had been executed for high treason in England. It was probably with some degree of satisfaction that Fenwick swung his shame and treason to the winds. Here, at least, was one of his enemies paid off. Yet Langhorne, a lawyer, had only been counsel for the coalition.

He mentions in his defense one legal fact which, only partly consummated at that time, became a reality on August 6th, 1680, and led to his final undoing and submergence as Lord Proprietor of the Salem tenth. This was the deed from the Duke of York to the six landowners of the coalition brazenly announcing that Fenwick had conveyed his land to Eldridge and Warner, and that they in turn had conveyed to Penn, Lawrie and their friends in order that they might make a division of the "Intire premises." This deed wiped out Fenwick's interest by a stroke of the pen. The deed, whose grantor certainly was not the man to worry over a little thing like extinguishing some poor Quaker's land right, was really an amplifying deed for the six gentlemen to enjoy West Jersey with a clear title—clear for them, at least.

The coalition was successful. In two years they calmly passed over Fenwick's head and succeeded in shearing from him his title of Lord Proprietor and his right to exercise proprietary rights. It was finally done by combining the Salem tenth with the new colony of Burlington, founded in 1677, electing an assembly and sending over a deputy governor appointed by the Proprietors.

At Salem, Fenwick had to put up with the humiliation of having commissioners appointed by Andross as his overseers. These commissioners served a double purpose. They not only reported to Andross in New York but they also kept the proprietors in England informed as to Fenwick's movements, his sales, and assertions of authority. These commissioners, Nevill, Guy, Bradway, Penton, Malster and Ward vexed and harassed him to the end.

By March, 1682, Fenwick saw he could not continue as Lord Proprietor. The end was at hand; his ex-friends and land speculators had the upper hand in every way. Furthermore, he was almost penniless. At his death a year or so later, the inventory of his estate yielded about twenty pounds. On March 23, 1682, he conveyed to William Penn all his right, title and interest in West Jersey except one hundred and fifty thousand acres, for the sum of ten shillings and "other valuable consideration." But Fenwick was a lord of the manor to the end. In the deed he reserved the right to maintain in his excepted tract, his court leets and court barons, two old English legal prerogatives which he could never forget.

The story of how Fenwick came to sell to Penn is still unexplained. Just a short time before he had hated Penn as much as the other members of the coalition. Penn was as much a party to the connivances of the group as were the others. He had signed everything the rest had signed, although he had couched his earlier letters to Fenwick in flowing unctuous phrases of religious and moral uplift. Why did he buy from Fenwick? There are several avenues of conjecture open. Fenwick probably needed money badly and Penn might have pushed the thought to a logical conclusion. It is unfortunate that the full consideration of the purchase was not given in the deed. Ten shillings is not a large sum of money. Fenwick, seeing he was cornered and about to be wiped out, picked Penn at random as the one of the coalition most likely to aid him. The fact that Penn gave him permission to keep his favorite toys of "court barons and court leets," discloses a possibility that Penn had bolted from his fellows and tried, very belatedly, to give Fenwick some help.

Fenwick's days on earth after the deed was signed and delivered were very short. He still had plenty of troubles. This time, it was on the religious side. The Friends came upon him, probably because he had absented himself from religious meetings, used profanity, hit Eldridge in the face, and other things. The Friends demanded to know of him "whether he had a desire to walk more circumspectly." He answered that he "loved the truth above all things," that he "loved honest Friends," but he had his failings as well as others; but he said that he could "freely forgive them that were the occasion of it," and desired to have his "love remembered to Friends," and that he "loved truth above all things."

His name finally disappeared from the minute book of the Society of Friends. The inference is that gradually losing his interest in the Society, he had neglected its requirements, and finally left it altogether. A great Friends' minister, no less than George Fox, on one occasion came to Salem and endeavored to adjust the difficulties between Fenwick and his fellow Friends. His journal reads:

"After meeting (at Chester) we took boat and went to Salem about thirty miles, where there lived John Fenwick and several families of Friends from England. We got Friends together and had a meeting; after which we had the hearing of several differences and endeavored to make peace among them."

Among the earliest immigrants at Salem was a man named James Neville. He seems to have been above the usual intelligence and delighted in making legal dissertations in the margin of his account books. He served Fenwick at first as secretary. Seeing Fenwick's cause waning, he became attached to the other side and served them far more zealously than he had his first master. After Penn's purchase from Fenwick, Neville wrote at least two letters to Penn. These missives, near the close of Fenwick's career, show only too well the duplicity from which he had suffered at the hands of those he had trusted most. They are exceedingly illuminating letters; the first, written soon after Fenwick sold to Penn, shows that his former friends in Salem, including Neville, wanted to exile him to Pennsylvania. The letter read:

LAST DAYS OF FENWICK 49

Deare Friend:

On the first day of this weeke, after ye meeting, I informed friends, That I had some matter of importance to impart to ye people, and desired them to give notice thereof to as many as they could, to meete at Salem on the next day; accordingly, there came together about 30 psons, to whom I read the inclosed, at wch George Deacon, John Thompson and seaverall others seemed highly displeased, Saying they would stand by the Concessions. I demanded of ye two foremensconed persons, whose leggs they would stand on, for their own legg had fail'd them formerly, &c.: they asked what I had to doe to medle in such Matters, wth out acquainting them; I answered, I thought yem not psons fitt to be of my Councill, &c: Some said, If the Governmt belonged to thee, thou might assume it without our peticoning thee thereto: I replyed, thou would'st rather have it by consent of the people also; for Wm Called ye Conquerr acknowledged he was chosen King, by the consent of ye people: ma'y words past, when it appeared yt some had not learn'd how to keepe Silence, not yet to speake to purpose: at last it was agreed that all ye Inhabitants should have Notice to meete on the second day of this instant moth, and about 60 psons came together; the most part willingly Subscrib'd, & all ye rest, except two psons (after a long dispute) did the like, All generally desiring thee to admitt, that the people may have the Nomination of thy Deputy Govrnor and the Justices of ye peace; John ffenwick did not appeare, his son Hedge told me he thought his father would not doe any thing until he had been wth thee; I have sent thee herewth his Commission, desiring it may never come to his hand, for the people have had so much experience of his ambition, &c, formerly and it is credibly reported that he hath boasted (Sincer thy being here) yt all is his: That very few or none of the Sober people can willingly recll him in Authority except I should acquaint yem with ye meaning thereof, wch I thinke will not be expedient; and I doe foresee yt he and his Tribe wilbe so arrogant, that the peace of ye people wilbe much disquieted thereby, if not prudentially prvented, it may be Expected yt all things will be in disordr when bad men hold the best places of Credit, Though I could veryly hope my enemy were reconciled, and that there resteth no malice in him towards me, Neverthelesse, blame me not to be so considerate and provident, That put the case he should have the will to hurt me, yet he shall not have the opportunity, or occasion to doe it, by any Act of mine; As for thee, I declared to the people that I doe Confidently believe that thou intend'st Such an establishmt that men shall not have a means or opportunity either to .... or prejudice the Publick without extreme hazard and Daingr to yemselves; And to remove (as much as may be) all disgusts and heartburnings, and to settle this country vpon the fairest probabillitys of a lasting peace and Contentfull establishmt: To Defend ye poore and fatherlesse, to doe Justice to the Needy, and to deliver yem out of the hands of those yt are too Strong and mighty for yem: This I declare wth integrity of heart, who am thy loving and Respectfull friend

JAMES NEVILL

Salem 33d jrst mo., 1682-3

I think it may be the best to setle Jon ffenwick in the Province of **Pensilvania,** and remove him, so that he have noe interest or Clayme here, least his pticular interest. I wish thyne and the people's felicity, and freely leave the ordering thereof to the Wisdom of God in thee J. N.

In the second letter, written a short time later, Neville wrote:

Govr Penn:
   I have herewth sent thee an acct of the Lands sold and taken vp in these ptes; I desire thee to take the towne of Salem into thy lott; John ffenwick has no acknowledgems due to him from any one in this towne; and if he should keepe his Courte Leete and Court Barron here, it would much weaken or Authority, and pties would be made, Some for Jon ffenwick's Court, othere yr Comrs, most out of ordr; I foresee the inconveniency that will attend this if J. ff. comes to Exercise Jurisdiction here; I hope the Neck of land between Oldmans-Creeke & Salem, is in thy remembrance, and wilbe brought into thy lymitts, otherwise both Towne and Country wilbe of little value; I cannot but be concerned for the people here, who earnestly desires to be vnder thy protection, being confidently pswaded thou wilt imploy thy powr for their good and make it thy worke to pcure their Safety.
                              Thy Reall and affectionate Friend
                                          JAMES NEVILL
Salem, ye 23d 3 mo 1683
For Govr Wm. Penn, These, with care & speed.

To his everlasting credit, Penn did not act upon the advice of his overzealous agent to remove Fenwick to Pennsylvania. He also had his troubles. Soon after his arrival in Pennsylvania, Sir John Warden says, "You should use great care to hinder Mr. Penn and the inhabitants of both Jerseys from obstructing ye Peltry trade from New York, and you should prevent all you can the uniting of either part of either Jersey with Mr. Penn who as you observe, is very intent on his owne interest in those parts."

But by this time Penn was busy with plans for his new commonwealth of Pennsylvania and, outside of his proprietary interest in the Jerseys, did not attempt to unite the two provinces.

In Salem Fenwick, poor, brokenhearted and shattered in health, prepared to die. On August 7, 1683, he wrote his will. In it he has a master stroke of Christian forgiveness, for he names William Penn as one of the executors of his last testament. The others were John Smith, Samuel Hedge, his favorite son-in-law, and Richard Tindall, his faithful surveyor. He forgot his wife in the will, not mentioning her at all.

Another thorn in his side, this time a domestic one, was the action of his granddaughter, Elizabeth Adams, whom he mentions in his will and says, "Lord, open her eyes to see her abominable transgressions, against him, her grandfather, and her poor father, by giving her true repentance; and forsaking that black that hath been the ruin of her." These few lines have given rise to a story concerning the founding of the village of Gouldtown, near Bridgeton, Cumberland county. It is said that Elizabeth Adams married a black man, and from that union the light colored people of the village are descended.

The writer does not believe this story to be founded upon

fact. Neither does Frank H. Stewart, one of the most painstaking and accurate historians of New Jersey. He has done a considerable amount of research on the subject and finds that Elizabeth Adams married a man by the name of Windsor within two weeks of the writing of her grandfather's will.

After the union of the two infant counties of Salem and Burlington, Fenwick was chosen to represent it as one of the Assemblymen at an election held in 1683, but he never served. Perhaps it was just as well that he, the one time Governor, was not called upon to participate in the loss of his own authority.

He died December of 1683, in his sixty-fifth year. His burial place is a point of much controversy. It is undoubtedly somewhere near the present Salem County Home, in Mannington township.

So died the man whom Fiske called "Litigious and troublesome." Nevertheless, he left behind him a settlement of which he would have been proud and which is proud of him. In late years there has been more attention given to perpetuating his name. A granite monument has been erected on the Salem-Woodstown road not far from where he is supposed to have been buried. At the two hundred and fiftieth anniversary of the founding of Salem in 1925, there was placed on the walls of the Salem Court House a bronze tablet with these words:

TO KEEP IN PERPETUAL REMEMBRANCE THE NAME OF
JOHN FENWICK
1618-1683
MAJOR IN THE ARMY OF OLIVER CROMWELL, 1648
PROPRIETOR OF THE SALEM TENTH
FOUNDER OF SALEM, NEW JERSEY, 1675
MEMBER OF THE ASSEMBLY OF WEST JERSEY, 1681
THIS TABLET IS ERECTED BY THE SOCIETY OF COLONIAL WARS
IN THE STATE OF NEW JERSEY, 1925

That my said colony and all the Planters within the same may be settled in the love of God—and in that peace which becomes all our great professions of being Christians.

CHAPTER VII

Of the Years Between the Death of John Fenwick and the Dawn of a New Century

Water courses were the main factor in determining the trend of Fenwick's Colony. It was a wide stream which brought Fenwick into Salem. Along this and the other streams of Fenwick's Tenth the colonists built their homes. Fenwick had originally planned a series of towns with the capital at Salem. This town and Greenwich were actually the only two built in his life-time. His ambitions for the towns which he planned to call "Finns Town Point" and "Bout Town Finns" were never fulfilled. He sold lots in "New Salem Town" and "Cohanzick," later Greenwich.

The majority of the early colonists, however, and those who came after Fenwick's death, did not bother with the towns, but pushed out into the wilderness. This colonization began at Salem and first spread up and down the small creeks which flow into the Delaware river. Later the colonists spread eastward and southeastward away from the navigable streams. They settled the banks of the streams because they had no roads, but they did have boats, and those boats served the early colonists well until roads were built. This accounts for the fact that many of the old homes of Salem County are built facing upon water courses. Before Fenwick's death, however, by order of the Proprietors, the first roads were built.

Transportation was an important factor in colonization. In 1682 the original King's road was constructed between Salem and Burlington. A little later the King's road to Greenwich through Jericho was built. It will be seen that the first attempt of these early road builders was to connect Salem with Burlington and Greenwich.

The favorable location of Salem is readily seen by the fact that it was the terminal of the road from Burlington which was the main colonial town of Central New Jersey. From Burlington or Bridlinton, as it was sometimes called, the road went on to Amboy, where the early governors of the Jersies had their residence. Salem was also the starting place of other roads no less important in West Jersey. From here led a road to Greenwich and another which eventually led to Cape May and the ocean.

But it must be remembered that the earliest means of transportation was by water. Salem, Alloway and Oldman's Creeks were the chief arteries of travel until the first roads were pushed into the wilderness. As the water courses yielded to the roads, their influence was still seen in the many landing roads which led to wharves on the creeks where the goods of the pioneers might be shipped. Many of the old trails of the county can be traced to these landing roads.

Another method of tracing the ancient throughfares is by locating the early taverns. Without doubt these hostelries were certainly situated on well-traveled roads. A third determining factor in tracing the old trails is the mills. The farmers had to take grain to the mills and return home with the product so that early in the colonization of the county, roads were built to enable the settlers to reach the various mills.

The study of the old trails involves endless research. Many of the landmarks have disappeared; the names and the titles used are entirely forgotten in many cases. The calls of the roads in their construction gives properties and not distances and with this method of description comes the necessity of studying all the various land titles back to the early years of the eighteenth century.

But with this problem there are some features which can be fairly well ascertained. The early roads of Salem were on the ridges. There was not money enough to erect bridges and to fill in causeways for approaches. The early surveyors avoided the swamps. It was their job to build without undue expense so they avoided the streams and the marshes to seek high ground whenever possible. For this reason, the early King's roads followed winding courses rather than straight lines.

As the colonies increased in wealth, the settlers found it possible to straighten out a great many of their winding roads and to build new thoroughfares instead of having to avoid all the natural barriers.

The King's road to Burlington started from Salem out through Gallows Hill or Claysville (Gallows Hill was the execution place for Salem's criminals) and then went past the present farm house of Michael Carmody, swinging back past the Pointers to a bridge at Mannington Creek, near the present bridge on the Salem-Woodstown road, thence over the Jesse Bond road and by Compromise schoolhouse, out to the Fenwick monument and to the county house at Major's run.

There the old trail is lost. It may have followed the present route from the county house to Sharptown, coming in that latter place by Kidd's harness shop, or it might have gone on into Woodstown at Hall's Mill and then across by some other route. From Sharptown, once called Blessingtown, the King's Highway is rather definitely determined by its present route past the Seven Stars Tavern and on to Porch's Mill, where it crosses into Gloucester County.

The King's road to Greenwich or Cohansey started in the upper part of Salem in the neighborhood of the present Baptist Cemetery, ran past Angelo's Landing at the back of it, near the present Kent street, Salem and then through Quinton township to the old Baptist church at Mill Hollow. Here it divided, the right fork continuing on to Quinton's Bridge. Here the road crossed Alloways Creek by a bridge and went southeast of Quinton down the Tattletown-Jericho road to the first cross road at Woodmere. There it turned eastward a mile, south to Gravelly Hill, one mile and a quarter out of Jericho, thence to Greenwich.

It is reasonable to suppose that there were numerous Indian trails in all parts of Salem County; that the colonists used these trails before the roads were built and that they incorporated parts of these trails into their new roads.

One of the most interesting features in Fenwick's Colony was the use of place names denoting the owner or some characteristic of the land. Most of the immigrants were comparatively poor people who had resided either in a large city or a town in England. For the first time in their lives they became proprietors of landed estates and they gave their new plantations names which reminded them of far-away England or else mentioned some particular application to their new homes. It is too bad that more of these names have not been preserved. They are as English and as colonial as any to be found in Massachusetts or Virginia. Samples of these names are Lumles Sawlay, Tyndales Bowery, Watsons Ranthrope, Provoes Holt, Paynes Pytle, Amwellbury, Hancocks Hurst, Whites Denes, Bradfield, Beriton Fields, Hollyborne, Grundel Hill, Lefevers Chase, Hedge Field, Pages Plantation, Braithwaite Hall, Petersfield, Webbs Arladon, Sandyburr Wood, Pilesgrove, Brothers Forest, Moseleys Shield, Bacons Adventure, Crawkerne Wood and Whites Vineyard. A few of these are existant today. Most of them have died with the lapse of the years, and are not ascertainable unless one goes back through two hundred and fifty years to the recital of the deeds.

The name Amwellbury has been preserved. It identifies that section of Elsinboro lying south of Salem between the Yorke street and Oak street roads. Hancock's Hurst is easily recognized; it is the present village of Hancock's Bridge. Beriton Fields, forgotten for at least two centuries, was happily revived by James J. Pettit to designate a real estate development on the Salem-Woodstown road just past Claysville. Lefever's Chase, commemorative of fox hunting and the like, extended from the present Mannington Mills to the present Penton. It too is quite forgotten. Hedge Field has never lost its identity. It comprised the estates of Samuel Hedge, son-in-law of Fenwick, and was the tract upon which Fenwick died in 1683. It is the first farm on the right after one crosses Mannington Creek at Mannington Hill, enroute to Woodstown. Pilesgrove is a Salem county township taking its name from Thomas Pile, the original purchaser, who called it his grove. Some of these names denote plantations in what is now Cumberland county. An example of this is Bacon's Adventure.

The modern townships of Salem and Cumberland county would be hard to recognize under the system of nomenclature existing in 1680. Fenwick had set up several precincts in the bounds of his colony. These were Windham, East Fenwick, West Fenwick, Monmouth, North and South Cohansey. Windham eventually became the township of Elsinboro. Windham was an early settler. Fenwick tried to use English names for his precincts instead of Swedish or Indian. After the purchase by William Penn from Fenwick in 1682, the township lying along the Delaware river and inhabited by many Swedes lost the name of the original governor of Fenwick's Colony, and took instead the name of its new purchaser, William Penn. To this day it has remained Penns Neck. This was West Fenwick because it lay towards the western side of the Delaware. On the other hand, East Fenwick was the founder's favorite township. It also lost its identity and became known as Mannington, in honor of the Indian chief Manito, from whom Fenwick bought the land. It was originally called East Fenwick because it lay in an easterly direction from Salem. Monmouth precinct, very English in its application because it remembers an English county, now comprises three townships, Alloway, Quinton and Lower Alloways Creek. Very few people today realize that when they cross the bridge at Quinton or Hancocks Bridge they are crossing a stream which Fenwick named Monmouth river. It lost its English name in order that it might commemorate a long forgotten Indian Chief, Alloways. Likewise, the land around it became the townships of Upper and Lower Alloways Creek. Today, Upper Alloways Creek has become divided into the two townships of Alloway and Quinton, but Lower Alloways Creek, around the mouth of the creek, has retained its name. On the Cumberland county side, precincts of North and South Cohansey comprised at that time what was known and settled of Cumberland county. Today it takes in the city of Bridgeton, the townships of Stow Creek, Hopewell, Fairfield, Greenwich and Maurice River.

* * * * *

The government of the Salem Tenth in the years from Fenwick's death to the beginning of the eighteenth century was the same as before. The proprietors in England ruled the counties of Burlington and Salem, which were the principal settlements at that time. Before the beginning of the eighteenth century Gloucester and Cape May counties had also come into existence. Most of the owners of the land were in England. Byllynge was over here in charge of West Jersey but died in 1684, only a year after the death of Fenwick. Laurie had been installed as deputy governor of East Jersey but was subsequently recalled in disgrace for his governmental actions. Penn was busy in Philadelphia with his plans for his new colony in Pennsylvania.

The facts that the principal rulers of West Jersey ruled from across the sea; that the colonial assemblies were subject to supervision in England; and that disputes continued over land titles (disputes had never stopped since 1675), all had their direct effect in starting the constant squabbles between the colonists on the one hand and the constituted authority consisting of King, Council and proprietors on the other. These disputes finally ended in the American Revolution.

Dr. Carlos E. Godfrey, director of public records in the State of New Jersey, is authority for the statement that Salem county was organized on March 25th, 1681. In other lists in the state, Salem is given as the first county organization in the confines of both West and East Jersey. However, it must be remembered that Fenwick had his own organization of his principality from the very time of his landing. But by 1681 he had been pretty well shorn of his power by the other proprietors and his old enemy James Nevill was elected register or clerk at this organization in 1681.

Until 1706 no court records were preserved in Salem County. This fact has led many to believe that there were no courts prior to 1706. This is not true. There were courts of some variety beginning with Fenwick; witness his court barons and court leets. Andros set up in 1678 a court of his own commissioners, named by him to exercise his authority against Fenwick. It is true that the records, except a few fragments, have been lost. The reason for this may be taken from a grand jury record of 1712 which follows:

"The Grand Jury of Salem, say at December term, 1712. Whereas some years ago, the Grand Jury of the County of Salem, made application that the records should be delivered to

A STRANGE MURDER

Mr. Basse, to be bound and put in order, and then returned to the County again; but we understanding, that the records are not bound, nor returned to our County, we humbly make application to your Worships, that speedy care should be taken that the said records may be again brought to our County, and here to be bound, and kept for the good benefit of the public. (Signed) William Clows, Foreman."

In 1696 there were two commissions issued for judges of the Court of Oyer and Terminer for Salem county. One was to a man named Hunloke and the other to Jonathan Beery. In the first case, Judge Hunloke was to hear the trial of Thomas Yorke, accused of burning and robbing a widow's house at Salem. In the second case, Judge Beery was to hear the trial of Jerimiah Bacon and wife Mary accused of murdering a child of Charles Angelo of Salem. Unfortunately, there is no record of the disposition of these cases.

But in this period there is one remarkable criminal case which deserves far more attention than it has been given by jurists and historians. It was the case of Rex et Regina versus Lutherland. That the records of this most strange and startling murder case have been preserved at all is due to the indefatigable efforts of John Fanning Watson, native of Greenwich and immortal preserver of the annals of Philadelphia. In his two-volume history, preserving all the little anecdotes of Philadelphia, the author briefly refers to a primitive trial at Salem, W. J., in 1691 and then notes for the future historian who might follow in his footsteps, that he had preserved the original in his manuscripts at the Pennsylvania Historical Society in Philadelphia.[1]

Watson had painstakingly copied from the original pamphlet describing the events, which was published by Philadelphia's first printer, William Bradford, in 1693, data sufficient to give information on this lost page of Salem's history. So, from the archives of the Pennsylvania Historical Society comes the record of Salem's first criminal case, trial and execution on which the Salem court records, begun in 1706, are of course silent.

Because of the superstition revealed, because of the social customs referred to and moreover because of the amazing precedent and conduct of the court and freeholders, rather than as a murder story, the whole is reproduced here.[2]

[1] "The Annals of Philadelphia," Vol. I, p. 306. Happy man, who had the forethought to tell us where we could find it; what heartbreaks would have been avoided if Johnson, Shourds and others had done the same.

[2] Instead of rewriting from the longhand of Watson in his manuscript, the writer deems it better to reproduce the story in exactly the same form in which it came from the archives and, where necessary, to intersperse it with pertinent notes.

Says Watson: I have seen a pamphlet of 19 pages printed by William Bradford in 1693 containing the first case of this nature (criminal trials) happening in this part of the county before .... The whole is published under the name and sanction of the clerk of the Court, Samuel Hedge (Fenwick's son-in-law). It elucidates several points of local history and is therefore useful to be preserved so far as I hereinafter extract. The pamphlet is entitled "Blood will out, or an example of justice in the Tryal, Confession and Execution of Thomas Lutherland, who murthered John Clark of Philadelphia, trader, executed at Salem, West Jersey, the 23d of February, 1691-2."

It reads: "At Salem Town the 16th and 17th days of February 169½ before John Worlidge, President, and George Deacon and Roger Carrary, Justices. The jury took their averment and the Indictment was read saying, 'Thou standist here indicted, by the name of Thomas Lutherland, late of Pennsylvania, carpenter, etc. The clerk asketh art thou guilty.' He answers, 'Not guilty of the murther but of the fellony'.

"The clark reads: 'In the beginning of November last John Clark, late of Philadelphia was trading at Salem with goods according to his usual manner. On the 12th November his boat was found on shore at Sandy Point (near the mouth of Salem Creek on the south side) without the person of Clark aboard, and the goods he before had missing, and having just cause to suspect the Prisoner at the Bar, he being convicted in England, at Sea, and at Philadelphia, being otherwise of evil name in Salem, he was apprehended and the goods found to the value of 15 pounds."

Beng thus examined before the justices, he said he bought the goods of John Clark and they cost him eight pounds for which he paid him all but 35 pence. Question: "What specie did you pay him?" Answer: "I paid him 36 shilling in wampum, one piece of eight, two half pieces, and one single and two double bits." He was committed to prison and from there escaped but was soon retaken.

At the final trial he confessed and made his final story. When first apprehended he was confronted with the corpse and bid to touch it which he did, saying "If I have murthered him he will bleed afresh," and saying "poor innocent man why should I destroy him? If I hurt him I wish the earth may open and swallow me up." [3]

The King's attorney then addressed the jury. The jury went out and were kept without meat and drink till they agreed and the next day they brought him guilty. [4]

The Attorney General then demanded judgment but a case of this kind never happening in his part of the country before, the court was very cautious in passing sentence of death. Whereupon the Grand Inquest, the Jury of Life and Death, the Coroners' Inquest, the most part of the country there present, caused the following petition to be presented to the Justices—to wit—"Whereas, Thomas Lutherland is found guilty, etc. by the judgment of 52 persons, Jurors, doth appear, and for as much as Justices of the Peace are not empowered to pass sentence of death, where there are superior court, but we having moved in this Province, we must apply ourselves to you for justice. The charge and trouble of keeping such a felon and the hazard of his again escape and our danger from him in that event constrain us to call

---

[3] Observe here, one of the last lingering cases of the medieval superstition which persisted even at this day and time.

[4] Note again one of the rude survivals of English trial procedure, the old, old custom of keeping the jury foodless and drinkless until their verdict was obtained.

on you to sentence him to Death. In witness of our unanimous consent we severally sign our names on the 17th of February 1691. 5

The aforesaid justices and president pronounced his sentence—The prisoner being asked what time he would wish to prepare to die, answered "so soon as you please", saying also, "I never knew that a king's attorney should plead against a person for fellony." The court granted him five days; to wit, the 23rd of February, 1691. 6

The first day of the week after his condemnation he sent for the High Sheriff and confessed to him that he "murthered" John Clark and the next morning sent for Samuel Hedge, the clerk, to take his confession in writing, a part of which confession Watson gives;

"I have been a great sinner to this my 40th year and have been a follower of Drunkeness: Whoring, Swearing, Tempting young women to Debauchery and then leave them. I was convicted of fellony in England for which I was transported into Pennsylvania. I was convicted of several thefts. When I touched the corpse of John Clark I was afraid the blood would have flown in my face.

"When I sold Clark the empty cask I felt tempted while he showed me his goods, to steal them; but I knew I could not take the goods without killing the man. This was three or four days before he went to John Gillman. I began to bless God that he had prevented the wickedness in my heart—but when I met him again, I was sorry for seeing him; for again the temptation came strong upon me. I bought some thread buttons of him—told him he had a cold boat, and should wrap himself up warm in his cabbin —As I was going home my heart misgave me and I thought why should I destroy the innocent creature? I went to the Beer House and drank with N. Philpott two pots of beer and one gill of rum—As I parted from him the temptation came strong upon me—I however hesitated as I put my foot on the fence.

"When I came to the boat the man was in the cabbin. I counterfeited my voice and asked him whose boat it was? He answered, etc.—I then said I wanted to go with him to New Castle. He said I must pay and I said I would not. Then he put up his head I suppose to cry out. I bid him put it down. He said he would be still. So, I took the end of the roap and put it around his neck. He cryed, 'Friend, Do not destroy me—He that created him, created thee; Remember thy creator and redeemer and have mercy upon me as you expect mercy from God.'

"So, I told him I wouldn't destroy him, but he said, 'I think you intend to choke me'. I asked him if he had got any money? He said he had some wampum and cryed, 'Spare my life and take my goods,' but I pulled both ends of the roap together, while he cryed, 'Lord have mercy upon my soul, have mercy upon my soul,' even til he was dead.

"When I took the goods and money and leapt ashore by Sandy Point, having set the boat adrift after I had in vain endeavored to sink the body which thing put me in great fear. I hid the goods in a haystack and three days after brought them home unknown to my wife.

5 There were 100 signers but Watson did not preserve them from the original pamphlet. Nowhere else in the study of colonial and American criminal procedure has the writer such a remarkable proceeding as the above. It seems absolutely without precedent that the assembled court room and the freeholders of the county should petition a court for a death sentence.

6 All of this time is by the Julian calendar, hence the ambiguity of dates.

"I confess my great sin in marrying a wife in this country, having a wife and child at Clay Cotton in England. I have been very disobedient to my parents and a great neglector of the Lord's Sabbath. I pray to young people to take warning by me. I had great oppression on my spirit while in prison. I thought I should never repent and confess, but God has softened my heart and given me grace to repent."

As Sheriff Thomas Woodruff and his men were conducting him to execution he made a repetition of the confession and gave good exhortation to all people to take warning of his example. He prayed about a quarter of an hour and desired the prayers of all present and having forgiven the executioner, the court went away, and he "dyed" immediately. Watson adds the following as his own comment on the peculiar case:

It is remarkable that there were no witnesses against the felon and yet he was convicted. He had two examinations about the same time, one before the Coroner's Jury and one before the Justices. His confused and contradictory testimony ensnared him enough for commitment. When he came to trial he confessed the theft of his own accord in a fictitious story. He had declared in the story that he landed in a canoe at Windham Landing at an early hour and it happened that many at the inquest were then there and never saw him so land. It does not appear that there was an attorney or pleading in behalf of the prisoner. He said he was with his wife the night of the crime and she, examined apart, said he was from home until early next morning.

* * * * *

The division of domestic relations in jurisprudence was probably not known to the lawyers of that day. It existed however, as the fragmentary record of the Salem Surveys of 1688 show. It is probably the county's first order of filiation. There has been preserved an affidavit by one Peter Bilderbeck concerning a conversation had at Lawes Hendrickson's wake with Woole Woolson and Stephen's daughter Annacka. Annacka was the one concerned. She said at the wake, according to Bilderbeck, "she had a young Youdas, which is by interprataceon a divill in ffinns language".

One of the earliest acts of the Assembly permitted the Quakers who were conscientiously scrupulous of taking an oath to qualify as officers in the province of West Jersey. This act passed May 12, 1696, runs as follows:

Whereas, some persons, out of a principle of conscience, have not freedom to take oaths: Be it enacted by the Governor, with advice of his Council, and consent and agreement of the representatives in this present Assembly met and assembled, and it is hereby enacted by the authority of the same, That their not having freedom to take oaths shall not disable or incapacitate them for want thereof to hold or enjoy any office of the government within this province, whether magisterial or ministerial, to which he or they are duly elected, nor exclude him or them from any right or privilege which many of his majesty's subjects are capable to enjoy, he or they signing the declaration of fidelity, and profession of the christian faith, following, to wit:

EARLY COURTS

By virtue and in obedience to the said act of Assembly, we, whose names are subscribed, do sincerely promise and solemnly declare, that we will be true and faithful to William, King of England, and the government of this province of West Jersey. And we do solemnly profess and declare, that we do from our hearts abhor, detest and renounce, as impious and heretical, that damnable doctrine, that princes excommunicated or deprived by the Pope, or any authority of the see of Rome, may be deposed or murdered by their subjects, or any other whatsoever; and we do declare that no foreign prince, prelate, state or potentate, hath or ought to have any power, jurisdiction, superiority, pre-eminence or authority, ecclesiastical or spiritual, within this realm.

We profess faith in God the Father, and in Jesus Christ his eternal Son, the true God, and in the Holy Spirit, one God blessed forevermore. And we do acknowledge the Holy Scriptures of the Old and New Testaments, to be given by divine inspiration.

Coincident with the passage of this act there has been preserved the names of the first officers of the town of Salem. They were: the justices, Johnathan Beere, Richard Darkin, Obadiah Holmes, Rayneer Van Hirst, John Holmes, William Rumsey, John Bacon, Thomas Woodruff, Samuel Hedge, Jr., and Thomas Killingsworth; the recorders, William Hall and Samuel Hedge. The sheriff of that period was Hugh Middleton. (The first sheriff seems to have been Thomas Woodruff, who presided over the execution of Lutherland.)

The office of burgess seems to have ceased in New Jersey after the end of the proprietary period in 1702. The justices of the peace have of course survived to this day and are now constitutional officers. The recorder has become a clerk. The sheriff is still the same. Samuel Hedge, son-in-law of Fenwick, was not only a burgess and a recorder, but seems to have been the first coroner of this county. According to the records there were no surrogates until 1710 when Isaac Sharp was so appointed.

* * * *

So much for the political side of Fenwick's Colony in the years from his death to 1700. There is much more to be considered. Agriculture was of course the first industry in this county, but other trades and businesses prospered along with it. For instance, the immigrants had brought with them from England hand-mills for the purpose of grinding their grain, but their use was found inadequate to supply the needs of the rapidly growing community. Therefore they, in the early days of the colony, erected a grain mill in the upper part of Salem near what is known now as Kent's or Nittinger's Corner. This was a horse mill. Later, there were several tide mills. Mill Creek in Elsinboro derives its name from one of them. There was another in

Mannington on Mahoppony Creek (near Acton Station); one on Coopers Creek in Beasleys Neck, on the south side of Alloways Creek, and another at Carneys Point. According to Johnson there were at this time three windmills, reminiscent of Holland, in the county. One of these was in the lower part of Salem and another at Kinseyville, now Pennsville, in Lower Penn's Neck. A year before Fenwick's death, one William Hampton started a saw mill.

In this same year of 1682, a law was passed by the Assembly of West Jersey providing for a weekly market, to be held on Tuesdays, at the wharf. The provisions were that no sale should take place before eleven o'clock in the morning; anyone buying goods before that time should be subject to a fine. The informer, no stranger to British law, would receive half the fine.

Fairs were established about the same time, to be held in Salem in May and October of each year, at which time all persons might buy and sell goods, wares and merchandise. The law governing these fairs gave the added inducement that all persons were exempt from arrest during the fair days and two days before and after. This respite from jail was much abused and by 1698 the town fathers, declaring "it being then taken into consideration, that since fairs have been held in this town, that foreigners do flock from other parts, not only of this county, but of the neighboring province, do sell liquor by retail during the time of such fairs, thereby encroaching upon the privilege of the inhabitants of this town, who only are authorized, and none else, to sell by retail as aforesaid," enacted an ordinance which provided that only inhabitants of Salem might sell liquor on the days in question, and if any foreigner should dare to compete with the inhabitants of Salem in the liquor selling business their stock of wet goods would be seized. In this case the informer received one half of the bootleg liquor. The Salem fairs seem to have been the earliest in existence in this part of the state of New Jersey.

Suggestive of the western part of the nation is the interesting information that as early as Fenwick's day, rangers were appointed to roam through the woods and waste lands and confiscate horses and cattle not having proper marks of ownership. A law provided that no person should place his mark on beasts unless witnessed by a constable, justice of the peace or a ranger. All these precautions against improper marking were taken to prevent horse thieves and other dishonest persons from appropriating these beasts to their own use. Furthermore, no horse dealer might pass his drove of beasts out of the colony unless given a certificate by the ranger or a justice of the peace that such export was proper. The brand marks of the early horse and cattle owners have been preserved.

As soon as the population increased a demand arose for the exchange of commodities, and with this demand came the inception of stores at Salem and Greenwich, the two towns of importance in the county. The first articles exported from Greenwich and Salem for foreign consumption were deer skins, pelts, cedar posts, shingles, staves, wheat, corn, beef and tallow. Most of these export goods were sent to New York, and on the return trip goods and merchandise much needed by the inhabitants was brought back. Small as it was in the beginning, this trade was to make Salem influential and prosperous, on this score alone, for over a century. In 1682, Salem received its royal permission to be a port of entry, one of the most prized prerogatives a colonial town could enjoy. As a matter of fact it remains so to this day, although the British government has lost its interest in the collection of one shilling for each vessel under one hundred tons which uses the port; and all vessels of more than one hundred tons, two shillings. While the port of Salem has dwindled in the course of two centuries to a faint shadow of its former self, it still possesses the ancient glory of having been one of the oldest ports of entry of a far flung empire in the early days of the American colonies. It is older by some few years than the port of Philadelphia, whose customs house now exacts the toll for the shipping on the Delaware.

With the revival of interest in things antique, it is most interesting to note that the reason for the durability of many of the old brick houses of Salem county rests on the fact that the early settlers submitted to a law passed in 1683 which regulated the size of bricks. The early masons seemed to have been unusually careful of their handiwork and the materials they used. The brick law required that bricks must be 2¾ inches thick, 4½ inches broad and 9½ inches long, and that they must be well burnt. There were, in those days, brick appraisers whose duty it was to view the bricks made and to destroy those that they found faulty.

There are many stories existing in this locality that such and such a house was built of brick which came from England. In a few instances it may have been true, but there were not enough ships out of England to carry the huge amount of brick needed to build the colonial homes of that day. As a matter of fact, the vast majority of Salem homes were built of brick made and manufactured on the premises. The early colonists soon mastered the art of brickmaking and supplied their own needs. The raw materials were at hand, and the brick kilns were not hard to construct. On the subject of enduring memorials of brick of that period in Salem county, there are at least five houses, still standing, that were erected by the master masons of that period.

There may be and probably are more. But in the confines of this county these five examples of the brick layers' art before 1700 still remain: the Bradway House, erected in 1691, now the office of the Gayner Glass Works in Salem, bearing on its east wall the oldest date of erection of any house in the state of New Jersey; the John Mason house in Elsinboro, better known as the R. M. Acton farm, built in 1696; the Isaac Smart house, now known as the Kiger farm, mid-way between Salem and the Salem Country Club on the River Shore road, built in 1696; Guilford Manor or the Richard Johnson house, on Johnson street, Salem, erected in 1687; and the Redroe Morris house on the banks of the Delaware river near the Salem Country Club, built in 1688.

CHAPTER VIII

Being the Story of the Organization of the Earliest Religious Societies in Fenwick's Colony

The Swedes, with their Protestant faith, no doubt established the first religion in the confines of Salem county. However, the chief dissemination point of their religion was at Christiana Creek in Delaware, although they undoubtedly had branches of their church in the territory known as Penns Neck and Raccoon (Swedesboro.) In later years the Episcopal Church under the Society for the Propagation of the Gospel took over the members of the Swedish congregations who had remained in this section from the settlements which antedated the English occupation. St. George's Episcopal Church at Churchtown in Lower Penns Neck township is a direct outgrowth of these first families of Swedes. The principal families who comprised this congregation were the Joansons, Hendricksons, Wolversons, Nielsons, Woolysons, Sinnicksons and others. In addition to the Swedes there were a few French Hugenots, the Jaquetts, the Philpots and others who joined the Swedes in this congregation.

The vast majority of the colonists who came with Fenwick in 1675 were English members of the Society of Friends. Like their leader they had been subjected to religious persecution in England; their meetings of worship had been broken up, and their members arrested and fined. They were concerned not only with the prospect of a new deal in America, whereby they might increase their worldly wealth, and enjoy prosperity hitherto unknown in England, but they also had in mind the fact that they might find freedom from persecution and liberty to exercise their religious beliefs in this new land across the sea.

It is not surprising, therefore, to find that once having established themselves in perfect freedom from all fear and religious persecutions, they were willing that other religious sects should come to their new colony and enjoy the same measure of religious toleration that they themselves had sought. Like the relations with the Indians, Fenwick's colony never marred its religious record. Many congregations have settled in this county without fear of religious persecution. To this colony in West Jersey came a large number of families of varying religious faiths who had settled first in New England and who had been forced to leave that section on account of religious persecutions. A case in point is that of Obediah Holmes, a Baptist, or as they were called in those days, Anabaptists. Holmes, who came from Rhode Island, was the son of the minister of the same name who was flogged in the streets of Boston for his religious opinion, by the Puritans. Holmes, Sr. moved to Rhode Island along with Roger Williams and others who were forced to flee the inhospitable terrain of Massachusetts. The son eventually moved to Fenwick's colony and settled in Cohansey precinct, now Cumberland county.

The Friends, once they had comfortably settled in their new town of Salem, made haste to organize their meeting. At the house of Samuel Nicholson, pioneer with Fenwick, the first organization took place early in 1676. Their committees reported from time to time on the advisability of securing a proper meeting place and a burial ground. They did not succeed in getting a place to suit them until 1681, when Samuel Nicholson and his wife Ann deeded their town lot of sixteen acres for the use of the Salem monthly meeting forever. The part of this lot fronting on Broadway, containing the Old Oak Tree, is still the burial ground, and on the same lot, a little to the east of the tree, was built the first Friends Meeting House.

The minutes of the first organized monthly meeting are still in existence. They read as follows: "At a meeting held last day of the fifth month, 1676, it was unanimously considered that the first second day of the week, in the 6th month, that Friends do meet in the town of New Salem, in Fenwick's Colony, and all Friends thereunto, do monthly meet together, to consider of outward circumstances, and business. And if such that has been convinced, and walked disorderly, that they may in all gravity and uprightness to God, and in tenderness of spirit and love to their souls, be admonished, exhorted, and also reproved, and their evil deeds and practices testified against in the wisdom of God, and in the authority of truth, that may answer the witness of God within them. Signed, Samuel Nicholson, Robert Zanes, Robert Wade, Richard Guy, Isaac Smart, John Fenwick, Richard Johnson, and others."

Over a period of seventy years the Society increased their membership to such an extent that the meeting house in the grave yard was not large enough to accommodate them. In 1770 a new meeting house was erected on the same side of the street some distance to the east. This house, completed in 1772, still stands, and is still used. An architect from Philadelphia by the name of William Ellis drew the plans. This venerable building has seen the greater part of the history of Salem. In front of it during the Revolution the British army had its headuqarters, and within its walls a year later, was held the court which confiscated the estates of the Tories.

From the original settlement of Salem the Friends stretched their meeting houses over the colony. There was a meeting in Elsinboro conducted on the Darkin estate as early as 1680. The Friends meetings were started in the Alloways Creek section in 1679. There seem to have been meetings on both the north and south sides of the creek, finally resulting in the erection of the meeting house in the present village of Hancock's Bridge in 1756; an addition to this was built in 1784. Shourds says that this meeting house is the oldest church now standing in Fenwick's colony. Two burial grounds were established in connection with these early Friends meetings; one on the north side of Alloway Creek, and the other at Harmersville. In this county the Friends were the first religious organization to establish their own burial grounds. Most of the settlers buried their dead on their own plantations in what were called family burial grounds.

Families that were members of the Alloways Creek meeting included the Whites, Bradways, Wares, Hancocks, Stretches, Barbers, Denns, Oakfords, Daniels, Abbotts, Tylers, Stubbinses, Mosses, Waddingtons and others. The land on which the Alloways Creek Meeting House in Hancock's Bridge was built had been deeded to the society by William Hancock, builder of the famous Hancock House at Hancock's Bridge.

The Friends of Greenwich, in what is now Cumberland county, held their meetings in private homes until 1698, when with the assistance of the Salem monthly meeting they built a meeting house which stood near the present meeting house adjacent to the wharf on the Cohansey. Families which comprised the Greenwich meeting included the Stewarts, Tylers, Bacons, Harmers, Dennisses, Bricks, Tests, Sheppards, Woods, Millers, Davises and Reeveses.

Another Friends meeting which eventually died out was that near the head of Alloways Creek at the village of Thompsons Bridge, now Alloway. The meeting house has long since gone, but the burying ground near it remains, although it is in disuse and disrepair. The Thompson family, with the Foggs and the Oakfords, were instrumental in the forming of the Alloways meeting.

Pilesgrove meeting, which is still flourishing and active in the borough of Woodstown, was established in 1725. The families which comprised this meeting were the Lippincotts, Davises,

Dunns, Silvers and Bassetts. Over a period of two hundred years this meeting, which at its beginning was very small, has grown to large proportions.

Fifteen years before the Revolution and after Cumberland county had been set off from Salem county, a meeting was established at Port Elizabeth. The families of Jones, Buzby, Dallas, Elkinton, Townsend and Bradway were the organizers of this meeting. By 1876, this meeting had died out.

The last of the Friends meetings in Salem county was established at Pedricktown in the latter part of the eighteenth century. It was a branch of the Pilesgrove meeting at Woodstown. This meeting, too, has died out and the meeting house has been torn down. The families in this meeting were the Pedricks, founders of Pedricktown, the Greens, the Somerses and the Kirbys.

Smith, in his history of New Jersey, mentions that fact that in 1765 the Friends had four meetings in Salem county. These were: Salem, Hancock's Bridge, Allowaystown and Woodstown. Two great names among the preachers in the Society of Friends in these early days were George Fox and George Keith. Fox was here before Fenwick's death; George Keith of Perth Amboy appeared here ten years later. Keith was a wandering minister and a preacher in no less than three congregations. He left the Quakers to embrace the Baptist faith and later became a minister of the Church of England.

In the year of Fenwick's death, the first of the Baptists settled in the precinct of Cohansey. Among these pioneers of the Baptist faith in Fenwick's Colony were David Sheppard, Thomas Abbott, William Button, the previously mentioned Obediah Holmes and John Cornelius. At this time there came to Salem county the Reverend Thomas Killingsworth, the first Baptist clergyman in this section. Killingsworth was not only a clergyman; he was also an early judge of the Salem county courts. He was probably the first genealogist of Fenwick's Colony, because he kept a record of the Baptist families of this period of 1690. He was also instrumental in organizing the Baptist congregations of that day.

In 1690, the Baptists formed the Cohansey Baptist Church at Roadstown in what is now Cumberland county. The church used by the Baptists at this place was built in 1802 and is still in use. Killingsworth served this church as pastor until his death in 1709. Three years before the organization of the Cohansey Baptist Church another group of Baptists, fleeing from Massachusetts for religious reasons, came to this section and settled at what is now known as Bowentown. The families which constituted this group were the Bowens, Brookses, Barretts and Swinneys. Among these was the Reverend Timothy Brooks who in 1713, according to the records of the Salem county courts, took the oath and signed the declaration according to the law, made in England in 1689, regarding the Protestant faith. In the Roadstown Baptist Cemetery there is a stone which claims the birth of the first white female child born in Cohansey precinct, that of Deborah Swinney. Killingsworth, in addition to the Cohansey Church, held meetings throughout Salem and Penns Neck in the homes of his religious constituents as early as 1705.

In 1743, long after Killingsworth's death, a new congregation of Baptists was organized at Mill Hollow, midway between Salem and Quinton, and a Baptist meeting house was built at that place. Job Sheppard, a member of the Cohansey family of Baptists, was the first minister. A monument has been erected on the site of the old meeting house in memory of the first persons to sign the church covenant: Job Sheppard, Catharine Sheppard, Edward Quinton, Temperance Quinton, Edward Keasbey, Prudence Keasbey, Abner Sims, Sarah Sims, John Holme, Daniel Smith, Jr., Seth Smith, Samuel Simms, Joseph Sneathen, John Whittal, Sarah Smith, Phebe Smith, Rachel Sneathen, Patience James and Kerenhappuch Blackwood. Some of these first organizers are buried in this ground. This church was abandoned in 1790 and the building moved into Salem where it was used as a barn and later as an African church.

The Baptist congregation of Mill Hollow became associated with the Baptists of Salem and in 1790 built a Baptist Church on Yorke street, Salem. It stood within the limits of the present Baptist burying ground. In 1845 the present First Baptist Church was built. Its members are the successors of the congregation which worshiped in the churches at Mill Hollow and Yorke street. The Baptist sect in this city grew rapidly, and in 1869, another church was erected, known as the Memorial Baptist Church.

Another congregation of Baptists, known as the Seventh Day Baptists, settled in the vicinity of Shiloh in 1687. They were under the spiritual leadership of Timothy Brooks, previously mentioned, and they seemed to have worshiped first with the Cohansey Baptist Church. These early Baptists seem to have split on the doctrinal question of the correct day of worship, some contending for the seventh day, or Saturday, and others for the first day of the week, or Sunday. The first day Baptists throughout this county were known as antipedo Baptists, as being opposed to the immersion of infants, while the Seventh Day Baptists derived their name from the day of worship. This colony of Seventh Day Baptists has persisted throughout the years, and the inhabitants of the borough of Shiloh in Cumberland county are largely members of that faith.

The third and the last of the religious societies to set up an organization in Fenwick's Colony prior to 1700 were the Presbyterians. Like the Baptists, the first Presbyterians came to this colony from New England and New York. Like the Baptists and Quakers, they were satisfied with log houses for their first places of worship. The first Presbyterian church erected in Fenwick's tenth was built in Fairfield (Fairton) in 1695. These Presbyterians settled on both sides of Cohansey Creek, and a large number of them purchased land in the neighborhood of Greenwich. About 1705, they established the Presbyterian Church at Greenwich. The names of the families instrumental in the forming of the Fairfield and Greenwich churches were: Denn, Miller, Maskell, Watson, Ewing, Seeley, Dare, Fithian, Sayre, Sheppard, Moore, Peck, Vickers, Woodruff, Lupton, Bacon and others.

These three religious sects, the Friends, the Baptists, and the Presbyterians, were the pioneers of the first twenty-five years of Fenwick's colony. The next century finds them increasing their organization and membership in other parts of what are now Salem and Cumberland counties. The next century also finds newcomers in the field of religious activity; the Lutherans, the Church of England and the Roman Catholic Church. For the time being we shall leave these first organizations and later take up their activities and the new ones as well, throughout the course of the eighteenth and nineteenth centuries.

CHAPTER IX

OF AN EARLY POLITICIAN, AND OF THE MURDER OF THE HIGH SHERIFF OF SALEM COUNTY

In 1702, the proprietors of West and East Jersey surrendered their rights to the government in England. Politics in those days were as acrimonious as they are today, and this story concerns a wealthy land owner of Salem Town, who became involved in this political battle of the early eighteenth century. It deals with the fortunes of William Hall, an early resident, judge, and land owner. With this narration runs an interesting commentary on early colonial life, political and otherwise. In 1702, there came to New Jersey as governor, and he was governor of New York as well, one Edward Hyde, better known as Lord Cornbury. He was a member of the British family which had contributed two Queens to that nation, Anne and Mary. Cornbury's chief claim to fame was not as governor, but as a successful female impersonator; he loved to dress in women's clothes.

With the coming of Lord Cornbury as governor of the combined Jersies and New York, the provincial Council and Assembly began. These two bodies, with the governor, enacted the early laws, subject to the oversight of the Lords of Trade of the Plantations and the Queen. The Council was appointed by the Queen; the Assembly was elected by the voters, but suffrage was not universal, as property qualifications were necessary in order to vote.

In 1709, William Hall of Salem was appointed by Queen Anne as a member of the Council. He had been a Quaker but we find him as a Church of England man in later years, when the controversy broke out.

With the beginning of Cornbury's rule, disaffection broke out in the colonies, chiefly set up by the Quakers, who considered that they were discriminated against and that insufficient laws were passed for their protection. They largely controlled the Assembly but the Council, composed of four men from each section of the Jersies, was against them and lined up with Governor Cornbury in opposing their measures. Chief to feel their antagonism was Hall, who they claimed had deserted their faith to align himself with the governing faction, who were largely Church of England supporters. It must be stated, however, that the controversy, which continued through the administrations of several governors, was not altogether a church fight, although strong elements of that enter into it later.

The main cause of the political fight arose from the fact that the crown governors were sent across the sea with no knowledge of local conditions and no particular interest in them except to wrest whatever they could from them. The Council, including Hall, was extremely amenable to these predatory tactics and aroused the ire of the people in not combating more strongly these aggressions. Only from the Assembly came the roar that never ceased entirely until New Jersey, with the other twelve colonies, obtained its freedom from crown governors.

The Assembly contended that the majority of the poor farmers were unrepresented in its deliberations and that aristocracy and not democracy was the political order of the day. Loyal to the British crown, but intensely antagonistic to the royal governors, the minority of New Jersey raised as early as 1710, the cry of taxation and no representation, which finally culminated in the Revolution.

Those who celebrate the Fourth of July and acclaim the patriotic action of the forefathers who slapped the British king in the face and got away with it should never forget that the struggle started far earlier than 1775. In the early 1700's there were many men in the Jersies who contended bitterly against aristocracy in colonial government. One measure they did secure before the Revolution was the separation of the crown government of New Jersey from that of New York, a thoroughly needed step which is directly responsible for the separate government of New Jersey today.

In 1708, Cornbury went back to England. He was succeeded by Lord Lovelace, who died suddenly in a few months, and was succeeded in turn by Lt. Governor Ingoldsby. During this time the same state of political mismanagement continued.

However, in 1709 there came to the Jersies and New York a new governor, Brigadier Robert Hunter, who deserves far more credit than he has been given, for having tried to harmonize political conditions in the colonies. Although it has been contended that he, too, was money mad, yet he did try to placate the warring factions and took a great deal of notice of the class which up to that time had been given little part in the government. He looked upon Perth Amboy, East New Jersey, as his home, and even after he returned to England in 1720 wrote long friendly letters to his friends in this province.

WILLIAM HALL

From the time of the convening of the first Council and Assembly the aristocratic faction soon sensed that Hunter was not another Cornbury; that he was determined to establish tranquil government in his colony as well as to demonstrate that the people he governed were free men and not slaves. The Assembly at this session of 1711 drew up a courageous document setting forth the injustices the people had suffered at the hands of the previous royal governors and asking for redress.

The Council, who had indited a pompous letter to the new governor before the legislature convened, were amazed to find him espousing the cause of the complainants. They dropped the flattering attitude they had assumed and resorted to open warfare. The fight was on, and the Jersies witnessed for years a continual struggle between the wealthy land owning class, backed by the Church of England, and the smaller farmers, a great many of whom were Quakers.

Members of the Council during this period, some of whom figure in this story, were William Pinhorne, Daniel Cox, Peter Sonmans and Colonel Townley of East Jersey; and William Hall, Hugh Huddy, Robert Quarry and Roger Mompesson of West Jersey.

At the very outset Hunter, sensing that he could do little with these political opponents, asked the Lords of Trade to remove them and put in their places men who could carry out the popular will of the people. It was a long time before any action was taken on this request; meanwhile, the maneuvers of William Hall occupied the stage.

The Assembly and the small farmer party, seeing that the governor was sympathetic to their cause, immediately singled out Hall as one of their chief enemies for political decapitation. Here is their opening gun.

"The Humble Address of ye genl Assembly of said province of New Jersey Humbly Shewth, that we ye Representatives of this her majesty's Colony of New Jersey find ourselves under a necessity of addressing your Excellency against William Hall, Esq., one of her majesty's Council and Judge of ye Inferior Court of Common Pleas for ye county of Salem, who has appeared to this house to be guilty of High Crimes and Misdemeanors wch need not to be aggravated by us they appearing so plain that we can't think her majesty's subjects safe in either their liberties or properties while he is continued in power to Oppress them at Pleasure.

We therefore herewith lay before your excellency ye Matters of Fact with ye proofs and Humbly pray for Excellency to remove him from all places of profit and Trust within this province. WILLIAM BRADFORD, CLK."

Appended was the list of the several articles and list of crimes and misdemeanors of which Hall was accused and which he later answered count by count. The first was that as judge of the Salem court he had extorted unreasonable fees from several people prosecuted before him at the Court of Common Pleas.

Second, that he had forced one Thomas Bartlett to bind himself by indenture to a friend of Hall's, one Morgan, in fear of a prosecution to be brought against Bartlett by Morgan.

Third, that one Francis Godbolt and his wife were arraigned before Hall on a burglary charge and in fear of the prosecution, Godbolt consented to bind himself as a servant and was sold aboard a New England sloop. Moreover, the accusers alleged that Godbolt's wife remained in Salem as the "servant" of Hall.

Fourth, that a man by name of Reeve lost four barrels of flour in the Delaware, that they were found and recovered by Hall on his boat some days later and sold by him to some one in the Morris river section, now Cumberland county.

It was also alleged that Hall went around Salem county under the alias of George Trenchard, Sr., but for what purpose was not disclosed.

Hall was not long answering the accusations of the Assembly and in a lengthy manuscript defended himself from the charges. In Volume IV of the New Jersey Archives may be found Hall's open letter, preserved with all the curious spelling and tedious verbiage of the time. It is one of the first examples of an office holder defending himself by means of a public letter, an art which is not altogether lost in these days when so many public officials are compelled to defend themselves from attack.

Answering the first allegation Hall said regarding the extortion charge, "I am not yet sensible of any mistake much less Extorcon in ye first, but can very well justify it by ye ordinances for ye Regulation of ye Fees.

"In ye two others if there by any mistake in ye fees I have taxed for myself it is but five shillings in each one of wch I restored as soon as I was made sensible of my error."

He went on to add that any aggrieved person should not have bothered the governor with such a petty detail but should have made "his applicion to ye Court."

Concerning the second charge Hall said it "appears like a confused Dream," and added that it was "an Unitelligible Jumble of Indentures, threats and Felonies." Hall claimed that Morgan and Bartlett had an understanding between themselves and that the court was no party to any indenture or threat of prosecution.

Regarding the Uriah-like accusation of shipping Godbolt before the mast and retaining his wife at his plantation manor house at Salem, Hall declared that both the man and his wife were indebted to him for certain amounts and that both of them voluntarily entered into indentured servitude until the debt was paid off. Said Hall, "The woman continuing some time a Scrvt to me until she had wrought out a further debt of about 40s. was then discharged, has been at her own disposal ever since, And still continues at Salem."

Concerning the four barrels of flour, Hall declared that full accord and satisfaction had been made by him and the master of his sloop for the converted flour.

Hall spent the rest of his defense in a long criticism of the belligerent assembly and declared that he was a "victim of the violation of those inestimable Jewells, Lyberty and property then to be Arraigned Tryed and condemned without being heard" and in conclusion said: "Your Excellency will be pleased to observe from what I have been obliged to trouble you with, how severely and yet how unjustly ye said articles load me, and that ye pretended Crimes and Misdemeanors, even when they are endeavored to be forced up to ye height, if they were as true, as they are false, amount to noe more than ye value of Ten Pence, a sum so mean that it ought to be below ye Observation of ye Genrl Assembly of a whold province and not worthy to build an address to yor excellency upon."

Thus Hall ended his defense, which was forwarded to England with Hunter's comment that it "was a most curious and unusual document," but the storm against the other provincial officials continued unabated. In the midst of the correspondence during this troubled time we find one of Hall's friends in Council, Daniel Cox, belabouring the governor and the Assembly for their attack upon Hall and declaring that he had been "fired" by the governor as judge of the Salem Court and one Middleton, a poor Quaker, appointed judge in his stead.

Cox shed further light upon Hall's career and added that as Hall "was a reputed Quaker, that party relied upon him for their tool and that he was at first highly caressed by the governor but he could not be prevailed upon to betray his party, meaning the Council, and that as a result the Quakers gave him a surfeit (in these days a fit, or a large pain) so that he went constantly to church during his stay in Amboy."

While Hunter was waiting for the Queen to act upon his recommendations for appointing new Councilors and the Council themselves were moving heaven and earth to keep their jobs, a further discordant note was tossed into the proceedings by one Jacob Henderson, a missionary of the Church of England who told the Lords of Trade just how bad the situation was in New Jersey. Henderson intimated that if the present Council were not retained, Hunter and his desired new Council would give the Quakers power to oust the Church of England entirely from the province, which "will be of the worst consequences to the Church in our province." Of William Hall, Henderson said he "was once a Quaker, but now a Church man and very zealous to serve the Church and that the governor desired in his place or room, one Thomas Reading, a man of no principles who joyns with the Quakers in all their measures."

Henderson's letter brought the famous retort which classified Hall as "once a Quaker, then a Church of England man, and now of no religion."

Finally, after two years of bickering which marked the appeal to the court at Whitehall, the Queen assented to the demand of Governor Hunter and ousted those members of the Council of the Jersies whose discharge he had previously requested. Two of the members objectionable to the governor and Assembly had died and two had resigned, but Pinhorne, Cox, Sonmans and Hall, who had remained to the end, were summarily discharged by the Queen in an order dated April 23rd, 1713.

This ended the hectic career of Salem's first member of the provincial Council and marked the triumph of the small land owner and Quaker faction against the wealthy proprietor and Church of England faction in the affairs of the colonial government.

Hall died in 1715, apparently meeting financial reverses as well as political setbacks in the remaining two years of his life, because an act was passed by the legislature in 1717 settling the distribution of his estate among his minor children as the great bulk of his lands had been sold to pay debts.

* * * *

In 1717 the county of Salem was thrown into a great state of excitement by the fact that in one of the early months of that year, the body of James Sherron, high sheriff of Salem county, was found buried under a pile of dirt on his farm in Mannington.[1] He had been beaten to death with a hatchet. The detective methods used to apprehend the criminals are not available, neither is any reasonable motive given for the crime. We do know that five persons were indicted for the murder and that the trial of some of them commenced on April 16th, 1717. The

[1] This farm is now the Carpenter farm on the King's Highway two miles from Salem.

justices were Isaac Sharp, John Mason and Alexander Grant. The freeholders who aided the justices in the trial were Joseph Gregory, Daniel Rumsey, John Brick, Andrew Hopman and John Lloyd.

It must be remembered that the courts of New Jersey were then in their infancy, that no elaborate court system had been evolved, that there was no Supreme Court and no Court of Errors and Appeals, and that the Salem Court of Record was only eleven years old. Despite all these handicaps the trial was undoubtedly fair and just. The defendants were allowed to tell their own stories without interruption and one of them was discharged as soon as it appeared that the evidence in no way connected him with the murder.

The justices and freeholders ordered Mr. William Griffin to prosecute the prisoners on behalf of "Our Sovereign Lord the King," meaning George I of Hanover, who had only been on the English throne a little over two years.

There appears to have been no counsel assigned to the slaves but in view of the prevalent English custom this was not unusual. Hager, the female slave of Mr. Sherron, was first brought to the bar and being accused pleaded not guilty, yet made the acknowledgement that she knew of the intended murder and was present when her master was murdered. She was followed by John Hunt, another slave but apparently not owned by Sherron, who declared in quaint language that the said murdered person had been a living person only for the said Hager, who met the said Hunt the evening the murder was done.

John Hewett declared that one night being upon watch of the said Negroes and others, he heard a conversation between Hager and Hunt in which Hunt asked Hager "did she remember the poison she proposed to put in her master's broth?"

The negro boy Ben, who testified and pleaded at the same time, confessed that he had brought the hatchet to Hunt, the person who actually committed the crime, at the request of Hunt, just before the murder was committed and he heard the victim cry out in agony, and that he knew that when he brought the weapon that Hunt intended to kill Mr. Sherron.

This seems to be the entire case offered in court because in the next entry the justices in conjunction with the freeholders found the slave Hager guilty and condemned her to be burnt. They likewise determined the boy Ben to be guilty and condemned him to be hung by the neck until dead and then to be chained up in gibbets.

The second trial of this case was held by adjournment on May 21st and 27th, 1717. This also presents some curious features of early colonial justice. This time they proceeded with two judges, Isaac Sharp and Richard Johnson, and four justices, John Mason, Alexander Grant, Samuel Smith and David Rumsey. Present also was a petit jury, which was lacking in the first case. After the presentation of the grand jury and the usual proclamation for silence John Hunt, the actual murderer, pleaded not guilty. Mary Williams, the last of the defendants, also pleaded not guilty. The record of this cause is without summarized evidence and all we have is the bare declaration that Mary Williams was found guilty of knowing of the intended murder of James Sherron before it was committed and of concealing the same. Despite the fact that she was undoubtedly an accessory before the fact, she was only fined 100 pounds and ordered to remain in jail until the amount was paid. Hunt was convicted and sentenced to death, being first allowed to show cause why the sentence of death should not be passed upon him. One other negro slave by the name of Kizar was released from custody during the trial and absolved from blame.

It is a matter of regret that the records of this case were not more fully stated and set out. The lack of it makes it necessary to do a great amount of conjecture in studying the trial, which even in its paucity of detail is a picturesque case in colonial trial procedure. It is evident that the female slave Hager was convicted and burned at the stake under a very ancient English statute of 1351, [2] which provided that a servant who killed his master, a wife who killed her husband or an ecclesiastical person who killed his superior was guilty of petty treason. The breach of civil connections coupled with murder constituted the offense. The jurists of that early day classed it as small or petty treason because of the violation of the private allegiance. The penalty provided by the law for female servants was drawing and quartering, but in Hager's case this variety of medieval punishment was evidently not imposed. Salem county justice was satisfied with burning at the stake.

Evidently the boy Ben and Hunt were not slaves of Mr. Sherron because their penalty seems to have been hanging and gibbeting without recourse to other gruesome punishment. Yet it is by inference only that we can conclude that they did not add petty treason to their crime of murder. The act under which Hager was convicted was in force in England up to the passage of the Offenses against the Person Act in 1861 and no benefit of clergy obtained in this particular species of crime. The antiquity of Salem is emphasized by contemplating such punishment in this county. The fact that this statute of 1351

[2] The statute of Parva Proditio—25th, Edward 3rd.

was extant to permit such a cruel and barbarous execution links early Salem with the Middle Ages.

Much has been written of the punishment of witchcraft in Salem, Mass., by burning at the stake, but it is little known that Salem, N. J., also burned a person at the stake, not for witchcraft but for petty treason.

The executions were carried out at Gallows Hill in Claysville. The site is close to the present state road on the right going North, just past the railroad spur and a short distance from the beginning of the old willow causeway.

CHAPTER X

OF MANY THINGS WHICH HAPPENED IN THE FIRST FIFTY YEARS OF THE EIGHTEENTH CENTURY

The year 1704 is an important date, both in the history of the colonies in general and Salem in particular. In that year the first American newspaper was published in Boston. From then on the history of Salem and the history of all communities in the colonies is reflected through the press. Before 1704 all history was gleaned from deeds, letters, old manuscripts, and the like. After that date it was no longer necessary to rely wholly upon these things. The newspapers at first printed weekly reports, then daily, and from these newspapers the historian of today may gather a picture of the sociological development of the colonies. And Salem is among those mentioned.

Even the most casual reader of the files of those early newspapers will notice the overwhelming majority of items dealing with ship news. Those were the days when the now humble ports of Perth Amboy, Cape May, Burlington and Salem ranked with New York and Boston. The first item relative to Salem in an early issue of the Boston News Letter of 1704, deals with the fact that the ship *Eleazer Darby* had arrived at Salem on the seventh of August of that year. The article goes on to say, "the French Privateer gave him his salute after they plundered her of a great part of her loading."

The importance of this shipping trade to Salem in the early decades of the eighteenth century cannot be overlooked. It was to a large extent the actual making of the community. The pages of the early newspapers are full of items concerning the ships which entered and left Salem on their errands of commerce. Many fortunes which enabled their owners to build stately, colonial homes in this section, were laid as a result of this shipping industry. Nor was this trade destined to die out in a short time. The use of Salem's port kept up until the Revolution. A hundred years after the *Eleazer Darby* arrived at Salem, a shipyard at Alloway was building ships for this same coast-wise trade.

The names and destinations of some of these ships which came into Salem are of interest. The list reads like a page from

Lloyds: the sloop *Beginning*; the brigantine *Success*, for Bilbao; the sloop *Dragon*, from Virginia, William Brown master; sloop *Tyrall*, from Maryland, George Deane master; sloop *Exeter* and sloop *Dolphin* from Tertudas; sloop *Morning-star* from South Carolina; brig *Dolphin*, William Hall master, from Barbadoes; sloop *Dove*, Thomas Crisp master, to Cork; brigantine *Amity* to Jamaica; *Joseph Filmore* for Oporto; *William Roby* for Bilbao; *Samuel Darby* for Medera; *Gale* for the Barbados, and *Perkins* for Portugal. From this very partial list it is easy to see that numerous nations traded with these early merchants of Salem. The wide diversity of these ports accounts in large measure for the success of Salem as a shipping center.

Probably second in the list of items which appeared most frequently in the colonial newspapers were those of runaway servants. The redemptionists were often a problem to their masters. These people, sometimes called servitors, were persons brought from England, often against their will, and sold for a term of several years into a modified system of human slavery to pay for the passage across the ocean. We are not speaking of negro slaves; these redemptionists were all white people. The name comes from the fact that they would redeem their freedom from their master after a certain number of years, after they had paid their transportation charges. Quite a few of the families of Fenwick's colony came to Salem in this manner. The great New Jersey historian, Smith, contends that a majority of these servants, once they gained a foothold in the new world and secured their freedom, outstripped in worldly wealth and position the masters who had once owned them. But still there were many of these redemptionists who took the easiest way out. They simply deserted their masters and left for parts unknown. For that reason the papers are full of advertisements offering rewards for the apprehension of these runaway servants. Added to these were a large number of items concerning runaway negro slaves.

The comic strips and the funny papers of today cannot improve on the descriptions of some of these runaway servants. The curious costumes worn by them, including relics of former finery, and the peculiar personal descriptions are all well worth the notation. For instance, "Leering down Look, proud hambling Gate, walks Crimplin, he is so prodigious a Lyar that if observed he may easily be discovered by it, with a long Nose and a wild Look, goes crooked and groans very much in his sleep, speaks by Clusters, talks West Country."

Another amusing description of a runaway from Richard Haynes of Salem is: "Run away, the first of this Instant December, from Richard Haynes of Salem, in West-New-Jersey, a

Servant Man named James Smith, about 24 Years of age, by Trade a Shoemaker, Tall of Stature and wellset, of a fair Complexion and short red Hair having a Cap over it, his Teeth decay'd before, had on a white Kersey great Coat, a striped Flannel Jacket, a pair of old Leather Breeches, grey Yarn Stockings, new black-grain'd Shoes stitched round the Quarters, a Felt Hat and two fine Shirts the one white the other chek'd. Whoever takes up the said Servant and secures him so that his Master may have him again shall have Forty Shillings as a Reward and all Reasonable Charges."

One more notice of a runaway servant is worth mentioning at this point, largely because it gives the residence of the owner as Indian Town, a long forgotten place name in Salem county. It runs as follows: "Run away the 6th of this Instant, from Benjamin Davis of Indian Town, in Salem County, near Cohansie, a Servant Man named Edward Jones, tall Stature, Aged about 35 years; having a Scar under one of his Eyes, short Hair, a Sandy Colur'd Beard, and had on when he went away, an old Home-spun Coat, patch'd and lined with Blue, & Pewter Buttons, no Cuffs, two pair of Breeches, two Shirts almost new, one Home-spun, the other Ozenbrigs, old Shoes, and a felt Hat. He has been in the Army and Professes himself a Drummer. Whosoever takes up the said Servant and secures him, so that his said Master may have him again, shall have 40 Shillings as a Reward, and reasonable Charges. Paid by me."

The indentured servants were not the only ones who ran away. For two hundred years and over, the sheriffs of Salem county have had difficulty in keeping their prisoners in jail. As early as 1720, three men at the same time left the peaceful confines of the Salem bastile for parts unknown, compelling the then sheriff, William Griffith, to advertise for them. The reasons for their incarceration are unknown, but their descriptions are interesting and illuminating. The sheriff who lost them writes of them as follows in the American Weekly Mercury of 1720: "Broke out of Salem Gaol, Reyner Johnson a Tall Thin Man, six foot six Inches high, about 22 years of Age, had then on a Cinamon Coloured Coat, Vest and Breeches, short black Hair. Henry Coulton, a Middle Sized Man, down look, black Curled Hair very like a Perriwig; had then on a light Coloured broad Cloath Coat, black Jacket and Breeches. He had a Pass from the Mayor of the City of Philadelphia, which he Obtained before committing the felony for which they were Imprisoned. The first is a Bookbinder, the other a Printer by Trade and were late Servants to Mr. Bradford of Philadelphia, Thomas Mehew, an Irish Man short Hair and Poor Cloaths." There is no evidence that any of these were ever caught. In addition, some seven or eight more felons wanted for various crimes left the Salem jail, never to return.

Sensations, even two hundred years ago, were still in popular favor, and the newspapers of that period paid ample attention to the startling statements which came to them through their country correspondence. In this regard three early newspaper accounts regarding sudden death, fire, and the eternal triangle, make interesting reading. The first, dated October 9, 1729 reads:

"By the Post we have the following Intelligence. From Salem we hear, that on Monday Evening last, Israel Porter, who was a strong lusty Man, came home from his Labour, and sitting down call'd for a Cup of Cyder; but had scarce taken his Draught before he started out of his Chair, and dy'd in about two Minutes."

The second:

"We hear from Salem that a few weeks ago the House of Mr. Samuel Smith sen. near that Place, was burnt down, occasioned by the Maid's leaving the Candle carelessly when she went to bed. Mr. Smith saved his Money and Writings, and some Beds, but the rest of the Furniture was destroyed, and the Maid burnt to death."

The third:

"We have the following remarkable Account from Salem, That two Men having been Partners in cutting of Staves, the Wife of one of them conspired with the other to kill her Husband; but her Heart failing her when the Thing was to be done, she run out of the House and cry'd Murder, upon which the designed Assassin was taken and committed to Prison. This enrag'd him so against the Woman, that having broken out in the night preceeding the Day of the Fair, he went and found her at the House where she liv'd, stab'd her in several Places in the Body with a clasp Knife, and having left her for dead, he came back to the Prison-Door in the day time, and made his Appearance in the Fair, all bloody, with the Knife in his hand, declaring that he had taken his Revenge and Kill'd the B———h, but that no body should put him in Prison again, tho' he would go in himself, if the Sheriff would toss him the keys! Nobody caring to go near him while he held the knife in his Hand, they persuaded him to clasp it, and then they seiz'd him and put him in. The Woman was not dead but its thought she cannot recover. The man has endeavour'd to kill himself with the Knife, but it meeting with the Breast Bone, he only cut and mangled himself in a miserable manner."

One of the earliest notes regarding the ravages of the Demon Rum appears in a correspondent's letter to the Gazette in 1737, showing that these colonists were quick to recognize the evils of intemperance. It says:

"On Sunday the 3d of this Instant July, about 2 a 'Clock in the Morning, one John Thompson, an aged Man, who lived in this Town of Salem in New Jersey, who was very Poor, but very subject to drink Rum; had been drinking Rum the fore-part of the Night till he was Drunk, or very near it; and being got in a Passion with his Wife, told her, he would pack up his All, and go to Carolina; and thereupon he took a Bundle of things in a Wallet, or Bag, and went to the Wharffe at the lower end of the Town, and by

Endeavouring to get into a Cannoe, (A Vessel he had chosen to make his Voyage in,) Accidentally slipt off the Wharffe into the Water, and was drowned. He had a Son drowned near the same place, about two Years ago, in the like condition of being drunk with Rum.

"This, and the like, often prove the Consequences of excessive Drinking, which, tho' however frequent such things come to pass, yet nevertheless People will not be deterred from the immoderate Use of strong Liquors; This certainly bespeaks want of due Conduct in the Use of Things, a Defect too frequent amongest Mankind, which is, I think, a perfect Blot in that Escutheon of Reason annexed to the Fabrick of Human Bodies."

Disease was prevalent in those days. Smallpox raged throughout the colony, and in 1730 the justices and freeholders of Salem county decided that in view of the prevalence of this disease and the mortality caused thereby, that the annual fair should be postponed. Again in 1737 the officials of the county cancelled the annual fair, which would have been held at Cohansey and Salem that spring, because of another outbreak of smallpox in Philadelphia. They were afraid that the visitors from Pennsylvania would "bring down that Distemper, and may perhaps occasion it to spread amongst the people in this Province". Twenty years earlier, the citizens of Philadelphia complained that "the measels begin to spread in our Towne: it was brought hither from Salem in West Jersey, where it proved very Mortal".

In this period it is quite evident that the royal governors of New Jersey had some contempt for this struggling colony. In 1721, William Burnet, the royal Governor, referred to Salem as a "small fishing village" containing twenty houses and only seven or eight voters.

Real estate advertisements were very common in the newspapers of that day. One, dated July 23rd, 1741 and signed by John Jones, attorney, offered a thousand acres of land for sale along Cohansey creek in what is now the city of Bridgeton. John Jones was one of the first attorneys of the Salem courts. His small towered office building, which still stands in good preservation, is one of the oldest law offices in the United States. It may still be seen behind the Salem National Bank on Broadway, Salem.

The end of an early romance is shown by a series of advertisements in the Mercury which air very decidedly the marital difficulties of one James Dunlap and his erstwhile spouse, Elizabeth, of Pilesgrove in the county of Salem. The first notice, signed by the outraged husband, notified the reading public that his wife Elizabeth had left him (her lawfully wedded spouse) and had eloped with another man and that her husband would pay no bill contracted by his hitherto loving wife.

A few days later, through the medium of the same paper, Elizabeth, the erstwhile loving wife, had her say. Said Elizabeth, regarding her spouse:

"These are therefore to certify all Persons whom it may concern that the elopement of the said Elizabeth is utterly false; for the said Elizabeth never eloped from her husband, but was obliged for the safety of her life to leave her husband because of his threats and cruel abuses for several years past, repeatedly offered and done to her and that she went no further to her Father's house in the said county where she has resided ever since her departure from her said husband and still continues to reside. And the Elizabeth hereby gives notice that she will not join in the sale of any part of any land belonging to her and her husband, but that she intends to claim her right of Thirds (Dower) in any and all lands owned or hereafter to be owned by her husband the said James Dunlap."

In this early case of shattered romance the husband had the last say. He countered with another letter in the Mercury in which he said in effect that his beloved wife was a liar, that she had actually eloped from him and that "sundry persons could prove it;" furthermore she had contracted bills which he had to pay even though "eloped from his bed and board;" and that still further, if anything more appeared in print from her or her friends, that the said James Dunlap would be "obliged to publish other matter for his justifications".

A curious case of psychomachy appears in the Pennsylvania Gazette of 1742: "About two Weeks ago, one John Leek, of Cohansie in West-New-Jersey, after twelve Month's Deliberation, made himself an Eunuch (as it is said) for the Kingdom of Heaven's Sake, having made such a Construction upon Mat. XIX 12. He is now under Dr. Johnson's Hands, and in a fair way of doing well."

Perhaps the most significant item appearing in the newspapers for these decades of the eighteenth century is one taken from the Pennsylvania Gazette for December 17, 1744, which gives the startling news of an Irish insurrection in Salem county. The exact item is as follows: "From Salem they write that at the last court four Irish men were found guilty of a misdemeaner having with others chiefly servants of that nation to the number of 15 or 16, been engaged in a foolish conspiracy to make an Insurrection in order to seize that county with an old Irish trooper at their head. They stood in the Pillory last week till their Ears and Fingers were nipped with the frost."

This is all the historian has been left except the four indictments, yellow with age, which remain in the Salem County Clerk's office. From these we find that John Gallachrone, Stephen Kenney, James McDaniel and John Burke were indicted for uttering seditious remarks and approving of the uprising of Charles Edward Stuart, better known as Bonnie Prince Charles, then imminent in England. Gallachrone was charged in the indictment as having said to one Dorothy Lecroy, "that he is a soldier in the army of the pretender and that the county in his behalf is as good as taken already". In another place he says, "we are loyal subjects of his majesty King Charles III, and we shall cut the throats of these Quakers in their bed".

They do not seem to have done anything about it except talk, though that talk, from the story of the indictments, was blood-thirsty enough. What the plotters intended to do, how it was avoided, and a number of other details are not known, but the significant thing is that in this county of New Jersey an attempt, foolish and inconsequential as it was, was made to raise the standard of the Stuarts over the ruling house of Hanover. The uprising of 1745 convulsed England and nearly led to the success of the Stuart pretender in his armed attempt to capture the throne of his father. In the colonies the subject lay quiet, and the newspapers are comparatively silent on the upheaval in the mother country. It is regrettable that so little is known about this "insurrection", but the fact remains that in this county of Salem there was some organized sentiment for the house of Stuart. As said before, the movement seemed to be little more than blasphemy against the king of England and a lot of empty talk, but its historical import must not be overlooked.

* * * * *

From the 1748 files of the Boston Weekly News Letter comes the hitherto unknown intelligence that the Spaniards attempted a raid on Salem county and the surrounding country in that year. In this year the war known as King George's War was being fought in the colonies. At the same time the War of the Austrian Succession was being fought in Europe.

Sardinia, Saxony, Spain, France and Prussia were arrayed against Austria and England. While the war on the continent dealt with the vexing question of who was to occupy the Austrian throne, King George's War, its first cousin, was simply a fight between England on the one hand and France and Spain on the other, each seeking to enlarge their colonial domain with the major war as a pretext.

Briefly, the war in the colonies resolved itself into an attempt to seize the French fortress of Louisburg which was finally captured by the English general Pepperill with his colonial troops in 1745. South of Canada there was little actual fighting but there was an attempt by the Spanish to raid the valley of the Delaware.

SPANISH RAID ATTEMPTED

On May 29th, 1748, the calm of Salem was abruptly shattered when there burst in before the magistrates an excited English sailor named George Proctor who swore before the judges that he had just escaped from a Spanish privateer off Elsinborough Point the night before and after hiding along the shore all night had made his way to Salem Town to inform the populace that the Spaniards intended making a raid on the Elsinborough farmers and the town of Salem.

Proctor was a seaman who had been captured by the privateer and pressed into service. His testimony revealed the fact that there were several other privateers, both French and Spanish, cruising off Cape May looking for British merchantmen to capture. The privateers of that period were little better than glorified pirates and only the fact that their respective nations were at war saved them the actual name of piracy.

Proctor in his deposition informed the magistrates that the boat was from Havannah and mounted fourteen carriage guns, six and four-pounders, with a crew of one hundred and sixty men. The town officers were impressed with his story. In time of war the Delaware coast has always been a subject of apprehension with the Jersey officials and this time was no exception. They made preparations for the attack and sent Proctor on to New Castle to warn the town there.

The seaman went to New Castle from Salem and told the same story. If the burgesses of New Castle doubted this yarn of Proctor's all doubts of his veracity were set at rest an hour after his arrival when the privateer under full sail swooped down upon New Castle and attempted to board a Jamaica-bound English frigate lying off New Castle. The British command, astounded at the sudden attack, rushed to the batteries which fortunately for the town had been recently erected, and fired a broadside at the pirate.

The Jamaicaman also responded with a volley and the intruder weighed and towed away with the ebb tide, firing as they left and hoisting the Spanish colors in defiance. The Spaniard took herself off down the river and anchored off Elfsborg Point for the night. Fearful of the morrow the citizens of New Castle summoned the entire countryside to their aid, strengthened the fort and put armed men on board the harassed merchantman.

Foiled at New Castle, the *La Fortune*, Captain Ramong, now tried to do what Proctor had warned he would. Putting off in small boats the Spaniards tried to land on Elsinborough Point, but the timely warning of the day before had convinced the officers of the county that they had better prepare for trouble.

During the night of the 29th and the early morning of the 30th of May, armed bands of farmers guarded the Point and when about daybreak the Spaniards sent their small boats ashore they found a warm reception. There was nothing but the exchange of a few harmless volleys but the Spaniards perceiving the armed farmers on the shore, decided to call it a day.

The privateer wasted no more time on the coast towns. She weighed anchor again and dropped down to the Cumberland county shore at Cohansey where, tired of the presence of twenty-seven comrades of Proctor who were still captives, set them adrift in a small boat. The boat landed safely in Cohansey and the sailors repaired to Salem and thence to New Castle.

The repulse of the *La Fortune* had salutary effects because, waiting for her outside the bay were more privateers, French and Spanish alike, who, tired of capturing English ships, were awaiting word of the success of the *La Fortune* in raiding the coast towns of Delaware and New Jersey. Apprised of their ill luck at New Castle and Elsinborough the pirates sailed away, leaving the river shores in peace and quiet until the slumbering guns re-echoed in the war of the Revolution.

* * * * *

These years were an era of building. As more settlers came, as the coast-wise and foreign trade touched Salem, as merchants started stores, and business generally became brisk, there came a boom in construction. Looking back over two hundred years, it is easy to determine that there are still standing in Salem county at least fifty houses built in this first half century and probably as many more in what is now Cumberland county. They present, these brick houses, an interesting study of early mason work and architecture. Nowhere else in America may the equal be found of these houses with their glazed red and blue brick design. If a parallel is to be drawn the nearest are those houses of the tide water section of Virginia and eastern Maryland. But the houses of those two places do not possess the intricate glazed brick design, the dates and the initials of the builder that Salem county houses have. Here the homes may have been mere shells inside, architecturally speaking, but their exteriors are a thing of joy to the antiquarian.

The designers of these splendid brick houses must have had some model. To Professor T. J. Wertenbaker of Princeton University the writer is indebted for the information concerning the original pattern of these Salem houses. A photograph of the inner gate house of Leighs Priory, Essex, England shows very clearly the same pattern of brickwork used in the houses of

Salem county. For instance there is reproduced on the Hancock House and the Chambless house, both at Hancocks Bridge, the same zig-zag pattern as may be seen in this English original, built about 1536. The diamond shaped design on the Priory is the same as that on the walls of the Abel Nicholson and Richard Smith houses in Elsinboro. The most fantastic design of Salem county brickwork is that gorgeous spread of figures covering the entire west wall of the John Dickison house at Oakland Station in Alloway township. To a lesser degress this fantastic design is reproduced on the walls of the Samuel Bassett house at Milltown in Pilesgrove township.

There are numerous others which not only have unusual scroll designs but bear upon their gables the date of erection and the builder's initials. The Hancock House and the Dickison house are perfect examples of the bricklayer's art which embraced not only a pattern in brick, but the dates and the initials as well. The Hancock House was built in 1734, the Dickison house in 1754. Unfortunately the names of these early builders cannot be ascertained to a certainty. From some accounts it appears that Richard Woodnut was the master bricklayer of this period, but the others who either worked with him, or independently, are lost.

The court records for this period, in addition to the famous Sherron trial, are most illuminating. The legal antiquarian may find in the Salem county court records things which have long ceased to exist in modern law. He may find also interesting examples of precedence which have survived.

The colonists took strong drink and Sabbath breaking seriously. Those guilty of these two offenses were punished with fines and forced to stand in the stocks for four hours. For illicit relations the penalty was five pounds fine, and if the offenders were unable to pay the penalty both man and woman were sentenced to receive from ten to thirty lashes on the bare back at the public whipping post. If the amour was adulterous, the fine was thirty pounds apiece for the offense, and the principals received thirty lashes on the bare back at the public whipping post.

The court had many cases presented to it. David Roach was whipped fifteen times for stealing a bag in 1708. A constable was fined ten shillings for letting an indentured servant escape from his master. Richard Hancock, constable of Alloways Creek, was ordered to watch at the house of Esther Sikes to apprehend several robbers of whom Sikes complained.

In 1711 the grand jury of Salem county said that the jail would not hold the prisoners, that the court house needed repairing, and that the town needed a pair of stocks. A playful gentleman by the name of Edmund Morphey was fined five shillings for holding John Quinton under water until he was almost drowned. In September, 1713, the grand jury presented Eliza Windsor, "with force and arms upon the body of Elizabeth Rumsey, wife of Isaac Rumsey, of Salem, in the peace of God and our said lady the queen, then and there being, an assault did make, and her with a paddle over the head did strike, and also over the neck, and her collar bone did brake, to the great damage of the said Elizabeth Rumsey, etc." The historian wonders if this is Elizabeth Fenwick Adams, granddaughter of John Fenwick who married a man named Windsor, and whether or not she became pugilistic in her old age.

Rumors of pirates on the high seas came to Salem in 1718 when the court records say that, "Upon application of Richard Johnson, that Thomas Hill had lodged in his hands, being a magistrate, a remnant of silk, quantity 5½ yards, which the said Thomas secured with a certain person to him unknown, upon suspicion of the said person being a pirate, which person afterwards made his escape from the said Thomas. Ordered, That the piece of silk in the hands of Richard Johnson, late sheriff, be delivered to John Rolph, Esq., collector of his majesty's custom, to be by him disposed of for his majesty's use."

Several attorneys were admitted by the order of the court, none of whom seems to have been resident here except John Jones, admitted in 1732.

In 1729 the court issued orders that "each tavern keeper take for their several measures of liquors hereafter named as followeth, and not more, viz: For each nib of punch, made with double refined sugar and one gill and a half of rum, ninepence; for each nib made with single refined sugar and one gill and a half of rum, eightpence; for each nib made of Muscovado sugar and one gill and a half of rum, sevenpence; for each quart of tiff, made with half a pint of rum in the same, ninepence; for each pint of wine, one shilling; for each gill of rum, threepence; for each quart of strong beer, fourpence; for each gill of brandy or cordial, dram, sixpence; for each quart of metheglen, ninepence; for each quart of cider royal, eightpence; for each quart of cider, fourpence. Eatables for men—for a hot dinner, eightpence; for breakfast or supper, sixpence. For horses—2 quarts oats, threepence; stabling and good hay, each night, sixpence; pasture, sixpence."

A long-forgotten provision of English common law comes to light in 1732 when Eliza Crook, found guilty of petty larceny, was sentenced to receive twenty lashes on her bare back. Eliza took advantage of the English statute which called for a commission *de ventre inspicendo*, because she said she was quick with child. A jury of matrons consisting of Susannah Goodwin, Sarah Hunt, Anna Grant, Mary Grey, Eliza Hackett, Sarah Test, Elizabeth Hall, Phoebe Saterthwait, Ann Woodnutt, Eliza Huddy, Eliza Axford and Sarah Fithian declared that Eliza was right. Therefore, the sentence was delayed until after the birth of a child, when the punishment was inflicted.

One Mary Kelly, who had the temerity to abuse the judge, Mr. Acton, in what is now known as contempt of court, received ten lashes on her bare back for this offense.

CHAPTER XI

OF THE GREAT COLONIAL INDUSTRIAL ENTERPRISE WHICH WAS CASPER WISTAR'S GLASS WORKS AT WISTARBURGH IN THE TOWNSHIP OF ALLOWAY, AND THE COUNTY OF SALEM

Driving over the Alloway-Daretown road, about a mile or so from the Alloway lake one comes to a gaudy painted frame dwelling. Old bricks may be seen in the foundation of the house. Back of the building, the ground slopes away in a graceful undulating valley barren of buildings.

The scene is pastoral enough and is typical of many portions of Salem county. Therefore, it is exceedingly hard to realize that you are looking on the remains of America's first successful glass house and that this pleasant slope of farmland once was the teeming colonial industrial site of Wistarburgh.

It is true that there were other attempts at glass making in the colonies before Caspar Wistar purchased the tract of land from Clement Hall. There are shadowy records of glass making at Jamestown in Virginia; there were small factories established under the patroons on Manhattan Island and there was an effort in Massachusetts contemporaneous with Wistar's. This latter was at Sandwich on Cape Cod.

But the first concern to manufacture glass and to stay in business was this firm of Caspar Wistar and his son Richard, at this historic spot two miles from Alloway and six from Salem.

Hard times engendered by the Revolution caused this concern to draw its furnaces and to close its doors after flourishing for forty-one years.

Caspar Wistar was an emigrant to this country in 1717. He was born at Heidelberg, in the duchy of Baden, in 1695, the son of Johnananese Caspar Wistar, the Fuistenjager or electoral huntsman. Young Caspar Wistar arrived in this country sadly depleted in funds but after working a few years in Philadelphia he possessed money and courage enough to start the manufacture of brass buttons in which business he was already a success when he embarked upon his glass venture.

In 1725, he joined the Society of Friends and shortly afterwards married an attractive young Quakeress from Germantown named Catherine Janson. From this union in 1727 a son,

Richard, was born, under whose management the glass works closed in 1780. The Janson family was very influential in early Philadelphia and thus occupying a high social and financial position, the young German immigrant felt encouraged to branch out in other lines.

With the rise of the young colonies the demand for better modes of living led to a widespread demand for window glass and table glass ware. From the early factories there had come a small supply of glass ware, but with this and some importation of glass from England, the demand far exceeded the supply. Therefore the time was ripe for another colonial attempt to supply glass. Even in 1738, the sandy soil of West Jersey must have been celebrated enough to have caused Caspar Wistar to come to this vicinity and purchase 100 acres of woodland from Clement Hall on January 7th, 1738. From Amos Penton and Amos Hilton, adjoining landowners, Wistar purchased an additional amount of wooded land. The properties lay on either side of the highway leading from Salem to Pilesgrove, as it was described in the old deed. A little branch of Alloways Creek is only two miles away. The old accounts describe Alloways Creek as navigable for shallops up to Thompson's Bridge or Alloway and it was by means of these shallops that Wistar moved both supplies and finished ware.

In this now vacant field Wistar laid out his new plant, consisting of a cordage pot and glass house, a general store, workmen's homes and for his own use a mansion house. Determined to do the job right and knowing that the colonies contained few workmen who knew about the manufacture of glass, Wistar entered into an agreement with a sea captain, James Marshall, who for a consideration of 58 pounds 8 shillings transported from Rotterdam, four experienced glass workers. These men were named Caspar Halter, Johan or John Halter, Johann Wentzell and Simon Greismeyer. They contracted to come to this land and show Wistar the formulas of making glass for money advanced, all expenses including land, homes, food and servants and also one-third of the profits from the sale of the manufactured ware.

Some authorities class these four pioneer American glass blowers as Belgian, others contend that they were either Dutch or German. The names suggest the Walloon or the Dutch rather than the Flemish. Two of these three names, Halter and Wentzell, remain in Salem county, indicating that these families remained in this region after the breakup of the glass works. In the next twenty years other foreign workmen came to Wistarburg, encouraged and stimulated no doubt by their connection with these first named families. To the student of genealogy, the others also present a fascination. Here are some of them: Ridman, Freas, Trollenger, Meyer, Hahn, Born, Mackassen, Heppel, Dillshoever, Sowder, Kniest, Tobel and Ziegler. Some or these, in an effort to be thoroughly American, changed their names to more popular and easier English derivations. Two examples are Trollenger and Ziegler. The first became Trullender and the second Sickler. Some of these names have of course died out but it is easy to place the Freas, Meyers and Hahn names for instance, as examples of remaining Salem families.

Late in 1739 the glass plant, under the careful eye of Casper Wistar, got under way and started on its course of being one of the very few successful colonial plants. Six miles from the nearest provincial town of any size, it was necessary for Wistar to have his own general store on the premises and here was centered also the community life of the little industrial city of Wistarburgh. From the old chronicles come stories of winter sleighing parties coming to the store for their balls, dances, entertainments and other diversions of those pre-Revolutionary days. No artist or novelist has saved or restored to the imagination the romantic picture of this half American, half foreign, glass making colony in the very heart of the West Jersey forests.

In reviewing the history of this pioneer industry it is only fair to state that few records of the works remain. Unlike Steigel at Manheim, the records of Wistarburgh have not been preserved and in only a few family letters and the New Jersey Archives are to be found any remaining records. For the subsequent history of this enterprise the Archives still give some very interesting economic and social aspects of Wistarburgh.

In 1740, Mr. William Fraser, Collector of His Majesty's Customs at Salem, reported to the Board of Trade in England that "there has lately been established a Glass Works within Eight miles of that Port by one Caspar Wistar, A Palatine, and is brought to perfection so as to Make Glass." This is in conformity with the Government's demands for knowledge of colonial industry. We shall see later how important this knowledge of manufactures was to the British home government.

In 1752, with the glass works prospering, Caspar Wistar died and his son Richard took over the business and we find him announcing to the world that he was moving to another central place in Philadelphia "next door to the Spinning wheel." Richard personally managed the ware rooms and the button business in Philadelphia while he appointed a Salem man, Benjamin Thompson, as the resident manager of the Alloway plant. During these years the pot capacity was enlarged, looking forward to a more extensive business. While Wistar was serenely going on his way at Wistarburgh the dark clouds of trouble were beginning to loom over the colonies. England, always jealous of the prosperity of her colonies, was starting to bear down on exports and by increasing taxes and imports was beginning to make life miserable for entrepreneurs of colonial enterprise.

Out of the Archives again we get a side picture of the industrial situation when in 1752 Belcher, the Provincial Governor of New Jersey, wrote to a friend in Boston, "I am fully in opinion with you and my friends in New England that there is no Wiser or better Measure to go into for Retrieving the Miserable Circumstances of Your Province than to promote Manufactures among Your Selves and at the same time to be practising economy and all possible Frugality and I have wondered that Gentlemen of Substance have not long before this Set Up a Glass House.—But you put me on a Hard task to procure any Tolerable Information as to the carrying on of these works here in which the Managers are very secret."

Some time later Governor Belcher writes again and says, "I have begun to make Inquiry about the Glass Works in my province wch are 130 miles from this town (Perth Amboy) & I know no person near them capable of getting the information you desire. I have hardly a Lean hope of rendering you any Service in that matter in which the Undertakers are very close and Secret. I was well acquainted with one Caspar, a German who lived at Phil. and was the first and principal Undertaker of the Glass Works in this Province and with whom I discoursed about them five years ago and He complained to me that the Clay for the Furnace Bottoms was but Poor and often gave way to their great damage and Complained also that they Cou'd make their Glass so clear for want of Help, their Works being near two hundred miles from any Quantity of it. This Caspar is lately dead and from a very poor person raised and left a Fortune of 200 to 300 pounds Stl."

Another slant on Wistar comes from the immortal Benjamin Franklin, combining with it an excellent case of American political misinformation. The colonial governors about 1768 were almost unanimous in attempting to minimize the colonial industrial effort so that the Georgian government would not become too wise and smother these attempts. Franklin in writing to his natural son, William, the last British Governor of New Jersey says, "I wish you would send your account before the meeting of the next Parliament. You have only to report a Glass House, coarse window glass and bottles, all the finer and better goods coming from England and the like. I believe you will be puzzled to find any other though I see great puffs in the papers."

So the young glass works becomes a miniature football in Franklin's campaign to keep all flourishing reports of industrial activity away from the King's ministers. What they didn't know didn't hurt them and Franklin was no exception to that rule. William Franklin, although a Tory, was at this time at least, amenable to his father and here we find the actual report to the Crown according to his father's suggestions.

"A Glass House was erected which makes Bottles, and a very coarse Green Glass for windows used only in some of the houses of the poorer sort of People. The Profits made by this work have not hitherto been sufficient it seems to induce any Persons to set up more of the like kind in this Colony; but since the late Act of Parliament laying a Duty on Glass exported to the Colonies there has been talk of erecting others, but I cannot learn that any are yet begun: It seems probably that notwithstanding the Duty, Fine Glass can still be imported into America cheaper than it can be made here."

By reading between the lines it is easy to observe the great game of bluff the early colonial leaders used in hoodwinking the mother country into believing that they were doing anything well at all. In 1760, the Wistar works probably developed to their greatest extent, for in that year, while opposing the importation of tea, merchants of the different seaport towns included glass as one of the commodities on which they would not pay tax and seeing this condition Wistar advertised extensively both ware and window glass to reap a temporary large profit.

The problem of labor has always agitated the American public and Wistarburgh was no exception. The pot furnaces were hot. No ventilation processes had been invented, and the work to the young and restless spirits was anything but pleasant. Indentured servants were of course prevalent in those days and if the indentured servant did not like his work, as he frequently did not, the only thing to do was to leave. Therefore, Richard Wistar spent a lot of money advertising for strayed servants and bound boys: These notices are still extant and as an excellent picture of American life at that period, a few of them are reproduced in their original spelling here:

TWELVE DOLLARS REWARD

Run away on the Second of this instant, from the Glass House in Salem County, West New Jersey, a Dutchman named Phillip Jacobs about five feet six or seven inches high, light grey eyes, sandy hair, thick lips speaks but little

WISTAR GLASS WORKS

English, had on when he went away, a blue cloth coat with Metal Buttons, red plush Jacket, striped Ticken Trowsers, good shoes with large brass Buckles and a Castor Hat about half worn, took sundry other things with him also a Fiddle, upon which he is much addicted to play: Both his Legs were sore.   Richard Wistar.
Wistarburgh, November 6, 1767.

Another classic description eloquent of the sartorial fashions of the time, minus some of the lengthy description, is as follows:

A Dutch servant named Charles Geisinger, had on when he went away, an old felt hat, brown linesey jacket and an under jacket, the foreparts of which are the same as the other but the back part red, a coarse shirt, a new striped trowsers and new shoes.   Martin Halter.
July 9th, 1767.

An interesting runaway case advertised is that of Jacob Stenger age 18, five feet and eight inches of height, well set, light complexioned, dark hair, etc. This young man ran away from Wistar to later set up his own glass plant in the woods which are now Glassboro, N. J. This plant was the forerunner of the Whitney Works which was a live concern during the civil war and largely responsible for the South Jersey Railroad construction.

Another fugitive from the terrific heat of the glass works is described as follows in what might well be called a "cute" description:

TEN DOLLARS REWARD

Run away from the Subscribers Glass House in Salem county, New Jersey, a Dutch Servants Man, named Adrian Brust, about 27 years of age, 5 feet seven inches of height, of a pale complexion has short light hair, two moles on his left cheek and on his right temple a scar, also on one of his feet near his ankle which is but lately healed, and the shoe mended where the cut was. Had on when he went away an old felt hat, a lightish colored upper jacket with a patch on one of the hind flaps where this a hole burnt; an under one with flat metal buttons, both of Linsey, leather breeches, grey yarn stockings, good shoes with brass buckles. A good shirt and generally wears the bosom part behind.

The last of these runaway ads indicates that some of the running was done towards Richard Wistar's plantation glass works in the Jersies and not away from it. Here we find an irate advertiser in Philadelphia summoning aid for his lost female servant.

FOUR DOLLARS REWARD

Ran away on Thursday evening the 3rd, inst. from the subscriber a Dutch servant girl named Maria Catharine Mammo, 18 years of age. She goes by the name of Caty and supposed to have gone with one Conrad Konigsford to Mr. Wistar's Glass House in the Jersies.

Subscribers name torn from old paper. August 5th, 1775.

It would be very interesting to know if the unknown subscriber ever located Caty.

Despite the hot furnaces and the runaways, Richard Wistar did keep in close touch with the social and economic aspects of the problems facing both him and his employees, and if this industry is studied closely it will be noticed that here was an early attempt to introduce cooperative management into a manufacturing plant and by use of their store house for dances and parties, encourage the recreation of their employees. It is a pity therefore that the ravages of the Revolution did not spare this promising industry but even the prestige and financial resources of Richard Wistar were not enough to stem the tide of this trade depression. With 1780 and five years of awful war wastage the end came, and after Wistar had attempted to save the situation by selling his acres of cultivated fruit trees, the Pennsylvania Journal of October 11th, 1780, contains this **valedictory notice.**

At the very end of its existence this last account gives the best description of the plant, so it is given here in full:

The Glass Manufactory in Salem County, West Jersey is for sale with 1500 acres of Land adjoining. It contains two Furnaces with all the necessary Ovens for cooling the Glass, drying wood, etc. Contiguous to the Manufactory are two flattening Ovens in separate Houses, a Storehouse, a Pot **house, a House fitted with Tables for the cutting of the Glass,** a Stamping Mill, a rolling Mill for the preparing of Clay for the Making of Pots: and at a suitable distance are ten dwelling Houses for the Workmen, as likewise a large Mansion House containing Six Rooms on a Floor, with Bake House and a washhouse: Also a convenient Storehouse where a well assorted Retail shop has been kept above thirty years, is as good a stand for the sale of goods as any in the county, being situated one mile and a half from a navigable creek where shallops load for Philadelphia, eight miles from the County Seat. There are about 250 acres of cleared Land within Fence 100 whereof is mowable meadow, which produces hay and pasturage sufficient for the large Stock of Cattle and Horses employed by the Manufactory.

There is stabling sufficient for 60 head of cattle with a large Barn Granary and Waggon House. The unimproved land is well wooded and 200 acres more of meadow may be made. The situation and convenience for the Procuring of Materials is equal if not superior to any place in Jersey. For terms of sale apply to the Subscriber in Philadelphia. Richard Wistar.

Wistar died in 1781 before a sale was made of the property and for a while his wife Sarah and his son John attempted to carry on the business, but conditions were too chaotic for success and after a short trial the furnaces were closed and the glass making industry at Wistarburgh abandoned.

The writer has dealt at length with the economic and historical aspects of Wistarburgh rather than with the finished product and the technical description of the ware. The average

Salem antiquarian is able to identify either Wistarburgh or Glassboro ware by its main characteristic of bulbous bodies, uneven feet, wide mouths and large handle space. A recent book on glass gives this rather poetic description of the South Jersey glass, "Examples are generally wide, capacious and substantial of form, combining both utility and beauty—forms which suggest something of the forests of Thuringia and the expansive flow of the Rhine, which suggests the sturdiness of Amsterdam, yet hint at the delicacy of Venice and the subtleties of the Manchu in their manner of manipulation. Warring and clashing characteristics the world over have somehow been fused in the great American melting pot and have emerged with an air of freedom from restraint and tradition."

It is quite certain that few colors were used at Wistarburgh. Those authenticated and checked seem to be combinations of clear glass and light green, golden amber and shades of green, brown and opaque white, smoky browns and dull sea greens with a few more combinations not definitely proved to be those of the Wistarburgh plant.

Concerning the various kinds of ware manufactured Wistar's own advertisements in the later days of the plant offer the following articles for sale: flasks, demijohns, sweet meat and preserve jars, mustard pots, spice jars, measures, snuff canisters, medicine phials, tubes, globes, laboratory equipment and apothecary's supplies.

There is very little authenticated Wistarburgh glass in existence. The Wistar family, notably Wyatt Wistar of Salem, have some pieces of Wistarburgh glass blown at the factory of their ancestors. William B. Sickler of Salem has three pieces of Wistarburgh ware, which has been handed down from father to son since the original Sickler was a glassblower at this plant in the 1760's. An authority on glass in New York once stated he had never beheld an absolutely authenticated piece of Wistarburgh glass. The collectors of glass often dig in the field which was Wistarburgh, hoping to find broken bits of ware that were made in this old colonial factory. Eighty years after Richard Wistar drew his furnaces for the last time, Salem Glass Works, founded in 1862 by Hall, Pancoast and Craven began the manufacture of glass in the city of Salem. It is today one of the largest and most prosperous glass works in America. A few years later the Gayner Glass Works, founded by an English family, began operation and has since continued.

So Salem has at least two companies which are modern successors to this great original enterprise of Caspar Wistar in the woods in Alloway nearly two hundred years ago. Even the two sycamore trees which for years watched over the vacant field of the Wistarburgh glass works have gone and only the field is left to commemorate the greatest Salem county industrial enterprise of colonial days.

CHAPTER XII

OF THE NEW RELIGIOUS CONGREGATIONS IN FENWICK'S COLONY UP TO 1800

Governor Andross, in the days when he and Fenwick were contending, derisively called Salem "Swamptowne." In 1722 those inhabitants of Swamptowne who were members of the Church of England wrote a very earnest and pleading letter to the Society for the Propagation of the Gospel in England asking that a missionary be sent to them for the purpose of advancing the interests of their church in these parts.

The Reverend John Holbrooke, a young man and a new clergyman of the Church of England, was selected to be the missionary to Salem, and in 1724 arrived at the scene of his missionary labors. His letters are not only a history of his own struggles and those of the Episcopal Church, but they are also valuable for his splendid contemporary pictures of the other religious congregations in this county. They give also much important data concerning Salem generally. Soon after he arrived he wrote:

"The place lies between two branches of a large creek that falls into the lower part of ye River Delaware. The shores of this creek are prodigiously rotten, marshy and fenny for several miles, and are as bad as any of the hundreds. My constitution being but weak, I am persuaded I shall never be able to outweather ye unwholesomeness of this place, and therefore do desire leave from ye honorable Society to remove to some healthier place. There are several settlements in this country that want a Minister, as particularly Trent Town (Trenton) in this province, the people of which I hear design to address Ye Society for a missionary.

"If I might have the liberty of removing to this place, I hope I should enjoy better health. I am indeed concerned to think of leaving Salem, having settled a congregation there, some of which are a kind people, and seem to be well disposed. The congregation is but small, Quakerism having overrun this country and 'tis thought that ye Quakers in this country are five times the number of all other sects."

Later he wrote to the society in England that some gentlemen of a firm constitution be sent to Salem in his place, but nevertheless he stayed on and labored hard for the Church of England. He did not think much of the Quakers, although giving a good account of the other sects in the county who were competing with him and his faith. Of the Quakers he wrote:

"This part of ye country being first settled by Quakers, Quakerism has taken such root here that of all ye weeds of Heresies and Schism, this is by far ye most flourishing. The Quakers are about five times ye number of those of ye Church of England who are about seventy adult persons. Besides Quakers, there are no other sort of Dissenters near Salem Town except three families of Anabaptists, and as many of Independents. I do not know if there is one Papist in ye whole country. There is at Cohansie, a place twenty miles from Salem in ye same county, a numerous New England colony that principally consists of Independents and Presbyterians, among whom is a congregation of Anabaptists and five families of ye Church of England that are of my congregation. There is twenty miles farther a settlement upon Prince Maurice's River ye people whereof are of ye Church of England, amongst whom I sometimes officiate. There are six Quakers brought over to ye Church of England, and several Presbyterians, and Independents are better affected to it than before my coming, some of them having declared to me that they had been prepossessed with a wrong belief of it."

Holbrooke reported that although his congregation was poor yet they had contributed toward the building of "a neat brick church". People outside of Salem in both Pennsylvania and New Jersey had contributed to the building of a new church. He mentioned the three leading members of his congregation, John Rolf, collector of customs at Salem, Captain Vining and Dr. Gandovit. He spoke highly of the Reverend Ledenius, a Swedish minister who had ministered to the Swedes in Salem county for fifteen years before Holbrooke came. The Society of England in 1725 gave him permission to move from Salem to Burlington, but he found that the people of Burlington were not as anxious to have him as the poor people with whom he had originally settled. He wrote again in 1727, giving progress of the church and with it another good picture of Salem county in those days. He said:

"Our Church built in the town of Salem was founded May 7, 1725, the year following my arrival here, but is not quite finished, the window being yet unglazed. It is built of good brick and for ye materials and workmanship is reckoned a very neat church. It is forty feet long and twenty-eight broad. It was built by the contributions of the people of my congregations and of certain of ye adjacent inhabitants, among whom the people of Philadelphia were the most eminent contributors. His excellency, William Burnett, our Governor, gave ten pounds toward it. Divine service hath been hitherto performed in the Court House. The church is altogether unendowed, no house or glebe belonging to it, so that I am forced to pay a rent of 15 pounds per annum for a tolerable house. The salary I have from the people is 20 pounds per annum.

"The number of inhabitants at first usually resorting to our service at Salem were about seventy. They were and are now generally poor. Their business is chiefly husbandry. Some of them were strictly professors of the Church of England, and some of the Independent or Presbyterian persuasion, but of these latter, the main part now appear as hearty conformists. We have a town Salem, in which is a Court House and gaol, consisting of above thirty dwelling houses. There are likewise in Salem County two places called towns: the one twenty miles from Salem, called Greenwich, a town of above twenty houses in the north part of Cohansie precinct; the other called New England Town, alias Fairfield, on the south side of Cohansie, wherein are about twenty houses; between these two towns runs a creek called Cohansie Creek, but the bulk of the people live dispersed up and down a large compass of ground.

"In all the distance between Burlington and Cape May, which is about one hundred and forty miles, there is only one church, viz: at Salem, erected for the service of the Church of the State of England, and in this space there lie two counties that are without one, viz: Gloucester and Cape May.

"There is in Salem County in a precinct called Pennsneck a Swedish church twelve miles from Salem Town; between them lie a creek and marsh which make it incommodious for those of our side to go thither. There is another Swedish church that lies on the hither side of Gloucester County seventeen miles from Salem to which is a good road, even in the winter time, generally speaking. Both these churches have a minister apiece.

"I cannot say that the present number of people joining with me at Salem do much exceed the number at first, nor do I perceive that they are much bettered in their fortunes and conditions. Beside my congregation at Salem, I have a small one, Cohansie. In this place Independents and Anabaptists are by far the major part of the people, as the Quakers are of the people about Salem.

"I have another congregation at Maurice River about forty miles from Salem where the people are almost all church people and are above one hundred. They are poor people.

"There are in our county of Salem four Quaker meeting houses viz: one large brick one in the town of Salem, one in a precinct called Piles Grove, another in the precinct of Alaways Creek, and another on the south side of Cohansie, and another on the north side on which side is an Anabaptist meeting house. The number of the Quaker teachers is indefinite. There are two Independent ministers in our country who are maintained by the voluntary subscriptions of their respective hearers. There is an Anabaptist teacher who I believe depends more upon his secular than spiritual calling for a maintenance. By a computation lately made by the Governor's order, it appears that there are about four thousand inhabitants in this county, from which deducting five hundred of the Swedish settlers and two hundred and fifty that are up and down in the county profess themselves members of the Church of England, the remnant are dissenters of different denominations viz: Quakers, Independents, Presbyterians, Anabaptists, Seventh Day men, etc. There is but one Papist family in the county.

"There is a man that teaches school in Salem Town, but being but an indifferent schoolmaster, he has but few scholars. He has no settled maintenance. There is another school on the north side of Cohansie for the maintenance whereof a house and lot was left but I believe it is not appropriated to that use as the Testator designed.

"There have been no donations made to our Church, no benefactions to the minister, unless ye salary of 20 pounds per annum be reckoned one, nor any to a schoolmaster at Salem, nor have we any library but what I brought with me from the Society.

"The number of negroes and other slaves in this county lately given in to the Sheriff was one hundred and fifty, of which twelve belong to the people of my congregation. I have baptised one negro woman lately; as for the rest, I have endeavored what I could to procure their baptism, but thro' the remissness of their masters, and through ye stupid unconcernedness of the negroes, it is yet uneffected. The people in these countries take little or no care to instruct either their children or their negroes. Such a strong spirit of fanaticism and giddiness reigns here that I must confess I see but little hopes of gaining over many to a sober sense of religion, and the practices of the people are generally as bad as their principles among whom hypocrisy, bondage and oppressions, not to mention other vices, are common. The men that act with great candour and integrity are, I think, those that join with us, but among those there are some I fear are only nominal brethren. I hope Sir that I shall be forgiven if I utter a wish that we had the administration of our spiritual discipline here for the want of which we are derided by our sectaries. It is an uneasy reflection that when all the Sects have the exercise of their discipline according to their several schemes, the poor Church of England, the National Church, should be without the exercise of hers. I hope for this I shall not be thought posset (pampered.)"

A year after this letter he wrote again to England that his church was finished and they were holding meetings in it, having done so since the twenty-fourth of June last, the day it was opened. Thus the church received the name St. John's in honor of the Saint of that day.

Holbrooke added other notes of historical importance in his letters. He mentioned that Mr. Windrufea, pastor of the Swedish Lutheran church in Penns Neck, had died of pleurisy and that this epidemic was sweeping the county. Mr. Windrufea was the Swedish pastor of the church which later combined with the Episcopal faith and became St. George's.

He complained of financial straits and said the subscriptions to the church were always larger than the payments. He claimed that at Burlington there was both a nice house and glebe with a large congregation and well-to-do people, while at Salem the the congregation was small and the people poor. Again he paid his respects to the Quakers, saying that they were very numerous, obstinate, and irreclaimable, and that as soon as new settlers arrived from England they turned renegades from the religion they were brought up in and joined the Quakers. The missionary concluded his letter with a note of hope in that "with God's blessing" he might "send a more comfortable account later."

Several other missionaries in the colonies wrote the society asking that financial aid be extended to the struggling minister at Salem. But apparently no aid was forthcoming for in 1732 Holbrooke removed himself and family to Northampton county on the eastern shore of Virginia, and wrote the society in England of his great disappointments experienced at Salem. But in 1736, again from Northampton, he wrote that he returned to Salem on a visit and found that the people in Greenwich loyal to the Church of England had built a brick church there and wanted a missionary. He also encouraged the society by saying that

THE EPISCOPAL CHURCH 105

the Presbyterians of Cohansey (Greenwich) had shaken off their prejudice to the national church and were willing to join communion with it. Holbrooke hopefully asked that he might be allowed to remove to Salem. This location would be nearer to his wife's family, who lived in Salem.

No record is available concerning Holbrooke's subsequent activities, but to his efforts, in the face of great difficulties, the Episcopal Church in this section owes its origin.

A missionary named Nathaniel Horwood was sent to America to succeed Holbrooke but he went to Burlington and stayed there instead of coming to Salem. It seems that the Reverend John Pierson actually succeeded Holbrooke at Salem. He wrote that he arrived on January 30, 1734, and found the people rejoicing to see him. Mr. Tranberg, Swedish minister in Penns Neck, had tried to keep the congregation together in the absence of a minister. Pierson complained that some of the more inconsiderate had joined the Quakers but hoped they might be reclaimed in time. He preached also at Greenwich where there were many Presbyterians but where a small church had been started some years before, as mentioned by Holbrooke.

Pierson gave one of the first census takings of the colony, listing the number of inhabitants as 2,700; number of the inhabitants baptized, 1,400; number of actual communicants, 23; number of those who professed themselves of the Church of England, 207; dissenters of all sorts, 2,430; Papists, 60; number of heathen and infidels, uncertain.

Ten years later, in 1744, he wrote that he was trying to instruct the negroes and servants but found little improvement. He reported that the Greenwich church was declining but that the prospects for the Salem church looked better. By 1746 he wrote an account of his baptisms and noted that he was now serving Penns Neck and spoke in high terms of the people of that section. Like Holbrooke, he did not care much for the Friends and said "this place has a deep tincture of Quakerism". He died about 1747 and is buried in the Salem churchyard.

The church at Greenwich which both Holbrooke and Pierson refer to was erected about 1728 by the brothers Nicholas and Grant Gibbon. They resided at the time in Greenwich, were members of the Church of England and made money in the coastwise shipping trade. The church was named St. Stephens, but within a few years the congregation dwindled away and the house of worship was removed. This ended the attempt to maintain an Episcopal Church in Greenwich.

Following the death of Pierson in Salem, a man by the name of Thompson was named a missionary but did not stay there long. From then until long after the Revolution there was no regular clergyman stationed at St. John's and the services were spasmodic and irregular. During the Revolution the British troops took over St. John's church, quartered their troops there and by the time they left had completely wrecked it. It was not until the second decade of the nineteenth century that the church was repaired and a regular clergyman obtained. During some of these years from 1750 until 1800, the Swedish ministers at Penns Neck did their best to supply the struggling church at Salem.

It has been previously mentioned that the Swedish Lutheran Church was the first within the confines of Fenwick's colony. However, their organization as a church did not occur until 1714. Before this and in the years prior to Fenwick's arrival they had worshiped at Christiana, now Wilmington. On December 3, 1714 a meeting of the members was held and it was determined to build a church on the land of John Jacquet in Penns Neck. This is now Churchtown and the land is where St. George's Protestant Episcopal Church now stands. From that time until 1786, when the Reverend Nicholas Collin, the last Swedish minister, departed, the church was under the auspices of the Swedish Lutheran church, with ministers sent out from Sweden and the church records kept in that language.

The Swedish Lutheran church is to all intents and purposes, despite its name, the same as the Church of England. The organization is very similar, and bishops rule over it as in the Anglican church. But until after the American Revolution the ministers of this church came from Sweden, and were responsible to the bishops there. The church at Raccoon, now Swedesboro, was closely connected with the parish at Penns Neck and in 1720 the joint congregations purchased a farm or glebe for the use of their minister. This farm is situated in Pilesgrove, Salem county, and is still known as the glebe farm.

This church also had its struggles. At a vestry meeting in 1722 the Reverend Abraham Ledinius told the congregation that he would be obliged to leave unless they could subscribe a sum that he could depend upon for his support as his circumstances were wretched beyond all measure. The congregation responded with an immediate subscription. Among the names of those who came to the rescue of the poor pastor were many names known in Salem county today, Peterson, Jacquet, Vonneeman (Vanneman), Seneck (Sinnickson), Johnson, Hendrickson, Bilderback, Casperson, Stanley and Lampson.

The history of this congregation was not entirely devoid of humor. In 1729, at a parish meeting presided over by the Reverend Mr. Tranberg, the following matter was discussed: "How

THE EPISCOPAL CHURCH 107

the disturbance may be settled which has arisen between Raccoon and Pennsneck about Mr. Windrufa's horse, which was bought with the understanding that it was to be left to the congregation at his departure, but later it was the universal feeling that he should have it for his own. They were very decided that as they had given Mr. Windrufa his horse, so gave they Mr. Tranberg, his, and that if he, Mr. Tranberg, should die in the congregation, like Mr. Windrufa, and have no one to leave it to, it should belong to the congregation, but notwithstanding this seemed to be equitable, the Raccoon folks would not agree to it. Finally, it was resolved that Pennsneck should buy a horse for the use of the Priest and Raccoon another, and one was bought of Anders Peterson, down in Pennsneck for 7 pounds."

The same Mr. Tranberg was transferred to Christiana in 1740. The new minister was a supply, Mr. Olof Malander. Mr. Malander only stayed a year, and being very poor left the ministry temporarily and went to work in the print shop of none other than Benjamin Franklin. Mr. Malander then joined the Moravians, and due to his influence Pennsneck became a hot bed of Moravianism although Reverend Tranberg sometimes came across the river to hold Swedish services. A new minister, the Reverend John Sandin, in 1748 succeeded in returning some of the converted Moravians to the Swedish faith. Sandin died suddenly in August, 1748.

The Moravians contested the Swedish Church with every effort they could put forth. The Swedish Church was aided in its struggle with the Moravians by Professor Peter Kalm,[1] one of the great botanists of his time. Kalm, who was not a minister was touring this country studying plants and seeds, when the death of Pastor Sandin occurred. He became a preacher temporarily and supplied the Pennsneck church at this time. In February, 1750, he married Sandin's widow and returned to Sweden. There follow other Swedish pastors until the last one, Nicolas Collin, arrived on August 19, 1773. The Reverend Mr. Collin was rector of both St. George's at Pennsneck and Trinity at Swedesboro.

It was this worthy minister's fate to be the rector of Raccoon and Pennsneck during the long years of the Revolution. He has recorded his sufferings, and they were most severe. He reported that the rents of the church farms were insignificant due to the rapid depreciation of continental currencies. The congregations could help him but little. They had financial troubles of their own. At Swedesboro, while conducting a

[1] The mountain laurel the technical name of which is Kalmia latifolia, was named for Peter Kalm.

funeral, it is said that the great Lord Cornwallis left orders that his soldiers were not to disturb the rector of the Church of England. He was an eye witness, too, at the skirmish at Swedesboro, and to the depredations of the British in Salem county. Patriot and hero that he was, he stuck it out until 1786 when he was recalled to Philadelphia, and the king of Sweden gave permission that he and Lawrence Girelius, the last two Swedish missionaries in America, should return home.

Thus ended the Swedish mission in America, a mission which had lasted since the days when Johan Printz in 1643 had ruled the Delaware river in the name of Gustavus Adolphus and the people of the kingdom of Sweden. Collin stayed in this country, where he died in 1831.

In 1789 the Reverend John Wade became the first English pastor of St. George's and in 1794 the Episcopal church of St. George's in Pennsneck became incorporated under an act passed a few years after the Revolution. Since that time the church has been English, not only in its pastors, but also in its records. The log church built in 1717 was replaced by a brick church built in 1811 and remodeled in 1877. The rectors of St. John's Episcopal church in Salem, whose history through the centuries has been so entwined with that of St. George's, now serve it.

* * * *

In all the years prior to the American Revolution, there was one church which had been none too welcome in Salem county, although as far as the historian can discover there were no open steps taken against it. But the laws of England provided heavy penalties against the worship of its ritual, and the colonies were no exception to the mother country. This religion, banished from England because of the rigorous prosecution of the statutes of George II, and worshiped in silence and seclusion was the faith of the Roman Catholic Church. True, the Catholics had settled Maryland, but in most of the colonies along the Atlantic seaboard their path was stony. The government of England still hated popery, as they called it, and the colonies manifested the same antipathy. The Hanoverian government of England, remembering the battle of the Boyne, the "15" and Bonnie Prince Charlie, were afraid of the influence of a Catholic church in England and enacted laws to that end. The Georges saw no distinction between politics and religion and acted accordingly.

Fenwick's colony, free from religious persecutions, had little need of worrying about the Catholics and the statutes against them until Caspar Wistar established his glass works at Wistarburgh in 1739. Then for the first time, French, Belgian, and German families who were Catholics came into the county

THE CATHOLIC CHURCH

to work at the glass house. According to Holbrooke, the Episcopal missionary, there was at least one Catholic family in Salem county around 1725. But the large number of families who came with and after Caspar Wistar raised a new problem in religion.

Under the laws of England, the celebration of the Mass was forbidden under extremely severe penalties. It must have been an anxious time, spiritually, for those Catholics who had settled in and around Wistarburgh.

Two intrepid Jesuit priests, Father Schnider and Father Farmer, braved the authorities to celebrate Mass in Salem county. The first record we have is that of Father Schnider, who disguised as a doctor, celebrated Mass at the home of one Maurice Lorentz at Wistarburgh. The house has long since been demolished.

There is, however, a shrine dear to Catholics which is still in existence. In June, 1744, Father Schnider was invited to visit the house of Matthew and Adam Kiger, on the banks of Salem creek midway between Courses Landing and Sharptown. This house is still standing. For a great number of years after that date, the two Jesuit priests celebrated Mass and conducted their missions. By the time of the Revolution most of the old religious prejudices had gone, and the priests were free to move at will and celebrate their Masses as they pleased.

A description of this earliest Catholic Church in Salem county is well worth mentioning here. It is reached by taking the Pointers-Sharptown road, better known as the King's Highway. About a mile out of Sharptown facing north, there is a road to the left which leads past two farm houses, across the front lawns of both of them, and after several turns ends before the Kiger house on the banks of Salem creek. The house is in Mannington township, a short distance below Majors run, the dividing line between Mannington and Pilesgrove. The house is known as the Truitt Perry house from the aged man who now owns it. [2]

---

[2] It is said that one of these priests, probably Father Farmer, who was a noted botanist, planted the seeds of the Tsuga canadensis at the Kiger house. The tree in question is the Hemlock and this is the only place in Salem county where it has been known to grow. Likewise Father Farmer has been given credit for bringing into this county the Nelumbo lutea or Pond Lilies which grew in beautiful profusion in the Sharptown mill pond a short distance from the Kiger house. Other naturalists dispute this and say the Indians were the only planters.

The Kiger House was the recognized Catholic Church in this section until Masses were actually conducted in the homes of Catholic citizens in Salem about 1847, but it was the refuge of the faithful at a time when that faith was decidedly unpopular. It would be appropriate for some patriotic Catholic society to place a marker on the Kiger House and hold appropriate ceremonies at a shrine which must be very dear to them. [3]

It was not until many years after the labors of the two Jesuit priests that the first Catholic Church in Salem county was actually organized in 1852.

* * *

Meanwhile another faith had entered Salem county. This was the German Lutheran church, called Emmanuels, at Friesburg in Alloway township. It was established in 1748. The organizers of this church had come, like the French and Belgian families, to work at Wistar's glasshouse. The constituents were all Germans. The family names were Freas, Trollenger, Meyer, Hahn, Born, Wentzell, Mackassen, Heppel, Ridman, Dillshoever, Sowder, Kniest, Tobal and others.

This church at Friesburg has existed for almost two hundred years. The great Muhlenberg, preacher of the Revolutionary period, once ministered to this church. Like St. George's in Pennsneck, the records of the Lutheran church were kept in a foreign language, German, until a hundred years ago when English took the place of the German. It is the only Lutheran Church in the county of Salem and it has a proud record of distinguished ministers and prominent laymen over the period of its long existence.

The Presbyterian and Baptist Societies both had their origin in the Cumberland county section of Fenwick's colony. These two, with the Friends, were the pioneer religious faiths in this section before 1700. While the Quakers started in Salem and later organized in Cumberland county, the Baptists and Presbyterians settled first in what is now Cumberland county, and then worked towards Salem county.

The Presbyterians, established first at Fairton and Greenwich, founded in 1737 their church at Deerfield which for years was presided over by Andrew Hunter. Hunter was one of the most illustrious ministers of his day. The Presbyterians of the eighteenth century had their own dissensions regarding the doctrines of the church. The Fairfield congregation adhered very closely to the views of Calvin while the members at Green-

[3] Beside the house is a view well worthy of the journey to reach it. In the whole panorama there is nothing to indicate the passing of two hundred years. The aged house, the wooded ravine, the virgin territory of the creek at this point all indicate that this place has changed little since the Jesuit fathers looked from the windows of the Kiger mansion on this same scene in the days when the "King Over the Water" was their secret toast.

THE PRESBYTERIAN CHURCH   111

wich and Deerfield were more liberal. The struggle between them was known as the fight between the old side and the new side congregations which were represented by Greenwich and Deerfield.

There were other eloquent ministers in this section besides Hunter. The greatest divine of the age, George Whitefield, came into this section on a ministerial tour in 1740, and in a letter from Salem said to a friend, "Yesterday, at Cohansey, (Greenwich) the Spirit of the Lord moved over the whole congregation; what reason have we to be thankful for the great things that we both see and hear!"

Earlier that year, Whitefield had been scheduled to preach at Salem on April 16. Instead there was an error in the preacher's schedule and his diary tells us, "Went by water about four miles and then rode in company with many others to Greenwich (Gloucester county) in the West Jerseys about twelve miles from Philadelphia. There being a Mistake in the Place when I was to preach, I had not over 1500 hearers."

The congregations of Greenwich and Deerfield had many celebrated ministers work among them. Others beside Whitefield and Hunter were Charles Beatty, Gilbert Tennant, Samuel Finley, and John Brainard (brother of David Brainard, the celebrated missionary among the Indians).

In 1770, a Presbyterian church was built on the line between Salem and Cumberland counties, two miles from Friesburg. But the congregation was small and did not last very long. The families which participated are all of them still in this section, the Sowders, Wentzells, Piersons and Fosters. There is no trace of the building today but the old graveyard remains.

A year after Whitefield's visit in this section, the first Presbyterian church in the confines of Salem county was organized. This was Pittsgrove church, located at Daretown. This church has taken the names of the township rather than that of the town in which it is actually situated. It was organized April 30, 1741. The first pastor was the Reverend David Evans, a Welshman. The families which contributed to it were the Van Meters, Newkirks, Duboises, Garrisons, Millers, Sparkses, Mayhews and Coombses. David Evans, the first pastor, was also one of the first schoolmasters in this county. He was famed for his learning, and it is said that he built a log cabin on the church ground and conducted school there.

Evans died in 1751 and was suceeded by the Reverend Nehemiah Greenman, who was an ardent patriot and who was forced to take to the woods around Egg Harbor when the British came to Salem county in 1778. It was during his pastorate that the old Presbyterian church, still standing at Daretown, was built. Although it is no longer used for services it is still in good repair and shares with the Friends Meeting house at Hancock's Bridge the honor of being one of the two oldest church structures in Salem county.

William Schenck became pastor in 1780. He had graduated from Princeton thirteen years before and he stayed at Daretown for seven years. While he was pastor there came into a short existence the only college this county ever possessed. The old account says that "during years of trial and poverty a flourishing school was maintained at Pittsgrove to which parents from long distances sent their children." Pittsgrove College seems to have ceased after Schenck's pastorate ended, but during its brief term educated such responsible citizens as Drs. James and Robert Van Meter, John Moore White, attorney-general of New Jersey, and Salem's historian, Col. Robert Gibbon Johnson. The Pittsgrove congregation is flourishing today and is using a church built about the time of the Civil War to replace the colonial one mentioned above.

The other two Presbyterian congregations in Salem county founded before 1800 have both gone to decay. These were the Quihawkin and Logtown churches. Quihawkin was located at Obisquahasit on the banks of the Shanangah river. The melodious Indian names have gone and the English translation would be Pennsville in Lower Penns Neck township on the Delaware River. The church was founded in 1748. The families which made it up were Nevils, Philpots, Dunns, Wrights, Lippincotts, Stanleys, Burdens, Healys, Gil Johnsons, Lambsons, Congletons and others. Another great patriot and orator, the Reverend Samuel Eakin, was pastor of this church during the stormy years of the Revolution. He, too, was a graduate of Princeton college. Some critics place him next to Whitefield in his oratorical abilities. He is said to have addressed a militia company and the soldiers whenever they drilled, urging them to fight for their country. A line of one of his patriotic sermons implores the Lord "to teach our people to fight and give them courage and perseverance to overcome their enemies". Eakin died in 1784 and lived to see the Revolution a success. However it is said before his death, the Tories in his congregation forced him out. After his removal or death two or three other pastors ministered to the Penns Neck church, but about 1807 the last of these removed to Cape May, and soon after that the church died out. The graveyard still remains; it is located at the intersection of Main street and Salem road in the center of the village of Pennsville. A devout member of this extinct congregation

THE BAPTIST CHURCH

was Francis Miles, who left a farm for the purpose of educating the children of that township. In his memory the school children of Lower Penns Neck erected a monument about 1880 calling attention to his benevolence.

The Logtown Presbyterian church was founded in 1750. It was located in Harmersville, Monmouth precinct, now Lower Alloways Creek township. It was closely allied with the church at Penns Neck and in many cases had the same pastor. The names of the organizers were James Sayre, Joseph Hildreth, Richard Moore, Thomas Woodruff and Thomas Padgett. Later some of the Duboises and members of the Grier and Wood families joined the congregation. It died out about the same time as the Penns Neck congregations. The church building was taken down about 1815. The cemetery that once belonged to the Logtown Presbyterian church is now a part of the Baptist graveyard near Canton.

At one time the Swedish Lutheran church had a congregation at Buckshutem, near Leesburg. This church came from the early settlement of Swedes on the banks of the Morris river at Buckshutem, Dorchester and Leesburg. Johnson in 1839 said that at that time there were no traces of the church left, and no Swedish families in the vicinity. However, an old graveyard near Leesburg indicates there was a large settlement there at one time.

* * * *

The Baptists also spread into Salem county from Cumberland. While Nathaniel Jenkins was pastor of the Cohansey Baptist Church at Roadstown, branches of the church were established at Salem and Pittsgrove. The Salem church, first organized at Mill Hollow, was later moved to Yorke street, Salem; in 1845 the present building was erected on West Broadway. In 1743, the Baptist church at Pittsgrove was organized. The families which comprised it were Reeds, Elwells, Cheesemans, Pauldings, Mayhews, Dickisons, and Wallaces. This church is located at Daretown and like the Presbyterian takes its names from the township. The old brick church of this faith, erected about 1840, is still standing although not used.

This church also had vexing questions of doctrine. Just before the Revolution, one William Worth became pastor and continued for about twenty years. It is said that the pastor caused the division of his church into two factions. It seems that the women members of the congregation resented the unisersalist tendency of Worth, and opposed him vigorously, while the male members of the congregation accepted his doctrine. Worth became a speculator in western lands, and for his heresy was finally ousted from the ministry. It is said that Worth remained a universalist until approaching death induced him to renounce his error. This record comes from Shourds, who goes on to say that "the female members maintained the doctrine of the mother church at Cohansey. Their names were Susanna Elwell, Catharine Harris, Ruhama Austin, Ann Robertson, Tabitha Mayhew, Priscilla Blue, Abigail Joslin, Ruhama Moore, Rachel Robison, and Rachel Brick. Being deprived from meeting in the church by the apostate pastor and, which was more trying, by their husbands and sons, these sterling women frequently held their meetings in private houses and, in pleasant weather, in a contiguous grove. Ancient Rome was saved at one time by a heroic band of women and the fundamental doctrines of the Baptists were maintained at the Pittsgrove church by those faithful women, whose names, I have no doubt, are held in greatful remembrance by the congregation up to the present time."

The Baptists also seem to have had a mission in Penns Neck at the home of one Jeremiah Nickson. There seems to have been no organized congregation but in the family record kept by the man who preached there, Judge Thomas Killingsworth, it is mentioned that the families to whom he ministered were the Baldwins, the Lambsons, and the Copners. There were scattered Baptist families on Oldmans creek but there was no regular congregation. Some of them went as far as the Cohansey church at Roadstown for services and some went to Daretown. These Baptists did purchase a piece of ground at Auburn, then known as Sculltown, and erected a log meeting house in 1771. There is no trace of it today but the burying ground which went with the church remains and is used as a common ground by families in that vicinity.

CHAPTER XIII

Of Benjamin Abbott, Whose History Is the Story of the Methodist Church in Salem County

"I saw nothing but devils and evil spirits which tormented me in such a manner that neither my tongue nor pen could express it. There were scorpions a fathom long with stings in their tails. An inch and a half of the tail was stuck into me and the devils roared like thunder. I saw a lake of fire with devils blowing up the flames. One took me by the head, another by the feet to throw me in. I woke up."

Thus Benjamin Abbott records one of his dreams. This man, whose name is little but a faint memory today, was in the late eighteenth century one of America's most celebrated itinerant preachers and the father of Methodism in West Jersey. Picturesque, startling, flamboyant in his religious zeal, a weaver of spells and trances of religious ecstacy, a memoir writer of crude style and simple charm, this native son of Salem made a definite impression on the people of his day and still remains after a century and more, a mythical, mysterious figure.

Time has dimmed his glory, obliterated the epitaph on the tombstone beneath which he lies in the Walnut street graveyard, Salem, but above loom the walls of the First Methodist Church which he organized, a memorial to the work of a religious pioneer and the most powerful spiritual firebrand who ever trod the ground of West Jersey.

As an example of high-powered, evangelistic religion Herbert Asbury, relative of Bishop Asbury, wrote an article on Abbott in the *American Mercury*, classifying him as a sorcerer and a magician with ability to exorcise devils and cast cataleptic trances. Asbury of course writes with the modern tendency of the day to "debunk" famous characters who have in one way or another acquired haloes of fame.

The Methodists on the other hand claim him as one of their most gifted spiritual leaders and have written a great deal about his life and work. Somewhere between these two extremes the truth probably lies.

At least he was in his day one of Salem's most distinguished sons so that his life record and personality along with his unusual magnetic qualities are well worth a brief sketch. From the Chesapeake to the Hudson, he was famed as an evangelistic orator in days when religious feeling was hard to develop and maintain. He left behind him a series of memoirs that reveal his innermost feelings and reactions to the cause in which he was engaged. It is a story well worth reading if only for an excellent contemporary picture of post-revolutionary American life.

His early career and the place of his birth are uncertain. He is supposed to have come from the Long Island family of Abbotts, not the same family of Abbotts who have been in Salem county for over two centuries. Of Benjamin Abbott's line there are descendants today in the northern part of Salem county and in Atlantic county. Benjamin married young and lived for a while in Pittsgrove township, where he was employed as a farm hand by Benjamin Vanmeter. Vanmeter hired him largely on account of his great muscular strength but otherwise found him objectionable, often drunk and very troublesome when in liquor. Abbott spent his early days in gambling, drinking, fighting, swearing and other sundry vices. He was no stranger to the grand jury and was fined several times for assaults and batteries in his various fights. It is also admitted that he was almost illiterate, barely able to read and write.

Prior to his conversion in 1772 at the age of forty he had bothered the churches but little, occasionally going to the Pittsgrove Presbyterian Church of which his wife was a member. Abraham Whitworth, a travelling Methodist minister, in 1772 conducted a series of meetings in the home of John Murphy, in Pittsgrove, and here Abbott happened in and acquired the foundation for his subsequent conversion to the Methodist faith. His journal in quaint, picturesque language describes his emotions and varying feelings in experiencing the first awakening of religious interest. After several visits to Friendship Church during which time the "Devil and the Lord wrested for my soul", he finally realized he was "saved from sin and filled with unspeakable raptures of joy."

This episode was the beginning of his career as a preacher and a proselyting influence in the Methodist church. For the next twenty-four years he was destined to travel over a broad area, conduct meetings and experience physiological and religious phenomena that were to make his name a household word to those who valued strenuous evangelistic methods. He made many enemies also in the course of his long career and was often saved from violence at their hands by his overwhelming power of personal magnetism.

As an exhorter and a weaver of spells over his listeners he had no equal in his time or possibly at all in the history of the evangelical Methodist church. After the lapse of a century even his appreciative supporters in the church are unable to account very clearly for his great power of swaying audiences. The amazing feature of his leadership was that he could cause men and women in his audiences to drop on the floor as if slain by a bullet and remain there for hours in a trance. On his route through the Jerseys and Maryland after holding these remarkable meetings he would organize a small society of converts, often the nucleus of many a modern Methodist church.

The Reverend Abel Stevens in his monumental four-volume history of the Methodist Church, pays more attention to the record of Abbott than that of any other pioneer of that faith save only the giants of the cause, Wesley, Whitefield and Asbury. Thomas Shourds in his history of Fenwick's colony gives a conservative Quaker view of the famous exhorter and concludes that if Abbott possessed some of the education of his contemporaries in connection with his vast amount of zeal and exhortatory ability he would have ranked with the greatest pulpit orators of his time.

Stevens, loud in his praise of Abbott, compares him to John Bunyan and indeed there were parallels in the two lives. Both lived a thoroughly wicked early life, both had an originality of mind and character, both possessed rude but robust souls, profound in the mysteries of spiritual life. Stevens says: "He was subject to marvelous experiences which baffle solutions of clairvoyance and somnambulism. His marvelous dramas and visions were often verified by the most astonishing coincidences. He was an evangelical Hercules and wielded the word as a rude irresistible club rather than a sword."

John Firth of Salem, one of the original members of the First Church in Salem, was the author of the "Experience and Gospel Labors of the Rev. Ben. Abbott," including a narrative of his life and death. To that account, largely in Abbott's own quaint reported style, we are indebted for the actual record of those phenomenal meetings which so stirred his auditors that they "fell to the floor as if dead."

Concerning his dreams and the accuracy of their predictions, Abbott writes regarding Abraham Whiteworth, the preacher, who had converted him, "In a dream, I saw the preacher under whom I was awakened, drunk and playing cards, with his garments all defiled with dirt. When I was awake and found it a dream I was glad, although I still felt some uneasiness on his account. In about three weeks I heard that the poor, unfortunate preacher had fallen into sundry gross sins and was expelled from the Methodist connection."

This was indeed the case. Stevens regretfully states that Whitworth's case was the first instance of apostasy that dishonored Methodism in the new world. Liquor was his chief downfall and he apparently drifted into the British army where he met his death in battle.

But his most illustrious convert was carrying on. Brooking no opposition he carried his meetings and listeners by storm, causing the unfaithful to flee "in fear and trembling."

Conscious of the great amount of sin prevalent in his home district near Salem, Abbott made one of his first pilgrimages as a preacher to the part of Lower Creek below Canton, where he states the place for its notorious depravity was called Hell Neck. His journal records the modest assertion that he was able to save some of the inhabitants from further vice. Whether this is the beginning of the name Hell Neck or not, it is at least interesting to know that Abbott in his new zeal firmly believed that the whole country was in the same condition. This being his first field of endeavor, possibly the name lingered when the missionary moved on to other territory.

At a meeting in Lower Penns Neck where he charmingly states he found "a set of as hardened sinners as were out of hell", he was confronted one night by a skeptical Presbyterian who rose to heckle him and question his good faith. The Presbyterian declared that Abbott was possessed by the devil and throughout the meeting sat on the front row and sneered at the preacher. Going to a meeting in a nearby farm house Abbott was again confronted by this same man, who still sneered and accused him of being diabolically influenced. Abbott prayed and exhorted and the listeners fell one by one to the floor in trances and exultations of joy until soon none were left standing but Abbott and the doubting Presbyterian. The meeting ended with the skeptic still unconvinced. A third and fourth time the Presbyterian followed Abbott from meeting to meeting in the various parts of the county until at last on the fourth encounter, Abbott says, "after exhorting the multitude, I said, I can speak no more, who should arise but my doubting Presbyterian friend, now free from the shackles of Beelzebub, who said he was convinced of his error in doubting us and who gave a warm and fervid exhortation lasting an hour."

On the eastern shore of Maryland Abbott conducted a funeral service during which dark clouds appeared over a hitherto clear sky. While exhorting his congregation thunder and lightning broke in heavy volume over the countryside. He set before them, "the awful coming of Christ in all his splendor, with all the armies of Heaven to judge the world and take vengeance on the ungodly." The crowd shrieked, scrambling on all fours around the house with Abbott's terrible strident voice screaming that here was the judgment at hand. Before his awful eye and powerful voice some fell unconscious on the floor or ran screaming into the pouring rain storm. This was one of his greatest spell-weaving experiences and the followers on the eastern shore always referred to it with awe and admiration as Brother Abbott's thundergust sermon.

Abbott frequently had to face dangerous men in his various meetings, especially in his home county of Salem. Once at Perkintown in Oldmans, then Upper Penns Neck, he was scheduled to speak at the meeting house by which ran a road used for running horse races. One was listed for that particular Sunday. Out of deference to Abbott the race was called off but two angry and dangerous looking men came in the church, one bearing a truncheon in his hand. Abbott accused people of that locality of being full of vice. The defender of the community, he carrying the weapon, called out that it was as good as some other places. Abbott said: "He had broken the law of God as well as the civil law and was liable to a fine. I poured out the terrors of the law in the most awful manner. I saw his countenance change and he cried aloud. He went out. He had met his match."

Another time in the old court house at Salem some of the lawyers and clerks jokingly invited him to give them a sermon. He went into the court room, barred the door and proceeded for two hours to warn them of punishments. His text was, "Woe unto you, ye lawyers. Ye lade man with burdens grievous to be borne. Ye yourselves touch not the burden. Ye take away the key of knowledge." He rebuked them hard enough and long enough to stop any future jest.

In a controversy with some Quakers who would not allow him to use their meeting house unless he was a member of that sect, Abbott said; "I love and speak real heart religion; let me find it where I may."

On Margaret Lane in Salem where Abbott and his followers met in a rude edifice no better than a barn, gangs of Salem revelers beseiged and annoyed the worshippers until the magistrates of the town were forced to protect the feeble society. Several historians recall the case of a club formed to burlesque the preacher and his excitable methods. At one of its meetings, a female guest climbed on a chair and started to imitate the minister shouting that she had found peace and was ready to die, whereupon she fell to the floor and did die. The Methodist historian assures us that this disbanded the club and its members joined church.

Out of his curious, sometimes egotistical memoirs one gleans the following favorite expressions. His most repeated ones, which sound somewhat bloodthirsty, were: "The slain lay all over the house"; and "I left the slain and wounded on the field of battle." Again, "She could then talk Canaan's language; An old lady was on the wing for glory; We had a powerful, melting, shouting time; They heard as for eternity and Several were lost in the ocean of love."

In midsummer of 1796 back in Salem after extensive tours in New York and Maryland, health failed him and he died on August 14, as his biographer Firth says, shouting "Glory, glory, glory," and "Clapping his hand in the greatest ecstacies of joy imaginable."

Bishop Asbury wrote in his journal in 1781: "I met with and heard Benjamin Abbott. His words came with great power. In Chester, he tells me, twenty were renewed in love and eight on this side; people fall to the ground under him and sink in a passive state, helpless, stiff, motionless. He tried to attach himself to two other sects, but had such struggles within, that he was forced back; the Lord would not let him be anything but of a Methodist faith." To them his singular yet effective life remains a marvel if not a complete mystery. Some of his superiors were doubtful about his propensity for causing fits and trances to his followers, but hearing of no evil results, allowed him to continue uninterrupted.

To him almost single handed the Methodists owe the establishment of the church in Salem. In 1784 his small congregation appealed to the affluent Society of Friends for aid in building a meeting house. The Friends divided on the propriety of aiding them and left it to the individual conscience of their members. He and Henry Firth, his chief lieutenant, did receive some pecuniary aid and finally erected a small frame structure on Margaret's Lane, later South and now Walnut street.

Directly behind the west wall of the church lie the bones of this man who despite bitter criticism and hatred did succeed in his life time in keeping religion from stagnation in this community. Space forbids the recounting of the upheaval of religious thought and controversy that this apostle of declamatory religion started, but he stands today as one of the most unique and unusual men ever known in this locality.

Apparently no artist has preserved the towering form and shaggy countenance of the preacher with the penetrating black eye that could prostrate his listeners and cause them to shrink with fear at his exhortations.

On the tombstone, worn with the flight of time, one may read: "Sacred to the memory of Rev. Benjamin Abbott, 25 years a member, 16 years a local preacher, 7 years a traveling preacher in the M. E. Church. He died August, 1796, aged 61 years. A holy, zealous and useful man of God."

CHAPTER XIV

OF DIVERS HAPPENINGS BETWEEN 1750 AND THE WAR OF THE REVOLUTION

After the turn of the seventeenth century, the residents of the Cohansey precincts began agitation for a new county to be set off from Salem. The reason for this was quite obvious. It was a considerable distance from Greenwich, Fairfield and the line of Cohansey creek to the county seat at Salem. The roads were indifferent, and communication tedious and poor. It is small wonder therefore that the citizens of the lower precincts, after the population had increased, wanted a county of their own. In 1733 an attempt was made to pass a bill through the provincial council and assembly to create a new county out of the southern part of Fenwick's tenth. It failed. But in 1747 the agitation was renewed and this time was successful. Late in that year a commission was appointed to run the bounds of the new county which was given the name of Cumberland. The name was given by Jonathan Belcher, governor of New Jersey, apparently to please the reigning house of Hanover in England, in honor of the Duke of Cumberland, brother of King George II. In view of the attempt of Galachrone and his Irish confreres to establish the house of Stuart in Salem county three years before, which was fomented at Cohansey Bridge (Bridgeton), it is extremely significant that Belcher should impose his gubernatorial will upon the colonists and have this county named Cumberland in honor of the man better known as the "Dutch butcher," who defeated and slaughtered without mercy the survivors of the battle of Culloden. The name of the victor in the battle which ended the enterprise of Bonnie Prince Charlie and his Stuart followers on a Scottish moor at Culloden in 1746 was selected by Belcher as the name for the new county. So the name of William Augustus, Duke of Cumberland, was perpetuated in history.

Due to the ambitions of one John Brick, Jr., Salem county lost a large part of its territory. It was the intention of the partition commissioners to divide Salem county into two equal parts; their first proposition was to make the mouth of Stow creek (Unknown creek) the starting point, follow up this creek until they came to a small tributary, on which the mill pond known as

NEW COUNTY FORMED

Seeley's is located, thence up to the head branches of the creek, and then by direct course to the Gloucester county line. But John Brick was at that time a judge of the Salem county courts, and he was anxious for various reasons that his possessions at Jericho on the south side of Stow creek should be included in the new county, and to that end therefore he insisted that the lower branch of Stow creek known as Gravelly Run should be the line between the two counties, and although there was much protest it was made the boundary, thereby giving Cumberland county much more territory than Salem, the parent county. Had Brick not prevailed with the politicians of that day the country north and west of Roadstown, Shiloh and the village of Deerfield to the Jewish settlement of Rosenhayn and just missing the northern limits of the City of Bridgeton would still be in Salem county.

The first court of common pleas of the new county was held at Greenwich, Fenwick's old town of Cohansey, in May of 1748. The judges were Brick, who had the unique honor of being a judge in both Salem and Cumberland counties, Richard Wood and John Remington. The first sheriff was Ananias Sayre. The first clerk of the court was Elias Cotting. Soon after the county seat was moved to Cohansey Bridge, now known as Bridgeton, where it has remained for almost two hundred years. Thus at one fell swoop over four hundred thousand acres were taken off Salem county, and the original domain of John Fenwick became reduced to less than one-half its original size.

* * *

The shipping trade which had been so beneficial to Salem during the first part of the eighteenth century continued unabated up to the time of the Revolution. Indeed, the newspapers of the 1760's contained little Salem news except that of the large procession of ships which entered and left the port of Salem. In 1763 one Francis Hopkinson, Esq. was appointed collector of the king's customs at the port of Salem. It is very ironical that this same man who in 1763 received a political position under King George III was, thirteen years later, one of the signers of the Declaration of Independence.

The new collector of the customs reported to England that smuggling was prevalent in his section. The English authorities always had trouble with smugglers from France, and the colonies in America were no exception. Hopkinson called attention to the fact that rum, sugar and molasses were the chief goods in which the smugglers dealt. The chief charge was that they had failed to pay the king's duty.

William Hancock, builder of the Hancock House and for

twenty years a member of the assembly of New Jersey, gets into the news in 1762 by being chairman of the house committee which told His Majesty that New Jersey could raise no more men to recruit the regular forces. Hancock's report to Governor Josiah Hardy showed that the French wars had so drained New Jersey of servants that labor was so scarce that in some cases money could not buy it.

In 1764, an institution which had lasted almost a hundred years was abolished by the legislature of New Jersey. Fairs had been held at Salem since Fenwick's death. They had been postponed for health reasons such as epidemics, and they had been abused by illicit selling of rum and drunkenness. But for all their ups and downs they had persisted until this year when, because of the abuse of privileges, they were abolished. While the Salem fair was the first to feel the axe of disapproval, others followed, and by 1797, all fairs in New Jersey including those at Greenwich, Burlington and Princeton were abolished.

The newspapers of 1760 carry frequent notices of runaway servants, of sales of land and, especially in Salem county, of the large number of prisoners who broke out of the Salem jail. In 1764, Sheriff Budd of Salem county advertised for one of his erstwhile guests, John Cleaver. Mr. Cleaver, according to the description put out by the sheriff, "wore a blue jacket, made out of an old Surtout coat, with metal coat buttons on it, Check Trowsers, old hat, old shoes and stockings; he is a tailor by trade, and plays on the Fiddle; he is very talkative and much adicted to drink." Many of these runaways and jail breakers took women with them, and the old advertisements frequently said, "he has a Woman with him which he calls his Wife."

A pathetic note and one significant of the troubles of indentured servants appears in 1765 in the Pennsylvania Gazette. It is entitled "Enquiry after a Lost Husband," and speaks for itself. It says, "Magdalene Bayer, came into this Country, last Fall, with her Husband Erhard Bayer, and her Brother Hans Sax, but as she was Sick, and sent amongst others to the House provided for Sick, and during the Time of her Confinement there the Merchant's Cruelty was so great as to sell her Husband from her, but to whom, or to what Part of this Province, she cannot find out. And after her Recovery, to sell her, big with Child, to John Ray, living in Alloway's Creek Precinct, near the Glasshouse, West New-Jersey. These are therefore to request any Person, who shall read the above and know any Thing of the aforesaid Erhard Bayer or her Brother, to give Notice thereof to Richard Wistar, in Philadelphia, who will take Care to inform me thereof, and will very much oblige the distressed Magdalene Bayer."

Colonel Johnson contended that Joshua Huddy, hero of Monmouth county, whose murder by the British in the Revolutionary War caused a delicate international situation,[1] was a resident of Salem. This contention is borne out by a legal advertisement published in 1766 by Edward Test, Sheriff of Salem county. It reads: "By Virtue of His Majesty's writ of Venditioni Exponas to me directed, will be exposed to Salem, on Saturday, the 30th of December next, on the Premises, a valuable Plantation, situate in Haynes's Neck, Salem County, Containing 300 Acres and upwards; late the Property of Joshua Huddy; seized and taken in Execution . . ."

A plea for higher morality in school teachers appeared in 1767, relative to the adventures of one James Weldon, who posed as a school master and turned out to be a second-story man. The Pennsylvania Journal said: "We hear from Salem, in New-Jersey, that on the night of the 12th inst. a person who had undertaken to officiate as a school master near that place, and to have opened his school the next day, as a specimen of his learning and ability, broke open the store of Messrs. Test and Johnson, and stole from thence about a hundred dollars in cash. This capital performance being discovered, he was conducted to proper lodgings, and will receive his trial at the next assizes, when no doubt his merit will be properly considered. This may serve as a caution against admitting persons to form the morals of our youth, without having a true knowledge of their principal and character." For his activities, ex-curricula, he was sentenced to be burned in the hand.

Old age records were shattered when in this same year of 1767 a negro slave, the property of Clement Hall of Elsinboro, died at the age of 120 years. The first notice of a stage line to Salem appears in December of 1767, in which one Aaron Silver advertises himself as a common carrier between Salem and William Cooper's ferry, now the city of Camden. His rates were three half-pence a mile for passengers and merchandise at four shillings and three pence for each hundred. The line ran from Salem to Cooper's ferry in one day. The driver rested a day, then returned to Salem the third day.

Not all the runaways mentioned in the countless advertisements were male. Here is one of the other sex, illuminating in its description. The owner of the runaway indentured servant was John Firth, the Boswell of Benjamin Abbott. "Run away from the Subscriber, in Salem County, West New-Jersey, on

[1] The case of Captain Asgill, "New Jersey, Colony and State," Francis B. Lee, Volume 2, page 243.

Friday, the 30th of October last, an Irish Servant Girl, about 17 or 18 Years of Age, named Mary Ann O'Bryan, but commonly calls herself Mary Bryan, short and thick, of a fair Complexion, has light brown Hair; had on, and took with her, one striped Camblet Skirt, two Linsey Petticoats, one striped with red, blue and white, and one black, blue and white, a homespun blue and white striped short Gown, blue Yarn stockings, new Shoes, and old Pinchbeck Buckles. She is much given to drink, and very impudent when so."

The colonists had heavy storms. On July 7th, 1768, a hail storm in Penns Neck destroyed all the growing grain, and on March 19th of that year, a high tide, "the highest that has been known by the oldest man now living," caused the death of many hundred cattle, hog and sheep and did great damage to the tide banks raised by the inhabitants of that township.

The missionaries of the church of England were still complaining in the Pennsylvania Journal for 1768 that "at Cohansey in West Jersey stands a church, but there is not the shadow of a congregation in the county. At Salem the Episcopal cause is almost as low."

Fire had claimed its toll early in 1769. The house of one Spenser in Salem county was burned and two of his small children "unhappily lost their Lives in the Flames; it being out of the power of their distressed friends to save them. About a week before, the House of one Cox in the same county, was burnt to the ground, and one of his children, a son, also perished in the Flames."

One of the most unpopular men of this period was John Hatton, who followed Hopkinson as collector of customs at the port of Salem. Incidentally, he was the last collector of his majesty's customs at Salem. He seems to have made everybody angry and as far as Salem county was concerned, became a contributing source to the Revolution.

Colonel Johnson, whose father probably knew him well, pours the vials of wrath upon him and calls him "a petty, overbearing and insolent tool of the British government." Johnson says, "He became despicable in the opinion of the people generally—so that recrimination and hard words often passed between him and even persons in authority. He made no scruples of charging the owners of the vessels with carrying on an illicit trade and defrauding his majesty's government out of the revenue, and that the justices of the town and county connived at it."

In 1768 he complained to Governor William Franklin that Grant Gibbon and Edward Test had abused him in the conduct of his office. A hearing was held on this matter and Hatton's charge against the two citizens of Salem was thrown out.

Hatton was himself investigated, the witnesses to the hearing alleging that there were many irregularities in Hatton's public conduct and furthermore, that his private life had occasioned the quarrels which actually started his complaint against Gibbon and Test. Hatton had charged also that one William Pike had cursed the king and used profane language while Mr. Hatton was exercising the duties of his majesty as collector of the port of Salem, but the governor threw this charge out also and advised Mr. Hatton to go back to Salem and treat his people civilly and decently.

At the same time one Jacob Scroggin entered the lists against Mr. Hatton with a scathing denunciation of the collector in the Pennsylvania Chronicle. It seems that Hatton sold a negro boy to Scroggin and had warranted him free of fits. As soon as Scroggin took possession of the boy he had several fits and Scroggin demanded his money back, but Hatton refused to pay. In an essay of over two pages Mr. Scroggin paid his respects to Mr. Hutton and said in closing, "I have been represented, by Hatton, as a contentious man, a character my neighbours will acquit me of; but if a perpetual state of litigious cavilling, or the universal voice of a people can give a just title to that character, I am sure no man can, with equal demerit, claim it as John Hatton, Esquire, Collector of his Majesty's Customs, of the port of Salem."

As the storm clouds of the Revolution broke over New Jersey, Hatton realized that he was not popular with the people of Salem and removed himself and his goods to Swedesboro where he built a brick house which is still standing. This house of John Hatton's may still be seen on the right of the King's Highway as one enters Swedesboro from the south. Swedesboro also made life miserable for the erstwhile collector of customs at Salem and he finally became a fugitive from the justice of the state of New Jersey and joined the British army in 1778.

In these hectic days before the Revolution, trade and industry seemed to prosper. There was much building of brick houses, as the large number standing today, built between 1750 and the Revolution, will testify.

From the earliest days of the colony and the first sessions of the legislature, various petitions had been presented asking for permission to run tide banks in the low places near the river and creeks in order to protect the lands against the encroachment of the tides. There are many of these in the New Jersey Archives. One asked permission for a tide bank in a territory well known to local gunners. It reads as follows: "This is to give notice to all persons concerned, that the several owners of the Salt Marsh, lying between Stow and Alloway's Creeks, called the Back Marsh, in the County of Salem, intend to petition the General Assembly of this province, at the next sessions, for an act to enable them to run a tide bank from a point near John Stretch's called Bear Point, to Eagle Island, and from Eagle Island to Deep Creek, up the several courses thereof to Little Creek; and so up the creek called Thoroughfare Creek, until it comes opposite the lower end of Ragged Island; and from the said Island to Home Island; and from Home Island to the lower end of Alloway's Neck, where Samuel Smith now lives."

Another stage line appears advertised in the Pennsylvania Gazette for 1771. William Shute and Jacob Paullin (now Paulding) informed the public that they would run a stage wagon from Pilesgrove near the glass house through Woodstown to William Cooper's ferry (now Camden).

Benjamin Holme had one of the first ferries in the county, which ran from Elsinboro Point to Port Penn. Holme was later a colonel in the American army and had his ferry house and home burned by the British in 1778 for his participation in the war. Eight years before this event he advertised for a lost ferry boat as follows: "A ferry boat, belonging to the subscriber, living in Elsinborough, with one James Canaday on board, it is said, set out from Port Penn, to come home to Elsinborough, the 9th instant, about sunset, and was seen to cross over as far as the upper end of Reedy-Island, the wind blowing very fresh at Northwest, has never been heard of since, as we know of; the boat would carry about four or five horses, rigged sloop fashion, with a poplar mast, and decked before the mast. Whoever takes up and secures said boat, so that the owner may have her again, shall have Forty Shillings reward, or Three Pounds if brought home, and reasonable charges, paid by Benjamin Holme."

By 1770 the influx of settlers had been such in the northern part of the county that a new township called Pittsgrove was formed out of Pilesgrove township. The new township lay to the east of Pilesgrove and today takes in the modern townships of Pittsgrove, Upper Pittsgrove and the borough of Elmer. Its name was given in honor of a great British statesman. The public proclamation on the subject, given on October 8, 1770, read: "As there has been lately a Division from the Township of Pilesgrove, and new Township chartered; and as there are various Monuments erected to the everlasting Remembrance of the Name of that truly noble and venerable Patriot, Mr. Pitt; out of a grateful sense—we, the Freeholders and other Inhabitants of the new patented Township, did apply to the Government for the Name, as well as the Patent, which Government, in its benign Goodness, did admit, and think we cannot immortalize that noble and venerable Patriot's Name, nor transmit it to Futurity better, than to apply it to the Township, therefore the new Township is called Pitts-Grove, in Commemoration of that great and noble Friend of American Liberty, Sir William Pitt, now Earl of Chatham."

Another note of longevity appears in this same year with the death of Mounce Keen of Pilesgrove, aged 105 years. He was of Swedish extraction and the death notice says that a short time before his death he rode alone on a horse three miles and back to his home. The progress of medical science is displayed by an item in the Pennsylvania Packet saying that one Isaiah Mills of Salem, West New Jersey, who had been blind of both eyes with a confirmed Gutta Serena, was restored to his sight by the ability of a Philadelphia doctor named Graham.

The colonists were still having domestic difficulties. Most of the notices appearing refer to runaway wives and husbands unwilling to pay their debts. This one, in 1772 is slightly different. It says, "I am very sorry for advertising my wife which was done through the heat of Passion and Inconsideration; which I now retract," and signed by John Elwell. There were tragedies also. Two men named Richard Hackett and Samuel Smith were drowned off Penns Neck when a sailboat was upset. Another passenger named Joshua Huddy escaped. Again the frequent mention of Joshua Huddy in the Archives leads the historian to believe, as Johnson says, that this hero of the American Revolution once lived in Salem county.

Two murders occurred in the county in the same year. The first is reported as follows in a letter to the Pennsylvania Chronicle, February 10, 1772: "Talbert, The Shopkeeper, at Quinton's Bridge, is in Gaol for the Murder of his Wife. She had been buried three Days, when she was taken up by the Coroner. The inquest brought their verdict in 'Guilty of shortening her days.' He is to remain in Prison till the Chief Judge comes down to try him for his Life." Talbot was later exonerated of complicity in the crime by a grand jury which found no bill against him.

The other murder was that of a farmer, William Gwin of Pilesgrove, who became involved in a fight with one David Sheppard, also of Pilesgrove. Sheppard killed him and fled to parts unknown. He apparently was never caught. The notice to apprehend the fugitive was signed by Jechonias Wood, coroner of Salem county and first settler of the modern Woodstown.

By 1772 there was competition noted in the newspapers of stage coaches both bidding for public favor. One line run by Samuel Bowen who apparently succeeded Aaron Silver was in competition with another line run by Samuel Brick. Both lines ran from Salem to Cooper's ferry. Brick, however, diverted his line one day a week to include passengers and mail to go to Quinton's Bridge from Salem. Many columns of the Pennsylvania Chronicle throughout 1771 were taken up with a long controversy between two high sheriffs of Salem county, John Budd and Edward Test, both asserting that one owed the other large sums of money.

Just prior to the Revolution Bennomi Dare inserted in the Pennsylvania Gazette an advertisement of a new stage line which also served Salem. It is as follows: "The Subscriber begs Leave to inform the Public, that he now designs driving a Stage-Wagon, from the House of Mr. Michael Lee, in Greenwich, Inn-keeper, starting from said House on Mondays, at 12 o'clock, and to proceed from thence to the House of Mr. John Dickenson, Inn-keeper, in Salem; to set out from said house on Tuesdays, at Sun-rise, and proceed from thence to Mr. William Cooper's Ferry; he then crosses said Ferry to Captain John Hyder's, in Philadelphia, and returns from thence to the Town of Salem on Thursdays, and on Fridays to the Town of Greenwich as aforesaid. Rules of the fare as follows—For a single Person from Greenwich to Salem 3s.—From Salem to Philadelphia 5s—and luggage, per 100 wt. from Greenwich to Salem 1s.—from Salem to Philadelphia 42 6d.—Letters 4d apiece, the money to be delivered with the Letters. All Gentlemen and Ladies, that please to favor the Subscriber with their Company, or Orders, may depend on the most civil usuage, and punctual Execution of their Commands, by the Public's humble Servant."

The year of 1774 saw the clouds of war definitely hover over Salem county. Johnson says, and no doubt correctly, that the Boston Port Bill excited the feelings of this community to the highest pitch. The struggle had long been brewing. The Stamp Act, the Navigation Acts, and now the Boston Port Bill had all caused concern and unrest in the colonies. Salem was no exception. Although it had profited greatly from the English protection of its coastwise shipping and had not suffered in the colonial wars as had New England, many of its citizens were willing and anxious to throw their support in the impending struggle against the mother country. The Town Meeting was called upon for aid at this time. The first of these was held in Salem at the court house on July 15th, 1774 "to consider of some proper measures to be taken in support of American freedom at this alarming crises."

The meeting was the Declaration of Independence as far as Salem was concerned. The resolutions of that meeting, presided over by George Trenchard, ancestor of a present Supreme Court Justice of New Jersey, are well worth the attention of every patriotic citizen:

1. That fully sensible of the important advantages derived to us from a continuance of that harmony, confidence and connection which, till of late has subsisted between the parent country and these Colonies, we, from inclination as well as duty, under free enjoyment of our constitutional rights, liberties and privileges, will ever render all due obedience to the Crown of Great-Britain, as well as full faith and allegiance to our most gracious Sovereign King George the Third, and his Protestant successors.

2. That it gives us inexpressible grief, when we consider that the machinations of those, who would wish to destroy the liberties of this country, have so far prevailed against us, as to induce our most gracious Sovereign to believe, that we are wanting in affection for his person and government and to give a sanction to laws respecting us, so contrary to the known humanity and goodness of his heart, so destructive of our rights and privileges as British subjects, and so manifestly tending to destroy that affection and dependence, which we sincerely wish to maintain.

3. That we conceive the Boston Port Bill, and the Bill for the impartial administration of justice, &c. in the Massachusetts-Bay, to be a most arbitrary exertion of tyranny over a free and loyal people, and of the most dangerous and alarming tendency, not only to that province in particular, but to all the British colonies in general; and therefore we think every well-wisher to the liberties of his country is now loudly called upon to promote, without delay a firm union of all America, without which it will probably soon cease to be a country of freedom.

4. That this meeting think it their duty to declare, that they consider the acts of the British Parliament, for restraining the erecting slitting-mills, plating-mills, &c in America, an absolute infringement of the natural rights of the subject, and of an equal tendency to enslave America.

5. That we think a Congress of deputies, consisting of men of the first character in every province, in point of fortune, integrity and abilities, having full powers delegated to them to act for the good of the whole, will be the most probable and proper means of obtaining redress of our grievances, re-establishing, on a constitutional foundation, our rights and liberties, and of restoring that confidence and harmony so much wished for: And we now declare, that we will cheerfully co-operate in any general plan of union, that may be thought most conducive to the public good.

6. That a subscription be immediately set on foot for the relief of the poor of the town of Boston, now suffering under the operation of the Boston Port Bill; and monies raised to be appropriated by the committee hereafter named, in such manner as to them shall appear best calculated to answer the good purposes intended.

7. That this meeting do return their unfeigned thanks to those truly patriotic members of both Houses of Parliament, who have so warmly espoused the cause of American liberty.

8. That the following gentlemen, viz. Grant Gibbon, Benjamin Holme, George Trenchard, Andrew Sinnickson, Samuel Lynch, Elisha Bassett, John Mayhew, William Hancock, John Holme, Robert Johnson, Edward Keasbey,

and John Carey, Esquires, and Messieurs William Goodwin, Bartholomew Wyatt, Nathaniel Hancock, Thomas Sinnickson, Dr. Samuel Dick, Robert Wilson, Joseph Champneys, Thomas Carney, sen., Dr. Isaac Harris, and Benjamin Thompson, be a committee to correspond with the other counties of this province, and with the Committees of the other provinces, and to transact all kinds of business in our behalf, which the urgent necessity of the times may require; and also to delegate a certain number of their body, to represent this county at the provincial meeting, at New-Brunswick, the 21st inst. in order to choose deputies to represent this province at the General Congress.

Another public meeting was held on October 13, 1774. At this meeting Grant Gibbon was named chairman and entrusted with the difficult task of raising money for the distressed, poor and starving patriots of Boston. It is said that a sum of one hundred fifty-seven pounds was raised by subscription and forwarded by Thomas Sinnickson, a member of the committee, to Boston. Three years later when Salem county was under the heel of the invader there is no record that Boston reciprocated in raising this sum for the distressed farmers of this locality. But in 1774 this charity was widespread. As yet the battles of Lexington and Concord had not been fought, but Boston was under the heel of the British army, and sympathetic patriotic feeling extended throughout the colonies on behalf of the inhabitants of Boston.

In the early winter of this same year occurred a most startling event which materially precipitated the Revolution in West Jersey. This was the Greenwich Tea Party on the night of November 22. It happened at Greenwich, in what was once Salem county, and the participants were practically all sons of men who were residents of Salem county before the division. A brig named the *Grayhound*, Captain J. Allen, with a cargo of tea headed into Cohansey creek and discharged her cargo at Greenwich. Some accounts say that the cargo was destined for Salem but that because of storm and fear the captain decided to dock at Greenwich. Emulating the Boston Tea Party, a band of young men disguised as Indians learned the whereabouts of the stored tea and seizing it, pubicly burned the cargo. There are several lists as to who comprised the tea burners. The list of Colonel Johnson seems to be the one most commonly followed. At least, his list is used on the monument at Greenwich. They were Ebenezer Elmer, Richard Howell, afterwards Governor of New Jersey; David Pierson, Stephen Pierson, Silas Whitecar, Timothy Elmer, Reverend Andrew Hunter, Philip Vickers Fithian, Alexander Moore, Jr., Clarence Parvin, John Hunt, James Hunt, Lewis Howell, Henry Stacks, James Ewing, Dr. Thomas Ewing, Josiah Seeley and Joel Fithian.

One of these men, Philip Vickers Fithian, deserves more

than passing attention. Prior to the tea burning he had graduated from Princeton College and was an ordained Presbyterian Minister. His diary or journal published about 1900 by Princeton University is a literary work of art. He was not only an ardent patriot; he was one of the few scholars of his time. At the outbreak of the war he left his young bride, Elizabeth Beatty, daughter of another famous Presbyterian clergyman, and joined the American army and became a military chaplain. He died at White Plains, New York of disease at the youthful age of thirty.

The destruction of the tea caused consternation in this section. Especially indignant were the owners of the tea and the Tories who sympathized with them. Attempts were made to prosecute these men for their act, but a convenient Whig grand jury in Cumberland county refused to find bills. Civil suits were also brought against the participants, but as the colonies drifted into the Revolution these suits were abandoned and the tea owners had to bear the loss.

As the Revolution became imminent frequent meetings were held throughout Salem county not only for military purposes and for raising money, but for the economic purpose of encouraging home manufacture. The colonists knew only too well that their trade from England would be shut off, and that they, only too soon, would be thrown upon their own resources. They decided to extend the production of flax by sowing more seed than formerly. The patriotic ladies of the colony were urged to work overtime on the spinning wheel and the loom. One resolution urged "that our young women, instead of trifling their time away, do prudently employ it in learning the use of the spinning wheel."

In 1775, a committee of observation chosen in the meeting by the several townships of Salem county was formed. The chairman of the committee was Andrew Sinnickson. The members of it were the leading patriots of the day; their names are worth remembering. They were Robert Johnson, John Carey, Bateman Lloyd, John Mayhew, William Hancock, Andrew Sinnickson, John Holme, Jacob Scoggin, William Mecum, Thomas Sinnickson, Dr. Samuel Dick, Robert Wilson, Samuel Nicholson, Aaron Bradway, Richard Smith, Jr., Whitton Cripps, William Smith, Allen Congleton, Henry Jeans, George Somerville, Thomas Carney, Jr., Joshua Shinn, James James, Isaac Harris, Jacob Dubois, Edward Hancock, John Finlaw, John Dickinson, Sr. and Samuel Finley, clerk.

In June, 1775, after the war had actually opened in New England, William Patterson, secretary of the provincial congress, issued a public notice calling on each county to organize a militia company. In addition a fund of ten thousand pounds was asked for, the sum to be divided proportionately between the counties. Salem's share was near the top, it being asked for six hundred and seventy-nine pounds.

As the patriots of New England were fighting the British and those in Salem were raising money for their relief, there occurred a murder and two trials in Salem county which are of interest because it was the last important case in Salem county in which an indictment was found in the name of the King of Great Britian. This murder case was forgotten for years. A chance reference in an old newspaper brought it to light and the records of the Salem county clerk's office yielded up this most interesting affair.

The old yellow copy of the indictment written in a scrawling longhand is eloquent of the changing days near at hand when this paper was written. In the course of the indictment one reads, "Our sovereign lord the King, George III now king of Great Britain." George continued as King of Great Britian, but the day was not far distant when his royal writ and summons to answer to a criminal charge would be omitted from the proper documents and instead may be found, "In the name of Governor Livingston," and "in the name of the State." All this because the indictment was penned in June of 1775, and only a year later the embattled colonists met in Philadelphia and wrote the document which made George's name a matter of no avail.

* * * *

The fear of being arraigned for treason themselves had little weight with the staunch citizens of Salem in those June days of '75 when the grand jury solemnly convened and handed to the judges and justices of the Salem Court of Oyer and Terminer, two indictments charging Ceasar and Kile, two male slaves of Recompense and Boston Sherry, with the murder of the first named master. Petty treason had reared its ugly head again and recalling the heinous murder of James Sherron fifty-eight years before by his slaves, the freeholders of the county of Salem were not disposed to waste any time in the punishment of this offense.

As may be expected with the flight of time the facts are meager and exceedingly hard to ascertain. About all we know is that Recompense Sherry was a farmer living in the forests of Upper Alloways Creek township, Salem county. Boston was either the brother or son of Recompense. The relationship is not clear. In the New Jersey Archives of 1775 may be found an advertisement signed by Recompense Sherry in the Pennsylvania Gazette, offering for sale a negro slave who had had the smallpox. Whether this was the slave who a month or so later was destined to kill his master is a matter of conjecture.

The present location of the farm and the murder is fairly ascertainable. In 1875 the farm was owned by John Garrison. It is east of Friesburg and southeast of Aldine in the corner where Upper Pittsgrove and Alloway townships and Cumberland county join. In the old account it is designated as Watson's Corner but on the map of 1875 the Garrison farm is a half-mile below that place.

The historical fragment indicates that Sherry had sent Ceasar to the woods to chop and not coming back when he called him the master went in search of him and beneath a large white oak tree was surprised by the slave who set upon him with an axe and a club. The master was almost instantly killed, whereupon Ceasar and his accomplice, another slave named Kile, secreted his body in a hollow log nearby. How the murder was discovered is not known, but apparently it was soon found out and the slaves were arrested and brought to the jail in Salem. The date of the murder was May 31, 1775.

On June 14, 1775 the June term of the Salem Courts opened and as soon as the court was convened the return of the grand jury was given charging the two slaves with murder, petit treason and murder. Again the statute of 1351 of Parva Proditio was brought to light and used in a Salem murder case. The indictment reads:

"The jurors for our Sovereign Lord and King upon the oath and affirmation of at least 12 Honest and Lawful men do present that a negro man slave named Ceasar the property of Recompense Sherry late of Alloways Creek Township and the County of Salem, aforesaid, and one other negro man slave named Kile, the property of Boston Sherry of the same place aforesaid, not having the fear of God before their eyes but being moved and seduced by the Instigation of the Devil, on the 31st day of May in the 15th year of reign of our Sovereign, Lord George III now King of Great Britain, did with force and arms in the township of Upper Alloways Creek in the county of Salem and within the jurisdiction of the court did in and upon one Recompense Sherry in the peace of God and our Lord the King then and there being feloniously, wilfully and of malice aforethought did make an assault and that the said Ceasar contriving and contending him the said Recompense Sherry his master, to deprive of his life and here feloniously and traitoriously to kill and murder then and there feloniously, traitoriously, wilfully and of his own malice aforethought.

"A certain axe made of iron and steel and a certain wooden club of the value of 10 penny which he the said Ceasar in his hands then and there held and had in upon and through the body, skull and neck of him the said Recompense Sherry and there did feloniously, etc., strike and cut giving to the said Recompense Sherry sundry mortal wounds with the axe and club aforesaid in and upon and thru the body of the said Recompense Sherry of which said mortal wounds the said Recompense Sherry did then and there instantly die.

"And so the jurors upon their oath and affirmations say that the said Ceasar the aforesaid slave of the said late Recompense Sherry and his late master, in manner and terms aforesaid feloniously, etc., did kill and murder against the peace of our Lord the King His Crown and Dignity. And the jurors do further on their oaths and affirmations present that he the said Kile then and there feloniously, etc., was present aiding, helping abetting and maintaining the said Ceasar the treason and murder of the said Recompense Sherry in manner aforesaid, and commit against the peace of our said Lord the King, His Crown and Dignity."

There is also a separate indictment against Kile in substance as above.

The grand jury which returned the indictments against the two slaves consisted of John Dickeson, foreman; Thomas Sayre, Robert Sparks, Benj. Lippincott, William Hancock, Peter Ambler, Ezra Firth, John Craven, Andrew McCollum, Samuel Elwell, William Young, Samuel Fitzpatrick, John Denn, Daniel Smith, George Dunham, Thomas Hancock and Robert Walker.

The judges were Elisha Bassett, John Holme, Andrew Sinnickson and Robert Johnson. The justices were John Mayhew, William Mecum, Bateman Lloyd, Jacob Scoggin, Isaac Harris and Robert Howard.

The indictment having been read and the prisoners having been brought to the bar and being charged declared that they were not guilty and put themselves upon God and the country. Carey, the King's Attorney, moved the case against Ceasar and with no sign of delay the petit jury was empaneled for the trial. Thomas Carney was foreman; other members were Jacob Freas, John Wood, Joseph Dunham, William Murphy, Abner Penton, Donald Russell, Herman Richman, Thomas Hopman, Michael Walker, Erasmus Kent and John Smith.

A long procession of witnesses was called but since the procedure followed was that of the English crown no counsel was assigned to the defendants and there was no constitutional provision for witnesses in their behalf. On the afternoon of June 14, a day which was soon to have a patriotic significance all its own, and a date only fifteen days from the time of the murder, the first of the slaves was found guilty of murder, and treason and murder. Says the court record, "The jury having returned to the bar and being called over appeared and say, that they find the defendant guilty in manner and form as he stands indicted and so say they all."

The next day Carey moved the indictment against Kile. Members of this jury were Robert Sparks, John Helms, Thomas Carney, William Parret, Aaron Beetle, James Flanagan, William Conklin, Michael Hover, Isaac Garrison, Samuel Van Meter, Malachi Jarman and Christopher Lynnivi. Came the same verdict and immediately afterwards the pronouncement of the death sentence upon the slaves. The warrant is not greatly different from that in use today.

"It is ordered that Ceasar and Kile the two Negro slaves be taken to the place from whence they came and then to the place of the execution on Wednesday the 20th day of June and there the said Negroes are to be hanged by the neck, between ten o'clock in the forenoon and three o'clock in the afternoon until they are dead, dead, dead, and the court order that the sheriff so do see execution done accordingly."

Edmund Weatherby was the high sheriff of Salem, the last under King George. Where he carried out the executions cannot be ascertained. It might have been at Gallows Hill in Claysville where Hager and her accomplices suffered or it might have been elsewhere.

It would be hard to find in the court history of New Jersey a quicker and more expeditious case of the traditional Jersey justice. From the murder on May 31 to the execution on June 20 is as short a span of time as will be found in any recorded judicial history for trial and execution. A historian bent on finding the origin of the term "Jersey Justice" might direct his studies here with great success.

The slaves were convicted and hanged for petty treason as well as for murder and it is rather an ironic commentary that some of their judges and peers were soon to be pursued throughout the province for another species of treason which was far from being directed at a master but was aimed at the British fountain of justice himself. Only twenty-four hours after the verdict was returned against Kile, fellow countrymen of the Salem freeholders dragged cannon to a certain hill in Charlestown and fired on His Majesty's men and ships in Boston, to give rise to the joke that although the British might have our guns from Bunker Hill, we had the hill.

The tradition which enveloped the crime is that the tree under which the deed was committed never grew again but that the grass was always green at the base of it and that leaves would never collect under it. Like all ghostly places, strange and ominous voices would be heard at night in the vicinity of the tree and long after its fellows of the forest had been removed for cultivation, this relic of a ghastly crime was allowed to remain unmolested. Not until the tree died completely some time before the Civil War, was the superstition disregarded and its withered trunk removed.

CHAPTER XV

OF THE REVOLUTION AND HOW IT CAME TO SALEM COUNTY

The war of the Revolution, which began at a Massachusetts bridgehead, in April of 1775, did not find the citizens of Salem county unprepared. As told in the preceeding chapters, the militia companies had been organized. There were destined to be many of these in this county and their history is really the history of Salem county in the Revolution.

On August 16, 1775, it was decided that the militia forces of this county should consist of one regiment including three companies of minute men. The idea of this came of course, from New England, where the minute men were comprised of those who took up arms at short notice. As early as June 3, 1775 the Provincial Congress of New Jersey recommended the formation of militia companies. The Salem county representatives to this Congress were John Holme, Edward Keasbey, John Carey, and Colonel Benjamin Holme. The first military company formed at their suggestion came from the modern townships of Pittsgrove and Upper Pittsgrove. The muster roll of this first company formed within the confines of Salem county included these men:

Jacob Dubois, captain; Peter Dubois, First lieutenant; Abram Dubois; second lieutenant; William Conckling, ensign; Joel Garrison, Benjamin Vanmeter, Elias Craig and James Stratton, sergeants; Jacob Vanmeter, Benjamin Burroughs, Ezeckiel Rose, Elijah Johnston, William Murphy, Isaac Dubois, Joseph Thompson, James Murphy, Robert Tullis, Jr., Francis Tullis, George Wagoner, Philip Titus, John Burroughs, George Fauver, Henry Huet, John Craig, Jr., Thomas Rose, Robert Patterson, Cornelius Dubois, Isaac Vanmeter, John Johnson, Benjamin Hughs, Henry Johnson, Ezekiel White, Reuben Langly, William Crum, Aaron Brown, Samuel Dubois, John Dinklespike, Alexander Steel, David Weeks, James Johnson, John Dubois, Benjamin Dubois, William Thompson, C. Niewkirk, Jr., William McClung, John Ricker, Joseph Jones, James Bourroughs, Giddon Tullis, Jacob Tullis, John Nealy, Joseph Nealy, William Nealy, Samuel Swing, John Miller, Cornelius Wollsey, John Crum, Isaac Newkirk, Jacob Steelman, Joseph Abbott, Abdon

THE STORM BREAKS

Abbott, John Burroughs, Isreal Elwell, Alexander Jones, Moses Nickles, Cornelius Burroughs, privates.

It is ironical that two of these militiamen of this first company in Salem county later became Tories and were three years later sentenced to die for high treason. They were Reuben Langly and Abdon Abbott.

This was not the only company of militiamen or minute men organized in Salem county. There were militia companies formed in Upper Alloways Creek (now Alloway and Quinton). Elsinboro and Upper Penns Neck. These soldiers called themselves "Associators". The language of their compact is worth recording here for it is an example of the motivation of the patriots of that day;

"We, the subscribers, Freeholders and inhabitants of the Township of Upper Alloways Creek in the County of Salem and Province of New Jersey having long viewed with concern the avowed design of the Ministry of Great Britian to raise a revenue in America, being deeply affected with the cruel hostilities already commenced in the Massachusetts Bay for carrying that arbitrary design into execution, convinced that the preservation of the rights and privileges of America depends under God on the firm union of the inhabitants, do with hearts abhoring slavery and ardently wishing for a reconciliation with our parent State on Constitutional principles: Solemnly Associate and Resolve, under the Sacred ties of virtue, honour and love to our Country that we will personally and as far as in our influence extends endeavor to support and carry into execution whatever measures may be recommended by the Continental and Provincial Congress for defending our Constitution and preserving the same inviolate."

But war was still to come to Salem County. The first taste of it, however, was on May 5, 1776 when the British ships *Roebuck* and *Liverpool*, appeared in the Delaware river after chasing the American brig *Lexington* off Cape May. The subsequent naval battle between the British ships and row galleys furnished by the Pennsylvania legislature electrified the citizens of the river counties. It was probably at this time that the cannon ball which lodged in the old Summerill House at the cove in the borough of Pennsgrove was fired. The neighboring county of Cumberland suffered from the depredations of the British after these two warships had beaten off the patriot attack. The vibration caused by the cannon in this engagement informed every citizen of Salem county that war was near at hand. This battle extended roughly from Red Bank to Bacon's Neck in Cumberland county.

The story of this battle, one of the first naval engagements of the Revolution, has been woefully neglected by American historians. Few students of the public schools have ever heard of this affair. The dozen or more row galleys were aided by three small ships, the *Reprisal*, the *Hornet* and the *Lexington*, previously mentioned as being chased by the British.

The alarm which came into the city of Philadelphia concerning the arrival of these two warships was given by means of alarm stations scattered along the west side of the Delaware river. Through the firing of guns and the employment of express riders, the news was conveyed to Philadelphia in remarkably short time.

This battle of the Delaware, which lasted two full days, May 8 and 9, caused every able-bodied citizen of this county to flock to the river banks to watch the unique and unequal struggle.

The invasion of the enemy stimulated enlistments of the militia. The county was organized by townships into Associators. At this time Captain William Smith, later destined to become engaged with the British in the skirmish at Quinton's Bridge, obtained his commission as captain in the foot militia for Upper Alloway's Creek township.

There were many preparations for war. At various times during 1776 the secret committee of the Constitutional Congress was directed to sell powder for the use of the inhabitants of this county. There was a shortage of guns. Congress was informed that the Salem militia could not drill properly because of the lack of firearms. As a matter of fact, most of the patriot soldiers had to furnish their guns, cartridge boxes, swords and horses at their own expense.

The first colonel of the Salem county militia was John Holme. He resigned because of ill health in May of 1777 and was succeeded by his brother Benjamin Holme, who was destined to command the American militia when the British came to Salem county a year later.

The barracks of these troops were situated in Elsinboro township and were erected for the temporary purpose of housing the militia. They were built in 1776 and must have been abandoned by September of 1778 because at that time the council of New Jersey offered them for sale. Where these barracks were located in Elsinboro is a matter of conjecture, but the reasonable thing to suppose is that they were near not only the home of Colonel Benjamin Holme but near the river shore as well. With the British fleet in the river and the early alarms of war coming from that section it is natural that the troops should have been as near this front as possible.

While all these preparations were being made the theatre of war had moved from Boston to New York and finally to Philadelphia. On September 11, 1777, Little Lydia Smith, aged 14, the daughter of Captain William Smith, stood under a large sycamore tree at her home on the Tattletown road and heard the guns which told of Howe's advance on Philadelphia and the battle of the Brandywine. At the same time old Jonas Cattell, an ardent patriot, also hearing the guns is said to have rowed his small boat across the Delaware river and walked overland in his haste to offer his services to Washington's army.

Salem county soldiers were present in this battle. One William Huffman, a drummer boy of Penns Neck, only 14 years old, was bayoneted and shot in this battle but he lived until 1841 when he died in Seneca county, New York. George Farney, possibly the ancestor of the Salem family of that name, also served at the Brandywine. Salem county soldiers participated in all the major battles of the Revolution. There were many of them who took part in the three great battles on New Jersey soil, Trenton, Princeton and Monmouth. The brigade of General Silas Newcomb, which comprised the men from Salem county, has never received the credit it should for its services with the decimated army of Washington. The writer agrees with Stewart that college students in search for a thesis for a doctor's degree would find profitable employment in writing of the activities of Newcomb's brigade.

It is interesting to note that there sprung up in Salem county in the year 1777 a custom which prevailed in this nation for over a hundred years afterwards. It was the hiring of substitutes. Captain William Smith submitted a list of some sixteen names of men whom he had hired as substitutes at the Elsinboro barracks early in 1777. Each man who served as such received $50.00. The price was considerably higher in the Civil War.

A month after the battle of Brandywine Salem county again worried over the possibilities of war within their own borders. The militia was called out again on the river bank as Philadelphia had fallen to the British and their warships patrolled the Delaware river and this time there were no row galleys to interfere. Neighboring Gloucester county was overrun by the British. Billingsport was in their hands, Fort Mercer soon would be, even though Christopher Green and his ragged Continentals had beaten back the Hessians under Count Donop in the short but bloody battle at Red Bank. On November 20 of that year General Washington appealed to the officers and soldiers of the Delaware river counties from Hunterdon to Cape May to "Help rid your country of its unjust invaders."

The red hand of war had yet to fall on Salem county. But it was not far away. As the winter months of 1777-78 drew on the circle of carnage which had caused misery to so many parts of the colonies came finally to Salem. Unlike many parts of New Jersey, the southern counties had not yet been devastated by foraging expeditions or the march of armies, but their time had now come.

At this juncture of the Revolution, Howe's army was in Philadelphia and Washington's at Valley Forge. The first army mentioned was fairly well provided for by the people of the neighboring section, who were interested in selling their supplies for real gold and silver money. Moreover, the British army had the great advantage of the free and uninterrupted use of the Delaware river. The "Grand Army", backed by an indifferent populace and squabbling politicians, slowly starving to death on the bleak snow-covered hillside near Norristown, had little to hope for save the end. The sufferings of the men at Valley Forge has captivated the sympathy and admiration of a humane nation ever since the first encampment. True, two years later at Morristown, in our own state of New Jersey came a test more severe and dreadful than that experienced in the hills of Pennsylvania. But Americans still look on Valley Forge as the last word in human endurance.

The winter was usually severe. Snow and ice and lack of adequate equipment prevented food from the northward from arriving at Valley Forge. From the south and west the presence of Howe's army likewise prevented the importation of food supplies. Furthermore, many of the counties in these directions had been entirely despoiled of forage and food. It was only from the east and from the southern counties of New Jersey that could be found the one way out. The story has been repeated hundreds of times and with very little credit by American historians, that the cattle and the food from the three counties of Gloucester, Cumberland and Salem saved Washington's army at Valley Forge from starvation.

As the situation of the "Grand Army" grew more desperate there were many officers and soldiers who remembered with a glint of hope that there were thousands of cattle in the lower South Jersey counties and that with due caution and by a circuitious route the cattle might be taken to Valley Forge. When this decision was made on a gloomy February day in 1778 it marked the entrance of this county into the turmoil of the Revolution. Anthony Wayne, the great "Mad Anthony", left Valley Forge in the middle of February on this last long chance, that meant so much to the army he left behind.

Coming through Wilmington after a wide western detour to avoid Philadelphia, Wayne landed in Salem on the nineteenth of February. On the next day he dispatched his small force to collect all the cattle they could find. Stories still linger in Salem county of farmers hiding their cattle and livestock in swamps to save them from this levy. But Wayne did his job well, for within forty-eight hours he had collected one hundred and fifty head of cattle. He tried first to send them across the Delaware on the boats of Captain John Barry, first commodore of the United States Navy, but fearing for the result sent the cattle on to Haddonfield, preferring the eastern entrance to Valley Forge. Barry had proved to be of considerable assistance to Wayne and while cruising down the river had captured a couple of British hay boats, but was later compelled to burn them.

On February 21 Colonel Ellis at Haddonfield, the ranking military officer of the militia of the lower river counties, wrote to Wayne at Salem: "I am happy in just receiving your orders by express, which I shall be particularly careful in attending to. Such cattle, etc., as are fit for present use and the several horses for the immediate use of the cavalry in the neighborhood of Gloucester, Cooper's Ferries and my present quarters shall be taken and driven to some secure place as soon as the small detachment under my command can possibly collect them. You may depend upon my being so attentive to the motions of the enemy that you shall receive the earliest intelligence of their route. I shall be as well careful to prevent any insult or abuse whatever being offered to the inhabitants through which the militia may pass, as executing any other orders that I may receive from you."

The advent of Wayne in Salem had not gone unnoticed. Hugh Cowperthwaite, a Tory who lived in Salem, immediately went to Philadelphia and notified the British that "Mad Anthony" Wayne was loose in Salem county. It was this act of the British intelligence service which led to the British raid on Salem. Upon receiving this news General Howe wasted little time. He sent Lieutenant Colonel Abercrombie down the Delaware to Salem to catch Wayne at the source, if possible. Anticipating Wayne's northward journey he ordered The Queen's Rangers (loyalists) under Major John Graves Simcoe and the 42nd regular British regiment under Colonel Sterling to head Wayne off, if he had left Salem.

But Wayne, with the salvation of Washington's army depending upon the small number of troops in his command and the cattle in his custody, was not captured by the enemy. By February 25th Wayne was at Haddonfield and wrote Washington that the cattle were on their way to Mount Holly. He had marched his troops between the cattle and the river in order to "amuse the enemy." Meanwhile on the river Barry was burning all the hay that he could find. Wayne was moving his cattle by back roads from Mount Holly to Trent Town, with his eye on the British under Simcoe and Sterling who were trying to cut him off at Cooper's Ferry (Camden). He remarked in a letter to Washington that on the day he was in Haddonfield, two thousand of the enemy had landed at Billingsport and had gone on to Salem. This was Abercrombie, in fruitless quest of Wayne and on the first British invasion of Salem. Archibald Robertson, engineer with the British army, writes in his diary:

"February 24, 1778. Lieutenant Colonel Abercomby passed in the night to the Jerseys, landed below Billingsport in order to surprise General Wayne who was collecting cattle. He marched to Salem and returned to Philadelphia 1st March, General Wayne having passed before he went over.

"Lieutenant Colonel Sterling likewise went into the Jerseys the 25th at night and marched to Haddonfield, but found Wayne had passed. We got some forage from Cooper's Ferry, Went over to Haddonfield 1st March".

From Billingsport, the British marched directly to Salem down the King's Highway past the Moravian Church, which still stands a hundred yards within Gloucester county on Oldman's Creek. Of this expedition Pastor Frederick Schmidt wrote in his journal:

"February 25, 1778. Over 2,000 English troops passed on their way to Salem. The house was full of soldiers, polite but carried off all the trifles they could find.

"February 26, 1778. Nicholas Garrison and wife left Bethlehem having been here several months. The neighbors talk of flight. My self and wife have determined to remain."

From a patriot source and from one who suffered severely in both the first and second raids of the British, Benjamin Holme said of the Abercrombie affair;

"Wednesday the (25th) day of February 1778 a part of the British Army landed at Billingsport, supposed to be about fourteen hundred. Marched Thursday and encamped at Major Sharp's (Sharptown). Friday continued to Salem town, continued there until Saturday of 28th inst. They then embarked in their boats at Elsinborough which day they burnt a house at the Ferry, the property of Colonel Benjamin Holme."

Poor Margaret Hall whose farm faced the Delaware River lamented that "when Abercrombie's army was at Salem ye 2d Mo. 1778, there was taken, by the flat boatmen, 7 blankets, as good as new; 5 coverlets, three almost new; 1 bed quilt, sheets and pillow cases. I can't tell how many; 3 hats, 1 new great coat, several pairs of gloves, a new apron, a pair of stuff shoes,

5 or 6 pewter plates, 1 3-qt. burnt china bowl, and 1 2-qt. enameled ditto, and 2-pine ditto, a hide of neat leather, several crocks; a house torn to pieces."

After four days in Salem, with Wayne beyond his power of capture and having satisfied himself with minor plundering, Abercrombie returned to Philadelphia. Wayne, with the Salem county cattle still in his control and confident of his success in placing them at Valley Forge, whote to Washington:

"Mr. Abercrombie, who commanded the detachment that went to Salem—hearing that the militia were collecting in great numbers—and that we were advancing from Mount Holly—also took the horrors and embarking on board his boats and got safe to Phila.—three evenings ago leaving all his collection of cattle, etc., behind. Thus ended the Jersey expedition which has not been attended with that advantage that these North Britons expected of their first arrival."

So finally Anthony Wayne and his Salem county cattle arrived at Valley Forge. The balance of life or death for Washington's army hung on this expedition, which fortunately for the colonies was successful. It is high time that American historians give credit not only to Anthony Wayne, but to Salem county from whence the aid had come. Cattle on the hoof were actually at Valley Forge and famine had been averted but as yet Mawhood and Simcoe had not been to Salem.

CHAPTER XVI

OF THE AMERICAN DEFENSE OF ALLOWAYS CREEK

Abercrombie had gone from Salem late in February of 1778 and had failed to catch Anthony Wayne. Two weeks had sped before Howe in Philadelphia, seeing that his food and forage were running short and probably remembering the success of Wayne in obtaining it in the hitherto untouched counties of Cumberland and Salem, despatched one of his ablest officers, Colonel Charles Mawhood, to Salem for that purpose. On March 11th, 1778, the *Roebuck*, which had appeared in the naval battle of the Delaware in May of 1776, and the frigate *Camilla*, fell down the river followed by a detachment of a thousand men under Mawhood. The expedition consisted of three British regiments, the 17th, the 27th and the 46th, and the Queen's Rangers under Major John Graves Simcoe.

At Billingsport, the British detachment seems to have split up into two divisions. Simcoe stayed on the transports and landed at Redstrake's Island in Lower Penns Neck township early in the morning of the 17th. The present Fort Mott is the approximate location of the landing place. Proceeding down the Finns Point road, the British distinguished themselves by burning the house of James Smith after first helping themselves to breakfast and despoiling the house of its contents. There was no Griffith Street bridge to Salem then. So the British marched on across Penns Neck to Long Lane and from there over Lamson's Bridge into Salem. This bridge has long since disappeared but the roads leading to it on both the Penns Neck and Mannington sides may still be observed.

Meanwhile, Mawhood had landed at Billingsport in Gloucester county and marched overland to Salem over the Kings Highway through Mickleton, Swedesboro and Sharptown. On the way south Mawhood had a skirmish with some Gloucester county militia over the passage of Mantua Creek. Johnson credits the British with burning two more houses enroute, the residence of Doctor Bodo Otto at Mickleton, which was rebuilt and is still standing, and the house of Major Anthony Sharp outside of

THE BRITISH ARRIVE

Sharptown on the present Colson farm. Mawhood arrived in Salem at approximately the same time as Simcoe and laid plans for foraging throughout Salem county the next day.

The British took complete possession of Salem without molestation from the Americans. They established their headquarters in the home of Colonel Samuel Dick which occupied the site where the Salem "Sunbeam" is now located. They proceeded to occupy and later ruin beyond repair, St. John's Episcopal Church on Market street. Also they quartered some of their troops and men in the Yorke street end of Salem. The headquarters there was probably the house, still standing, known as the Zaiser House at the corner of Magnolia and Yorke streets. In the west end of the town they took over the home of Captain Thomas Sinnickson, whose wife was a daughter of William Hancock of Hancock's Bridge.

Mawhood and Simcoe are said to have used the house of Colonel Dick as their own residence and as headquarters. The Colonel was away at the time, being in the American service. He had, years before, rendered distinguished service for the colonies at the taking of Quebec and Fort Ticonderoga. The British banished Mrs. Dick to the upper floor of the house and gave her army rations of a quart of Indian flour a day. To add to Mrs. Dick's trouble, a portion of the family plate was buried in the back garden a few days before Mawhood arrived and a "trusted" negro slave had decamped with the buried treasure.

A word about the two chief British commanders. They were both distinguished men and later in life received high honor from their government. Mawhood afterwards became aide de camp to King George III. But he had rendered excellent service before this. On January 3rd, 1777, he had been in charge of the British detachment left at Princeton by Lord Cornwallis, and had aided greatly by his daring and cool headedness in assembling the surprised troops when Washinigton suddenly fell upon them that morning. All in all, he was one of the most capable staff officers in the British army.

John Graves Simcoe was a graduate of Eton and Oxford, son of a British admiral, and later in life Governor General of Canada and commander in chief of the British armies in India. His military journal, reprinted in this country in 1844, although he died in 1806, closely follows that of the great masters of military journals, Xenophen and Ceasar, whose student he was, in conciseness, clarity of detail and unassuming exposition of facts.

Speaking of Simcoe, it is unusally interesting that a commentary on the British raid of Salem should have been written and preserved by him, as one of the ranking British officers. His account of the raid is written with far less passion than that of the American authority on the same subject, Robert Gibbon Johnson. Of course, it must be taken into consideration that Simcoe finally turned the American flank and was the victor in this campaign, while Johnson represents the views of a community whose sons were destined to be ruthlessly slaughtered in cold blood.

The authorities differ on whether or not Salem countians, awed and inspired by the British offer to enlist "All Aspiring Heroes", on arrival in Salem did actually join the British army. Judged from the names Johnson uses and the long list of indictments found in September, 1778 for high treason, there must have been quite a number. At any rate, the British offered to enlist these Tories and to equip them with the accoutrements of the Queen's Rangers. Johnson says that this proclamation brought forth "an abandoned set of fellows, the very offscouring of the earth who joined up for two guineas a piece". The reference to the Queen's Rangers and the Tories is often that of the "Greens". This because they wore green faced uniforms with whitebound hats, entirely different from the red hue of the British regular army.

As the British officers, warm and comfortable in the Dick house in Salem, made plans for the foraging expedition, the Salem county militia were forming under Colonel Benjamin Holme, in defense of their homes and firesides. Seeing that Salem was in the possession of the enemy they took up their stand on the south side of Aloes or Alloways creek, determined if possible that the foraging expedition should not include the south and east portions of Salem county beyond this creek, and also the whole of Cumberland county, which also lay beyond it.

The American position consisted of three fortifications. The last word is a misnomer. They were simply defensive bridges guarded more by the waters of Aloes Creek than by military art. On the west was the bridgehead at Hancock's Bridge. The house itself was simply the barracks for the troops guarding the bridge. Three miles away to the east was Quinton's Bridge, where a natural bluff aided the patriots in making temporary breastworks. Three miles more to the east and still along the creek was Thompson's Bridge, where there again seems to have been nothing but the stream as a barrier. This last defense was

THE BRITISH ARRIVE

also known as the Glass Works, because of the proximity of the Wisterburgh glass house which then was still in operation. The Salem county militia, for a day at least, had their headquarters there as subsequent general orders will show. It today is the modern town of Alloway. And it alone escaped the fury of a British attack.

On Wednesday, March 18, 1778, the foraging on the part of the British started and ended for the day in the battle of Quinton's Bridge. It is evident that Mawhood did not leave Salem with the main body of his troops until a subordinate officer reported to him that while collecting forage near Quinton's Bridge, a large number of militia had gathered under arms and was opposing the foraging endeavors of the British. Hearing this Mawhood put his force in action. Taking the 17th regiment and the Rangers, he left Salem and started against the patriot militia at Quinton. His route was circuitous, partly by design and partly because the road did not run as straight as it does today. His passage was out Broadway, Yorke street, Kent street, and then by the ice houses and the back of the present Elk-Hannah farm to Mill Hollow, where the Baptist church was at that period and where the stone marking it is today. That was roughly the original road. At Mill Hollow, the road branched to Quinton and to Alloway. Mawhood, in order to outwit the militia, kept on the Alloway road, now better known as the Sandy Ridge road, to make it appear that he was moving against Thompson's Bridge or Alloway instead of Quinton. But half way to Thompson's Bridge he turned and came back toward Quinton. It must be remembered that the country was heavily wooded and detection of the movement of enemy troops was not easy to perceive. This natural advantage aided Mawhood. Meanwhile the British commander had a small force of Rangers deploy in front of the bridge, in open sight of the militia on the south side.

This was all a part of Mawhood's scheme and worked well for him but greatly to the detriment of the Americans. At this point Mawhood and Simcoe went into conference and decided on an ambuscade, throwing the small party of Rangers out as bait and holding the 17th regiment under cover to perfect the masking movement. Mawhood and Simcoe both were masters of two old military tricks, the feint and the ambuscade, because both of them worked well. There is a house, still standing, known as the Benjamin Weatherby farm which yielded itself well to the plan. It stood on high ground and was well concealed by the woods from observation at the bridge head.

Mawhood is said by Simcoe to have asked him, "If he left a party in the house the enemy would pass by it or not?" Simcoe, not very kindly disposed towards the rebels said, "He thought they were too cowardly to try it, but that the attempt could do no harm". And so it was decided. On this conversation Johnson waxes warm and indignant. He goes on to tell the story which is a tradition of long standing in this neighborhood that while the British were in and around this house in question, one of their adventurous soldiers exposed himself by leaning backwards out a window and was promptly nipped by a patriot soldier named Simon Warner, who hastening to the scene of action beheld the sight and spoiled the day for the British soldier by good aiming of his trusty flintlock.

The ambuscade decided upon, one Lieutenant McKay was delegated to stand by the door with a drawn bayonet, "to whet the curiosity of the first rebel who might be prompted to enter", as Simcoe says. The family was banished to the cellar, the house filled with troops and more soldiers assigned to lie down behind the bushes and fence rails in the vicinity of the house. While all this was being arranged, Mawhood sent orders to the detachment of British which had been deploying up and down the road in front of the bridge, exciting threats and scattered gunfire from the patriots on the other side, to retreat back up the road to Salem in full sight of the militia.

The geography of the terrain favored the British. Besides the hiding place afforded by the woods, the house was situated on high ground. Beyond the house towards Quinton the land immediately became marshy to the creek and then arose again on the other side to be used by the militia as their breastworks. It is much the same today. However the road now bears to the right, whereas in 1778, it ran straight and much nearer the house than it does now.

But as Simcoe and Mawhood conferred and the strategy was being arranged things were happening on the Aloes bridgehead at Quinton. The deploy of the British had naturally worked the patriots up to a high state of excitement. Colonel Holme was away at Bridge Town seeking help from Colonel Elijah Hand and the Cumberland militia. Captain William Smith was the senior militia officer and the command on this hectic day had fallen to him. The militia, seeing the British, dreaded as well they might, a frontal attack, although the geography was well in their favor. However, with the appearance of the enemy and with the desultory firing which was going on, they naturally felt apprehension as to the safety of their position, not knowing the full British strength which lay in the woods between them and Mill Hollow. While the excitement was at its height, one Andrew Bacon, who left his plow in a nearby field and engaged in the dual role of a Cincinattus and a Horatius, appeared upon the scene.

No poet has ever written "by the rude bridge which arched the flood" in Bacon's honor but nevertheless the history books of the United States of America should remember him. For with consummate courage and rather reckless daring and in the full range of the masking party's fire, he proceeded to step out from the American breastworks and hew with an axe upon the draw, so that the British might be foiled in any possible attempt to cross. The narrator of patriotism has an epic here in the picture of Bacon, in full sight of any one who wished to shoot at him, hewing with all his might upon the draw of Quinton's Bridge. But the gods of chance were good to him and the draw fell into the waters of Aloes Creek and the hewer of it still lived.

But the American triumph was short lived. By the time Bacon finished, the British ambuscade was ready. The deploy was retreating with all the honors of war towards Mill Hollow and Salem. Smith, whose orders from Holme not to quit the breastworks were explicit, was exuberant at the supposed retreat of the British. He was aided in this exuberance by one Francis Ducloss, a Frenchman on recruiting service who had "happened" in on this occasion. Johnson calls him Decou, but his name was Ducloss and there is little doubt that his fiery Gallic temperament saw the opportunities afforded by the feigned British retreat. He urged Smith "how easy it would be for them to go over and drub those insolent rascals" and Smith, his orders from Holme forgotten and blown to the March winds by the supposed opportunity now afforded him, yielded.

The draw was relaid by means of planks and the American militia left their safe quarters on the south bank of the Aloes to engage in hidden slaughter and red war on the north. Smith led his men on horseback, the troops following on foot. "We will have them before they get to Mill Hollow, boys," shouted Smith, as he waved his sword towards the fleeing British up the road. Intent on the pursuit of the enemy, no one took the trouble to investigate the Weatherby house as they passed it. Somebody on the British side, seeing the predicament of the Americans, laughed. The British arose from their hiding places and streamed out of the house, pouring fire into the startled and dismayed militia. The ambuscade was complete.

As the trap was sprung, exactly as the British officers planned that it should, Smith did his best to extricate his men from the ambuscade. The march to the hidden slaughter was disjoined and irregular enough and so was the retreat. But Smith turned back what he could get together of his scattered troops and made precipitate flight towards the bridge and safety. The din was terrific and was aided by the appearance of the deploying column which had come back from Mill Hollow to join the fray, but the casualties on the American side were not as bad as might have been expected. Ducloss and Bacon both were captured and Bacon was subdued with a bayonet wound. One John Stump, a militiaman, was killed in the retreat but before he died, killed a British soldier, probably the only enemy death of the day. Simcoe says that the soldier had given Stump quarter and that the "villian or coward" killed him. Johnson says that Stump asked for quarter but it being refused, sold his life dearly by killing the soldier, who had rushed upon him.

Some of the Americans threw away their guns and attempted to swim the creek, others surrendered to the British, some fought it out, hand to hand, in a skirmish which was marked by its fierceness, if not for its duration. Smith, the only man on horseback, fled towards the bridge, only to have his horse drop dead under him as he crossed to safety. Providence seemed to be with the patriots, for as the retreat became a rout, Holme and Colonel Hand arrived from Bridge Town with reinforcements to keep the British back on the other side of the creek.

Smith's escape was close. He had some hair shot from his head and a ball grazed his loins, but he arrived safely to tell his commander of the defeat of his forces. Accounts of the losses of the Americans in the affair at Quinton's Bridge vary. The British accounts say twenty were killed and twelve taken prisoners. Holme, who should have known best, said six were killed and gives a succinct report in his own language as follows:

"Which day unluckily for us, the emeny ambushed in the house of Benj. Weatherby, under fences, banks and deceived our militia, who thought them to be gone and harass their rear fell into the ambuscade, who firing unawares on the Militia broke and confused them so that each man seeking his escape in his own way; the Light Horse pursued and killed six, one drowned in the Creek who could not swim."

In this, the action of Quinton's Bridge, the following gave

their lives in the defense of their homes and American freedom: James Blackburn, John Couch, Lieutenant Elisha Edminson, Isaac Rains, John Stump, John Smith, Thomas Noble.

Thus, among the apple blossoms and the spring foliage, to the echoing sound of gunfire and open warfare, ended the battle of Quinton's Bridge. The embattled farmers, snared into a trap, had lost the fight and left their fellows killed, wounded or captured on the north side of Aloes Creek but the creek itself was still uncrossed and the British, in their failure to reach across it, had won but a "Pyrrhic" victory.

CHAPTER XVII

OF THE MASSACRE AT HANCOCK'S BRIDGE

According to Johnson, on the next day, the 19th, the British made another attempt to cross Alloways Creek at Quinton's Bridge. However, Johnson is the only historian to mention it. All the others are silent upon this point. It is possible that a marauding or foraging expedition came back to the bridge the next morning and seeing the patriots there left without any attempt to attack the American position.

Johnson in his inimitable language thus describes "the second day" at Quinton's Bridge:

"As had been anticipated, Col. Mawhood being exceedingly chagrined that Major Simcoe's fine battalion, with his advice and in his presence, could not subdue the independent spirit of our people, determined that they should no longer bid defiance to 'His Majesty's arms', marched with all his disposable force on the next morning, and approached the bridge in battle array at about 10 o'clock in the forenoon. They imagined that they would strike terror in the hearts of our people by playing upon all their martial instruments of music as they boldly advanced to the foot of the causeway in columns of battalions, where they displayed and formed their lines on the edge of the marsh. The refugees were there in the ranks on the right of the British regulars, and many of them were recognized by our people as men who had been inhabitants of our own county, then in arms against their neighbors.

"On the approach of the enemy Col. Hand and Holme had placed their men under cover in their entrenchments, both up and down the creek as far as the discharge of musketry would tell with good effect; the creek running circularly towards the enemy, and from the position in which their line was then formed, they became exposed to the certain and destructive fire of our people in front and on both flanks. In this position were they when our militia opened upon them such a well directed and destructive fire, that, brave as they were, they could not long stand it. They then saw to their woeful disappointment that they could make no impression upon our people; they were not to be intimidated, for they felt themselves secure under cover and upon a high bank with the creek between them and the enemy to penetrate along the causeway to gain the foot of the bridge, they were so galled by the incessant fire poured in upon their left flank from what is now the shipyard, as well as assailed by small arms and the two pieces of cannon in their front, that they were thrown into confusion, were obliged to retreat back to Salem and leave the small village of Quinton's Bridge in the possession of our gallant militia."

Meanwhile, the Americans were burying their dead. Young Job Simpkins with other boys traced the wagons carrying the dead, by the trail of blood, from Quinton down the Tattletown road to Captain William Smith's farm where they were buried.

On Thursday the 19th and Friday the 20th, Mawhood and his British foraged at will throughout Salem county west and north of Aloes Creek. One incident occurred during this time which has passed into history as the battle of Long Lane. It happened in Lower Penn's Neck and was the outcome of the foraging expedition. The British had collected several wagons full of food and having left them with an insufficient guard, they were captured by the militia under Captain Andrew Sinnickson. There seem to have been no casualties. The commanding British officer however, in his precipitate flight lost his hat and cloak which, Johnson says, Captain Sinnickson sent him the next day under a flag of truce. The worthy American captain, according to tradition wrote the unknown British officer that he "had to regret the sudden departure of the officer, the owner of the articles, but hoped that if he intended another visit into that township he might have the pleasure of detaining him until they became better acquainted."

There is a discrepancy about this affair as there is about practically all the accounts of the Salem raid. For instance, Archibald Robertson, engineer with the British army, wrote in his memoirs that this affair of Long Lane happened on the 25th of March. Johnson says the 20th. Robertson's exact account reads: "25th. Foraged on Pen's Neck. Some of the waggons taken by the Rebels but were immediately retaken. 4 Company's of 46th Regiment went to Pen's Neck. Stay'd all night with the waggons."

On Friday the 20th a small detachment of the British marched out of Salem via Quaker Neck to Guinea Town (Penton) probably with the idea of reconnoitering the eastern outpost of the American militia at Thompson's Bridge. It returned without any excitement, although it is quite possible that it was on this expedition the enemy seized the Pledger house near Salem and imprisoned the family in the house. Among those temporarily jailed by the British was a young lad seven years old by the name of Robert Gibbon Johnson who one day would right the wrongs done his family, in a scathing denunciation of the British in a little book which he called "A Historical Account of the First Settlement of Salem".

Mawhood continued his foraging during those two days of the 19th and 20th of March. Under various detachments of armed men, food supplies and forage were transported to the flatboats lying in Salem creek. Thus the rich farm lands around

Salem were carefully despoiled of their produce, which was sent to Philadelphia to augment the British food supplies.

It still irked the British that they had as yet been unable to cross Alloways creek. Simcoe writes that the rebels "Were still occupying the posts at Quinton and Hancocks Bridge and were probably accumulating, Col. Mawhood determined to attack them at the latter post, where, from all reports, they assembled to near four hundred men".

But the accumulation of the American militia was not the main reason for the British decision to attack Hancock's Bridge. If the British armies were to be able to say they had crossed Alloways creek and defeated the attempt of the Americans to prevent them, it was now necessary to take the next best tactical method and turn the patriot flank, since their frontal attack at Quinton, as far as crossing was concerned, had been unsuccessful.

Simcoe seems to have planned this flanking movement which was all too successful. Among the British forces in Salem were two regiments of British regulars who, while they fought at Quinton, seem only to have stood and watched at the Hancock House. Under Simcoe were the loyalists known as the Queen's Rangers consisting of both troop and horse.

Simcoe's plan was simplicity itself. For two days, Thursday and Friday, the 27th Regiment of the regular army paraded up and down the road from Salem to Hancock's Bridge on the north side of the creek, taunting the patriot militia stationed around the Hancock House to come out and fight. Profiting by the lesson of Quinton's Bridge two days earlier, the Americans stayed where they were but suffered complete exhaustion from their efforts at watching the British. Each evening the redcoats were taken back to Salem. On Friday, Simcoe with Mawhood and a patrol went to a farm opposite the guard house and there Simcoe climbed a tall tree to sketch the post which lay opposite.

That night, Friday, the Queen's Rangers embarked on flatboats and floated down the Salem creek and Delaware river into the mouth of Alloways creek but as Simcoe says in his journal somebody in the naval department miscalculated the tide in the creek and the troops were told they could not arrive at Hancock's Bridge by that means until midday. So Simcoe did the next best thing. Throwing himself upon the mercy of his Tory guides he landed at the mouth of the creek on the south side and trusting his command to the treachery of the marshes, struck boldly across them the remaining few miles to Hancock's Bridge. At the same time, the 27th British regular army regi-

HANCOCK HOUSE MASSACRE

ment had gone down the Hancock's Bridge road and taken up its old position on the north side of the creek to cut off the American retreat and aid Simcoe if he should be able to force the bridge from the south side.

It was only an hour or so short of daybreak when Simcoe arrived at the village of Hancock's Bridge and it was within a short distance to the west of the present village that he separated his command into two divisions, one under Captain Stevenson which proceeded through the village and came to the Hancock House in front and the other under Captain Dunlop which was to surround the rear of the house. With Captain Dunlop went another detachment under Captain Saunders, whose job it was to watch the crossing over Old Creek and in general to watch the line of the Beasley's Neck road by which help might arrive from Quinton or the fleeing militiamen from the house might effect an escape.

Thus far the stratagem was perfect. On the north side of the creek were the members of the 27th regiment, who had waited all night in the cold to support the flank movement on the other side; on the south side the house was entirely surrounded by troops, and the only possible means by which help might arrive were guarded. Taking further precautions, a patrol of the 27th regiment had seized the farm house of Samuel Abbott on the north side of the creek and had placed the family under guard so that no intelligence might reach the militia on the opposite side.

And yet with all these well laid plans, a chance remark by a British officer almost ruined the surprise attack. History is full of these "might have beens" and slumbering peacefully for years is the intelligence that had it not been for a pig-headed American sergeant at Alloway, Colonel Holme at Quinton could have laid another trap for the British and perhaps, had the fates been willing, ensnared the enemy in an ambuscade not of their own making.

On Friday afternoon a half dozen men composing an American scouting party set out from Thompson's Bridge (Alloway), the upper or eastern defense of the Americans along the creek, and penetrated to Guineatown, or the modern Penton, where they halted at a store kept by Nancy Cattell, grandmother of a future U. S. Senator, who told them that an English officer who had recently left the place had spoken of a British raid upon Hancock's Bridge. Having no one to send to the American headquarters with the news, she entrusted the information to Sergeant Samuel Gosling, who was in command of the detail. Unfortunately, the soldiers partook of the lady's hospitality and had a round of grog before returning to Thompson's Bridge.

They arrived after dark and had not learned the countersign, so the guard, perceiving the fact that they had been drinking, although there is no evidence that they were drunk, clapped them all in the guard house and refused to allow Gosling to communicate with Colonel Holme. In vain did Gosling beg the sergeant of the guard to allow him to see Holme, who told him that morning would be ample time.

Finally about four o'clock in the morning, after listening to Gosling's importunities all night, they finally sent him to Quinton to rouse Holme. The delay was all too fatal. There were three long miles to Quinton and several more to Hancock's Bridge and at the time Holme was getting a scouting party together at Quinton, convinced of the truth of Gosling's story, the British were bayoneting the American sentries and breaking into the house at Hancock's Bridge.

With clock-like precision, Simcoe's plans came to full fruition. Dunlop and Stevenson entered almost simultaneously at the front and back doors and the massacre was on. One account, which is probably pathetically true, claims that as the Loyalists poured into the main room of the tavern, the Americans, seeing former friends and neighbors, shook hands with some of them, unmindful of their errand. Their former friends were fully attired in the green regimentals of the Tory brigade, and they should have easily perceived their purpose was not peaceful, but yet, again, they might have conjectured they were surprised and were perfectly sure that their peaceful surrender meant no worse than prison.

But there was no such good fortune. It was the home town boys of Salem and Cumberland counties, wearing the uniforms of the British king, who brought death to their neighbors and with such apparent ferocity that the long annals of the Revolution show no parallel. Men were killed with the names of old acquaintances in their mouths, some begging for their lives and naming the men who were their murderers.

It is true that the Americans were not defenseless, and had they had some time, a feeble resistance might have been made, but their case was so hopeless that only the most unmitigated fury of slaughter can explain their destruction. With only a little effort, the respective captains could have disarmed and imprisoned the entire garrison but no such effort seems to have been made to lessen the fury of their men against their fellow countrymen.

I do not believe that Simcoe himself ordered the mandate of no quarter. I think it more likely that he felt he was moving

HANCOCK HOUSE MASSACRE

towards a trap and expected stiff resistance although he probably had little regard for the military ability of the farmers he was facing. His retreat was cut off, his boats had returned to Salem and he expected to face a force double that of his. These facts can be found in his journal and there seems to be no question about them.

When he scouted the place the preceding morning he saw a large number of militia there, and he no doubt figured he would meet that many in his attack as he rather regretfully remarks that he had planned to envelope a larger force, but that they had quitted the pace the night before. There is no doubt whatever that the blame for the massacre fell upon him as he had a right to order that in case of no resistance his forces should take prisoners. But apparently his Tory troops revelled in their blood lust and went ahead to kill all those they could find, not even sparing the owner of the house, Judge William Hancock.

With some semblance of crocodile tears Simcoe says that the killing of Hancock was one of the real miseries of war and that he had tried to ascertain that the judge would not be home, but had not discovered that he had made a practice of sleeping in the house at night. Yet, from that very statement, inference might be drawn that he expected to wipe out all he could find there.

Outside of the house, a British patrol watching the avenues of escape into the country, came across an American patrol near the creek bank and exterminated all but one of these. The firing caused by the action was apparently the first use of firearms in the affair, the slaughter in the house being accomplished by means of bayonets, although Shourds states that Judge Hancock was shot in his own doorway.

The sound of firearms, says Simcoe, was the first knowledge the regiment on the other side of the creek had that he had penetrated the marshes and was successfully engaged on the other side. With daylight, the bridge was relaid and the Queen's Rangers joined forces with the 27th Regiment. Simcoe was anxious to press on to Quinton and wipe out the rest of the colonials on the south side of the creek, but decided to go back to Salem, after having had his troops out in the cold all night.

Simcoe, his subordinate, yielded to his desire although it is quite evident that he was in the mood for further conquest, but he agreed and withdrew the ambuscade from Old Creek and the country approaching the Beesley Neck section and the Canton road.

Again the inscrutable forces of history intervened to save

more militia from the fate of those in the Hancock House. While the British were mopping up at Hancock's Bridge, Holme was on his way from Quinton with a good sized patrol to render what succor he could to the garrison. Behind him was a company of militia. Striking through the barrens below Quinton's Bridge he circled around into Hancock's Bridge by the present Canton road and within a short distance of the ambuscade. Providentially for Holme, Simcoe withdrew this detachment and was forming his command in line to march to Salem, in front of the bridge, when the American relief patrol swung into sight at the rear of the British column and perceiving the enemy, rapidly turned and rode away to head off the company which followed them.

Chagrined by the close escape of the American colonel and his men, Mitchell changed his mind and wanted to march on Quinton, but again they finally decided that they had better leave well enough alone and return to Salem. Their real reason probably was that they were afraid of an ambush on the back road to Quinton where the barren terrain offered a fine chance for such an operation.

Finally, about seven o'clock in the morning, getting news that the British had evacuated the place, Holme returned to find the tragic confirmation of the report of the massacre and to realize had Gosling been allowed to speak sooner that his slaughtered soldiers in the house might have had a chance to fight for their lives.

From the attic window of their home in Elsinboro, diagonally across the creek from the Hancock House, William Abbott and his son Samuel witnessed in the dawning morning light the British and Tory troops pursuing and killing the few American militiamen who had escaped from the scene of carnage, only to be shot down on the creek bank. The next morning, while driving to meeting in Salem, several British and Tory soldiers surrounded the Abbott carriage and after tormenting the occupants by thrusting their bayonets at them, showed them blood on the steel weapons and exclaimed "See the blood of your countrymen."

In the midst of the massacre, the wife of one of the soldiers, who in a short time expected to be a mother, was sleeping in the Hancock House. Awakened by the screams of the dying soldiers, she jumped from a small window in the second story of the house on the west side and made good her escape. Tradition says that within twenty-four hours, the child was born and that descendants of that child are living in Lower Alloways Creek township today.

HANCOCK HOUSE MASSACRE

Johnson is authority for the oft-told story of the militiaman, Dennis Dailey, who in some way effected an escape from the house and while being chased by two murderous Tories, ran into a British grenadier and throwing himself at his feet, begged for his life, knowing from some source that the British troops of the 27th Regiment were largely Scotch. Pleading "Save me, I am a Scotchman, I am your countryman," the astonished soldier recognized Dailey as a boyhood friend in Scotland and protected him from the refugees.

From this slaughter only one other man seems to have escaped. All of the rest of the militia company were either killed, wounded and left for dead, or taken prisoner. This man was Reuel Sayre, twenty-four-year-old son of Thomas Sayre, a noted patriot of this county. Reuel Sayre seems to have never discussed the affair until years afterwards, when he made an application for a pension. He then lived in Ohio, and died there about 1830. His account of his escape is as follows, "When the British were in Salem county, they came upon us by surprise, the guard was taken and every man killed or taken prisoner but myself. We were stationed at the Bridge, we had guards up and down the creek, they came through the marsh on the back of us at night, I got off by mingling among the British in the dark. All were killed, left for dead or taken prisoners but myself. This was the time our Captain was wounded and left for dead. I had one brother killed and one taken prisoner in this night affair."

The Sayre family suffered severely from the massacre. Their home seems to have been scene of a mass funeral held for the victims of the Hancock's Bridge affair. From their home near Harmerville the dead were taken for burial in what is now the Baptist cemetery at Canton. Johnson says of this funeral: "What a sight it must have been to old Judge Sayre and his wife, and how distracting to their feelings, to have eight corpses brought and laid in their house at the same time, among whom were a son, nephew, and other relatives and neighbors!"

It is a matter of everlasting regret that the full list of the American militia killed at the Hancock House has not been preserved. When the monument in the Canton Baptist cemetery was dedicated in 1928 an effort was made to get the correct names but because Johnson's list was used, and he was woefully incorrect in his detail, the attempt went for naught. However, four years later Frank H. Stewart by careful research ascertained what is nearly the correct list. For instance, it was always supposed that Captain Charlton Sheppard, commander of the little garrison at Hancock's Bridge, was killed. He was not, although he was bayoneted in one eye and left for dead on the floor of the house. The proof positive of his survival comes from a pension application signed by him on September 19th, 1778 and the grant to him of a tavern license, yearly up to 1784. About this time he died.

Definitely, the men killed at Hancock's Bridge were Walker Beesley, Captain Reuben Sayre and John Sayre. The early account of Beesley's death was that he was bayoneted by a man named Hanks, a local Tory who had been brought up in the Beesley family as a "taken boy" and to whom Beesley's entreaties for his life were in vain. The murderer is said to have remarked that for their former intimacy alone he was determined to kill him. Over the death of Reuben Sayre the authorities are in conflict. He was a member of the family referred to above. Johnson says he was murdered by a man named Ballinger, supposed to have been one of Simcoe's guides, while Shourds says he escaped from the house and was killed in his flight, falling into a swamp from which his body was later recovered. Another member of the same family, John Sayre, was killed outright.

There were four civilians massacred in the Hancock House. All were supposed to have been members of the Society of Friends and non-combatants. They were Judge William Hancock, Joseph Thompson, Charles Fogg and a man named Bacon. By Simcoe's order Hancock and Thompson were moved to a house down the creek and a British surgeon delegated to attend them. Simcoe stated in his memoirs that "among the killed was a friend of government, then a prisoner with the Rebels, Old Hancock, the owner of the house and his brother". Johnson in his 1844 or second account of the massacre waxes warm on this particular subject and rising to the patriotic defense of the Judge, used this language: "A great mistake, and a slander upon the character of that excellent man. Hancock was one of the County Judges, his son-in-law Thomas Sinnickson, then a Militia Captain, so was also as I have before said of his brother Andrew Sinnickson, who was also a Captain—the whole Sinnickson family and all their relatives were Whigs. It is true that the death of Judge Hancock was lamented by a large circle of his relatives. He had ten bayonet wounds in him, (Judge Hancock was a cripple in his left arm, having had it disabled some years before he was murdered). His daughter was then the wife of Capt. Thomas Sinnickson, in whose house in the town of Salem some of the British officers quartered. When the murder of her father was communicated to her, being almost frantic with grief and rage, she reproached the officers with unsparing language;

they threatened to hang her—she defied them, and persisted in her invectives against them for their horrid deeds."

Returning to the militia list, it is certain that Patrick Moore, a private, died of his wounds the next day. Others who were wounded were Abbott Sayre, Powell Carpenter, James Sayre, Anthony Lowden, James Finley, William Finley, Furman Sheppard, David Gandy and Waitel Snethen. Definite among the prisoners taken by the British were Dennis Dailey, Joshua Reeves, Joshua Williams and Joseph Sayre. This list is substantiated by the statement of Col. Holme which said, "Again on Saturday ye 21st, at night about 200 of the Greens with some Volunteers came up Alloways Creek in boats landed below Hancock's Bridge marched to the Bridge and surprised our Guard there and put them to the bayonet, killed four or five dead and wounded several more, several which are dead since."

The old Hancock house still stands. On its attic floor may yet be seen the blood stains of the slaughtered militia company who died or were wounded there on that March morning so many years ago. In 1931 the State of New Jersey purchased this house, which since that time has been a historic museum and has been visited by thousands of people. Its best epitaph comes from the words of the late Ellen Bradway Smith, M. D. in her speech at the unveiling of the D. A. R. tablet in 1903; "Look at me, remember the great sacrifice made here, remember the blood spilled within these walls that a nation might be free, remember the deeds of a sterner and simpler generation, who gave their all for liberty."

CHAPTER XVIII

OF EVENTS AFTER THE MASSACRE, THE BRITISH WITHDRAWAL FROM SALEM COUNTY, THE LONG COURT, AND THE END OF THE REVOLUTION.

There are two newspaper accounts of the Hancock's Bridge massacre which shed but little lustre on the British arms. The patriotic account was published in the famous newspaper of Isaac Collins, the *New Jersey Gazette* at Trenton. On April eighth, nineteen days after the massacre, it contained the following account:

On Saturday the 21st ult, about break of day our guard posted at Hancock's bridge, on Alloway's Creek, in Salem county consisting of about twenty men, were surprised by those the enemy call Jersey Volunteers: They, from their acquaintance with the country, had found means to cross the creek and come upon the guard from some unsuspected quarter and being undoubtedly led by some person well acquainted with the disposition of sentries, opened the guardhouse door and came in, many of the guards being, asleep, without giving the least alarm, nay, so far from it, that it is said some of them shook hands in a friendly manner with some of the guard with whom they were intimately acquainted, as indeed they were with most of them and O tempora, O mores!—immediately began bayoneting of them, without our people making the least show of resistance, not only reeking their fury on the guard but also on several of the peaceful inhabitants who were slumbering in their beds. One Bacon, of the people called Quakers, was inhumanly murdered in his own house and bed; old Mr. Hancock, beside his being of that society, was a cripple in both arms, was stabbed in his bed, and is since dead of his wounds. Another of that society is also since dead of his wounds; and the life of a fourth person is despaired of.

On the other hand, a Tory newspaper contained a flamboyant account of the British expedition and the massacre. While it is more editorial than historic, it does show, very clearly, the loyalist attitude. It is from the *Pennsylvania Evening Post* of April third, 1778 and reads:

Nothing can be stronger proof of the disaffection of the inhabitants of New Jersey, to the interest of rebellion, than their behavior to the troops, who went from this city on the 11th ult, under Col. Mawhood. When they landed at Salem none was found to oppose or impede them from collecting forage, excepting a few, who had been prevailed upon to abandon their houses, and on the third day after the landing of the troops, to show themselves in arms, but the number being insignificant, they were easily taken prisoners. Some days after, information was received that part of rebels were collecting at a place called Hancock's Bridge, on which the Queen's Rangers were sent off in boats, landed at the back of them and after killing and wounding a part, made prisoners of the residue. The rebels never afterwards appeared in force, so that the troops collected the forage without any interruption, and the inhabitants from all quarters flocked to them, bringing what cattle, provision, etc. they could spare, for which they received a generous price but lamented much that the army was to depart, and leave them again to the tyranny of the rebel faction. How far this may correspond with the pompous description which will be given to the world, by the immaculate Mr. Livingston, (Governor of New Jersey) is a matter of little amount, as truth will shine with superior lustre to misrepresentation. If it is said that the king's troops evacuated the place, before the militia could be called, it will stand the test; for it is an uncontrovertible fact, that in circuit of upwards of sixty miles, three hundred men could not be mustered; the people being fully sensible of their error, and heartily tired of the petty tyrants, who have galled and broke their spirits. This needs no further elucidation than that, in the place of fourteen hundred men who heretofore appeared and voted at the election of their assemblymen, no more than eight constituted the majority of the last electors, which is an evident demonstration that it is now a matter of indifference who now takes the lead, as tyranny and oppression is only to be expected from such as are willing to be of this number, who constitute that illegal assembly.

Mawhood did not run out of Salem county, as the patriots charged, but remained there for a full week, after the massacre of Hancock's Bridge. Robertson, his engineer, said that they foraged in Elsinboro, Lower Alloway's Creek, Penns Neck and other places on each day of the week following the affair at Hancock's Bridge. On the twenty-fourth of March, the British again distinguished themselves by burning the house of Col. Benjamin Holme in Elsinboro and in carrying off most of his household goods including a beautiful clock, since recovered by the Holme family, and causing other damage to this patriot's property.

Simcoe, the historian of the British expedition, says in his memoirs of the last days of the British expedition in Salem county:

Colonel Mawhood, in public orders, returned his best thanks to Major Simcoe and his corps, for their spirited and good conduct in the surprise of the rebel posts. Two days after, the Queen's Rangers patrolled to Thompson's bridge; the enemy, who had been posted there, were alarmed at the approach of a cow the night before, fired at it, wounded it, and then fled; they also abandoned Quinton's bridge, and retired to a creek, sixteen miles from Aloes Creek. Major Simcoe, making a patrol with the Huzzars, took a circuit towards the rear of one of the parties sent out to protect the foragers; a party of the enemy had been watching them the whole day, and unluckily, the forage being completed, the detachment had just left its ground and was moving off; the enemy doing the like met the patrol; were pursued, and escaped by the passage which the foragers had just left open. One only was taken, being pursued into a bog, which the Huzzars attempted in vain to cross, and were much mortified to see above a dozen of the enemy, who had passed around it in safety, within a few yards; they consisted of all the field officers and committee men of the district. The prisoner was their adjutant.

The enemy, who were assembled at Cohansey, might easily have been surprised; but Colonel Mawhood judged that having completed his forage with such success, his business was to return, which he effected. The troops embarked without any accident, and sailed for Philadelphia. The horses were given back to the inhabitants or paid for. On the passage, the ships waiting for the tide, Major Simcoe had an opportunity of landing at Billings Port, where Major Vandyke's corps was stationed, and examining it, they arrived at Philadelphia, March the thirty-first.

Thus Simcoe lightly attributes the retreat of the Americans from Aloes creek to Cohansey creek to the scare caused by one cow. The situation was more critical than Simcoe makes it appear. On the very morning of the massacre at Hancock's Bridge, Col. Mawhood, returning to his temporary home in the Dick House at Salem, issued the following proclamation, induced by "motives of humanity", so he said:

Colonel Mawhood, commading a detachment of the British army at Salem, induced by motives of humanity, proposes to the militia at Quinton's bridge and the neighborhood, officers as well as private men, to lay down their arms and depart, each man to his own home. On that condition, he solemnly promises to re-embark his troops without delay, doing no further damage to the country; and he will cause his commissaries to pay for the cattle, hay and corn, that have been taken, in sterling money.

If, on the contrary, the militia should be so far deluded, and blind to their true interest and happiness, he will put the arms which he has brought with him into the hands of the people well affected, called Tories, and will attack all such of the militia as remain in arms, burn and destroy their houses, and other property, and reduce them, their unfortunate wives and children, to beggary and distress; and to convince them that these are not vain threats, he has subjoined a list of the names of such as will be the first objects to feel the vengeance of the British nation.

Mawhood dated this March twenty-first, 1778, from his headquarters in Salem. He added as a postscript the names of the patriots whom he proscribed as enemies of the British nation. These men, all well known Salem county patriots actively engaged in the Revolution were Edward Keasbey, Thomas Sinnickson, Dr. Samuel Dick, Whitten Cripps, Dr. Ebenezer Howell, Edward Hall, John Rowan, Thomas Thompson, George Trenchard, Andrew Sinnickson, Benjamin Holme, Elijah Cattel, Nicholas Keen, William Shute, Jacob Hufty, Anthony Sharp and Abner Penton.

The next day Col. Elijah Hand, who shared with Benjamin Holme the command of the American militia forces, from the headquarters at Quinton's Bridge wrote the following dignified and cultured answer to the threat of the British colonel:

To C. Mawhood, Colonel.

I have been favored with what you say humanity has induced you to propose. It would have given me much pleasure to have found that humanity had been the line of conduct to your troops since you came to Salem. Not only denying quarters, but butchering our men who surrendered themselves prisoners in the skirmish at Quinton's Bridge last Thursday, and bayonetting yesterday morning at Hancock's Bridge, in the most cruel manner in cold blood, men who were taken by surprise, in a situation in which they neither could nor did attempt to make any resistance, and some of whom were not fighting men; are instances too shocking for me to relate and I hope for you to hear. The brave are very generous and humane. After expressing your sentiments of humanity, you proceed to make a request which I think you would despise us if we complied with. Your proposal, that we should lay down our arms, we absolutely reject.

We have taken them up to maintain rights which are dearer to us than our lives, and will not lay them down, 'till either success has crowned our cause with victory, or like many ancient worthies contending for liberty, we meet with an honorable death. You mention that if we reject your proposal, you will put arms into the hands of the Tories against us; we have no objection to the measure, for it would be a very good one to fill our arsenals with arms. Your threats to wantonly burn and destroy our houses and other property, and reduce our wives and children to beggary and distress, is a sentiment which my humanity almost forbids me only to recite, and induces me to imagine I am reading the cruel order of a barbarous Attila, and not of a Gentleman, brave, generous and polished with a genteel European education.

To wantonly destroy, will injure your cause more than ours—it will increase your enemies and our army. To destine to destruction the property of our most distinguished men, as you have done in your proposals, is, in my opinion, unworthy a generous foe; and more like a rancorous feud between two contending Barons, than a war carried on by one of the greatest powers on earth, against a people nobly struggling for liberty; a line of honour would mark out that these men should share the fate of their country. If your arms should be crowned with victory, which God forbid, they and their property will be entirely at the disposal of your Sovereign. The loss of their property, when their persons are out of your power, will only make them desperate and, as I said before, increase your foes and our army; and retaliation upon Tories and their property is not entirely out of our power. Be assured that these are the sentiments and determined resolution, not only of myself, but of all the officers and privates under me.

My prayer is, Sir, that this answer may reach you in health and great happiness.

Given at Headquarters at Quinton's Bridge the 22nd day of March, 1778.

Elijah Hand, Colonel.

On Saturday night the twenty-first, the American militia, doubtless fearing an attack at Quinton, now that their flank had been turned on the west side, withdrew their headquarters to the glassworks at Thompson's Bridge, now Alloway. On that same night, Hand and Holme formulated this letter to William Livingston, governor of New Jersey, beseeching him to send aid:

Glass Works, Salem County,
March 21st, 1778.

Worthy Sir:

These with our respects and would earnestly inform and recommend to your Excellency's notice the suffering state of our counties, viz, on Tuesday last a large number of the enemy landed at Salem Town as near as we can learn about or between two or three thousand and are advancing into the Country and plundering very fast; we have had two or three skirmishes with them and have lost on our side as near as we can yet learn about twelve killed and near forty taken prisoners; the loss on the enemy's side we cannot as yet positively learn, however, we are well assured we have killed some of them.

We have made our stand on Alloways Creek the lower side at Hancock's, Quinton's or Thompson's Bridges, but last night the enemy landed out of their boats below all the aforesaid bridges and surrounded our guard at Hancock's Bridge and took and killed almost all of them which is a part of the aforesaid loss, and we fear they will advance over all these lower counties (as we find our numbers at present are not large enough to make a proper stand against them) except you, Sir, by some means can help us to some relief which we desire you to do either by sending down some Militia or if that cannot well be done we desire you to inform General Washington of our necessity of some of the continental forces to assist us at this time and desire you, Sir, to use your influence with him to send some forces to our relief—we are under a disadvantage at present for want of field pieces and should be glad if we could be furnished with four or five of them by some means as soon as possible.

We are, Sir, your most obedient Servants
Signed,
Elijah Hand, Col.

Apparently the fear of a British attack on Quinton passed the next day for on the twenty-second, Hand dated his famous reply to Mawhood as "Headquarters at Quinton's Bridge." Simcoe said that the militia at Thompson's Bridge was alarmed by a cow, fired at it and then fled. The cow story was probably a bit of imagination on the part of the triumphant British major. However, it is true that some time after the twenty-second the American militia, still fearing a flank attack, did desert the line of Alloway's Creek to fall back some twelve miles in Cumberland county behind the shelter of Cohansey creek. Simcoe states this fact and the Americans confirm it by another letter to Governor Livingston dated at Roadstown on the Cohansey one week later.

This letter, honest and frank, is a most moving document calling attention to the pitiable state of the colonists in Salem and Cumberland counties and throwing themselves without stint upon the mercy of the new state government. The letter shows only too well the same state of mind which permeated the army at Valley Forge. It is a document which every patriotic American should read to realize the low ebb of this country's fortune in March of 1778. In part, the letter says:

A large detachment of the British army a few weeks ago made an invasion into the lower counties of this state on Delaware, and plundered a few of the inhabitants. At present a larger detachment are invading a second time. The enemy in this second incursion have, as we have been creditably informed, by the express orders of Colonel Mawhood, the commanding officer, bayonetted and butchered in the most inhuman manner a number of militia who have unfortunately fallen into their hands. Colonel Mawhood immediately after the massacre in open letters sent to both officers and privates by a flag had the effrontery to insult us with a demand that we should lay down our arms and if not, threaten to burn, destroy and lay the whole country waste and more especially the property of a number of our most distinguished men whom he named. He has since actually put his threat into execution in one instance by burning one of the finest dwelling houses in Salem County, and all the other buildings on the same farm the property of Colonel Benjamin Holme. Plunder, rapine and devastation in the most fertile and populous part of these counties widely marked their footsteps wherever they go. They are spreading disaffection. They are using every possible means to corrupt the minds of the people; they are publicly vending their goods to people who within their lines have so little virtue as to purchase from them.

We are in no state of defence. We are so exposed by reason of our situation that some of our officers civil and military have moved out of these counties for safety. Our militia during the last winter have been so fatigued out by repeated calls and continual service, and disaffection is now so widely diffused, that very few can be called out, in some places none. We have no troops of light horse regularly embodied; there is a scarcity of small arms among us and no field pieces. These two want of field pieces and artillerymen. The number of us assembled is so small that though we should use the greatest conduct and bravery we could only provoke not injure our enemy.

The extent of our country is so great, that our small number of men fatigued out, indifferently armed and without field pieces cannot defend it. As Delaware runs along these counties we are liable to be attacked in numberless places. The acquisition of these counties would be of great advantage to the enemy. They could nearly maintain their whole campaign by the plunder, forage and assistance they could draw from them. Although the United States might not need them, yet it might perhaps be advisable to defend them to prevent the advantage the enemy might receive from them. Our riches and former virtue make us a prey to an enemy whose tender mercies are cruelties. In short our situation is beyond description deplorable. The powers civil and military are daily relaxing and disaffection prevailing. We can neither plough, plant, sow, reap nor gather. We are fast falling into poverty, distress and into the hands of our enemy. Unless there can be sent to our relief and assistance a sufficient body of standing troops, we must be under the disagreeable necessity of leaving the country to the enemy and removing ourselves and family to distant places for safety. Although the present detachment may be fled and gone before the relief reach us, yet a body of troops are necessary for our protection as long as the enemy possesses Philadelphia and that these are the sentiments not only of us the subscribers but of all the rest of the officers civil and military and other good subjects of this state in these counties.

Your humble petitioners have set forth these few hints containing not the half of their distress and misery do humbly pray your Excellency to take the premises into consideration and give your humble petitioners just relief therein as to your Excellency shall seem meet—and your humble petitioners shall ever pray.

Dated at Roadstown in Cumberland
March 28, 1778 and signed.

Civil Officers: Joseph Newcomb, Joel Fithian, Samuel Leake, Ephriam Mills, Nathan Leek, John Holme, Providence Ludlam, John Peck, Jonathan Bowen, A. S. Sayre, Ebenezer Howell, Jonathan Elmer.

Military Officers: Elijah Hand, Benjamin Holme, Silas Newcomb, Abijah Holme, Samuel Ogden, Thomas Ewing, Edward Hall, Daniel Maskell, Henry Sparks, Robert Patterson, Enos Seely.

The pathetic appeal of the military officers and civilians had its immediate effect upon the commander of the New Jersey Continental line, Colonel Israel Shreve, for on the same day the letter was dispatched from Roadstown, he wrote to General Washington at Valley Forge, relaying the news of the British raid at Salem and the pitiable condition of the lower counties of New Jersey which lay upon the Delaware river. The letter is dated from Haddonfield, March twenty-eighth, 1778.

Haddonfield, March 28, 1778.

 The Governor desired me to join Col. Ellis and wait at this post until he could collect a body of militia; we have now one hundred and seventy foot, twenty horse and thirty-five artillery with two iron three pounders, besides my own Regiment—the last accounts from Salem by three deserters and several other persons were that four regiments commanded by Col. Mawhood, consisting of between one thousand and twelve hundred were at that place; the Militia to the number of three hundred were at Roads Town thirteen miles below Salem; all the county on the River between that post and this place, forty-five miles, is open to the ravage of the Enemy—the tories to the number of one hundred and fifty are in arms fortifying at Billingsport with the assistance of some marines; a great number of disaffected inhabitants are trading with the enemy. Yesterday, sixty tories and marines commanded by one Cox, went to Swedesboro, took Lieut. Lloyd of the fourth Regiment, Jersey, with two recruits, plundered the house of Capt. Brown in a shocking manner, stripped his wife and children, carried off or destroyed everything in the house. Several other houses shared the same fate. Every civil and military officer is forced to fly from home; many have been taken by the tories and carried off to the city. Three days ago, three of the militia took a covered wagon and three horses with baggage and stores belonging to Daniel Cozens a Tory Captain; yesterday Col. Ellis with a small party of horse took a certain David Chew one of the tory gang; he acknowledges he has borne arms against the States; they also took some marketing going to the enemy, but the owner fled; Captain Cumming has just returned from a scout, took a wagon and two horses at a landing; no person will own the wagon. I have ordered these things sold for the use of the captors.

 This country is in a miserable situation, the inhabitants afraid of every person they see. If marketing is found in any house the whole family, even little children, will deny the owners, not pretend to know anything about it. If your Excellency could spare part or all of the Brigade it would enable us to quell the Tories and collect a considerable quantity of privisions which otherwise, I fear, will fall into the hands of the enemy as it is collected in places near the River for that purpose. We shall do everything in our power to protect the virtuous inhabitants and suppress the tories; we have a negro man confined as a spy, as I believe it will appear he went to Philadelphia to give intelligence of my crossing the Delaware. I desire your Excellency's directions concerning the tryal of this spy and those of the inhabitants taken in arms against the States, as some examples seem highly necessary in this place, but I am too prolix and have only to say that a general defection prevails in many places, that from the situation of Haddonfield it must be in our possession or least it be the case with the lower counties—that the force here is too small for the purpose, scarcely enough to prevent surprise when large scouts are out.

 I would wish to march to Cumberland as many things are there to be had if the Enemy were terrified from thence, which I hope to effect when the militia comes in to secure this post and by a junction with me make me responsible in numbers. If your Excellency has orders, I should be happy to receive them and I am your

Excellency's very Humble Servant,
Israel Shreve, Col.

 N. B. As the tories have fallen in with our parties I hope I shall stop their trade of catching officers for whom they get a reward according to the rank of the prisoners. Ammunition is wanted for the Militia as they are not furnished for common duty—they cannot be supplied from the State; therefore I shall find a wagon to receive it from the stores in camp and beg your Excellency's order to obtain it.

TORIES PUNISHED

Governor Livingston, writing from Princeton on the ninth of April, also urged Washington to send help to the Salem county militia. But Washington, with his own troubles at Valley Forge, considering his fast diminishing army, famine, starvation, and lack of supplies was unable to send the slightest bit of help to the harrassed militia of the lower counties. By the time the American commander had received the reports from Shreve and Livingston, the British army had gone from Salem, leaving in its wake the hatred and disgust of a community whose sons had been butchered in cold blood.

It is true that war came no more to Salem county but the outraged citizens cried out for retaliation against the British invaders. There was little they could do about it except take action against the persons or the estates of those who had aided the British in any way. They were not long in doing this. On September 26th of this same year the Salem County Grand Jury returned numerous indictments against those persons who had either taken arms or otherwise aided the British cause. The court appointed Thomas Sayre, father of a family which suffered so severely at the Hancock House, and Daniel Garrison as commissioners to confiscate the estates of the Tories.

Following the indictments the court of Oyer and Terminer commenced at Salem on November 30th, 1778 and lasted without adjournment until the nineteenth of December, the same year. It has passed into history as the "Long Court." It was the act of desperate men who, grieved by their serious losses, were determined to take this action against the enemies of the state. True, the war was not over and the British army no further away than New York, but these local citizens were determined that someone should pay for these wrongs.

No less than two chief justices, John Cleves Symmes and Robert Morris, separately presided over the various sessions of the long court. The foreman of the Grand Jury was William Dickison. The local associate judges were John Holme, John Mayhew, William Mecum, William Smith and Andrew Sinnickson. The justices of the peace in attendance were Robert Johnson, Edward Keasbey, Isaac Harris, Thomas Sayre, Thomas Norris, John Summerill, Jacob Taggert, William Miller and William Dickison. It should be noticed that most of these judges had rendered military service. The court appeared to roam about the town of Salem. On many occasions it met at the Quaker Meeting House, still standing on East Broadway. Sometimes it met in Mrs. Burrows' house, exact location unknown, and naturally in the Court house.

There seem to have been two courts sitting at the same

time. They divided their crimes into three classes, the first for high treason, punishable by death, the second for seditious words, the third for misdemeanors.

On the charge of high treason four of the Tories who were so unfortunate as to fall into patriot hands were found guilty and sentenced to be hanged on February 12th, 1779. Ironically enough, two of these men, Rubin Langley and Abdon Abbott, Jr., had served in the local militia before they joined the Tories. The other two were Richard Whitaker and Joseph Hilton.

However, the death sentences were never carried out. Before the twelfth of February Governor Livingston of New Jersey, listening to the appeals for their pardon, gave all four convicted men a reprieve. Whitaker was forced to leave the United States in six months from the date of his pardon. The other three, Abbott, Langley and Hilton, were also pardoned on condition that they leave the state of New Jersey.

There were numerous convictions with trifling fines for seditious words and misdemeanors. Most of these loyalists fled to Nova Scotia and other parts of the British empire. From the West Jersey volunteers is taken the following list of men who enlisted in the British loyalist regiments: Abdon Abbott, Phillip Adams, John Cowman, Jerman Davis, Rubin Langley, Michael Miller, Richard Meade, James Sutton, James Dean, Israel Elwell, Joseph Hilton, Joseph Kendall, Henry Longbaugh, Jacob Sutton, Moses Sutton, John Sutton, Thomas Sutton, Robert Whitaker. This list does not include the names of Joel Daniels and John Hanks. These two men are mentioned by Johnson as the murderers of their fellow Salem countians at the Hancock House. Neither does the list mention Hugh Cowperthwaite, Jonathan Ballinger and a negro named Nicholson's Frank, who were reported to have been the guides who piloted Simcoe and his men across the marshes to Hancock's Bridge on the morning of the twenty-first of March. These men seem to have escaped the vengeance of the Salem courts in person although Cowperthwaite, a fugitive, had his estate confiscated by the commissioners.

The hatred towards these guides did not die down easily. As late as 1825 a man by the name of Sayre, son of one of the patriots of that name massacred at Hancock's Bridge, was the captain of a small vessel plying between Salem and Philadelphia. Becoming drunk one night he fell into the river off Market street wharf at Philadelphia. A young man standing on the wharf plunged in and saved his life. Upon being rescued, Sayre discovered that he owed his life to the bravery of the son of the Jonathan Ballinger who guided the British to the massacre at

Hancock's Bridge. Perceiving this fact, Sayre said "he would be damned if he would owe his life to such a double damned scoundrel as the son of Ballinger." Thereupon, he threw himself back in the river and with some difficulty was rescued a second time from a watery grave.

As late as 1803 at a dinner in Salem someone proposed the toast of eternal damnation to Major Simcoe. In 1933 a facetious writer in a Philadelphia newspaper, after visiting the Hancock House, commented after hearing the story of the massacre "that the Salem folks were still mad about the massacre."

* * * *

References to Salem county after the withdrawal of the British troops in the last week of March, 1778 are few and far between. But it does not mean that the sons of Salem county were inactive in the Revolution which by this time still had three years and a half to run. As a matter of fact the British depredations in this locality caused a rapid increase in the militia regiment. A large number of patriots, angered by the affairs at Quinton's Bridge and Hancock's Bridge, hastened to join the Continental army.

The hero of Quinton's Bridge, Andrew Bacon, was languishing on the British prison ship *Jersey* in Wallabout Bay, New York. His career on this ship, after he was taken a prisoner by the British on the eighteenth of March, is well worth notice. For three years this man held on to life in the plague ridden, vermin infested ship. While several thousands of his comrades died horrible deaths, Bacon lived until the British evacuated New York City. At that time the few survivors of these awful years were herded on deck and asked where they belonged. Upon Bacon's saying he was from Salem county, New Jersey, the officer put him in a small boat, had him left on the shore of Staten Island and told him to get home as best he could. Fearful of the refugees and pine robbers Bacon spent the night crawling on his hands and knees through the bushes until, discovering a pig pen, he drove the pigs out and made their home his bed for the night. The next day he crawled to the house near where the pig pen was situated and asked for aid. The family, fortunately for Bacon, were patriots and took splendid care of him, feeding and nursing him and finally giving him a horse to ride to Salem. He arrived here finally, only to fall exhausted from the horse at his own doorstep. His wife, believing him to be dead, thought this was his ghost. He lived some fifty-five years after his terrible experiences and died in 1836, a hundred years old. He lies buried in the Salem Baptist Cemetery.

The patriotic efforts in this county were not diminished during the last three years of the war. If anything, their attempts to aid the young nation were more devoted and vigorous than before. The year after the Salem raid a number of citizens, led by the Sayre's and the Sinnickson's joined hands with the Elmers of Cumberland county to build and equip a privateer, which in honor of the governor of the state they named *The Governor Livingston*. It made one successful trip in preying upon British shipping but on the second trip while returning to its haven at Bridgeton, was captured off Cape May by a British frigate.

The ladies of Salem county were instrumental in aiding the soldiers. The New Jersey Archives mentions Mrs. Mayhew and Mrs. Dick as the ladies auxiliary committee for Salem county. The sacrifices of all continued to the end of the war. In 1779 Salem county was assessed for fifteen thousand pounds of beef and mutton for the support of the American army. Salem county soldiers in the Continental Line served their nation with fidelity until the end came at Yorktown in October of 1781.

* * * *

At the close of such a struggle as the Revolution, it was only natural that a great number of stories, some quite impossible and some probably true, should arise, engendered by the hardships, the vicissitudes, and the emotional experiences of those who carried on the fight for American independence. It is interesting to note that the minds of these colonists ran towards the preservation of all sorts of stories regarding the war. Ghosts played a popular part in the mythology of the Revolution. The best surviving ghost story is the one which concerns the Oakford House at Alloway. The ghost caused by the Revolution is sometimes called the Alloway Ghost and sometimes the Ghost of Oakford House.

This house, still standing, is one of the old houses of Salem county. It was built by William Oakford in 1736. He was a hardy settler who pushed out into the forest beyond Aloes creek, a main and proud thorofare in those days, and built this house. Until the Revolution it pursued the peaceful tenor of its ways, undisturbed by ghosts and goblins alike. Then came the war and the crimson tide which engulfed the colonies swept down on peaceful Alloway.

When the British army marched into Salem county in 1778, they found Alloway the east end of the line of the patriot defense. The American militia fortified the three bridges over the creek to protect the eastern end of Salem county and the whole of Cumberland county. Alloway, then better known as

Thompson's Bridge, was the last of the three forts from Hancock's Bridge eastward.

But the countryside was terrified and old men, women and children fled into the woods on the south side of Alloways creek, leaving behind them the heads of their families to fight the British. Times of anguish they must have been to those whose homes were broken up and to those who were forced to flee, bearing with them what valuables they could carry away.

The old Oakford House held out its shelter to these refugees. At this time the ghost begins, for it was said that several of these families hid their jewels and silver plate in the cellar of the old house or nearby in the woods. Like most war refugees, in their precipitate haste they neglected to mark carefully the resting place of their treasure.

The British marched on Thompson's Bridge and added to the terror of the families sheltered in the Oakford house but turned off and attacked the Americans at Quinton's Bridge. The sounds of musket fire of that battle certainly must have reached the ears of those gathered in the woods at Oakford's.

Then came the massacre of the little garrison at Hancock's Bridge so that of the three American outposts, Thompson's Bridge was the only one which did not suffer. Although the patriots retreated to Cumberland county and left the people at the Oakford House within the British lines, the enemy did not bother to follow up their success but instead moved back to Philadelphia and allowed the refugees to return to their homes.

Then, the story goes, the owners of the buried treasure came back under more peaceful conditions but to their utter dismay failed to find their goods. Perhaps some dishonest member of the little band secretly removed the treasure; perhaps the owners themselves in their haste completely forgot the exact spot, but at any rate the goods were never found and a Revolutionary ghost in the buff and blue regalia of a continental soldier took up a vigil which has lasted for a century and a half.

Some, wise in their knowledge of the situation declared that one of the refugees, an old man who was certain that he knew the exact spot where his treasure was buried, was about to dig in the ground and fell over dead with a heart attack. To those who told the story came the firm assurance that with this unfortunate man's death the ghost appeared to guard the hidden gold. This version of the ghost pictures it as an old white bearded man armed with a shovel and a pick.

The years passed swiftly. The tenants of the Oakford House died and the refugees also passed on, but the ghost remained to frighten away all who might dare to disturb the treasure of the dead.

But there were those bold spirits in the region of Alloway who had heard this tradition of buried treasure and who determined to find it for themselves. The house became deserted and the cellar laid open to any adventurer who sought the buried lucre. The wise ones shook their heads and predicted trouble to those who were profane enough to disturb the dead. Many, so it is said, dug in the cellar of the Oakford House only to flee in terror and dismay at the sudden appearance of the ghost, which was always present. Then a bolder soul would appear in Allowaystown and boast that no ghost could keep him away from the treasure, but after a few minutes of digging in the cellar, a ghostly noise would be heard overhead and the ghost would fly across the darkened cellar with its warning. The brave individual would, like all the rest, flee and leave the cellar to the ghost.

There were other stories of buried treasure and lost goods. One story is that Col. Samuel Dick, a member of the Continental Congress, buried his silver plate in the back yard of his home in Salem where the Mecum building is now situated. The plate was never discovered and as late as 1905 small boys, including the writer, still hunted for the buried treasure in the remnants of Col. Dick's once fine garden.

On the Tide Mill farm in Mannington now owned by Neil Campbell, Whitten Cripps, an ardent patriot, drilled militia. Hearing of the British approach he sent his family and live stock under the care of a negro slave named Pompey to Wyncoops Woods for safety. These woods today are better known as Muttontown Woods. The family arrived safely but the negro carefully took the cattle and livestock into Salem where the British army gratefully appropriated them.

Many other stories concerning the Revolution come down to us. It is said that when Col. Mawhood entered Salem on the morning of the seventeenth of March a funeral was passing to the Friends' Burying Ground and that the British colonel thoughtfully took all the horses in the funeral procession except the one belonging to the widow, a Quakeress named Fogg. Many also are the stories of families terrified by the approach of the British who crawled under the sheets of their beds or fled in terror to the woods.

CHAPTER XIX

OF EVENTS FROM THE CLOSE OF THE REVOLUTION TO 1820

It was only natural, following the Revolution, that the victors should divide the spoils. The veterans of the American Revolution who had given their all to form the new nation demanded and received the political positions which were available. Fitness for office was not as important as the question of whether or not the man had served in the Revolution. An excellent anecdote illustrates this point exactly. About 1785, Whitten Cripps, whose house still stands in Mannington and on whose farm the militia drilled, was a candidate for sheriff. At the polls that day some scoffer asked, "What has Whitten Cripps done to deserve being sheriff?" Both Cripps and the scoffer happened to be carpenters. A by-stander sarcastically said to the one who asked the question that Cripps had at least buried his broad axe under the walls of Quebec, "where such a coward as you have never been."

So it was true that the principal office holders were veterans of the war. Cripps was twice sheriff and his son Benjamin also held that office. Doctor Samuel Dick, veteran of two colonial wars who had served under both the British flag and the Amercan, was a member of the Continental Congress in 1783. Thomas Sinnickson was a member of the first and fifth congresses. Bateman Lloyd, Curtis Trenchard, John Smith, John Rowan and Anthony Keasby were clerks of Salem county; Samuel Dick for twenty years after the Revolution was surrogate of Salem county and was followed by Artis Seagraves, also a veteran. By far the larger number of delegates to the legislature in both the Council and the Assembly were men who had served in the Revolution. All of these selections were made before the days when political parties nominated candidates. The first election along party lines did not come until 1798, when John Tuft, a Federalist, was elected sheriff. From then on until the present time all of the office holders throughout the county have had a party label. Undoubtedly the Federalist party had the largest number of office holders in the first twenty years of the republic. This was only natural, for the Federalist party drew its membership largely from the old soldiers. By 1800, with the elevation of Thomas Jefferson to the presidency, his Democrat-Republican party took control of the situation. For nearly sixty years the Jeffersonians elected the largest number of office holders in Salem county.

Without reference to party politics a petition containing seventy-five names was handed to the New Jersey Legislature in September of 1787, asking that they ratify the proposed new constitution of the United States. Some of these signers were Thomas Sharp, Peter Du Bois, Thomas Carney, James James, Bateman Lloyd, Jonas Keen, David Colson, Frederick Denelsbeck, David Austin, Moses Richman, Peter Culin, Enoch Ballinger and Isaac Garrison.

As early as 1802 politics started to become intensely bitter. Although the new republic was in its infancy there were at that early day quarrels and frictions over the right to hold office. A good example of this occurred in 1802 when the Democrat Governor of New Jersey, Joseph Bloomfield, removed from office Doctor Samuel Dick, surrogate of Salem county. Bloomfield put in his place Artis Seagraves and by so doing aroused a storm of newspaper comment. A Salem farmer, evidently a Federalist, wrote a scorching letter to the Trenton "True American" protesting against Dick's removal and saying that Seagraves was wanting in integrity, temperance, morality and capacity; that he was a reviler of Christianity and that the only reason that he got the job was because he owed the governor money. In the same newspaper, a friend of Seagraves came to his defense and said that even if Dick had been a soldier, which was admitted, Seagraves had also carried a musket at Trenton and Princeton, and that furthermore, he was not a reviler of religion but on the contrary was a clergyman in the Universal Church; that even though Seagraves owed the governor money, he at least was not behind in his account with the surrogate's office as was Dick.

Nor was politics possible without the ugly form of bribery raising its head. William Parrett, many times a member of the legislature and a most prominent citizen of Salem, wrote a letter to the Trenton "True American" saying that two men, one a governor and the other a chief justice, came to him and a man named Welsh offering them one hundred acres and a thousand dollars cash for their two votes, as members of the legislature, for a certain candidate. This was in 1803 and the newspapers of New Jersey were stirred by the revelation. But like so many bribery investigations it came to naught.

In the same year of 1803 John Firth, author of the "Memoirs of Benjamin Abbott," and at this time the leader of the Methodist

Church in South Jersey, wrote a long letter to the Trenton "True American" praising the Jefferson administration for its friendliness to the Methodist Church and saying that the administration was responsible for the large increase in Methodist membership. Firth was a regular correspondent of this Trenton paper and in most of his articles stressed the political side of the Methodist Church. In one of his other articles he called the Federalist newspaper of Trenton "The oracle of slander". But Firth lived long enough to see his fellow Methodists turn on the Jefferson party and became Federalists. It has been previously mentioned that the infant Methodist congregations were frequently subject to interruption and abuse by noisy mobs. This situation became so bad that the Methodists struggled to get a bill passed in the legislature to stop the annoyance of Methodists at their worship. The Democrats were against the measure, the Federalists for, and by this latter support gained the friendship of the Methodists.

For about ten years in the early 1800's the Methodist Church and the disturbance of their meetings was a live issue in the politics of Salem county. In 1808 one Jacob Murphy of Salem, a member of the Methodist Church, claimed that he lost an election for assemblyman because he was a Methodist. Out of these early struggles of Methodism it is interesting to speculate that many of the Methodist fathers of that day handed down to their sons a dislike for the party which, as Firth said, had once favored them and then had turned against them.

But in the first decade of 1800 the Jefferson party carried everything before it in the annual elections. In 1802, 1803 and 1804 there was no opposition to the ticket named by the Democratic party. Democrats like William Parrott, Jacob Hufty, Samuel Ray, Jed Dubois, Jerry Dubois and Hedge Thompson were elected to the legislature, year in and year out, without opposition. In 1805 the Federalists did run a ticket against the Democrats but were swamped by a majority of five hundred votes. A triumphant Democrat wrote to the Trenton paper saying, "I have the pleasure to inform you that in the County of Salem, Republicanism has completely triumphed over Anarchy; those who call themselves Federalists played all their old tricks; notwithstanding we won." In the election of 1818, the Methodist influence made itself felt and for the first time in two decades a Federalist, Thomas Murphy, was elected to the legislature. True, Hedge Thompson, James Newell and Morris Hancock, all Democrats, were elected but a mournful correspondent writing to the "True American" said he "hoped that the election of Thomas Murphy will teach the Democrats of Salem County a lesson that they should be eternally on guard".

Another Salem county official under fire was Clement Acton, clerk of Salem county, against whom charges of the neglect of his office were made. This lasted from 1800 to 1803 and was like the rest carried on through the files of the Trenton "True American". Finally he was removed and John Hall put in his place.

John Adams, president of the United States, had many supporters in Salem county. Just before the presidential election of 1800 there was a meeting at the Academy, which stood where the Salem Grammar School now stands, to further the cause of John Adams. Thomas Sinnickson, a Federalist, was chairman of the meeting. The Democrats had their meetings as well, although they made a little more noise about it. On July 4th, 1800 the Jeffersonians held a big party and street parade in Salem. Let the correspondent of the Trenton "True American" tell the story:

"As the County Court was sitting on the fourth (the epoch of our deliverance from the Reign of Terror) the Republican citizens of this town agreed to meet on this day in celebration thereof. Major Jacob Hufty was selected as officer of the day, the solemn assembly met at the house of James Sherron (now Green's Hotel) opposite the Court House at eleven A. M. where the processions formed which accompanied by a great concourse of citizens, paraded to Penny Hill. The procession consisted of a detachment of infantry, followed by the artillery then the colors and music followed by the citizens and military officials. Succeeding this grand procession a sumptuous repast was served to all and sundry at Mr. Sherron's house. Our most prominent citizens gave toasts to Thomas Jefferson, Aaron Burr and William Tell, all of which were received with salvoes."

Thus ended one of the first and certainly most elaborate Fourth of July celebrations in Salem. This celebration seems to have been run solely by the Democratic party. Ever since this time, annually on the Fourth there has been held some kind of celebration in honor of the day. Some years later the Whig party held its own Fourth of July celebration at Woodstown while the Democratic party held theirs, as they did this one, in Salem. About ten years before the Civil War local pride supplanted the giving of Fourth of July celebrations by political parties for their own interests, and the respective villages carried them on instead.

The War of 1812 brought dissension and trouble to the prevailing political party of Salem county, which was at this time the Jeffersonian party. For years now they had swept the annual hustings by majorities of 500 or more, and frequently had had no opposition at all. It took the second war with Great Britian to solidify the opposition to the Democratic party and prepare them for the beginning of the great struggle for supremacy which culminated in the Jackson campaigns of 1828 and 1832.

The Hartford convention and the opposition to the war found its echo in this county when the Friends of Peace of all West Jersey met in a monster convention at the Salem Court House on December 16th, 1812. Josiah Harrison, Thomas Sinnickson and others were the leaders of this meeting who bitterly protested the actions of President Madison and did not hesitate to call it a "foolish war". The elections of 1812 had witnessed a peace party victory for the congressional seats of the state, while in Salem county the huge majorities of the Democrats were cut from 500 to less than 100. The war tax on this county alone amounted to $6,528.17 and as the peace party formed of the remnants of the Federalists and opposition named a complete ticket for the year 1813, the Democrats, with a bitter battle on their hands, again carried the county by a scant majority of 160.

The war went on as British fleets appeared off Cape May, Lewes, Delaware and in Chesapeake Bay but Salem felt not the heel of the invader as it had thirty-five years previously. The legislature of New Jersey augmented by Salem's Democratic representation remained faithful to the administration although the Friends of Peace met frequently at Sherron's Tavern in Salem and other places in the county to protest the war.

Not due to the war but due to an outbreak of cholera morbus, the old jail was used as a hospital in the year 1812. One effect of the war however, was the freeholders' decision to move the county records to a safe place, no doubt fearing a British invasion.

The draft called forth by Governor Pennington in loyalty to the administration netted seventy-two volunteers out of a possible one hundred and ninty-five, the remainder of which was supplied by the well known process of drafting. Captain Peter Bilderback's troop of horse left Salem late in 1814 to spend a few days at Billingsport in the one military manoeuver which affected the county. The opposition and the Friends of Peace cried that Governor Pennington had so managed the camp at Billingsport that the militia of Salem county, largely Democrats, could go home to vote in the fall elections of 1814, while the regiments of Cape May county, mainly Federalists and opposition men, were forced to remain at camp and lost their chance to vote. Again in the election of 1814, Jediah Du Bois, Democrat, and his assemblymen were elected over the Friends of Peace ticket by about the same plurality as the year before.

By January of 1815 Andrew Jackson had shattered the

British forces behind the mud ramparts of the Rodriquez Canal outside New Orleans, the treaty of Ghent had been signed and the Salem troop of horse under Captain Peter Bilderback had come back from Billingsport, leaving the Democratic party to claim the full honors of having won a war, which had called forth possible threats of secession in the Hartford Convention, had seen the capital burned in Washington and had left the Friends of Peace totally without an issue.

So it continued in the politics of Salem county for another five years. With the exception of the election of Murphy, a Federalist, in 1818, the Democrats still swept the boards. Indeed their worst enemy was within their own ranks, for in 1816 open insurrection broke out between the upper and lower county forces of the dominant party.

The section around Salem had to face opposition on the part of the citizens of Pilesgrove and Pittsgrove. In 1818, the Democratic party split into two factions, both nominating candidates. A Union ticket, composed mainly of Federalists, also was entered. John Dickinson of the upper county faction won a bitterly contested battle for the Council while the new Salem "Gazette" uttered one broadside after another in behalf of the lower countians. Dickinson received 768 votes, Freas of the lower 488, and Hall, also from the lower part of the county, running on the Union ticket, polled 201 votes.

The Assembly contest was equally bitter. There were three sets of tickets here also. The upper faction elected two of the three, Yarrow and Mayhew, while Stacey Lloyd of Upper Alloways Creek, who ran on the lower county ticket, won the third seat. Flushed with their success the upper faction immediately rushed through the legislature an enabling act calling for an election to move the Court House and county buildings away from Salem.

After the election of 1817 when Messrs. Curriden, Lloyd and Bilderback were members of the Assembly the agitation for removal of the county buildings had started. All three voted against the enabling act and by so doing broke the Democratic party into the two factions previously mentioned. Lloyd had a change of heart and although he ran on the lower county ticket, promised to vote for the referendum on removal and when the time came fulfilled the promise.

1819 found Salem county visibly agitated over a proposition to move the county buildings from Salem to a more central location in the county. The year itself was significant of the spirit of unrest which had permeated even the marsh land fastness of Salem. The great riots of Manchester in which the disgruntled voice of labor spoke loudly for the first time, occurred in England; Napoleon's career on the rocky island of St. Helena had still a few months to run; the United States had stopped the importation of slaves; Monroe was about to promulgate the doctrine which bears his name, warning Europe to stay out of the Western hemisphere; and only a few years afterward, the marvelous invention of Stephenson put the miles at naught, and in Salem county put an end to agitation over inadequate transportation to the county seat.

Before the era of the locomotive and the railway cars, it was no news to say that transportation in Salem county and any other county was decidedly tedious. In the first place the roads were miserable, with few exceptions. Stage coaches were running, but to only one or two points such as Craven's Ferry (Pennsville) and Philadelphia. Gigs and light wagons were in use, but as late as 1819 were still considered a luxury; the saddle horse was still the best means of travel. It is not surprising, therefore, to find a growing sentiment that Salem was too far away from the rest of the county and that a change of the court house and gaol should be made to a more central location.

The first cry of change arose from Pittsgrove and Pilesgrove, the townships most distant from Salem. Upper Alloway's Creek, now the township of Quinton, and Alloway also put in a protest against the maintenance of the buildings at Salem. Salem, where the possession was nine tenths of the familiar percentage, resisted the move to reduce her glory of a hundred and forty years and the struggle was on.

There were three other places bidding for the honor of the new court house, two in Mannington and one in Alloway. Those interested ran a survey and determined that the south end of the present county farm on Major's Run was the most central, but the loyal citizens of Alloway pointed out that Alloway was nearly as central, and in addition was a town with an up-to-date tavern, whereas Pilesgrove was nothing but an empty field with no civilization nearer than Woodstown, two miles away.

Salem's inhabitants waxed wrothy over the proposal. What difference did it make if roads were bad and transportation difficult? Didn't John Fenwick in his wisdom donate one acre of land to Salem and will it in perpetuity for the residents of Salem and his colony to use as a court house and a jail? The old order from Samuel Hedge to the deputy surveyor, John Worlidge, dated 1688, is still in existence.

The objecting citizens presented a memorial to the freeholders in 1817 to hold up the proposed repairs and alterations to the building until it was determined whether they would be moved or not, but the board serenely went on their way and rebuilt it in the form existing, until the repairs of 1908.

Finally, to end agitation, the legislature passed an enabling act to allow the county at large to vote upon the proposal and Merriman Smith, clerk of the County of Salem, announced the election for two days, the thirteenth and fourteenth of April, 1819.

Shourds states in his history of Fenwick Colony that the election was held to decide whether the court house should go to Major's Run or remain at Salem. He is in error with this, as well as the statement that the election took place in 1817. There were four locations voted for; the present site at Salem, the Major's Run site in Upper Mannington, the central part of Alloway, opposite Hitchner's tavern, and another site in Mannington, for which no one cast a vote, which was described as being a few rods from Samuel Applegate's farm.

With only eight voting districts, it is easy and at the same time interesting to enumerate the results in each township. Salem, as was to be expected, voted almost solidly for the old location. It polled 193 votes to two for going to Major's Run and one for Alloway.

Mannington, the chief beneficiary of the change, surprisingly gave 35 votes to Salem, while it cast 191 for its home site and none for Alloway.

In Lower Creek, the stalwarts of the marshes upheld the honor of Salem by casting 169 votes for Salem and none for the other contenders.

Upper Alloways Creek, containing Alloway, voted 77 for the Hitchner tavern site, 68 for Major's Run and 125 for Salem.

Pittsgrove, the farthest away of all the townships, gave 233 for the location near Woodstown, three for Alloway and twenty-four for Salem. Pilesgrove gave 262 for the county building locus, twenty-six to stay in Salem and none for Alloway.

Upper Penns Neck, also rather far from Salem, supported the time honored county seat with a vote of 119 to 76 for Upper Mannington. Lower Penns Neck loyally supported Salem with 170 votes to six for Major's Run. Elsinboro, also loyal, cast 78 to zero for any of the others.

The total vote was 1,095 for Salem, 672 for Major's Run, and 81 for Alloway, then called Thompson's Bridge.

At the freeholders' meeting on May 12th, the same year, Clerk Smith read the results, freeholder Stacy Lloyd was paid $8.00 for printing the notice of the election and the ballots, and

EARLY NEWSPAPERS

the ghost of John Fenwick probably chuckled when he beheld the defeat of the move to take away the ancient capital of his little principality.

* * * *

These years from 1783 to 1820 might properly be called the "dark" ages of Salem's history. Not because there was anything gloomy or disastrous in the history of those years, but because there is so little information which may be gleaned on the history of the county in that time.

Johnson concluded his history with the end of the Revolution as far as narration was concerned, and Shourds busied himself with the chronicles of the families of the time. The Philadelphia newspapers would occasionally favor their readers with a brief extract of some event occurring in Salem but these accounts were few. The Trenton "State Gazette" probably did better by Salem than any other newspaper until the Trenton "True American" began publication in 1801. This latter paper apparently hired a correspondent to inform them of happenings and named James Sherron in Salem, Lewis Yorke in Hancock's Bridge and Isaiah Shinn in Woodstown as agents for the paper.

So it was not until 1801 that the student's opportunity of reading consistent and current news articles in a regular newspaper presents itself. Until 1816, when Isaac Kollock started his "West Jersey Gazette" in Salem, this county was dependent for its news and its recorded history, upon out-of-town newspapers. There was one exception, however, in saying that the "Gazette" was the county's first newspaper.

For many years it has been believed in Salem and stated in such historical publications as the Salem County Handbook, that his "West Jersey Gazette" in Salem, this county was dependent Salem in the year 1817. Recent researches have proved that such is not the case and that the first newspaper within the bounds of Fenwick's colony was the "Observer," issued in 1798 and continued throughout a part of 1799 by an Englishman named William Black and his partner North, first name unknown.

The history of the "Observer," meagre as it is, is not without fascination and romance. In the fall and late summer of 1798 the city of Philadelphia was swept by an epidemic of yellow fever. Disease, death and pestilence stalked at will through the desolate national metropolis and hundreds of citizens fled to the suburbs of the city for relief against the plague. Many accounts of fugitives coming as far south and west as this county will be found in the records. One isolated case of these plagues is that of the "lone tombstone" near Eldridge's Hill where Major Christian Piercey of the Revolutionary army died while fleeing from the yellow fever peril in the year of 1793. More fortunate were the two young enterprising journalists, Black and North, who vacated Philadelphia with their printing press and came to Salem during that same period. Black fell in love and married a lady named Smith from Elsinboro.

In December, 1798, the partners started the "Observer" and used the old Salem Academy on Market street as their printing office. It was a weekly paper and continued for thirty-six issues until 1799 when the proprietors took their press and stock in trade and went to Dover, Delaware.

There is one single issue of this rare paper left in South Jersey, as far as is known. That is the one numbered Vol. 1, No. 19, dated Saturday, May 4, 1799. It is preserved by the Camden County Historical Society.

It contains numerous advertisements of the United States treasurer and of the treasurer of New Jersey. Several advertisements of new books for sale at the "Observer" office appeared together with another advertisement offering for sale at the same place a cure for rheumatism. W. Black of Salem also offered for sale a cure for worms prepared by Benjamin Shaw of London and of pectoral balsam of honey prepared by the late Sir John Hill.

Of news there is little of interest, mostly foreign. The only local news is the marriage of Benjamin Wright of Mannington to Miss Ridgway of Gloucester county on May 4th, and of John Gill and Prudence Thompson, both of Mannington, at the Friends Meeting House on Wednesday, May 1, 1799. The paper consists of four pages, sixteen by ten inches.

Beginning in 1817 and continuing, with possibly a few weeks' interruption, the news of Salem is complete to the present day. Before that year there is little for the historian to grasp. True, there were wills made and probated, people died and people were born, deeds passed and mortgages were given, men were elected to high office and life went on generally as it had and would continue to do, but these events may be covered by a mere notice in a big deed book or an election return. It is the usual run of newspaper story, of events usual and unusual which are missing from the history of these years. So the historian bent on getting below the surface of dry statistics, vital and otherwise, has scant reward in researching this particular period. With all the lack of information they were important years and had much to do with the subsequent history of the county. And just because they have been ignored and forgotten, it does not say that these events were not vastly important.

The chief of these events and one which has a most direct bearing on the nation's history is that movement, overlooked by historians, known as the great western emigration. Salem was only one of the many creeks which fed the sea to contribute to this great tidal wave of migration to the western lands. But few towns and cities in the east from which came this movement of people can lay claim to so much paternity of nomenclature as Salem. The ones who came from here remembered the town which gave them birth to the extent that Salem, Ohio; Salem, Indiana; Salem Iowa, and the state capital of Oregon owe their names to Fenwick's colony on the Delaware.

But the names of Western towns is aside from the point. Following the Revolution came depreciated currency, tight money and all the resultant features of hard times. Coupled with this was the failure of the soil. Thomas Shourds, whose ponderous history is not always easy to read, is invaluable on this point of the western emigration. With painstaking care he describes the large number of families from Salem who helped, in the years from 1795 to 1860, to build the west. While this volume is not a geneological study as was Shourds, it is only simple justice to those pioneers that some of them be mentioned. There is scarcely a chapter on one of the families of whom Shourds writes that does not mention some member as having gone to a "Western state".

In the Salem newspapers for years afterwards may be found many death notices of people dying in the middle west and south who claimed Salem as their home and whose relatives were so notified.

Nor was this emigration restricted to the middle west. Thru the Kentucky and Tennessee mountains, the wanderers from the Delaware penetrated to the new states of Alabama, Louisiana and Mississippi. Henry Ellet, congressman from the latter state, was born in Salem.

The soil failure was not confined to Salem alone but because this was an agricultural county the effect was all the more severe. It resulted, first, from a lack of scientific education and secondly, from failure to rotate crops and use fertilizers.

All the damage which the war had left hung heavily over the heads of the local citizens. Added to this, the 1790's found them unable to wrest even a meagre living from the ground. The soil had been exhausted but they did not know this. Neither did they know the fertilizing value of marl, which lay at their very door. With the foreclosure of mortgages, with famine stalking their thresholds, the farmers of Salem, harassed and worried, did exactly what so many of their comrades in other counties of the state did, they moved west.

Farms were left deserted, the mortgagees taking them as they were, the fields were left unsown and unploughed as the heart-sick natives, whose sires had lived on this soil for a hundred years, left their poverty stricken ancestral estates in Lower Alloways Creek, Elsinboro and Pittsgrove to seek a new living elesewhere. The tide was first directed towards western New York and western Pennsylvania. As the Indians fled westward, the hardier pioneers penetrated to the forests of Ohio in the very start of the winning of the west. Thus, it was that Salem, Ohio, was founded in 1803 by Zadock Street of Salem, New Jersey.

It was the same idea, the hope for gain in the west, and the failure in the east which motivated William Wayman and Samuel Jones of Woodstown to advertise in 1800, "their grist and saw mill near Woodstown for sale and their hope that the purchaser would exchange lands of Western Pa. and New York in part pay."

Meanwhile farms were depopulated and left standing idle while the erstwhile occupants were pushing along the Ohio in the new western country in search of homes. The new frontier states acquired hardy, sturdy and worthwhile citizens who were used to adversity and whose Quaker stock stood them in good stead in their new homes.

To show the vast spread of these Salem emigrants who poured westward and southward in these years the writer has culled from Shourds and others a partial list of men and women, native born, who settled, lived, married and died in lands afar from their native Salem.

The Streets, Straughns, Cattells, Harrises, Bradways and others were the settlers of Salem, Ohio. Some of these pushed on to other points of the west in after years. Two of the descendants of Captain William Smith went west, John P. Smith to Illinois and Washington Smith to Kansas. The Coles family, inter marrying with the Strings, went to Ohio and from there to Indiana. Joseph Hall settled in Dunkirk, New York, other members of the Hall family went to West Virginia and the writer believes that Mannington, West Virginia received its name from these people. Edward Smith, who was sheriff of Salem county in 1825 and married a daughter of Andrew Sinnickson, emigrated to one of the western states. Edward K. Gibbon and A. K. Gibbon also found a home in the middle west. Members of the Challis family settled in Atchison, Kansas, and by the time Shourds wrote his book were reported wealthy. Clement

Acton and his kinsman Thomas Woodnutt entered the mercantile business in Cincinnati, Ohio. In fact Cincinnati, in the first five decades of the nineteenth century was populated by a large number of Salem families. There were Burts, Carlls, Campbells, Harrises, Reeveses, Whitakers and others in this city. Here also lived Louis Eugene Yorke, son of Congressman Yorke of Salem. This man had the distinction to be not only a great civil engineer, but also to rise from a private to a general during the Civil War.

Sarah Yorke of Salem with her family emigrated to the Tennessee Valley; she later married Andrew Donaldson Jackson, adopted son of President Andrew Jackson. Another Yorke, first name Patton, married a Miss Coleman of Louisiana and was elected to the legislature of his adopted state. There were more members of the Harris and Carll families who settled in Huntington county, Indiana, and also in Cincinnati.

Isaac Ogden went to Ohio, Jedidiah Ogden to Fairfield, Indiana, Louis and David Whitaker to Logans Port, Indiana, and Oliver Whitaker to Clinton county, Ohio. In fact, the Whitaker family seems to have been the most numerous of all the families coming from Salem in the great Western migration. Summerill Whitaker went to Illinois, Rachel Whitaker married and settled in Iowa, Isaac Whitaker in Carlinville, Illinois, and Mary Whittaker Perton in Bunkerhill, Illinois.

Jacob Ware went to Mechanicsburg, Ohio. Robert Reed and wife (Sarah Maria Green), and his widowed daughter, Sarah Reed Ware and two children, Jacob Reed Ware and Anna Ware migrated to Springfield in 1822. In 1825 Jacob Reed Ware went to Mechanicsburg, Ohio. In 1829 he married Amira Wallace. Members of the Cripps family settled in Michigan. Catherine Tyler of Salem married William Walker, soldier of fortune, who was killed in the American army at the battle of Buena Vista. Prior to this they had lived in Cincinnati and in Indiana. Salem Pledgers settled in North Carolina, Rumseys in Portsmith, Ohio, Vanmeters in Virginia, and Foggs in New Orleans. Peter Bilderback became a traveling Methodist preacher in Ohio.

Christopher White was one of the pioneer settlers in Fenwick's Colony and owned a large tract of land in Lower Alloway's Creek township. This county was destined however, to lose these citizens who were some of the most useful men of their time. Josiah White, feeling that he had been defrauded of just accounts by fellow citizens of that township, left Salem. Joseph White in 1811 made a historic trip west on a flat boat down the Ohio river and has left behind him an exceptionally good account of his travels. Another White, Josiah, was the founder of the Schuylkill Navigation Company. By this means the first coal mined from the hills at Mauch Chunk, Pennsylvania was brought to market in Philadelphia and made White one of the first wealthy coal producers of the United States.

As the early settlers moved into New England bringing with them their Bridgewaters and Tauntons and Exeters, so did the Salem folk take their place names west with them. Mannington, West Virginia, is a sample. So is Ohio Pyle in western Pennsylvania, which commemorates the Pyle family of the township of Pilesgrove. Zanesville, Ohio, was founded by the Zanes family from Salem.

The Street family of Salem were particularly adventurous and especially dissatisfied with staying in one place too long. In 1834, John B. Newhall wrote his sketches of Iowa in which he gives Aaron Street credit for founding the town of Salem, Iowa. This book was circulated back home and caused the editor of the "Freeman's Banner" to write an article concerning the empire building proclivities of the Street family. It reads: "It is somewhat remarkable that the father of the present Aaron Street (Zadock Street) emigrated from Salem, New Jersey, to Salem, Ohio, father and son came and built up Salem, Indiana; from Salem, Indiana, the subject of this article came and built up Salem, Iowa. When the Street family shall cease to build up Salems is more than the writer can divine. It is probable, however that some future generation will find in the curve of some beautiful bay, indenting the shore of the vast Pacific, another city of Salem, reared by the posterity of Zadock and Aaron Street."

The prophecy was more than fulfilled ten years later in the founding of Salem, Oregon.

Another member of the migrating Whitaker family settled in Muskingum, Ohio. Lewis Whitaker at Hennepin, Illinois and his son John from this place, were some of the founders of the Constitution of Illinois. David Sheppard went to Springfield, Missouri. Shourds unfortunately does not always tell just where these settlers finally located. For instance he says Thomas Bowen, Benjamin Goodwin, members of the Kelsey, Sheppard and Shourds family simply "went west". Leonard Sayers settled in Cincinnati, Ohio, in 1803. Reuel Sayers who married Hope Sheppard also settled in Ohio. This migratory note deserves extra attention because it was Reuel Sayers, who in a pension application to the state of Ohio, years after the Revolution, set forth the true fact that he was the only member of Captain Charleton Sheppard's company neither killed, wounded nor taken prisoner in the massacre at Hancock's Bridge.

It seems that Lower Alloway's township was especially hard hit by the crop failure of 1790. At least large numbers of people comprising entire families moved west. The Harrises, Sayers and Whites were only a few of the families who left their native county. There were still others. The Stretches who married into the Test family, settled Richmond, Indiana. One of the descendants of this family, Samuel Test was a Quaker preacher in Indiana. He also was very wealthy. Aaron and Jonathan Stretch settled in Nashville, Tennessee. John Test, who married Hannah Sheppard, became a Congressman from Indiana during the administration of Andrew Jackson. Reubon Sheppard located in Hillsboro, Ohio, Samuel Griscom in Galveston, Texas, and Mary Griscom married Samuel Stewart, settling in Indiana. John Denn joined the gold rush to California in 1849 as did Charles Edward Pancoast of Elsinboro, the author of the celebrated "Quaker 49'er." John Griscom of Lower Creek traveled eastward instead of west, going to England as a school teacher to study the Lancaster system of public education. He was one of the few Salem countymen of the early 1800's who risked a trip across the sea.

William Perry of Salem migrated to the west in 1815, became wealthy and was such a reputable citizen of Cincinnati that Perry street of that city is named after him.

Anthony Patrick of Salem died at Urbana, Ohio, in 1806. Shimps, Davises and Hinchmans of this county settled in Ohio. James Riley became a judge in Crawfordsville, Indiana. Sometimes the western movement would not go any further west than Pennsylvania. In the rolls of Philadelphia society there are many people who came from Salem because of the post war depression. The Wistar, Clement, Hall, Thompson, Carpenter, Sinnickson, Griscom and other families if traced far enough back claim Salem as their native heath.

Salem residents were moved to laughter in 1916 when some enterprising individual in Salem, Oregon, wrote to the Mayor of Salem, New Jersey, suggesting that since Salem, Oregon, was a state capitol and the "most flourishing of all the twenty-six Salems listed in the postal guide" that it would be nice if all the other Salems in the union would change their names, leaving this youngster by the Pacific in solitary possession of the great name of Salem. Needless to say, the suggestion was not acted upon and the second oldest Salem in the union was not obliged to change its name to Glenview, Delaware Heights, River Park or some equally foolish cognomen. Andross had named us "Swampetowne", years ago and possibly that name would have

HISTORY OF SALEM

suited the "parvenu" Chamber of Commerce member of Salem, Oregon.

Religious activities were many in the years following the Revolution. There was a decided impetus in this direction, largely because of the influence of Benjamin Abbott and the new Methodist Church. It will be remembered that Abbott did his proselytizing and organizing work for the Methodist Church in the twenty years from 1776 until his death in 1796. With him and following him came the circuit riders, preaching the doctrine of the Wesleyan faith. The Salem circuit under his direction was commenced in 1788. The first Quarterly Conference was held in Salem in 1789. Eleven years before Abbott's death, he organized and dedicated the Methodist Church in Penns Neck from which came the modern congregations of Pennsville and Pedricktown. The original building has long since gone to decay. This was a flourishing church organization in Abbott's time as was also the one in Pilesgrove which Abbott formed, aided by Anthony Atwood, Lorenzo Dow and others in 1791. This old church stood until 1905, when it was torn down. The graveyard of that church, although covered with briars and brambles, may still be seen a mile out of Sharptown.

In addition to the churches in Salem, Pilesgrove and Penns Neck, there were numerous homes of loyal Methodists where Abbott and his circuit riders were welcome. Revival followed revival, many class meetings were organized and slowly but surely the Methodist Church started on the road which led it to become the largest congregation of any faith in Salem county. In Pittsgrove Abbott left behind him the Olivet Methodist Church which is now located at Palatine Lake. This and Friendship Methodist Church in Upper Pittsgrove are two of the oldest churches in the eastern part of the county. The present Olivet Church was erected in 1851.

On this scene of growing Methodism, came in 1783 and again in 1785 and 1802, Bishop Francis Asbury, the head of the Methodist Church in America. A half century later devout Methodists produced the chair in which Bishop Asbury sat on his last visit to Salem in 1802.

Along with this growth of religion came the first camp meetings in various wooded groves of the county. A good example of a camp meeting is found in the Trenton "True American" for July 20th, 1807, which comments that "at the camp meeting held by the Methodists on the 18th of June last past there were eleven traveling, seventeen local preachers, twelve exhorters and a vast concourse of over six thousand people. The power of the Lord was eminently displayed in the awakening,

RELIGIOUS ACTIVITIES

convicting and converting of nearly two hundred souls."

Associated with Abbott as a circuit rider and organizer of Methodist churches was Thomas Ware, a veteran of the Revolution and a pioneer in the new faith. Thomas Ware lies buried in the same graveyard as Benjamin Abbott on Walnut street, Salem. His period of activity lasted for several decades after the founding of the republic. His devotion to his church and abject poverty caused by his unselfishness finally moved his friends to obtain a pension for him in 1824. The family of which he was a member contributed many worthwhile citizens to the community of Salem, among them a future United States Senator, his nephew, Alexander G. Cattell.

In 1818, the Baptists organized a new congregation at Canton in Lower Alloways Creek township. One of the early pastors of this church was the Rev. Dr. Jayne, father of the David Jayne of patent medicine fame. The Friends' Meeting House at Woodstown was erected in 1785.

* * * *

While the French Revolution was entering its last mad stage, life went on as usual in Salem. On March 20th, 1793, the mildly excited citizens beheld the opening of the new post office, incidentally one of the earliest post offices of the new republic, under the charge of Thomas Jones. It was located on the present site of the City National Bank, opposite the Court House. Later on, during the postmastership of Samuel Sherron, it was located next door in what is now Green's Hotel. For years the mail stages made this their leaving point on the long trek to Philadelphia. It is interesting to note that the desk used by Jones, together with the original orders by Timothy Pickering, Postmaster General, is preserved by the Salem County Historical Society in Salem.

By 1804, there were only three post officers in the county, two of which are in existence today, Salem, Woodstown and Pittsgrove, better known as Pole Tavern. This last office was closed several years ago.

The observers of unusual events in these years record an earthquake and a visitation from a meteor. Concerning the first, the papers record an earth tremor on January 23, 1812, which shook the ground at Haddonfield and stopped every clock in Woodstown. It seems to have been part of the earth disturbance which wracked the Mississippi Valley at the same time. The "Salem Gazette" of 1819 thus describes the meteor of November 20th of that year:

> The citizens of this place were alarmed by the near approach of a meteor on Thursday last. It descended for some distance almost perpendicularly

and then passed off with rapid flight in a horizontal direction from east to west and was lost to sight. The light was such that a pin might be discerned on the ground. About two minutes after its disappearance, a sound of an explosion was heard, attended by so considerable a concussion of the air as to cause a clattering of the windows and a slight trembling of the earth.

There were severe storms in Salem in 1810 and again in 1817 which did considerable damage to crops and to property. But storms were not so terrifying as the frequent outbreaks of yellow fever in Philadelphia in the 1790's. Salem was not far away and many of the refugees from that city sought this town for escape from the plague. There was always the fear of contagion with the kind hearted folk of Salem who held out hospitable latch strings to the fugitives, but Fenwick's capital city escaped the infection.

Escaping yellow fever, Salem had its suffering ahead of it. In September of 1819, the "Salem Gazette" with mournful truth told its readers that sickness and the long drought of the summer had brought disastrous results to the town. "The deaths per day were unusually alarming," said the newspaper. There was no rain, the weather continued warm late in the fall, the potato crop was small and the Indian corn dried up entirely. Salem faced its worst sanitary crisis in years. One day, September 11th, 1819, found dead in the homes of Salem, Andrew Sinnickson, Stephen Hutchins and wife, Joshua Thompson, Richard Tyler, Mary Hall, Eliza Maul, Edward Long and infant child. Finally cooler weather prevailed and Salem recovered from one of its worst spells of illness and death.

Melancholy references were the order of the day. A good specimen of the newspaper styles of the day, in treating of such cases, is found in the following from the Trenton "True American", dated November 6th, 1802:

On Monday October 15th, a very melancholy and mournful accident occurred in the County of Salem. Joseph Shinn Esq. on his way from Quinton Bridge to a neighboring saw mill (being within half a mile of the former) unfortunately having not taken precaution enough to fasten the swivel, it worked out of the swiveltree, falling on the horse's heels, frightened him amazingly (being naturally very skittish) and immediately threw Mr. Shinn in violent manner off his chair upon the ground, which fall he survived not longer than fifteen minutes. Mr. Shinn, possessed the greatest candor, amicableness, goodwill and probity and almost every virtue that rendered him happy in himself, and useful to society which made his life worthy and esteemed, but alas! now makes his death universally regretted and lamented.

Repeating the foray of 1747, another Spanish privateer appeared off the shores of Salem in the Delaware, penetrating as far north as New Castle on July 18th, 1797. She carried fourteen guns and ninety men but unlike the *La Fortune* of fifty years before did not attempt to land any men. Warlike activities had not stopped with the Revolution. The Salem militia, organized into several companies of foot and horse, met regularly for drill and just as regularly had ceremonious dinners at the various taverns throughout the county. One of these drills in the summer of 1818 went off so badly that a disgusted citizen writing to the "Gazette" dubbed it the "Broom Stick Corps" and said "the militia was armed not with guns but with pocket bottles pouring off the life giving stingo!"

The Quakers were not exempt from either attending drill or paying a fine in lieu thereof. It was several years before the New Jersey Legislature granted exemption from military duty to the Friends. A lady in Haines Neck, Mannington township, had eighteen sons but another contributor to the "Gazette" remarked, "We regret to state that the parents are Quakers and that the army is not to be benefitted by this increase."

With better roads and improved means of transportation it was not surprising that the city "slickers" should catch up with the sleepy provincial town of Salem and endeavor to practice their "arts". The "Gazette" in 1818 tells of this visitation: "On Saturday evening the 13th instant, a strange woman and a man in a gig tandem made their ingress at Salem, their appearance was genteel tho' their behavior was such as to excite much inquiry; they appeared anxious to borrow money, in large and small sums, and on the whole their conduct was suspicious and even mysterious, as they kept pretty much incog- the public have not been able to fathom their design or discover their names. Their egress was separate and distant, she started in the tandem and two mornings after he went over in the mail stage".

On the soberer side of life in the county of these years, it is interesting to note that immediately after the great western emigration, which reached its peak in 1803, marl was discovered in the soil deposits of Salem county and by proper use saved the day for the local husbandmen, checked the western movement and quite definitely established Salem as one of the leading agricultural counties of the state. The importance of this discovery saved Salem county from rapid depopulation and more than that, laid the groundwork for its future prosperity. Farmers took heart now, mixed the marl with the worn-out soil, and reaped for the first time in years a substantial recompense for their crops.

Trade increased with the improvement of the farm situation. More doctors and lawyers came to Salem and in 1820 the first Medical Society was formed consisting of Doctors James Van Meter, Thomas Yarrow, Charles Swing and Charles Hannah.

It was still before the days of steam and the Industrial

Revolution but the hand artisans were making progress. In 1817, Edward Hanes opened his machine shop at Eldridges Hill. Hanes was a blacksmith who worked on a new invention for a percussion cap. This machine shop under successive generations of this family lasted until 1897.

In 1807, Colonel Robert Gibbon Johnson, who had served under Washington in the Whiskey Rebellion of 1794 and who was probably the wealthiest man in the county, built his new brick mansion on Market street in Salem. This house, now owned and used by Salem county, is one of the finest architectual specimens in the state. True, Johnson had owned many farms in the county but the revival of farming aided by the discovery of marl, had greatly increased his revenue and enabled him to build this splendid mansion with its fine interior hand carved woodwork. That times were getting better is shown by the fact that the carpenters working on the job demanded seventy-five cents a day and an eleven-hour day, and struck till they had received their demands.

In 1807 Richard Hunter began his tannery in Salem. For a hundred years this was to be an important industry in this locality until the supply of tan bark was exhausted. The Tyler family, tanners on their own estate, about this time went into business on a larger scale. It was over twenty years ago that the last vestige of Tyler's tannery on Fifth street, Salem, disappeared. At one time it was the largest tannery south of Newark. In addition, Woolmans in Woodstown ran a large tannery; altogether, there were some fourteen throughout the county. Meadow companies were organized, the first of these being the Stony Island Meadow Company in Elsinboro in 1794. Other companies organized later were the Tide Mill Meadow Company, Mannington in 1796, the Keasbey Meadow Company, Salem in 1796 and the Denn's Canal Meadow Company in Mannington in 1820.

Ship building was begun early in the nineteenth century but it was not until twenty or thirty years later that Allowaystown became the ship-building center it was for some years.

In 1796 the Legislature of New Jersey passed a relief bill for the distressed inhabitants of this county and in the next year opened a loan office for the relief of agriculture. Colonel Robert Gibbon Johnson was placed in charge of this office and states in his history that he closed it on March 1st, 1797, after Salem county had subscribed to the amount of sixteen thousand dollars. Coincident with this relief measure the Board of Freeholders purchased Bassett's Tavern two miles from Woodstown and established the first poor house. This building, erected in

1797, was burned in 1845 and the present county home stands on its site.

The most far reaching event on the mechanical side in this era was the advent of the steamboat "Aetna". She ran to New Castle, Del., connecting with the stage line running to Frenchtown, en route for Baltimore and Washington, making two or three trips each week. She was withdrawn in a short time and sent to New York. In that harbor her boiler exploded May 24th, 1824. This was the beginning of steam navigation connecting Salem with the outside world. Six or seven years later a regular steamboat company was formed and organized opposition was given to the slow and cumbersome overland mail stages.

Despite the western movement the County of Salem held its own, and in fact, gained a little population. The figures for the first United States census in 1790 show a population of 10,437 and in 1800, 11,371. 1810 showed 12,761 and 1820, 14,022.

CHAPTER XX

SALEM IN THE 1820's

1820

The first year of the third decade of the nineteenth century saw another innovation in agriculture which was as important to Salem farmers as was the discovery of marl a few years previous. It was as far reaching and revolutionary as the other discovery. This was the importation into this county by Colonel Robert Gibbon Johnson of the Salernum Lycopersicum. Today, people call it the tomato; some call it "termats." At that time it was known as a love apple or Jerusalem apple and was considered poisonous and totally unfit to eat. Johnson patiently educated the natives as to its qualities, showing that it was edible and nutritious, and furthermore explaining by scientific practice that it would grow abundantly in these regions of sandy soil. The famous historian and farmer was completely justified in his claims for this unpopular vegetable. Now it ranks as one of our first crops and has proved a source of revenue to many farmers who have cultivated it since 1820.

In 1826 Johnson in his laudable zeal to promote the agriculture of this county reorganized the county fairs, first held in Fenwick's day. With them was joined an agricultural society which sought to develop the farm products of this section. Johnson has received much praise as a historian but it must not be forgotten that he did as much, if not more, for agriculture in a county which sorely needed help, as he did for history.

The annals of 1820 show also a peripatetic feat on the part of one Furman Cooper, who in a walking contest covered forty miles in one day between dawn and sunset, making him the champion walker of Salem county. It was a crude beginning possibly, but feats of strength such as this marked the beginning of athletics here. In addition, during this decade frequent foot races were held at Sculltown (now Auburn) in which men competed for prizes of money and for honor as well. In a flax dressing contest in Lower Penns Neck, Benjamin Robinson and Sinnickson Dilmore dressed 115 pounds of flax between dawn and dusk on March 16, 1820.

February 23, 1820 brought the melancholy news to Salem of the loss of the brig *Le Tigre* with all its crew off Barnegat. This was a Spanish privateer captured off Cape May and towed into Bridgeton where a prize crew was put on her to take her to New York. Most of the crew were Bridgeton boys but there was one Salem citizen, Edward Lawson, who was lost when the ship foundered off the Jersey coast.

This year, 1820, witnessed also the manufacture of cigars by Joshua Kirk in Salem. Kirk advertised in the new "Salem Messenger" started the year before by Elijah Brooks, that fast sailing vessels brought the best Virginia leaf tobacco here from Norfolk in quick time. The Missouri Compromise was worrying the local citizens to the end that they held a meeting to consider a new state in the Union "without a conditional prohibition of negro suffrage." 1820 had a warm winter. A fisherman reported catching three shad in Salem creek cove on February 26th. Simon Sparks ploughed up five hundred Spanish dollars on his farm in Lower Neck, said the gossips, but it turned out to be only seven instead of five hundred.

Brooks, who took a prominent part in Salem life with his "Messenger", attacked the conditions of the debtors' prison and imprisonment for debt generally, which were badly in need of reform. He deplored in this year the fact that he was forced to delete a "most interesting letter which contained insulting and disrespectful terms not admissible." Newspaper advertisements showed a new attorney in Woodstown, Oliver Freeman, and that Delzil Keasbey made good hats and W. G. Beesley manufactured fine chairs. This was the era of skilled work; Hollingshead in Woodstown was famous for his beautiful grandfather clocks, some of which are today the proudest possessions of a few Salem families. Likewise Beesley's chairs are the pride of those antiquarians who have them. The election of 1820 passed off with "less noise", said the "Messenger". Monroe was elected President without strenuous opposition and there was no contest to the election of John Dickinson, Morris Hancock, Zaccheus Ray and John Mason to the legislature from this county. If so, it was the last quiet election for years to come.

St. John's Episcopal Church had, since the Revolution, experienced a grim struggle for existence. The congregation had dwindled, the church had been wrecked by the British soldiers, but worse than that, the spirit of the congregation had been broken by the numerous reverses that they, as a church, had suffered.

However, the courage of the faithful returned. The church was repaired and a little later on, a new one was erected. On

November 8th, 1820, the Rev. Richard F. Cadle was ordained to the order of priest in the church. The discourse was delivered by Bishop Croes. Cadle did not remain here long; he later became a missionary in the Wisconsin territory where he is honored as a pioneer in the Episcopal faith of that section.

A stage line from Salem to Craven's Ferry, now Pennsville, was established in 1820. From here the passengers could get a sail boat or row boat to New Castle and a brand new river steamer from there to Philadelphia on Mondays, Wednesdays, and Fridays with passengers "landed at their homes."

Burglars entered the new Ferryhouse of Craven at Cravens Ferry and stole $80 in cash, muslin, sheeting, 2 pairs of woolen suspenders and a row boat with oars.

* * * *

1821

When the Episcopal faith revived in Salem following the dark years of the Revolution the Presbyterian Church, powerful in Pittsgrove, had yet to settle a congregation in the county seat. For some years previous the few Presbyterians in Salem had jointly used the repaired Episcopal church for their services. On a night in 1820, Colonel Johnson had invited Ashbel Green, his old college mate and at that time president of Princeton College, to speak at the Presbyterian services in the Episcopal Church. For some reason the Episcopalians decided to allow no more Calvinist services in their church and had barred and locked the doors so that when Green, Johnson and the Presbyterians appeared there was no edifice in which to worship.

Locked out, the indignant Presbyterians met in the CourtHouse and immediately formulated plans for a church of their own. Johnson gave the land and aided by Dr. Van Meter and others, the necessary funds were soon raised, to the extent that the corner stone of the new church was laid with impressive ceremonies on March 6th, 1821. Rev. Freeman, Rev. Ballantine and Rev. Janvier, the latter of the neighboring church at Daretown, officiated.

It was still long before the era of public schools but private schools were beginning to flourish in Salem. There was one conducted by Isaiah English in the year 1818 in an old brick building which stood on the site of the Jeffers house at Griffith and Market streets, Salem. There was another in the Salem Academy, which Joseph Stretch conducted, and a seminary on West Broadway in 1822. The Baptists under the Rev. James Challis started a seminary in 1824, but it lasted only a short time. It was located on West Broadway opposite the church.

FIRE COMPANY ORGANIZED

With the dedication of the new Presbyterian Church came the opening of Grant street, Salem, from Market street across lands of Col. Johnson to Quaker Neck.

In the same year the "Messenger" was authority for the information that six slaves were sold on the auction block in front of Sherron's Hotel. This is the one and only slave selling case in Salem county, under the republic, that the compiler has been able to find. In the same issue, the "Messenger" advocated the culture of tobacco in the county. That this newspaper, entering its second year in Salem, was flourishing is attested by the fact that in 1821 it erected a building of its own next to the county jail on Market street.

Inhabitants of the remote township of Pittsgrove, probably disturbed by the results of the Court House election of 1819, began agitation for, first, annexation to Cumberland county and secondly, a demand for a new township.

The first was not granted until 1867 and then the inhabitants protested so much that the township was returned to Salem county but in the second case, a law was passed by the legislature enabling the inhabitants of Pittsgrove to form a new township called Centerville. In Revolutionary times this had been Daytons Bridge, then it was Centerville, and now it is Centerton. Therefore from 1821 to 1828, when a hostile legislature returned it to Pittsgrove township, the voters of the town of Centerville had seperate municipal privileges.

"The young men of the town of Salem who are desirous of joining themselves into a fire engine company are to meet at Hacketts tavern this evening at 7 o'clock, where all who are friendly to this object, are especially invited to attend." So ran a notice in the "Salem Messenger" on November 5th, 1821, calling for the formation of the Union Fire Company, which is one of the oldest in the State.

The Union Fire Company came into existence in 1821 in response to a demand for a more youthful and active fire company in Salem. The older semi-organized company with a large membership of old men had failed to please the populace, who firmly believed that younger men should be in charge of this very necessary protection of the citizens.

The meeting was held in Hackett's Hotel with William T. Mulford as chairman. The secretary of the meeting was later in life one of Salem's most distinguished sons, Richard P. Thompson. A brilliant lawyer and a statesman of ability, Thompson was twice attorney general of New Jersey and as such was the prosecutor in the famous Treadway case in 1852.

The old company whose members resigned on account of

public pressure included such well known sons of Salem as Robert Gibbon Johnson, who was past fifty years of age when this step was taken; Hedge Thompson, father of Richard P. and in 1828 a congressman of the United States from this district; Thomas Sinnickson, a former member of Congress and of the state legislature, and James Sherron.

The old members resigned and the new organization which at that time called itself the Union Fire Company, elected Joseph Miller as president and Richard P. Thompson as secretary. Committees were appointed to collect the buckets from the old members and to select a suitable badge for the organization. The bucket committee reported little progress as they said "irresponsible" persons had taken the buckets. The insignia committee, however, reported the purchase of linen badges with a yellow background, blue space and black and yellow letters which read, "The Union Fire Company."

In this year came the dedication of the Baptist Meeting House, Woodstown on July 4th. A member of the Friends Meeting in the same place, William Lippincott, wrote and offered for sale at six cents a copy "A description of the Custom of Marriage with the Authors Views and an Address to the Unmarried Females of the Society."

This was the period of the celebrated will case of Rowan versus Sinnickson which went to the United States Court of Appeals for decision and which as Elmer says in his "Reminisences", "Split the Sinnickson family into two separate camps."

The election in this county, says the "Messenger", "has terminated in favor of the ticket selected and is of course, Republican, except one member—Robert G. Johnson, a federalist is elected to the assembly a well maneuvered election trick by a majority of two votes over Mr. Vanneman."

1822

That the majestic Old Oak in the Friends Burying Ground in Salem was not the only survivor of the primeval forest is shown by the following news item in the "Messenger" in May, 1822; "How are the Mighty Fallen! We refer to the great oak at the corner of Elsinboro Road, a half mile from the Court House, whose branches extend in every direction and which was destroyed by fire on Thursday last. It has been a land mark for several generations and its branches covered a quarter acre. Some bad boys tried to burn bumblebees out of its limbs and by so doing, ignited the entire tree, the greater part of which was hollow, so with the fire bursting out of this crevice, the tree was entirely consumed with a roar that was heard for at least a hundred rods distant."

MILITIA ACTIVE

There was a big stir in Sharptown this year when the assembled militia company met at Brundage's Tavern to court-martial Captain Erasmus Morton. He was charged with neglect of duty in that he went fishing in Salem creek during the nice weather instead of attending to his official duties in the militia. Brigadier General Du Bois presided over the trial. Outside of the fact that Captain Morton was officially "bawled out", nothing much seems to have been done about it.

An obituary notice for the year mentions the fact that the "poor deceased had 150 fits in five hours, all of which greatly contributed to his untimely end." A stick of lumber drawn by thirteen horses passed through Salem on its way from Elsinboro to the Navy Yard at Philadelphia. William N. Jeffers, whose career as a stormy petrel of Salem politics was just beginning, was within five votes of the Attorney-Generalship of New Jersey in the joint session of 1822. As a consolation prize he received the prosecutorship of Salem. The "Messenger" accused its contemporary, the "Saturday Evening Post", of stealing stories they had published, pointing especially to the "Toll Gatherers Daughter."

The "Messenger", commenting editorially on the large number of crimes charged to blacks, said, "Why not send them to Santo Domingo or the African settlement? We think the subject demands attention." The election showed John Dickinson elected to Council without opposition. In the contest for sheriff, there was a four-cornered fight between Kille, Hackett, Humphries and Craven without respect to party. Joseph Kille won, thus calling attention to the fact that this man was born under a lucky political star. Thirty-four years later, when he was an old man, this leader of the Salem democracy would again win in a four-cornered fight for the assembly.

In the northern part of the county, especially in Pilesgrove township, there was a big revival among the Methodists in 1822. This led to the formation of the New Bethel Methodist Church. It still stands, a weather beaten and forlorn frame building near the Gloucester county line in Pilesgrove township. The church was organized by Samuel Atkinson and members of the Stites, Wallace, Carter, String and Peterson families. The church originally had a high pulpit and three galleries encircled the interior of the building. There was a huge ten-plate stove for heat. In 1847, St. John's Church was built in Harrisonville, Gloucester county, and the congregation of New Bethel abandoned it to worship in the new church.

1823

An additional transportation line commenced in 1823 when

Thomas Reeves started a regular stage line from Salem via Allowaystown and Roadstown to Bridgeton.

A bad storm in March wrecked the New Castle packet off Fort Delaware and blew down many trees in Salem. There seems to have been no replacements of the trees and by June an indignant land owner wrote to the "Messenger" that "unless trees are planted, this town will be destitute of shade."

Job Tyler's ox has been famous for a century. He raised many oxen on his farm in Quaker Neck, but the ox of 1823 has always held the prize. Its picture is preserved in the Hancock House at Hancock's Bridge and its fame is legion. When dressed it produced 2111 pounds of beef, 365 pounds of tallow and 176 of hide. Tyler had sold it to a firm of butchers in Philadelphia, so on March 12th, 1823 a special steamboat accompanied by a band came into Salem creek to give the prize ox a last ride to Philadelphia. It is said that Tyler, riding with his ox on the boat, objected to the band playing, he being a Quaker, so that the band was forced to wait until arrival in Philadelphia when they proudly paraded up Market street hill with the ox in tow.

July of 1823 saw a sorrowful wife write to the "Messenger" in rebuttal to a previous notice by her husband which refused to pay her bills. She said in scornful language, "Where is his bed and board? The information is badly wanted and my poor miserable husband adds insult to injury in asking—Where am I to find his bed and board? I would be willing to do all that I could to support the board and keep the bed provided it be outside of the prison walls."

Two years before, thirty members of the Salem Baptist Church had organized a new church in Allowaystown. They immediately began erecting a building, digging the clay on the end of the lot and burning the bricks nearby. It was finished and dedicated on Sunday, August 10th, 1823. The first pastor was the Rev. M. N. Hopkins.

The "Messenger" announced that the election of that year would be held on October 14th and proceeded to state its views on holding office, a view which a great many politicians both before and after have often conjectured on, themselves. Said the "Messenger": "The election will probably be conducted without any other object than personal promotion. To get a legal right to sit and yawn, stretch one's limbs and sleep away a month or two in the state house at Trenton is the height of some men's ambition. How silly it is to persevere and suffer through all the torturing rains of anxious hopes and glory just to attain the privilege of a three months' exposure to public opinion and to say Aye to a proposition to dig a ditch thru a salt marsh and to say nay to a petition for a law to preserve oyster beds."

The election was held "with no regard paid to old party distractions" and Josiah Reeve, Robert Gibbon Johnson, Aaron O. Dayton and Charles Swing went to the legislature.

1824

This was the time of Lafayette's visit to the United States. Throughout the original thirteen colonies every town was anxious to do honor to the distinguished guest of the new nation. "Washington," writing to the "Salem Messenger", suggested the complete illumination of the town of Salem in his honor. The Salem Light Infantry met at Sherron's Hotel to discuss plans to meet Lafayette. The great Frenchman, of course, did not come to Salem but he was in Philadelphia and New Castle, so that the citizens of Salem had ample opportunity of seeing him. Salem was completely deserted as folks went to Philadelphia on his reception day there to see the "true triumphal entry of the nation's guest." Mr. Brooks, editor of the "Messenger", wrote at length on the event and then mournfully added, "the editor had the ague, could not attend the festivities, but felt better by taking a large dose of Marshall's powders."

Another slavery note appeared in the minutes of the Board of Freeholders. Stacy Lloyd was paid $150 for moving negro Daniel to his master in North Carolina and $50 for taking negro John to his master in Virginia. Camp meetings were held this summer of 1824 at Craven's Ferry in Lower Penns Neck. Mr. Sansay, fresh from Paris, opened a school for polite dancing in Salem at Ward Wilson's Hotel.

As the shadows fell around Pole Tavern on the night of Saturday, March 27th, an unknown horseman wheeled his steed against the window of Joseph Cook's house in that place, fired through the window and mortally wounded the owner and occupant thereof. "A most dastardly and highhanded crime," said the "Messenger". "Joseph Cook was shot at his home in Pole Tavern and is not expected to recover." After lingering he died on April 12th, 1824. Two men were arrested as suspects, a Mr. Zane and Mr. Austin. The latter was brought to trial on December 10th, when the indictment against him was moved by Prosecutor Jeffers. The defendant, Cornelius Austin had been heard to mention expressions leading to the belief that he had murdered Cook. The court and jury later found out he was an awful liar. He was speedily acquitted. The crime has never been solved.

Salem county had its own "Gretna Green". Three weddings

in one week at Pedricktown caused a local "poet" to write, in the "Messenger":

> "Scarce a week or month or year,
> But we have a wedding here,
> Weddings now so oft are seen,
> Wags have dubbed it Gretna Green."

This was a presidential year and politics became stormy among the citizens of Salem. There was still no hard and fast political party allegiance but the voters were split into two factions, one of which owed allegiance to Andrew Jackson and the other to John Quincy Adams. Early in the summer of 1824 the lines were drawn for the political battle which ended in a vote in the House of Representatives to determine the new president. The ladies of Salem held a straw vote with Adams receiving nine, Jackson one and Calhoun two. Loyal Jacksonians wore black vests with a print of Jackson's head on it, thus giving a new sartorial touch to the campaign. Frequent meetings were held and the "Messenger" contained column after column anent the controversy between Jackson and Adams. Editor Brooks favored Adams but gave ample space to his opponent. Joseph Kille, sheriff, was named an elector for Jackson and David Du Bois for Adams. The election results as far as the president was concerned were not known until February 12th, 1825 when Adam Sickler's stage entered Salem with "President Adams" written on it in chalk.

1825

Adams' victory was celebrated by a huge banquet at Ward Wilson's Hotel in Salem. The packet sloop *Marianna*, about the last of the sailing sloops out of here, advertised that they had fixed up the forecastle of the sloop for colored persons exclusively. Samuel Allen established his iron foundry in Salem, which seems to have been the first in operation in the county. Congressman Daniel Garrison, a pioneer in the field, publicly announced that he would be glad to meet his constituents and hear their problems before he voted in Washington.

Religious revivals in March of this year exceeded past records in conversions. There was a large one in Lower Penns Neck and twenty-five persons were baptised at one time in the Baptist Church at Salem. Richard Stockton Field comes to Salem as a young printer and attorney. Col. Johnson started his agricultural society as previously mentioned.

The hotel business in the county had two additions. Horatio Lawrence advertised that he had taken the hotel at Cravens Ferry and said in his ad., "This hotel is 7 miles from Salem to slow travellers but near enough to those who stir their stumps briskly." Thomas Andrews opened his Sportsmen's Hotel and Steam Mill Hall on the banks of Salem creek and advertised that for sportsmen he kept two fine pointers.

As to steamboats, we find the following advertisement: "The new steamboat Lafayette will leave Market street wharf, lower side, on Monday morning, 11th inst., at 8 o'clock, and continue to run on Monday, Wednesday and Friday from Philadelphia to Salem, and leave Salem every Thursday and Saturday. Signed by B. & B. Cooper, April 8th, 1825." Many of the Salem citizens were at that time much opposed to the steamboats, as the following paragraph from the Salem "Messenger" shows: "The farmers will take their butter, cheese and eggs away, and buy groceries, dry goods, etc., and we will have nothing to eat. The merchants' trade will be destroyed, and our packets rot for want of freight." Again April 20th, 1825, the editor said: "In consequence of the great opposition and even hostility to a steamboat in Salem, the proprietors of the Lafayette have determined to withdraw her and run to Mount Holly." We quote again from the same, "We should be sorry to say anything tending to encourage the running of a steamboat to this place, should it tend in the least to retard the growth of the town, but we cannot, like some of our friends, believe such will be the effect."

By far the most startling event of 1825 was what the "Messenger" called the "Foray of Fort Delaware." It was only a social event, although it had a warlike appearance for a while and considerably upset the citizens of peaceful Salem. It all happened out of an innocent enough Fourth of July celebration. Bigger and better Independence Day festivities were becoming in order so the local committee for that celebration invited William N. Jeffers, the president of the bank, to be the orator and in order to augment the occasion had invited the garrison of Fort Delaware. There was to be a big military ball and it was planned to make this affair long remembered. It was.

Jeffers orated, the parade was held and everything went on swimmingly until the evening. Then in the shocked words of the "Messenger" this is what happened: "Some of our prominent ladies and gentlemen were enjoying a private dance at a private home when suddenly Lieutenant Strong and Band (consisting of common soldiers) from Fort Delaware burst in upon the startled assemblage.—A lady was insulted by a common soldier. —Mr. Strong was asked in polite terms to withdraw his troops. He assumed a pert air and said he would do so, only on a proper request. He was quite flushed in the face and gentlemen present believed he had been drinking.—He said he only brought the band in to keep them all together.—Finally he left taking the common soldiers with him."

But the "Messenger" assures us that this was not the end of the affair. Continuing, "The music started again but alas, after the night was over and in fact, two days later Fort Delaware made a sortie on the town. Lt. Gardiner of that place with a sutler and Surgeon Smith, came back to Salem. While the government of the United States rested firmly in the belief that these young men were performing their duty at Fort Delaware they were actually engaged in the nefarious business of arranging a duel. The sutler entered a gentleman's home here and announced himself as Captain Farley. The readers will please remember that he was and is, just a common sutler. He had the audacity, on behalf of Lt. Strong, to challenge this gentleman to a duel. Lt. Gardiner also challenged another gentleman to a duel. Both challenges were respectfully declined. The obnoxious lieutenant and common sutler, calling himself Captain Farley, remained in Salem until eleven o'clock.—On Saturday night, a common sergeant foraged upon this town and thrust placards under the doors of these gentlemen, again taunting them to fight.—Unsatisfied, the gentry slunk away unperceived to the den of desperadoes.—No doubt the public paid for their education at West Point."

Jeffers was one of those challenged to fight on the field of honor. He respectfully declined, but did set forth his views on dueling some few days later in which his declination was buttressed by public opinion of several other citizens. So, the great "duel" came to naught, but for years afterwards, the people of Salem would discuss the mad sortie upon their town by "desperadoes from that den of iniquity, Fort Delaware."

The summer of 1825 was very hot and dry. Countless fish were found dead in Alloways Creek. Brooks complained in the "Messenger" not only of the heat but of the noise as well. It seems that the colored folk held a camp meeting in the woods near Salem and that some whites joined in to make the affair very "tumultuous". Brooks said "if it was the purpose of these worshippers to avoid hell, they certainly raised enough of it here first."

The election of 1825 was exceedingly close. William N. Jeffers lost by thirteen votes to Robert Gibbon Johnson who won to serve his last term in the Assembly. Edward Smith, Whig, won the office of Sheriff by a seven vote margin over Hackett, the Jacksonian candidate.

That fall witnessed the divorce of the steam mill from the

bank, Jeffers, Mark Miller, Richard Craven and others retaining the mill while John G. Mason followed Jeffers as president of the banking institution.

Fire bugs were loose in Salem and several suspicious blazes took place. The citizens had a habit of blaming such things on the blacks. The township Council passed a law that no colored person should be on the street later than 9 P. M. The Reliance Fire Company was started, giving the town of Salem two companies instead of one.

1826

The fiftieth anniversary of American independence was celebrated in proper style by Salem countians. This time the lads from Fort Delaware were not invited. The jubilee was held in Allowaystown with fitting ceremonies. At the dinner in Paullins Hotel that night, Sheriff Edward Smith of Salem in replying to a toast, recalled what so many of our people had forgotten. Raising his glass, Smith cried, "To the memory of our ancestors who fell at the battle of Quintons Bridge and the Massacre of Hancocks Bridge during the Revolutionary War."

With the spread of population inland into Salem county there had been a demand for better mail service. There were still only three post offices, Pole Tavern or Pittsgrove, Salem and Woodstown. But President Adams' administration created a whole handful of new post offices. They were Cravens Ferry, now Pennsville, Canton, Allowaystown, Sculltown, now Auburn, Pedricktown and Helms Cove, now Penns Grove. All of these are in existence today except Auburn. This office was placed on a Swedesboro rural route a few years ago.

When the Masonic lodge building was rebuilt in 1857, documents were discovered which had been placed there thirty years before at the time of its erection. The following excerpt is enlightening because at the time the anti-Masonic movement was in full swing. Elijah Brooks, in conjunction with Dr. James Van Meter and Alphonso Eakin were, even at this time, publishing the Anti-Masonic Courier. Along with the disappearance of Morgan, the Masons were considerably under fire. This document from the pen of Richard Parrot Thompson is exceedingly illuminating. It is addressed to "Ages yet Unborn" and reads as follows:

"This Masonic Hall which in elegance of design and in beauty of construction owns no rival in our State was erected by a Commission of Loans under the direction of Salem Lodge, No. 19 Commenced in June A. D. 1827 Finished in Jan. A. D. 1828. Architect—Mr. Thomas Sharp. Mason—Mr. John W. Challis. Painter—Mr. Wm. G. Beesley. Workmen at the Temple— Messrs. Robt. Moore, J. Bacon, I. Smart, T. Oliver, J. Sharp and others.

To the Master of Salem Lodge No. 19
(When found, if ever)

Dec. 21, 1827. The sect of Freemasons is now reviled in consequence of the fate of one William Morgan, who, as is alleged, has been murdered in the state of New York, by some Masons, to prevent the publication of a pamphlet containing as was believed by "those who have not received" to contain the Secrets of our order.

In the political world anxiety is felt to an unusual degree for the next Presidential contest, which shall elevate either John Q. Adams or General A. Jackson to the chair. Heaven send the former may preside!

These scraps are committed to paper with the belief that the many years may roll away, the heart that dictates and the bonds that pens them may moulder into dust. yet, some of the unborn may when the pillar shall decay in which many years may elapse and Time's eventful progress may find the above names no more known on the earth, yet whosoever shall find this let him remember that we once, like himself, existed and draw from that fact a moral lesson.

Be thou also ready,
    Edward Smith, P. M. of S. L. No. 19
    Thos. Jones Yorke, Sec.
    R. P. Thompson, S. D.

Dec. 21—1827

Officers for 1828—R. S. Field, W. M.; T. A. Maskell, S. W.; G. W. Connarroe, J. W.; D. Jayne, Treas.; T. J. Yorke, Sec.; R. P. Thompson, S. D.; J. M. Brown, J. D; J. Plummer, Tyler.

Deposited by R. P. Thompson, Dec. 21, 1827.

They are placed, read them with feelings of surprise when you look into "by past times" and find that these things were.

                            Richard Parrot Thompson
Attorney at Law and S. D. of Salem Lodge No. 19

The health of Salem was good, wrote Editor Brooks in the summer of '26. "It should be a great health and summer pleasuring resort. The bilious fever and the ague have quite departed." A sea turtle weighing 43 pounds was exhibited at Sherrons Hotel. It came from the far distant Galapagos Island. Professor John Griscom, of Lower Creek, who had been all the way to England to study the new methods of education, lectured in his home town on the Lancastrian system.

The only reference the compiler can find to the old Trap Tavern is in the files of the "Messenger" for 1826. Even then, it does not tell much of this place which has been handed down in rumor and tradition as a famous hostelry. In 1826, three colored men were tried for arson in connection with the fires of late 1825. Brooks apparently had no great affection for the principals involved because he said in the "Messenger": "One of these is Sutey Cato, far sunk in the scale of moral degradation." One of the defendants at the trial testified that the plot to burn the barns and houses was formulated at the Trap. Brooks says of it, "Cato and the other Black Hellions of the Trap—once a tavern but lately occupied as a place of entertainment, yclept, a dance hall for all the Samboes and Physillis who could raise enough money to get in." The Trap, which went back to Revolutionary days, was located on the Penns Neck side of Salem Creek at Lambson's Bridge. The building of the Penns Neck bridge in 1811 had opened a quicker way from Salem to Penns Neck. The Mannington-Lambson's Bridge route was therefore little used and the Trap suffered by the change.

Congressman Garrison, probably as public minded as any representative this county has had, was instrumental in securing the new post offices. He likewise was in 1826 doubly engrossed in the study of improving the streets of Salem by a new process named after its inventor, "Macadamizing."

The election of 1826 beheld the Democrats split again. Two of the leaders, Jeffers and Wm. J. Shinn, had a quarrel at the county convention with the result that three men ran for council, Clawson winning over Ray and Sinnickson. Robert Gibbon Johnson went down in defeat trying to retain his assembly seat. Losing with him was Joseph Kille. Humphreys, Archer and Freas were the three successful assemblymen. Hedge Thompson of Salem ran for congress on the Adams ticket, being opposed by Congressman Daniel Garrison on the Jackson ticket. Thompson won.

1827

Hog killings are still much heralded in this county. In 1827, one reads of a hog killing contest in Salem in which Mr. J. Thompson's hog won the prize, before it was slaughtered, at 697 pounds.

Attorney F. L. McCullough introduced the silk worm to the county. The business, like other schemes for amassing quick wealth, only impoverished those who entered it on a large scale.

Trade and prosperity seem uppermost in the annals of 1827. A new wharf was built at Cravens Ferry, regular steam lines were proposed, stud horses were freely advertised, the Famous Round Mill House at the foot of Broadway was built. There were five doctors and five attorneys practicing in Salem county.

Elias Hicks' name was on the tongues of all the Quakers. The great separation was on and his sermons were for sale in the book stores of Salem.

The Rev. John Burt of the Presbyterian Church protested so much against the running of the steamship *Essex* on Sundays, that it was withdrawn. A fierce controversy between the Sabbatarians and the open Sunday people started at this time. A scornful open Sunday man informed the populace through the "Messenger" that two hundred Wilmington Sunday School scholars had come to Penns Neck via a steamboat for a Sunday excursion. The Methodists organized a committee to protest against an old evil, that of buying votes.

Protests were in order that year. Citizens of the entire state were beginning to agitate the formation of a new Constitution. At that period the governor had to be a lawyer, since he was chancellor of the equity court as well. There were only five men in Salem at that time capable of being governor and they of course were the five attorneys.

Two Presbyterian ministers of the county, Rev. John Burt of Salem and Rev. G. W. Janvier of Daretown published in this year a few numbers of a short lived church magazine entitled the "West Jersey Evangelist". It was published by the "Messenger" press and ran for about a year.

Mary Elwell was the servant maid of Thomas Lambson. She complained that her wages were low and her board consisted of bad food. In the fall of 1827 Mr. Lambson had missed household goods and he blamed Mary Elwell. His wife, who had a great belief in the stars wrote to an astrologer in Philadelphia to discover who stole the goods. They told Mary that they had "consulted the stars." One morning Mr. Lambson, sitting at the breakfast table absorbed in the new edition of the Salem "Messenger", neglected to stir his coffee. He sipped it instead and became deathly ill. However, he did not die and had Mary Elwell arrested for the attempted murder. She fully admitted her guilt, said that she had purchased ratsbane or arsenic of the local apothecary and hoped by placing it in the coffee, "that it would settle the star business and her master at the same time." Because of her tender age—she was but 16—Justice Ford gave her a six months sentence and advised her not to play the Lucretia Borgia again.

The polls of 1827 showed another Adams victory. Clawson of that party defeated Nelson of the Jackson faction by 726 to 650. The Jacksonites claimed a partial victory in the election to the assembly of William N. Jeffers. This was his first term and the beginning of the grand fight involving him and the Salem Steam Mill.

1828

Since a number of other towns had asked for and received post offices from the Adams Administration, the town of Quintons Bridge early in 1828 asked also for a post office. In addition they named their postmaster, David English, and received not only the office but the official they desired. This was the year of Jackson's election to the presidency. Denied by a close vote

POLITICS IN 1828

in 1824, the Jackson adherents left nothing unturned this year to make his election possible. The county convention met early that year at Allowaystown, long a citadel of the Democratic faith. Paullins Hotel was too small for the crowd, so they met in the newly erected Methodist church instead. About the same time the Adams party met in Woodstown, long a stronghold of Republicanism, and finding Fisher's Hotel too small, used the Baptist church. So enthusiasm in both parties ran high early in the campaign. The campaign was extremely bitter throughout the county but traces of humor often appear. A loyal Democrat from Salem wrote to the "Messenger" near the close of the campaign: "This is a good Jackson ticket," and,

> "God of love look from above,
> With pity and Compassion
> And cut the throats of all the folks
> That won't vote for General Jackson."

Despite the precatory offering, Adams carried Salem by 265 votes but in the nation at large, the hero of the War of 1812 swept the boards and was elected president. The Democrats held forth in great style at Sherron's Hotel, Salem, which was "totally illuminated" for the grand occasion. The county went Republican except for the sheriff. John Hackett, twice defeated, won this time in a three cornered fight, only to die in office two weeks after he had assumed it.

Jeffers in 1828 came again very close, but not close enough, to high honors. He missed the United States Senatorship to Mahlon Dickerson by five votes in joint session. Isaac Johnson was elected sheriff for the unexpired term of the late Sheriff Hackett.

Henry Clay, the great Whig leader, received his share of fame as far as Salem county was concerned, in 1828, when the "Messenger" said, "Near the town of Salem within a quarter mile of Salem old Bridge and at the old windmill, a respectable village has sprung up within a few months past and has received the name of Claysville in honor of that great but persecuted man, Henry Clay."

The Fourth of July was celebrated again at Allowaystown with the great Benjamin H. Latrobe as the orator of the day. The Truth Teller, (Richard S. Field) appeared for the first time in the "Messenger" in July of '28. He would worry Jeffers and the Democrats to a great extent. The "Messenger" advertised a circulating library "of recent good books," to be had at moderate rentals from their office.

1829

The winter of this year was the coldest in Salem since 1780. The Delaware and all the creeks feeding it from this county were frozen over for a long time.

The hard winter did not deter the citizens of Pedricktown from meeting at John Sooy's Inn in that place to design ways and means for a steam boat line between Wilmington and the Jersey shore.

Samuel D. Ingham, relative of the Salem Inghams, and at that time secretary of the treasury under Jackson, visited Salem to be followed by gaping crowds on the streets who were proud to say that they had actually seen a member of Andrew Jackson's cabinet.

The Rev. Henry M. Mason of St. John's Church, Salem wrote and published an Ecclesiastical History of the Episcopal Church in North America.

Two slaves were given thirty lashes apiece by Sheriff Johnson for petit larceny. A poor unfortunate in his cabin near Salem rolled into his cabin fire place, after consuming a jug of rum and was speedily cremated. The bachelors of Salem met to find some way to make themselves comfortable for the coming winter of 1829-1830.

Late in 1829, the "Messenger" said: "There was so much lack of interest in this election that we forego publishing the election returns. The Jackson ticket carried all except Elsinboro where only 29 votes were cast." Two weeks later, Brooks said; "There appears to be a demand that the returns be published," and so he did. Jeffers won his second term in the Assembly, with Jacob Wick and David Hurley as his associates. All were Jackson Democrats. Henry Freas of the same party won the Council election over Clawson of the Adams faction. Defeated Adams candidates for the Assembly were Foster, Shinn and Field.

CHAPTER XXI

SALEM IN THE 1830's

March of 1830 saw the breaking of the scandal over the Salem Steam Mill Company. The company was formed in 1822 for both the Steam Mill and the Bank but in 1823 the bank and mill were divorced and they then continued under separate management. William N. Jeffers, who was twice elected to the Assembly in 1827 and 1829, had been the moving spirit in the organization of both bank and steam mill and the bank had been erected on part of Jeffers' property. For years there had been undercover gossip and rumor concerning Jeffers' activities in various fields. By March of 1830, prompted by several reasons, the scandal broke and left Salem for almost a decade in the throes of a great controversy over Jeffers' activities with the wreck of the steam mill company.

In 1828, Jeffers and his associates had changed the name to the Salem and Philadelphia Manufacturing Company. It was this corporate change which made all the trouble. The bank notes issued by this new company had Philadelphia in large letters and Salem in such small letters "that it was necessary to use a magnifying glass" to see them. There were no rotating numbers used on the new bills and the opponents of the company argued that they had infringed upon their legislative powers by even issuing the notes. A quo warranto was issued but to no avail. The company was soon insolvent and all the suits against it were covered by one judgment in favor of an individual—William N. Jeffers. There were no stockholders available and no dividends were ever declared. "They robbed the widow and the orphan," declared the committees report early in 1830.

The committee which investigated the matter thoroughly was composed of several prominent citizens, among them John G. Mason, who had followed Jeffers as president of the bank, Thomas Sinnickson, William J. Shinn, Morris Hall, Joseph Hancock, David S. English, Jacob W. Mulford and others.

Elijah Brooks publishd the report of the committee in full in the "Messenger". He did more than that. He issued or caused to be issued a hand bill which did not treat Mr. Jeffers. Mr. Miller or Mr. Craven very lightly. It said in part:

SALEM STEAM MILL
Come ye to the market!

"The capital necessary is a few bales of honesty, several tons of brass and a Miller Cravening Employment.

"Come then to the sale on Wednesday ye poor stricken souls that are laboring under the burden of poverty and secure to yourself a fortune. The term of payment will be easy and but one condition will be annexed—He that grows rich, thus loses his reputation . . ."

Brooks in his bitter attack alleged that Jeffers permitted his brother John to escape and had even chartered the steam boat *Essex* to get him from Salem. Brooks said, "Jeffers was hung in Effigy, he was absent. If he had not been absent, he might have been hung actually."

Jeffers was not idle under this onslaught. He called Elijah Brooks "an under-strapping quill driver to a scandalous paper," and then proceeded to sue Brooks for libel to the amount of $5,000.00

Brooks said in the next issue of the Messenger, "As soon as we have recovered from our excessive fright, we will submit a proper answer—We are dreadfully afraid it will never come to trial—The writ has not yet been served."—

Faced with a libel suit which was never tried, Brooks kept on with his crossfire and barrage against Jeffers. He printed with gusto, letters from Rockland, Maine and De Witts Valley, New York showing that a man named John E. Jeffers had been selling notes of the Salem and Philadelphia Manufacturing Company. Similar complaints later came in from Ohio and Mississippi valleys. John Jeffers was a brother of William. "A man by name of Jeffers swindled a poor peddler near Oswego, New York", another complaint said.

Jeffers published a pamphlet in his own defense citing within an incident which has often been referred to by elder citizens of Salem who heard it from their fathers. This was the horsewhipping of his brother John, who had the ill luck to come to Salem at this particular time. Jeffers wrote, apropos of the assault, "This man, John Hall, came up behind my brother in the dark, knocked him down and beat him with a whip in the most shocking manner."

The Messenger was moved to scorn in answer. "No, it was not his face and eyes which were disfigured but an entirely different part of his body—which is sometimes designated as the seat of honor—But be this as it may, he certainly did receive a most severe flagellation."—

John Hall was fined five dollars but the horsewhipping affair on Star Corner remained a choice bit of gossip.

Jeffers blamed all the attacks upon him to politics and petty jealousy. Seeing that his prompt answer to his maligners did not have effect he took the attack into Brooks' own territory and started a new paper called the Statesman, which made Brooks see red. Brooks had enjoyed a profitable monopoly on the newspaper business in Salem and did not relish opposition. In May of 1830 the Statesman appeared under the editorship of Henry H. Elwell backed, of course, by Jeffers. Brooks got a bit excited and cried, editorially: "This is a base, inhuman thing to do and there is universal indignation over this latest manipulation by the trickster."

In this same period of 1830 James S. McCalla had come to Salem and started a newspaper called the New Jersey Farmer and Literary Gazette. It only ran a few weeks before Brooks and McCalla, being kindred spirits in their antipathy to Jeffers, joined forces and merged the Gazette into the Messenger under the firm name of Brooks and McCalla.

Blasts continued from one side to the other while the Salem and Philadelphia Manufacturing notes continued to circulate over the eastern part of the United States with no value for their redemption.

Jeffers claimed that some of the committee signing the hand bill against him were directors of the company and had full knowledge of all arrangements. But still the burden rested on Jeffers to prove that the company had exceeded its legislative power and issued notes which were not redeemable and consequently worthless. A suit was brought against Richard Craven, a director of the Salem and Philadelphia Manufacturing Company by Augustus Taylor for deceit in the issuance of the notes, in which Taylor recovered a small sum.

The Messenger used the case to advantage but spent most of the time in this hectic year of 1830 in lambasting Jeffers. "His frauds are unparalleled in the annals of iniquity;" "Watch the Masonic lodge for he holds office therein;" "His handbill in defense is a gross outrage,—an unblushing villany—a poor drunk was made to sign it." Thus spoke Brooks in some of his attacks on Jeffers.

The bitter opposition to Jeffers did not come from the Steam Mill note affair alone. Part of it came from politics. Jeffers was a Jacksonian Democrat, even though the Messenger had accused him of wanting to run as an Adams elector in 1828. As a member of the Assembly in the session of 1829 he had voted with his Jackson colleagues, Wick and Hurley, against the new railroad which was designed to compete with the original Camden and Amboy road. The cry of monopoly had already been heard against this road. The citizens of Salem had planned to construct a new road running from Delaware Bay to Raritan Bay but it was years before it was completed. At any rate, the Salem delegates leagued with the monopoly to kill off any competing roads and for the time being were successful.

This was the burning issue in the election of 1830. Running for re-election, Jeffers had to face this as well as the steam mill scandal. The Messenger dubbed Jeffers and his followers the "Steam Mill Democrats". It combined to defeat Jeffers and his complete ticket.

Gloating over the victory of Zaccheus Ray, John Summerill and Joseph Nelson, the Messenger said, "He, (Jeffers) converted this quiet village into a theatre of strife and contention,—but we have him on the hip now."

This election of 1830 probably surpassed all previous ones in bitterness. Someone had dug up a conviction of Jeffers in Cincinnati, Ohio Territory, in 1811 on a conspiracy charge. This was dangled before him by the vituperative Messenger and undoubtedly injured him. Jeffers denied it but the merry battle went on.

Finally Jeffers pulled his trump card. He had been a Jackson follower and had seen both Marcy and Jackson declare that "to the victors belong the spoils". And he had obtained his. Influential with the new administration, he had asked for and received the post of *Charge de Affaires* to Central America. Thus, he has the distinction of being the only Salem citizen ever made a minister or ambassador to a foreign power.

Brooks raved at the "perfidy" of Jeffers and Jackson. So bitter did he become that when Jeffers, enroute to Central America, became ill at Pensacola, Florida, and was reported dead, Brooks said, "Good, that is the best news we have yet heard."

He was not dead, but he never reached Central America as an ambassador. The furore the Steam Mill and the Cincinnati affairs had kicked up, penetrated to Washington and President Jackson, fearing political reprisals in the election of 1832, had him recalled from Pensacola.

The Statesman, backed by Jeffers, issued a prospectus before it commenced publication. Following Brooks' blast about the "inhuman" idea of starting a new paper, Mr. Elwell of the Statesman cordially saluted him in the following fashion:

"We hold ourselves under no obligation whatever to make any reply to the friendly notice taken of us by the Messenger. We shall be quite content, for the present, to pursue the course which we ordinarily avowed it to be our intention to follow, without turning out of our way to repel abuse, which as yet, has only resulted to our benefit, by swelling our subscription lists. We can't be always stopping to brush away insects."

It was the era of the sea serpent. Everywhere off the Atlantic shores of the nation some one was seeing a monster in the waves. Elwell in the Statesman beat Brooks of the Messenger to it by dubbing the party Brooks represented the "Sea Serpents". Brooks, a master of abuse, said Jeffers, Elwell and their friends were not even fit to be sea serpents, they were "small snakes".

But little by little the steam mill storm blew over. Small industry and agriculture continued to prosper in the county of Salem and as the years passed in the fourth decade of the nineteenth century, the great agitation over the Steam Mill was gradually forgotten.

1831 saw another bitter election. The Steam Mill Democrats, as Brooks called them, undaunted by their defeat the preceding year, proceeded to elect their ticket this year. Again the vials of wrath were poured on the heads of Jeffers and his followers. But Freas for Council on the Jackson-Jeffers ticket defeated Sinnickson of the opposition 997 to 884. Hurley, Johnson and Butcher, all Jeffers followers, were elected to the Assembly by substantial majorities.

The Statesman could throw a few bombs itself. The Truth Teller has been referred to before. He was a columnist in the Messenger and his name was Richard Stockton Field. Later in life he was a United States Senator and a Federal Court Judge but in these days he was the author of many articles in the Messenger attacking Jeffers. In retaliation, Elwell let loose this blast at Mr. Field:

RICHARD S. FIELD—It is perfectly well known to the citizens of the county, that Richard S. Field, a profligate and unprincipled young man (who ran for the Legislature and obtained only 300 votes) is the editor of a filthy paper, printed in this Town, called the Messenger. Although this paper and the conductors of it are so well known here, that nothing said in it can affect the reputation of any one, yet the vile scribbler is not as well known elsewhere. It shall henceforth be our business to make him better known. We have several communications on hand and the proof of his baseness and depravity as exhibited in the late election. Several of his circulars and papers are on file, and it is time to let the public know what sort of man he is. Had he courage he would in truth be a dangerous man!

None but the cowardly and profligate offer to disturb the repose of the dead! This Field has done by insulting the grave of a man who has been honored by the people with the office of High Sheriff of his native County— one who has held the office of Judge of the Court and Justice of the Peace, and whose honesty has never been doubted by his fellow citizens. Yet the tomb of such a man must be invaded, and the feelings of his afflicted family be outraged by a profligate adventurer who stands before the public accused of numerous acts of depravity—and especially with having withheld the money of the widows and orphans of Masons in the late transactions respecting the Salem Lodge. This much for the present! He shall hear from us again! When it has come to this—that the dead can no longer rest, forbearance ceases to be a virtue.

November of 1833 saw Elijah Brooks resign as editor of the Messenger. With this event ended the long controversy between Jeffers and Brooks. The Messenger became the Weekly Visitor and was run for five weeks by James M. Hannah and Dr. Ware. On March 28, 1834 the Weekly Visitor and the Statesman united under the new name of the Union, edited by James M. Hannah. The new combination announced that "it hoped the Union proved acceptable to the great Democratic party." So the dove of peace settled over this newspaper war. Three days after the Union appeared the Freemans Banner, owned by Sisty and Prior, whose object was anti-Jackson and consequently anti-administration, announced they were "opposed but not foes." This arrangement continued for two years when Hannah sold the Union to Prior. It was merged with the Freemans Banner in 1836.

In the early part of this decade Penns Grove received its name. It was given to the village, then chiefly a steamboat landing, by the Wilmington and New Jersey Company. Prior to this it had been called Helms Cove, although that part of the village was a mile away. The name of course remembers William Penn who once owned Penns Neck, and the groves in and around the Landing, which were many. At this period of its history Penns Grove boasted a first class tavern, "The Sign of the General Wolfe," which stood across from the grove where French's Hotel later stood. Other groves near here were frequently used for camp meetings and the steamboats loaded and unloaded hundreds of worshippers at the nearby landing.

In 1831 or 1832, due to much agitation against them, the Masons surrendered their charter. There was no Masonic lodge in Salem after that date until the formation of the Excelsior Lodge on January 19, 1868.

A new post office was established at Mannington Hill with Dr. Samuel Githens as postmaster. George W. Connarroe was winning fame and fortune as an artist in Philadelphia. A heavy snow storm which spread over fences and piled up against farm house doors came to the county in January, 1831. The next month saw much excitement in Salem when the powder magazine exploded on Fort Delaware and the ensuing fire destroyed the buildings. The "largest hog" in the world was slaughtered at Allowaystown in April. Samuel Dare was the proud owner. The hog weighed 1074 pounds.

February of 1831 beheld a controversy on a religious question. In that month there had been a baptism of new members of the Alloway Baptist Church. The ice had to be chopped away in Alloways Creek to allow the immersion. Brooks in the Messenger was aghast at the news and said he "thought they could wait". The members of the church thought the matter was none of his business and some of them promptly cancelled their subscriptions. Soon after, Brooks hastened to say in the Messenger that "he regretted his untimely remarks and believed that the rite of baptism should be administered whenever the hungering soul demanded".

On December 29, 1835 the residents of Salem were roused from their beds at four in the morning by cries of fire and murder. The Banner said, "It was neither fire nor murder but the heart rending cries of eight miserable human beings, chained and naked being carried through Salem in a wagon." A Mr. Dannenhower, Philadelphia agent for a North Carolina slave owner, had come into South Jersey and recaptured near Stow Creek the eight fugitive negro slaves. The citizens rushed from their homes and stopped the wagon, taking slaves and agents alike to Sherron's Hotel.

Magistrate Bush was summoned from bed and a charge of disorderly conduct was filed against Dannenhower. The hearing itself was an uproar. Bush, backed by public opinion, held Dannenhower for breach of the peace and released the slaves. Before he rendered his judgment, some one liberated the negroes and they fled into the street, "emitting loud voices of joy". Dannenhower drew a gun and rushed upon the magistrate. Some one seized his arm. He then tried to stab Sheriff English with a dirk. Dannenhower seems to have been well armed in this emergency. Joseph Hancock seized a chair and attempted to strike Dannenhower, exclaiming, "Kill the ——— ———, kill him." They knocked him down, dragged him out of the hotel and robbed him; at least that was Dannenhower's story. Joseph Kille, Samuel Clement and W. G. Beasley of chair fame, who were all present, testified that Dannenhower was in error and that they all thought if he had been subdued, it was done lightly and that his pocketbook was taken from him but restored to him in the jail. Dannenhower spent the rest of the night in jail together with the negroes, who were rounded up off the streets of Salem. The Philadelphia papers were indignant at Dannenhower's treatment in Salem. The Salem papers were indignant at Dannenhower.

Steamboats came into their own in Salem in this decade. In 1830 the *Essex* ran to Delaware City to connect to Baltimore via the new Chesapeake and Delaware Canal. Then came the *Salem*, the *William Penn*, *Robert Morris* and *Ohio*, all running to Delaware or Maryland points. It was in 1834 that the *Pioneer* came to Salem and was advertised to run direct to Philadelphia. Competition came the next year in the *Flushing*, owned and operated by the Boon family of Salem. In 1838 the Boons replaced the *Flushing* with the *Clifton*, a very fast boat. The *Clifton* was moreover a staunch sea going vessel and the Boons were good seamen.

Epidemics were loose again in Salem in 1832. Cholera raged and there were some cases of smallpox. Dr. Tuft was accused of bringing smallpox germs into Salem. He indignantly denied the foul charge in both newspapers and was exonerated therefrom. Captain Alexander Orr, a Revolutionary veteran aged 80, died at Allowaystown.

The election of 1832 saw Jackson and Henry Clay opposed to each other for the presidency. Joseph Heritage of Salem was a Clay electoral candidate. James Newell was a Jackson elector. Clay carried Salem county by 277 votes and his ticket was successful. Clawson defeated Freas, a Jackson adherent, for Council and the Clay ticket also won. The Messenger frothed because President Jackson, playing politics, removed the postmasters at Allowaystown, Woodstown and Sharptown. In 1831 Salem received its third postmaster when Henry Elwell of the Statesman, thanks to Jeffers' influence, succeeded Samuel Sherron.

1833 saw the Rev. Thomas Ware receive a Revolutionary pension. It was justly received and was rather tardy recognition for an aged man who had served his nation. He had been for years a Methodist circuit rider and preacher, one of the best loved of the Methodist congregation. Back in 1821 he had helped organize the Methodist church at Allowaystown and had been one of the first ministers stationed there. The Sharptown Methodist Church was built in 1835. It took the congregation away from the old Pilesgrove Methodist Church, a mile distant from Sharptown and eventually caused the decay of the first church.

Cholera returned again in 1833. This time it raged more furiously than the year before. Eighteen people died in one day in the town of Salem alone, and the only place of business open was a cabinet maker's shop, manufacturing coffins. The separation between the Hicksite and Orthodox sects of the Society of Friends filled the papers. The legal outcome of it all was the law suit of Hendrickson vs. DeCou. The decision favoring the Orthodox branch had its political repercussions. The Hicksite voters, mainly Anti-Democratic, voted to a man for legislative candidates to unseat Justice Drake. Drake had not only judicially decided against the Hicksite Friends, he had openly in Court told them what he thought of them. Swing, a Democrat, defeated Clawson of the opposition for Council 1108 to 882 and proceeded to carry out his constituents' desire by voting against Drake for a new term on the bench in the joint session.

John M. Brown of Salem in 1835 solicited funds for erecting the Washington Monument. Baker's Tavern in the Hancock House at Hancock's Bridge was in flourishing existence. The editor of the Banner lamented the lack of news articles. He was quite correct and if there had been more happenings narrated, the task of the historian would have been easier. Thomas Keen of Gloucester county won a foot race at Sculltown and a purse of $30. A huge bone was dug out of the marl pits at Woodstown. Miss Anna W. Maylin, whose name is on the drinking fountain in front of the Salem County Clerk's office, opened a ladies finishing school in the Salem Academy. She was also a poet of parts. St. Johns Episcopal Church installed a new organ in 1833. In 1835, vandals entered the church building and wrecked the new organ. The great New York fire of Dec. 27, 1835 was visible from Salem, 120 miles away.

This decade saw a distinct increase in trade in the county. The steamboat had much to do with it, affecting not only Salem but aiding the smaller towns on the creeks, Alloway, Sculltown, Pedricktown and Quinton's Bridge. Numerous county stores, utilized for post offices sprung up and in addition became meeting places for those in the rural districts. In 1830, William J. Shinn opened the first livery stable in Salem. Still dependent on tallow for illumination, George M. Ward operated a candle manufactory on Ward street. There were many tailoring establishments, boot and shoe manufacturies, and harness and saddle stores in this section. Mr. Shinn of the livery stable also opened a horse mill which the paper complimented as a great boon to the town. Dr. Jayne, the local boy from Canton who made good, started to flood his home county with advertisements of his Carminative Balsam and Health Restorer. Hazlehurst's saw mill was located on Cool Run in Alloway township. The Oakland Mills at Allowaystown were destroyed by fire in April of 1835. Ship building had started under the Reeves family at this place in the same decade.

The juveniles of Salem were delighted in 1833 to behold one of the first travelling menageries to visit this section. An excerpt of the advertisement in the Banner read:

WILD BEASTS
A MENAGERIE
OF WILD BEASTS

Will be Exhibited at Salem, in the Rear of Mr. Mulford's Hotel,
On Monday and Tuesday, the 10th and 11th of June, consisting of the following animals:

THE FULL GROWN
AFRICAN LION

The Zebu, or Wild Cow
The only one on this continent.

A PORCUPINE

Recently imported to this country from Spain

A GOLDEN EAGLE
A PAIR OF BRAZILIAN CAVIES
SOUTH AMERICAN LION
TWO PANTHERS
PECCARY, OR WILD HOG
THE
REAL MAN MONKEY

This animal was lately imported into Philadelphia from Africa and is termed

THE WILD MAN OF THE WOODS

When standing erect, he measures about five feet in height, and possesses the strength of two ordinary men. He is secured with two strongchains, so that he may be viewed with perfect safety.

In the same year the Erie Canal Boat Museum, housed on a canal boat fifty-six feet long, named "Superior of Albany," E. Wilcox, proprietor and master, visited Market street wharf, Salem. It had thirteen glass cases of curiosities and a variety of paintings, engravings, Indian war clubs, and similar articles. It also had a Cosmorama.

A circus enroute from Wilmington to Penns Grove had the misfortune of losing its elephant. The elephant broke away at the landing and proceeded to visit the farmers in the rural districts of Upper Penns Neck. One of these farmers, an Irish man celebrating a Saturday night, had the misfortune to come in contact with the elephant while recovering from his potions. He fled to the woods, "emitting loud cries of anguish and terror." What happened to the Irishman is not known but the elephant came back to the Delaware river for water and it is said, "took a row boat from the shore and rowed back to Wilmington where he was captured by his owners." Apparently the newspaperman who wrote that in 1837 was suffering from the same disease as the Irishman who saw the elephant in the woods.

In the '30s Salem gave competition to Trenton in the pottery business. William J. Diamond in October, 1833 opened an earthenware manufactory making high pots, flat pots, large pans, basins, black and red chambers, jugs, jars, pitchers and flower pots. It was located on Ward street.

Samuel Reeve of Mannington had a fine nursery containing 150,000 fruit trees of different varieties.

* * * *

A distinguished citizen of Salem participated in the rebellion of Texas against Mexico. His name was Doctor John Jacobs Sinnickson.

More than thirty years before Fenwick and the English colonists founded the town of New Salem in 1675, Anders Seneca with his sons, Broors and Anders, Jr., emigrated from Sweden to the new world. They located permanently upon a large tract of land on the east shore of the Delaware, which was bought from the Indians who at that time inhabited that portion of America. Anders Seneca, Jr., married and had two sons, one of whom was named John, whose last name was altered to Sinnickson, then to be the family name.

Dr. Sinnickson was the great-great-great-grandson of Anders Seneca, Jr. He was born in Salem September 11th, 1811, and at the time of his death, January 11th, 1889, in his seventy-eighth year, was the eldest descendant of the Swedish immigrant who settled on the east shore of the Delaware.

He spent his childhood in Salem and studied at the Salem Academy. In 1831, Dr. Sinnickson was graduated from Jefferson Medical College in Philadelphia. Having practiced medicine for one year in Pittsylvania county, Virginia, he moved to Washington, Texas, where he resided and practiced for several years.

When Texas rebelled against Mexico, Dr. Sinnickson joined the Texan army immediately after the battle of San Jacinto. He was detailed as guard over Generals Santa Anna (the same Santa Anna who commanded the Mexicans against the Americans in the war of 1846-47) and Ampudio, prisoners of war.

At the battle of Mier, Dr. Sinnickson was captured by the Mexicans, and after a terrible march to the City of Mexico, was imprisoned in the Castle of Perote. During this ordeal he received severe wounds which disabled him to the end of his life. He was unwilling to talk of the horrors of his imprisonment even to his best friends.

Dr. Sinnickson's brother-in-law, T. Jones Yorke, then a member of Congress; Waddy Thompson, U. S. Minister to Mexico; Daniel Webster; Prescott, the historian, a conciliatory intermediary with Calderon, Minister from Spain, and Madam Calderon; Senator Critendon, the father of his comrade and fellow prisoner, George Critendon, all united in their efforts for his release. They were successful only after almost insuperable difficulties and delays. Having been given his parole, with the understanding that he leave Texas, Dr. Sinnickson sailed from Vera Cruz for New Orleans on a dilapidated steamer, finally returning to his father's house in Salem.

* * * *

The papers were full of the panic of 1837 which had its effect here, as in other places.

Another slavery tumult took place in June of 1837. Mr. McKim of Philadelphia attempted to lecture in the Salem Court House on the subject of abolition. A minute or so from the start of his lecture, Mr. McKim was interrupted by several drunks, who apparently were in favor of slavery. A free-for-all fight ensued and McKim abandoned his speech and left the court house. A mob, beating drums and tin kettles followed him to his boarding house, the residence of Mr. Goodwin. Here they serenaded him in derisive fashion and invited the "d———abolitionist" to come out. He declined. The mob repaired to a tavern, got drunk all over again and satisfied themselves by burning McKim in effigy.

The church people were still protesting against the running of the steamboats on Sunday. Captain Boon of the *Pioneer* for a time cancelled his Sunday trips and yielded to public opinion.

The new church of St. Johns was dedicated on Feb. 8, 1838 with the Episcopal bishop of New Jersey, the Rev. G. W. Doane, officiating. This building, now in use, replaced the Revolutionary structure which had been sacked by the British and later repaired. Old prints of the early colonial church are preserved among the records of the Salem County Historical Society. A month later, the new Methodist Church on South street, now Walnut, was dedicated. The new building replaced the old frame structure erected by Benjamin Abbott. This building lasted until the 1880's when the present First M. E. Church was erected.

The elections of 1837 showed a Whig victory for the legislative ticket. William F. Reeve of ship building fame was elected to Council on the Whig ticket with all Whig assemblymen. Thomas J. Casper, a Democrat, was elected sheriff.

On May 1, 1838, after two years of litigation, the case of Culbreth vs. Griscom et al, was decided by the New Jersey Supreme Court in favor of the plaintiff, the owner of the slaves whose agent, Mr. Dannenhower, had been so badly treated, according to his story, in Salem many months before.

The Broad Seal War caused as much political excitement as the state of New Jersey has ever witnessed. One of the Congressional seats involved was contended for by Salem countians. Joseph Kille on the Democrat side and Thomas Jones Yorke on the Whig side were the Salem men involved. At that time, 1838, the Congressmen were not elected by districts as they are now, but in the state at large. The campaign of that year was very bitter and the election very close. Arbitrarily, the Secretary of State, a Whig, refused to allow the election returns from South Amboy and Millville, alleging election irregularities. Without those returns the five Democrats including Kille were defeated; with them they were elected by less than a hundred votes. Governor Pennington, also a Whig, certified the Whig Congressmen as elected. The Democratic House of Representatives refused to accept the "Broad Seal of the state of New Jersey" and instead accepted the five Democrats. Thus, Joseph Kille became a Congressman. In this same election the Democrats carried Salem county for their legislative slate, electing John H. Lambert to the Council by 38 votes over Johnson, a Whig. Lambert, a minority member of the Council, protested against the action of Pennington in giving the Whig candidates for Congress the Broad Seal approval.

This year of 1838 saw miserable roads in Salem county. It also saw the climax of silk culture, which ruined many a farmer who had attempted it. The Friends, always interested in education, opened their new school at the corner of Fenwick and South streets. Remodeled, it still stands in the rear of the corner of East Broadway and Walnut street. Clement Acton and George M. Ward were trustees and Thomas J. Saunders the first principal. It is interesting to note that Halliday Jackson was a teacher in this school in the following decade. His grandson of the same name became superintendent of the Salem system in 1933.

March 5, 1839 was a record day for the historian. On that day, Colonel Robert Gibbon Johnson delivered before the Salem Lyceum in the old Court House the first of a series of lectures which formed the basis of his book published the same year on the history of Salem. It formed a most valuable source book of Salem's past and is now eagerly sought by historians. Samuel Prior of the Banner, in reporting the first lecture said: "And after saying that the remains of Fenwick were in an open field overgrown with brambles and briars, beautifully did he utter the statement, 'sic gloria transit mundi.'"

Prior continued: "The speaker referred to Andrew Bacon, dead but a few years since. From motives of delicacy no allusion was made to the father of the lecturer, although it was well known that he was a most ardent Whig and did much towards driving the tyrant from the country, and the lecturer, himself but a lad, was compelled to become guardian and pilot to his mother and sister in conducting them at night through woods and swamps to a place of safety from British insolence."

Prior prepared to publish Johnson's lectures in book form but a quarrel broke out between him and the colonel with the result that the book was published in Philadelphia. Before it was done, however, many columns of the Banner were devoted to spirited recriminations between Prior and Johnson, the former alleging that the latter had broken faith with him in an oral contract to publish the book.

"The printer needs work and cash. Will the people have the goodness to bring it in?" said the Banner in the winter of 1839, calling attention to the plight of newspaper publishers.

The election of 1839 disgusted the editor of the Banner for he declared: "This campaign passed everything ever seen in crimination, recrimination, falsehood, invective, ridicule, and misrepresentation that we have ever beheld." The Democrats won again with John H. Lambert for Council over his fellow Allowaystown man, William Reeves, by a score of 1355 to 1220. The three Democratic assemblymen were also successful.

At a special town meeting of the inhabitants of the township of Salem on the sixteenth of April, 1839, it was ordered that the different streets of Salem receive the names listed below and that a board bearing the name of each street be erected thereon:

From the jail to the old Bridge—Market street.
From Market street to the Wind Mill—Broadway.
From Market street to the New Bridge—Griffith street.
From the Steam Mill to Broadway—Front street.
From Griffith street to Broadway (formerly Bond street)—
   Third street.
From Broadway to Howell's Landing—Penn street.
Fram Market street to Quaker Neck Causeway—Grant
   street.
From Market street to J. Tuft—Fenwick street.
From Grant street to Fenwick street—Johnson street.
From J. Tuft's to M. Keasbey—Quinton street.
From J. Tuft's to Elsinboro—Yorke street.
From Broadway to Elsinboro—Oak street.
Margaret Lane—South street.

CHAPTER XXII

SALEM IN THE 1840's

The period of the 1840's in Salem county was a period of restless activity. In it was massed a great amount of business progression and in it also was crowded a large number of startling events. Chief among the business enterprises foremost in that period and one which elicited a great deal of comment from the newspapers was the business of building ships. Salem county has never had the credit due her as a ship building center. At Thompson's Bridge, now Alloway, was one of the largest ship building plants in the Union. Reference has been made to it before but it was in the 1840's that this plant of the Reeves Brothers grew to its fullest extent. The papers of that day credited the Reeves Brothers for the growth of Alloway and indeed from the early accounts it was a busy place.

Launchings from the ship yards were frequent. Among ships which slid down the ways were the *Salem*, a proud ship of 550 tons; the *Towanda*, the *Stephen Baldwin*, the *Raccoon*, the *Columbus*, the *Belle of Mt. Holly* and the *Pons*. The launchings on Alloways Creek were glorified by one little paragraph written by Charles Perrin Smith in the National Standard in 1844 when he said: "Glory to little Alloways, a mere ditch, but a few rods in width and which looks as if it might be crossed by a couple of leaps, she has grown upon her banks and bourne upon her bosom some of the finest merchantmen that ever floated on the Delaware."

About the *Pons*, there is more than a brief account of its launching. It was built at Alloway in 1842, for a firm of ship owners in Philadelphia. At the time of its building all hands headed by Captain Graham who was to sail the new vessel, were invited to partake of a bountiful feast on its decks. It was not long after its launching that its owner sold it to some Spanish or Portugese men who converted it into a slave ship. Four years afterward, this bark was captured off Sierra Leone, Africa by the American sloop of war, *Yorktown*, Captain Bell, and a British frigate. Investigation revealed that under her decks were impressed 1896 slaves who were being taken to America to replenish the Southern slave trade. The description sent into

Washington by Captain Bell beggars description. When the slavers started they had over 2000 slaves in the hold, but some of them had been tossed overboard to make room for the others. If one wishes to read a vile story of men engaged in the slave trade, he has only to read the narrative in the Salem newspapers of 1846 concerning Captain Bell's discoveries when he captured the *Pons*. The remaining slaves were liberated, the ship confiscated by the American government and its name changed to the *Cordelia*.

Other ships manufactured by Reeves Brothers in the flourishing ship yard at Alloway had more creditable records. Up and down the coast of North America these ships plied their way bringing money, produce and goods to the ports of the young nation. It was not until later in this decade when the supply of white oak failed in the neighboring region that the Reeves Brothers were forced to give up this lucrative business. Little remains of the famous ship yard today but the older citizens of Alloway still remember, by location only, where this ship yard stood.

There were other ship yards along Alloways Creek and Salem Creek, some of which survived long after this one had gone. There were Bradstreet's ship yard at Quinton's Bridge and later Townsend's ship yard in Salem. Today, except for two small shops which build and repair small launches only, there is little left of this great industry which in the 1840's was on the front page of many American newspapers.

Twenty years before the Civil War the question of slavery agitated the people of Salem county. It has been noted that in 1835 there was a dispute in Salem City over the question of the re-possession of some negro slaves from Maryland. This agitation continued through the 1840's. In the neighboring county of Cumberland in Stowe Creek township, just across the line from Salem county in 1840, a number of slave owners from Maryland came across the river and seized an entire negro family of eleven people, dragging them back in chains to Maryland, this time undeterred by any commotion such as attended the affair of 1835.

But if the slavers were successful in reclaiming some few slaves from the eastern shore of Maryland there were those who, fugitives from their masters, found safe haven in Salem county. The 1840's was indeed the period of the underground railroad. It was in this decade that the Quakers of this county, long friendly to the slaves, formulated plans whereby these fugitive negroes from the South might be taken care of. Lee, in his history of New Jersey, describes the underground railroad as working successfully in Salem county because of the friendly feeling manifested towards the slaves by the Quakers of this section.

Briefly, the trail of the underground railroad ran thus: the Quakers would see the negro safe across the Delaware river at some point near the river shore in Elsinboro, then would convey him from farm to farm under cover of night from Elsinboro into Salem, from Salem into Mannington, from Mannington into Pilesgrove, and eventually into Gloucester county. It seems that the Quakers and farmers of this locality took upon themselves the responsibility of forwarding the slaves.

Along with the interest of the Friends in helping the colored slaves escape from their masters was the establishment of the first colored school in Salem county. It seems to have been established in a cabin on Yorke street, Salem, about 1843. The Friends were the leaders in this enterprise, setting up the school and installing Ismael Lock, a colored man, as the teacher.

On the religious side, the 1840's saw a large increase in the organization of religious societies in this section. In 1846, the first Methodist church in Penns Grove was dedicated, that being the Emanuel Methodist Church organized at Helms Cove, South Penns Grove, in 1846.

In 1848, the Roman Catholics met for the first time in Salem City in Ward's Hall, a building still standing on the corner of Griffith and Ward streets. It was loaned to them by the Quaker owner of the building, George M. Ward. Here, until 1852, when their church was completed, the Catholics held their worship.

The new Baptist Church in Salem was finished in 1845 and opened for worship, supplanting the old Baptist Church on Yorke street, the site of which is now a Baptist cemetery. The bell in the tower of the new church rang for the first time on September 26, 1846, and was heard as far away as Sharptown. Some time later the clock was installed and served until 1903 when it was replaced by a new one.

A cause which contributed to the division of the Baptist Church was the famous law suit of the antipedo Baptist Society decided in the middle of the 1840's by the New Jersey chancellor. This suit grew out of an argument over the election of two boards of trustees for this church, which at the time the suit commenced was located on Yorke street. The legal ramifications do not concern us here. It is sufficient to say that the original board were successful and the second board, descending from their fellow members, were instrumental in forming a new church.

Queer sects were in Salem in those days. First came the "Shakers," a branch of the Quakers who believed in emotional religion. They accompanied their religious exercises with violent dancing, hence the name "Shakers." Of this sect the editor of the Salem National Standard said: "We imagine such insane proceedings as were represented could not emanate from any place other than a mad house."

The Millerites were also active in Salem in 1844. This sect believed in the second coming of Christ and the end of the world on a certain day in 1844. While the Millerites were more powerful in New England, there seem to have been a number of them in this county. The Millerites believed that when the Angel Gabriel blew his horn they would go out into the fields, put on their ascension robes and prepare for the judgment day. In a small town not very far from Salem some bad boys, knowing that a certain middle aged couple were devout Millerites, aroused them at midnight one night with an infernal blowing of tin horns. The couple, firmly believing that this was the end of the world, as set by their leader Miller, arrayed themselves in their robes, which were similar to night gowns, and came out into the street only to be met by a gang of mischievous boys.

The Mormons were also active in Salem at this time. Several of their missionaries came here for the purpose of securing converts, but there is no record that they were successful. A new Methodist church was dedicated at Pennsville. It was then known as the Lower Penns Neck Methodist Church.

The temperance societies were beginning to make themselves felt in the life of the county. Throughout this decade, there were frequent temperance parades. The Sons of Temperance were a feature of the Fourth of July parades held in this county.

But on the religious side of the decade's history, by far the most appealing and piteous note of all is the simple description of the funeral of a German Catholic, Joseph Sefriet by name, who died "in foreign lands" and was buried in the cemetery of the Society of Friends. Charles Perrin Smith, with his gifted pen, wrote a description of this moving scene in the National Standard of May 27th, 1845. The modern writer feels unable to reproduce the beautiful sentiment and style of Smith, who was an eye witness. The entire story is reproduced here as it was taken from the files of the Standard:

When the Bard of Avon denominated the world a stage, and the people its actors, he merely spoke with his usual truthfulness. How many little dramas are every day enacted in private life that need no touches or romance —no gas lights and tinsel to give them absorbing interest; but which become

CHURCHES IN THE 1840's

oblivious from the fact that all are too deeply engaged in the parts of their own play to give heed, or take interest sufficient to note, those of their neighbors. Here and there the more prominent fragments of a piece are observed, but generally so disconnected are they as to cause but a passing remark. One of these fragments from a life replete with misfortune and poverty has recently been the occasion of some conversation in this town, and we give it to our readers as it was told to us:

A family of Catholic Germans, consisting of the parents and four small children settled in Salem last year, and from disinclination to permit their wants to be made known, existed through the winter in the most abject poverty. About the commencement of spring the husband sickened and died, and the family thereby became reduced to the last extremity of wretchedness. The grief of the widow at her bereavement was intense, and for a time she refused to be comforted. Alone, in a foreign land, and (with the exception of her helpless children) surrounded by none but strange faces, it seemed as if the last crowning misfortune had filled her cup of misery to the brim. As there is no Catholic Cemetery in this neighborhood, the Friends with their usual kindness, offered the body of the deceased a resting place in their burying ground. This was gladly accepted, but a new difficulty arose. The widow, strongly imbued with the principles of the sect to which she had always belonged, would not consent to its interment without the formula of the Catholic burial service. There being no priest of her persuasion at hand, she applied to a worthy citizen to perform the ceremony; but he replied that he could not conscientiously act in the matter. Misconstruing his scruples, she exclaimed with earnestness—"Oh do!—the Pope will absolve you." He endeavored to prevail upon her to apply to someone else, but without effect. At length he asked, if it was not, under the circumstances, entirely requisite that a priest perform the ceremony, why she, being a good Catholic, could not act on the occasion? After a few moments' consideration, during which she appeared to be forcibly struck by the suggestion as something that had not before occurred to her, she consented to undertake the sad office.

An eye-witness of the interment and accompanying ceremony speaks of the scene as most affecting. A number of fellow countrymen of the deceased had collected round the grave, when the widow, with a sense of duty amounting to enthusiasm, and rising above the intense grief which had convulsed her, stood forward, and taking the earth upon a spade proceeded to consecrate it. She then went through with the solemn burial service of the Catholic Church in a manner so impressive as to bring tears from the eyes of many present long unused to the melting mode. The ceremony was concluded by the widow's offering appropriate and extremely eloquent prayer for the rest of her departed husband; and she turned from the grave for her desolate home and starving children apparently with every spark of hope extinguished in her bosom. But it is said that the darkest cloud has ever a bright star near it, and she found that her home was to be desolate and her children starving no longer. He who hearkens to the cry of the widow and the fatherless had raised them up friends in the hour of their extremest need. The death of the husband and the peculiar circumstances attending his funeral directed public attention to the family, when its destitute condition became known and immediate relief afforded.

During this decade people were a little more mindful of the humanities than they had been in previous years. It was the era of Dorothea Dix and her investigations of the various poor-houses of the state. Salem county did not miss a scathing denunciation of the conditions in its own local poorhouse. Her scornful comment on chained inmates freezing in a cold building are written large on the pages of her report to the legislative committee which she represented. Nor was that all. She told of seeing an aged man, once a judge of the Salem county courts, then a pauper and lunatic, who was allowed to mingle with the other inmates, raving crazy and dangerously mad. Such was the condition of the Salem county poor house, described by Miss Dix as one of the worst in the state when it burned to the ground in 1845.

The investigation bore fruit. The wrath of the people of Salem county was visited on the board of freeholders with the result that a new almshouse was erected in the year. The inmates were better treated and the insane were segregated from the paupers. The exposures of Dorothea Dix throughout the state led to the foundation of the first state insane asylum at Trenton. Well might it be called Dix Haven in her honor.

Events moved rapidly in this span of ten years which embraced the Mexican War and the gold rush. The temperance forces, rising in their might against the onrush of the liquor traffic, complained that the newly organized temperance hotel was being neglected by the cold water forces and that all the people desiring hotel accomodations passed up this hotel for the hostelries containing a bar. Incidentally, the temperance hotel held forth, until its closing in 1847, in the Alexander Grant House on Market street, now the home of the Salem County Historical Society, where today the old numbers may still be seen on the bedroom doors. Another temperance hotel was started in Penns Grove, but it too had only a brief existence.

A widow, farming for herself, advertised for a husband, commenting as a form of inducement that her dairy herd had produced a 1700-pound cake of cheese by milk from six cows. Tom Thumb (Charles Stratton) appeared in Salem at a public exhibition, the admission price being twenty-five cents. A rattlesnake with fourteen rattles was killed on the Telegraph road in Alloway in 1844. The Salem streets were in bad shape, so much so that an inebriated Irishman falling in one of the holes was, by kind friends, extricated therefrom. The adventure led the editor to say,

"We have lots of mud and water
Which lie in the streets
But hadn't orter."

The first nudist colony was squelched in Salem when, upon complaint of outraged citizens, the constable arrested several small boys for swimming nude in the waters of Salem creek during the hot summer of 1844.

Business was on the upturn. Mrs. Hunt announced that she served up "ice creams" on Saturdays, which was probably the first of the popular ice cream saloons. Another popular business first came into being in 1840 when an enterprising farmer living on the shores of the Delaware river opened the first bath house. The National Standard, in boosting its advertiser, seriously argued that one should take a bath at least once a month, that is in the summer months, and that here was a splendid opportunity. There was a flourishing woolen mill at Alloway and Reeves ship yard in the same place was busy making boats. Upon the launching of the *Express* the editor of the Standard once more gave his blessing, concluding his editorial peroration by saying "Success to her say we, and to whatever clime she wends her way may she not prove unworthy of the sterling qualities which characterize those who dwell on her native banks of Alloway."

The watch making and jewelry business of the Wheelers was established in 1844. It is one of the three oldest firms in Salem under its original name.

Another is the Salem Sunbeam, the Democratic newspaper of Salem which first shed the light of its existence on July 30, 1844. It is one of the oldest newspapers of the United States which has never changed its name or political allegiance in almost a century. Its coming was none too welcome in Salem. The previously established National Standard, which was once the Messenger and later the Freeman's Banner, looked with disdain upon the newcomer and said, sententiously enough, "The first number of a newspaper bearing the title 'Sunbeam' was issued in Salem on Saturday last and bears the name of Mr. Isreal Wells as editor and publisher. It is established by the Loco Foco (Democratic) party for the purpose as its name indicated of throwing light into this benighted region."

The third firm is the Salem National Bank, established in 1823 and divorced from the Steam Mill in 1826.

It was in 1840 that the willow causeway, of which a few tattered stumps still remain, was laid out to protect the exposed causeway on the road from Salem to Woodstown. There was another reason for its construction; several intoxicated persons, thinking the road broader than it was, had driven their teams into the adjoining marsh. Needing room for expansion, Salem opened a new street and appropriately called it Oak street in honor of the Old Oak which stands opposite its entrance. In 1841 the first daguerreotypes appeared in this city with competent artists, who advertised that they had reproduced by their modern methods, the crown heads of Europe. And in the same year, the last whipping at the jail was done on the back of a colored convict by Sheriff Johnson.

Editors could be very nasty in those days. Remembering the Revolution, one of them commented in the following style on the marriage of Queen Victoria: "Married in London on the 4th ultimo by the Rev. Dr. Canterbury, Mr. Albert Coburg of Saxe Coburg to Miss Victoria Guelph of the former place—No cake received." The last line refers to a time honored Salem custom of those days of giving the editor a slice of wedding cake for publishing the nuptials. If no cake was received the wedding notice was very scant; if a piece was sent, there were fulsome accounts of the "brilliant and accomplished bride."

* * * *

Not all the stories of Salem's past are of crimes and murders. Almost everything in the gamut of human experience happened here at least once. And in the exciting days of '49, when people were chasing gold and fleeing from the cholera, the local literati were much concerned with a case of plagiarism.

It must be remembered that the 1840's was a period of violent and prolific literary output. Anyone who could write did so, and sent the effusions at once to the local editors for publication. Take a look at the Salem papers of those days and you will find a vast and varied assortment of what might be classed as literature. The entire front pages of these journals are filled with sonnets and short stories, most of them by home talent for home consumption. They form an epic literary history in themselves and are well worthy of an English professor's attention.

Someone has called this literary period before the Civil War, the honeysuckle-columbine era of letters and the flowery title is well deserved. The Victorian period was on its merry way to historical glory and even the small towns across the seas reflected the influence.

It was a sign of social distinction to be an author in those days. It was also considered bad form to copy another's writings and pass them off as one's own. This is exactly what happened in the winter of 1849 in Salem, leaving the population in two well divided camps arguing whether or not a certain Salem literateur and lecturer was a plagiarist.

The Prescott Institute was a club composed of young Salem men who discussed in an open forum the burning questions of the day; it also provided an outlet for the current literary production. Here one night a member of the club, a young writer who called himself David of York and whose real name was David P. Brown, gave a lecture on "Woman and Her Influence," which seemed to be a roaring success, so successful in fact that a pleased auditor wrote this letter to the Sunbeam:

"Mr. B. ascended the platform and poured forth a continued stream of eloquence which commanded the whole and undivided attention of the persons convened. I conceive Mr. B. as a young man possessing more than ordinary talent, which if rightly cultivated, few years only will have to recede and he will be added to the cluster of stars that shine in the literary firmament."

Mr. Brown's ascending literary career as prophesied by the letter writer suffered a rude jolt in the next issue of the National Standard, for another letter writer, Mr. X, scornfully wrote: "The writer was not among those present that participated in the intellectual repast of last Thursday, but may be edified by a few remarks upon it. For those of your readers who formed a part of the audience, may when the veil of plagiarism, is removed, appreciate with true merits, the bold, contemptible course of the speaker.

"Dr. Meigs of the Jefferson Medical College has often delivered lectures entitled, Some of the Distinctive Characteristics of the Female, and your correspondent by careful perusal of Dr. Meigs' manuscript has found that the young speaker of the other evening has offered without any credit to the author, the total amount of nearly five pages."

The writer stopped with this awful revelation and the storm broke. The Prescott Institute was torn asunder by this charge against one of its most aspiring members. A committee issued a report that they had investigated Mr. Brown's speech and found it to be a "coincidence." This report was signed by Edward A. Acton, Samuel H. Sherron, Caleb Wheeler, Jacob M. Lippincott and Nehemiah Dunn. An interesting feature of this report is that with Mr. Lippincott's name, his famous poem of the Old Oak Tree is recalled.

The outbreak subsided for a very short time, but in the next issue of the Standard the inexorable Mr. X. dashed into print again and delivered another blow to the literary ambitions of the beleaguered Mr. Brown.

It seems that Mr. Brown, under his nom de plume of David of York, had in a moment of exuberance written a four stanza poem in a young lady's album, which were all the rage in those days and although the young lady had given her heart to another, her album still contained the lovely sentiments conveyed by David.

Mr. X. in his second letter printed the following, which he had taken from the album:

LINES WRITTEN IN A LADY'S ALBUM

By David of York
For these may ever blooming spring,
New life and light prepare,
And every transient moment bring
Fresh roses for thy hair.
Or thought of ill or worldly care.
Ne'er may thy bosom know
Whose laughing eyes ne'er drooped a tear
But for another's woes.
May peace thy footsteps still attend
When past thy youthful hours,
Nor age steal on without a friend
To strew thy paths with flowers.
And when the allotted years have sped
By inspiration given.
May angel's watch around thy bed,
To guard the way to heaven.

This disturber of Mr. Brown's literary slumbers then submitted the same poem, by George Broome, with something like ten words changed, as published in Neal's Saturday Gazette for February 15, 1845.

This was too much. The excitement broke all over again and for a few weeks little was published except controversial letters over David and his alleged plagiarism. This time the Prescott Institute did not attempt to say that this was a coincidence. They left this warm issue alone, officially at least. But some of the members resigned, splitting the club into two parts, those for David and those against him. The town paired off much the same way and the two papers got on opposite sides of the fence. The Sunbeam, where David had found an outlet for his literary effusions, supported him, while the Standard gave space to the detractors of the poet.

Finally the much abused Mr. Brown turned on his tormentors and in an open letter to the public declared himself in no uncertain terms. He began, "I am Mr. David P. Brown, the humble author of the piece in question, now disprove it if you can."

After vigorously asserting his own original authorship of the lecture and the poem, he censured his "envious detractors" thus: "Yet there are some miserable beings in this world and for aught I know in this beautiful town of Salem, whose narrow minds and empty heads will not permit them to merit anything but what is low and mean."

Shouting defiance to the multitude, David closed his defense peroration in fine style: "Now, let them come on. I am ready, yea, in the language of one, always ready whilst truth is on my side. Charge! Chester! Charge! and if I fall I hope I shall fall defending my just claims."

It was apparently not necessary for "Chester to charge," as the Salem townsfolk soon grew weary of the contention and after a few more gasps, the literary episode of the gold rush year was over.

David of York, however, kept up for several months his barrage of contributions to the Sunbeam. He even started to write a novel entitled "Tom Holbrook," or "The Plagiarist," but after one installment in which he set out his own difficulties in that line, he started a new novel called "Kate Walton," or "Her First Love." The reason why "Tom Holbrook" soon ceased was because the Sunbeam hesitated to anger a prominent Salem dentist, Dr. Samuel C. Harbert, who was the one Mr. Brown was gunning for. Dr. Harbert, the mysterious Mr. X. who exposed David of York, was the brother-in-law of Charles Perrin Smith, the gifted editor of the National Standard. "Massianello," or "The Poor Fisherman of Naples," likewise had a start, but no finish. After a time, he devoted himself to courting the muse of Pegasus and weekly turned out a poem. One of his final efforts was this:

> I have a pretty blue eyed coz;
>   With pouting lips of red,
> No zephyr breathes more sweet than does
>   The music of her tread.
> As white as is the Alpine snows,
>   Are her bright brows as fair
> Like rose buds, which the south wind blows,
>   Her blooming cheeks are e'er.

Charles Perrin Smith was a good judge of literary works. To the young hopefuls who offered to fill his paper with literary effusions, he proved a friendly critic. To one such poet he said: "The lines by Orlando, addressed to his dulcinea, are excreable and we think the writer acted judiciously in with-holding his name. We give a few lines as a specimen:

> Oh, Mary the lustre of thy dark eyes,
>   Fairly puts me in extacies."

He complimented Alpha-Lita and Aloza upon their "lovely and moving" verse but said he published an effusion by Pithus only because he desired to give the ambitious writer another chance. One may find the "poetry" of Pithus in the National Standard for December 22, 1847.

December 8, 1840 saw a heavy snow storm hit this county. Mr. John M. Thomas of Salem and a Mr. Carter were journeying from Salem to Camden to visit the ill mother of the former on this day. Storm-beaten and snow-bound they sought admittance to the hotel of Matthew Knisell at Woodbury. Refused admittance to the hotel, they plunged through the storm. Thomas took his pen in hand and published in the Salem paper a blast at Knissel, urging all travellers to boycott his hotel. "The public will please remember what a cold and snowy night it was."

Lower Alloways Creek township was justly proud of the fact that for the five years between 1839 and 1844 there were only two indictments for crime against citizens of that township. One of these died before trial and the other was acquitted. Francis McCullough and Richard Parrott Thompson were the prosecutors for Salem county in this period. Thompson had the honor at this time of being a member of the Board of Visitors to the West Point Military Academy.

Thomas Ware died March 11, 1842. Well might the Methodist clergyman say at his funeral: "Well done, thou good and faithful servant." In the death notices also at this time was the obituary of Jacob Horner of Salem, aged 85 years, who drove a baggage wagon in the Revolution and crossed the Delaware in the same boat with George Washington on Christmas night, 1776. The well loved Prescott, rector of St. Johns, died at sea in the spring of 1844. A tablet in his memory is on the wall of the church.

John Jeffers died at Galveston, Texas in 1842. He was the man who was horsewhipped on Star Corner, Salem, after having "broken the steam mill," according to his enemies. His brother, William N. Jeffers, had some years before moved to Camden, where he died in 1853, but in this year of 1842 he was busy in the famous murder case of the State versus Mercer.

In July of 1847 Dr. Elijah Griffiths died in Salem. He had been an intimate friend of Thomas Jefferson. Jacob Bryant of Salem died at the age of 97. He had served the Continental Army in the battles of Trenton, Princeton and Monmouth.

Cholera swept Salem in the gold rush summer of 1849. Captain Boon of the *Clifton* died of it, having contracted the disease on his run to Philadelphia. In the house of one Brooks in Mannington four people of that home died in one day.

The Standard of August 15, 1849 contains a harrowing description of the escape of Eli Adams from a maniac. Adams lived on the Salem-Quinton road and was awakened one night by hearing someone crash a window. He investigated and found himself face to face with a madman wielding an axe. Crying for help, he defended himself until neighbors could subdue the madman.

The *Pioneer* arrived in Salem one summer evening with its captain highly indignant. That afternoon as the boat was passing Catharine street wharf in South Philadelphia a young lad stood on the dock and wildly gesticulated for the boat to stop. Hurriedly the boat went into reverse and churned water to make the stop. The boy then yelled to the captain, "Buy a Ledger?"

Steamboat racing was the order of the day. There were competing lines with fares as low as 12½ cents a round trip. The best story of what fearful chances these captains took to maintain the "honor" of their boats comes from William Patterson's paper on Salem steamboats delivered before the Salem Historical Society in 1891:

On Saturday morning, July 19, 1842, as the old clock on the Statehouse was telling the hour of 10 A. M., the steamboat *New Jersey* (a new and large boat put on the line in place of the *Pioneer*, by Jacob Ridgeway, on purpose to out-run the *Clifton*) was casting off her lines from Race street wharf. As she passed the *Clifton*, at Arch street wharf, she gave three defiant whistles, and then like a giant swimmer made her foaming path down the Delaware and was soon out of sight. Half an hour later the *Clifton* tapped her bell and quietly slipped from her moorings, then like a greyhound, straightened herself out for the chase. As soon as she passed the bend of the river the double pipes of the *New Jersey*, pouring forth clouds of black smoke, could be seen in the far distance. An hour before the *Clifton* left Philadelphia several drayloads of musty lard came on the wharf. The barrels were rolled on board and quietly placed near the fireroom, to be used with the fatpine wood, in order to increase heat without much smoke. When the two boats came in sight the excitement on board of each was intense. The stops at the various landings along the route were short and hurried. Every barrel, box or bag was on the barrows, and passengers, with satchel in hand, stood ready to jump as soon as she touched the wharf. And Robert M. Boon could bring his boat just where she should be in a few minutes. In looking down into the fire room one could see four men busy, putting in wood and throwing in shovels filled with large balls of lard, which would crack like a pistol when they touched the fire. The safety valve had been fastened down, and Platt, the engineer, stood at his post, ever ready to put his hand on the shut-off, that if anything should get wrong to throw the engine out of gear in an instant, and every now and then calling to the firemen below, asking the height of water in the boiler. When the reply came up, "all right," it was replied to saying, "then pass up the steam." The boiler was making all the steam the cylinder could use, and it took all that came. At New Castle the distance was but short between them, and they arrived at Delaware City together. Then it was certain, as the *New Jersey* was the larger boat, she must go down the river and follow the channel, while the *Clifton* could cross the flats and enter the creek first. Just then a Salem lady asked Captain Boon to run up the flags. He asked, "What for? Have we been racing?" Her reply was; "I had several friends with me going to Salem, who took the other boat, because they wished to go on the fast boat. So I left them to come with you, because I knew you would get home first. And now, Captain, if you decline to run up your flags,

I will not go in this boat again." So up the flags went. Soon after the creek was entered the fire was drawn, having enough steam to take her to the wharf, which fact gave the boys a pretext for saying, "the Boons for economy, have the fire always drawn at Broad Reach, and let Platt work the boat to the wharf with the starting bar." There was a crowd on the wharf when the boats arrived. Boon's firemen were on deck, with coats on, leaning on the rail, as if nothing like hot work had been done. But the crowd was surprised when someone took a peep in the fire room and saw little or no fire and no steam to blow off. The papers say, "The *Clifton* made this trip and all her stops, in three hours and four minutes." After this the company advertised, "No racing."

Speaking of steamboats, the streets of Salem were so bad in 1845 that someone made application to run a steamboat from the steamboat wharf to Penny Hill on Broadway.

More seriously, another application was entertained to start a steamship line between Allowaystown and Philadelphia, for Reeves' ship yard was flourishing at the time. There was also agitation to run a steamship between Pedricktown and Philadelphia. One finally started between Helm's Cove and Wilmington, which gave added impetus to the growth of Penns Grove. Not to be outdone, Pittsgrove residents agitated a canal to connect Muddy Run, Maurice river and the Cohansey, the purpose being to give steamship transportation to those parts.

A young man named Howe travelled on foot throughout Salem county in 1843 writing history. The result was Barber and Howe's Historical Collections of New Jersey which is now at a premium to secure. The charcoal sketches of Salem places are extremely good and the originals have changed little in nearly a century.

1844 witnessed the horrible riots of the "Native Americans" against the Catholics in Philadelphia. The burning of their sanctuaries caused page after page of space in the Salem paper. Colonel Robert G. Johnson delivered a lecture on "Popery" in the Salem Lyceum. Leonard Gibbon, a Salem man, but at that time an editor of a Kentucky newspaper, was murdered by a Kentuckian because of disparaging remarks made about the assassin in his paper.

A Salem citizen burning with desire to change the name of America, suggested that the name "Winnipisbogania," should be adopted and that it "most nearly embodied all the tribal and aboriginal Indian names in use."

The Mexican War attracted little attention in Salem. The opponents of the Polk administration cried out that this was a Democratic war and that only Democrats should fight. There was some recruiting done in Salem but the volunteers were few. At that, when the casualty lists poured in from the Mexican

THE 1840's

battlefields there were Salem men therein. John Humphreys of Penns Neck left his job on a steamboat to enlist and was killed at Cherubusco. The Odd Fellows Lodge paraded in his honor and a local bard wrote poetry in his memory. John Miller, a Salem drayman, was killed at Monterey. Charles Randolph of Upper Alloways Creek died of disease on the Rio Grande and John Winters died at Jalapa. More fortunate than his fellows from Salem, Amos Garrison rose to be a commissary general in the United States army and fought through to Santa Fe with Doniphan. Josiah Pancoast was also a commissary in Taylor's army. He brought home trophies of the war and in addition, a Mexican boy. In 1850, a fever stricken soldier, George W. Leeds, returned home to Salem after two years' absence. A neighbor from Mullica Hill whose family was also in this county, received immortality from this war. He was Samuel French, whose bravery won him a Congressional award and a sword from the State of New Jersey. French does not disappear from the history of this county. In the Civil War, when he was a brigadier general of the Confederacy, the home folks of Salem and Gloucester counties rose in fraternal hatred to blast him as a traitor.

* * * *

The brutal, coldblooded slaying of Irvin Hite, colored woodchopper, in 1932, which is as yet unsolved, recalls that in the same wild tract of the pine forest known as the "Barrens," another gruesome murder happened almost a hundred years ago, ending in the most celebrated murder trial held in Salem before the Treadway case.

Harrison had been elected president of the United States and had just passed out of the mundane portrait after his inauguration and the local papers were still carrying sable borders in token of the event, when one William Lovell, peacefully pursuing his way through the Barrens on a beautiful April afternoon made a discovery, the news of which the Freeman's Banner, the only Salem paper at that time, published and started the agitation destined to end in the case of the State versus William Cain for murder.

This is the startling intelligence the Banner flashed to the breeze on April 20, 1841, and gave the staid town of Salem something to talk about for the next few months:

SUPPOSED MURDER

Considerable excitement has been caused among the inhabitants of Upper Alloways Creek by the discovery of a human skeleton, which leads many to suppose that a murder had been recently committed in the vicinity. We are told that only a short time since a person had occasion to enter a lone piece of woods a few miles below Quinton Bridge near Turnip Hill where he discovered a skull and other bones belonging to the human frame. Upon examination he found evidence of a grave, one foot deep, where the body had been partially interred and had been dragged out and partially devoured by dogs or other wild animals. It is supposed that from the aspect of the bones, hair, and parts of clothing, that the body could not have been interred for a long time.

A coroner's jury at a properly declared inquest states that the bones were those of a human female and that the unknown came to her death at the hands of persons unknown.

The authorities are endeavoring to get the facts, fully and completely upon this shocking crime and when they are completed with their work, we shall be glad to give them the space the affair merits.

A week later, upon information given by residents of the Barrens section of Upper Alloways Creek Township, one William Cain, also a resident of that section, was arrested charged with the murder of Caroline T. Hull and was given a preliminary hearing before George Bush and John M. Brown, Esquires, magistrates. The Freeman's Banner, unlike the modern newspaper, which would proceed to try the defendant then and there, proceeded to say, "We refrain from stating any part of the evidence upon which the prisoner was arraigned so that the Grand Jury may act without prejudice in the case at the proper time."

The grand Jury found an indictment against William Cain for the murder of Caroline T. Hull, although the corpus delicti in the case was rather weak and no one identified the bones found near the grave as those of the aforesaid Caroline. Still, this was in an era when courts were not overcareful in the matter of the corpus as a previous New Hampshire case will testify. In this case, a certain man was hanged for the murder of his friend and neighbor with whom he was last seen and whose body was not found up to the time of the poor man's hanging.

The trial missed the spring term and came up for issue on September 24, 1841 before Justice Daniel Elmer of the Supreme Court with the usual array of "flower pot" judges, to wit: Thomas Sinnickson, Henry Freas and John M. Brown, who was the committing magistrate. For the state appeared none less than George P. Mollesson, the attorney general of New Jersey who was assisted by Francis L. McCullough, prosecutor of Salem county. Murder trials at that period were sufficiently rare to attract the attention of the attorney-general himself. For the defendant Cain appeared Samuel A. Allen, better known as an author than as a lawyer because it was he who wrote the famous, "My Own Home and Fireside," and with him as counsel was associated the man whom he pilloried so bitterly in the same book, Alphonso L. Eakin.

THE BARRENS MURDER

The jury deserves more than passing attention as we shall see later, so their names are given in full. The foreman was Bartholomew Coles and the rest of the panel was composed of William Pancoast, Henry Buck, Smith Dare, John Woodsides, Andrew Smith, Peter Stretch, William Fogg, Luke Dancer, David Shoemaker, Tobias Casperson and Eleazer Harris.

The evidence was purely circumstantial. William Lovell, whose walk took him to the fatal spot, testified again as to the finding of the bones. He said they were on the old Burden place, near the residence of Noah Cain, brother of William, and with whom the defendent lived, and beside the loose bones he found a stocking, quanties of hair and a part of a calico dress.

It seems that the entire medical force of Salem county was called into the case because the records show that Doctors Thompson, Yarrow, Sharp, Keasbey and Gibbon all took the stand to declare that the bones were that of a female, aged about 20 years and further, that the bones had been exposed to the elements a long time.

The next witness came very close to hanging Cain for it was on his testimony that the state almost proved its case. A reliable negro slave was called to the stand, one William Howard, who lived in the Barrens on the road to Quinton's Bridge and who told the following story: On a wild winter night approximately a week after New Year's, 1840, he and his wife, who kept a semi-public house, were at home entertaining two white men, Caleb Smith and the defendant, William Cain, when a girl aged about twenty appeared at the door and said she was Caroline T. Hull who was coming to visit a relative, Jim Fisher who lived nearby, but that she was exhausted and asked permission to spend the night at Howards, which permission was granted her. She came in and after talking with Mr. Smith a while passed him to chat with Cain and forgetting her "exhaustion", romped with him around the parlor of the Howard house. After a while she declared that she had decided to spend the night at Cain's house "so she could cook breakfast for him" and soon went out with Cain. The witness declared that the girl wore a calico dress and swore that the material found in the woods looked like the same cloth to him. Before leaving the negro's home Cain borrowed a cloak for the girl from Howard's wife, which he later returned.

The next day, when Cain returned the cloak, which had broken clasps and showed signs of misuse, he told the Howards that the girl changed her mind about going home with him and had left him to go to the home of Neddy Roberts, where she stayed all night.

James Fisher and his wife, who were the pair the missing girl had set out to visit, told the jury that they had never seen the girl despite the fact that Mrs. Fisher said that Caroline was a relative of hers. Maria Fisher went on to inform the jury rather damningly that Cain was "no good" and that he had told her recently while in his cups, that "it was no job to kill anybody because he knew how." Mrs. Fisher concluded that Cain was "fit to be hanged and rather wanted the jury to hang him." Mrs. Fisher, who seemed to be well up on the defendant's remarks, also stated that when arrested Cain had declared that "he was ready to be tried and would be glad to get hanged and to go to hell at once if the court fellows thought he was guilty."

One notices, however, that when the time came for the defendant's case that his willingness dissipated a little because he did not take the stand in his own defense. Sarah Cain, the wife of Noah, brother of William, with whom the defendant lived, denied all knowledge of William coming home that particular night and bringing "a lady with him" although she admitted it was possible for the brother-in-law to have come in the house without disturbing her or her husband.

The only other evidence in the trial to show that the bones of the corpus were really those of Caroline came from a shoemaker, John Moore, who testified that a shoe found in the rubbish near the grave had been one made by him for the late Caroline at the order of one Joseph Inskeep, who had hired Caroline as a domestic for a time and had given her a new pair of boots. Grateful for the boots, Caroline had stolen a bolt of cloth from Inskeep and had been arraigned in Salem before a magistrate for the offense.

With a chain of circumstantial evidence and no absolute identification the jury retired after a day and a half of trial at at noon on Saturday, September 25, 1841. Tradition has it that after an hour's deliberation, the venire decided to hang Cain and were half-way out of the jury room to return their verdict when John Woodsides called the jury back saying, "Boys, I think we better not hang this fellow on the evidence we have now, we had better talk it over again." So, the jury trooped back to remain in wrangled discussion for five more hours at the end of which time they finally gave a verdict of guilty of murder in the second degree. Justice Elmer gave the prisoner fourteen years in the penitentiary at Trenton and the case was finished in the courts, but not in public opinion. The Banner blazed forth in this strain:

"Such a monster of iniquity should have never gone unhung if the lives of peaceful men and women of this God fearing community are to be safe.

The circumstantial evidence in this case was full and complete indicating without doubt or cavil that this vile person was clearly guilty of murder and only a technicality in the law (which leaves some of us to doubt at times, the wisdom of such procedure) saved this man from the full penalty of the law. The public is fully convinced of the guilt of the defendant and although he has escaped the noose which was so fitted for him, yet the public is gratified that the disclosure of this crime in time to save another heinous offense. For we are creditably informed that had it not been for his arrest, the blood of another might have stained his hands."

The Banner, equally solicitous of the morals of its readers as it was of publishing the facts too early in the case, said that the recent disclosures of the case made it imperative that all the details should not be published in the paper but that a fully competent person had been engaged to write the "full details and facts in pamphlet form and in justice to them, would refrain from further publication." If the pamphlet contained what outside talk proclaimed, then it might rival the lurid magazines which one sees today.

It was said that Cain was a "Bluebeard," that he had lived with Caroline Hull for quite some time and tiring of her had strangled her and buried her in the woods near his home until the hogs had eaten her and thrown her bones out of the shallow grave. That, unsatisfied with one victim, he had imported another female housekeeper with whom he had lived for another period of time until the very night of his arrest when he had attempted to choke her and was prevented from committing another murder only by the timely advent of the constable with the warrant.

As with most "Blue beards," this one was successful in missing the gallows because he had taken a typical waif of society with no one interested in her behalf and for whom no one ever took the trouble to look and had disposed of her in a locality but little frequented in those days of limited transportation. The folk of the Barrens, then as now, minded their own business and if Cain's brother and sister had moved out to allow him to remain alone with a "housekeeper" then it was no one's affair but his, and the countryside paid no attention. Not until he was arrested did the stories of his queer behavior penetrate beyond the Barrens.

The actors in this tragic drama of nearly a hundred years ago are gone but among the older residents of Upper Creek, now Quinton Township, the story handed down by their forefathers, is still told of the hogs eating the dead girl and of Cain's mastery in crime. Among the more superstitious of the Barrens folk, the tradition lingers that annually on a night soon after New Year's the ghost of Caroline Hull, clad in a calico dress and a new pair of boots, stalks the woods on Burden's Hill.

Three years after the murder, Richard P. Thompson, attorney general of New Jersey, while attending the Constitutional Convention at Trenton, wrote to his home in Salem that William Cain had sent for him in the state prison at Trenton where he was dying of an incurable disease, and confessed to him that he had actually killed Caroline T. Hull. Cain died in prison about 1847.

* * * *

From the History of Salem, Cumberland and Gloucester Counties by Cushing and Sheppard, the following biographical note is taken:

Samuel A. Allen, Salem lawyer, was born in 1813. He studied law in the offices of Richard P. Thompson, Attorney General of New Jersey and was admitted to practice in 1841 as an attorney and as a counselor in 1844. Lacking the usual mental legal qualities for a good lawyer, he became successful for his untiring energy and in such a fashion built up a large practice. Perhaps one of the most noted circumstances of his life and by which he is best remembered is the fact of his having written a book, entitled, "My Own Home and Fireside," in which a number of the leading society people of Salem at that time were held up to ridicule. The book which came anonymously created quite a stir in the society circles of the town. The demand for it was so great that the first edition was exhausted and it was necessary to print a second edition. Mr. Allen moved from Salem to Burlington soon after this book was published and finally settled near Germantown in Philadelphia. He died there in his 67th year, December 8th, 1879.

The book was written in 1846, published in London and appeared to be written by "SYR," at least that was the name on the title page. It was not hard, however, to ascribe it to Allen and the rumor of passing years has always connected him with it, although he never admitted it.

The book was of absolutely no literary value. It is valuable only to show a contemporary picture of Salem in the 1840's and to illustrate the vast gulf of social cleavage existing between one class of society and the one which Allen tried to represent as being downtrodden. In fact, it was the inability to crash the gate of Salem's society which caused Allen to write this diatribe. Added to this was his disappointment in being refused by a certain Salem lady.

As a brief sociological study it might be well worthwhile to digress a moment to comment on the question of social snobbery. Many pages might be written on the distinction of different classes in the period immediately preceeding the Civil War. It must be remembered that the gulf of political social cleavage had been partially bridged by Jackson's election and the emergence of the masses in American political life for the first time.

But in the old provincial towns where tradition and custom

changed but slowly, it was not easy for men with social aspirations to gain the level of this old aristocracy. Deeply imbedded in the minds of the descendants of the first settlers was the thought that they were the chosen people in all lines of endeavor and even the surge of democracy from across the Alleghenies could not shake this conviction.

Up to comparatively a few years ago visitors were wont to criticise the attitude of the Salemites as one of contemptuous indifference to those not of their caste. With the years and the widespread growth of democracy the distinction has come almost to the vanishing point.

In addition, the 1840's and the 1850's were periods of national tight-fistedness, not to say, in some cases, plain stinginess. Labor only got what the mill owners thought they should have. The spirit of gentle charity in almost all human relations was very small indeed. Even in Salem county this spirit of venal gain is emphasized by two little anecdotes.

A farmer in lower Creek had two runaway slaves come to his farm for refuge about the time the fugitive slave law began to vex the nation. He kept them during harvest season, used them in the fields, profited by their labor and then when the crops were gathered casually remarked to them that he had heard their master was in Salem looking for them. It was no doubt an excellent way to get rid of them without payment for their services. In all events it worked. Another traditional tale is that of the tight-fisted Salem farmer who used one mackerel for ten farm hands for their breakfast.

At any rate, Allen wrote and published "My Home and Fireside," which rated as a literary effort in these days, but now strikes the reader as a pretty fearful book. One hundred of this three hundred-paged effusion are amply sufficient for anyone to read through. It is alleged that Allen furnished a key for the edification of his readers who might want to know who certain characters, dressed up in early Victorian nomenclature, might actually be. If he did, although it seems unlikely, it would have been very easy to sue him for criminal libel, of which there is much in the book.

Regardless of this, it was fairly easy for the Salemites of that day to recognize themselves and their friends in the guise of such high flown names as Colonel Norissima, Alexander Grimbane, Dr. Lackumsmack, and others.

The publication of this book did at least draw gasps of horror from the dramatis personae contained within. While not admitted into the inner circles, Allen knew a great deal and what he did not know was easy to invent. The sale of the book was frenzied and for good reasons. Many a bonfire was lit with the blazing corpse of this awful publication and as soon as the second edition appeared, more found their way to the funeral pyre. So thoroughly did these outraged Salemites do their work that today it is exceedingly difficult to find a single copy throughout Salem county. One public spirited citizen who was also attacked by the book but enjoyed his "ride," donated his copy to the Salem Library but it soon disappeared from there.

The volume abounds in love-making of the most approved Victorian type. Some of them are violent enough to cause need for a restorative. In one of them Grimbane, the master fiend of this melodrama, rigs up his hostler as a Southern gentleman, in order to court and marry a certain young lady whom Grimbane is desirous of possessing himself. So he arranges it by proxy. The hostler appears in the garb of a cotton planter and utters the most marvelous effusions of love to the object of his attentions.

Here is a sample: The scene is at the seashore where in a beautiful sylvan bower overlooking the sea, Colonel Norissima says to his fair lady who "hangs swooningly upon his every word"; "Come with me, my darling, to that beautiful Elysian shore, where the reverberating waves croon a lullaby of eternal everlasting love and the nightingales sing all night long their lyric of unending bliss. By those waters, we may spend our days in the joy that knows no ceasing. Again I beseech you to come with me to the vale of happiness. Wilt thou not away?"

The eloquence of the colonel, we are glad to say, was not wasted. The fair lady married the southern gentleman and was all set to go where the "nightingales crooned," when she discovered that he was only a hostler and the real power behind the throne was the dreadful Grimbane. She then fainted "swooningly away" with a mixture of shrieks and sighs.

At the end of the book, if the gentle reader can last until the end, all the wicked characters meet their just dues and all the good men and women who display the admirable characteristics demanded by the exacting author are rewarded with peace, prosperity and happiness just as it should be in all such well regulated homes.

* * *

The Salem Academy was flourishing under Henry Freeman as principal. Back in 1787 the Johnson family had deeded land to the Salem Academy. Col. Robert G. Johnson, the son of one of the donors, was now a trustee, along with Thomas Sinnickson and Josiah Harrison. The colored schools, fostered largely by the Friends, had started. The earliest teachers were John S.

Rock and Ishmael Locke, both of whom Shourds remembers in his History of Fenwick's Colony. Rock was a leader in calling a convention of colored folk in 1849 to obtain equal suffrage with the whites. Lock went to Liberia on the west coast of Africa as a teacher in the cause of educating his race.

Harrison, defeated by Van Buren, was boomed for president early in 1840. Whig Young Men's Clubs were formed. After his nomination a thousand people paraded from Woodstown to Sharptown with a canoe, log cabin and a barrel of cider prominently displayed.

The Whigs did not toil in vain. Harrison carried Salem county by 1582 to Van Buren's 1302. Kille, the Democrat survivor of the Broad Seal War, went down to defeat for his congressional seat to Thomas Jones Yorke, a Whig. Seventy-six guns were fired in honor of the Whig president.

The joy over Harrison's election was short lived. A short month after his inauguration he died. John Tyler, really a Democrat, succeeded him and the fight was on for the next three years between Tyler and the Whigs. Funeral obsequies were held for the late president in Salem. Rev. William Prescott of St. Johns Episcopal Church gave the sermon and the ladies attending were requested to wear a black band of mourning on their left sleeves.

The Democrats won in 1841 in an extremely close contest. Alexander G. Cattell essayed to win a place in the State Council, now the Senate, but failed by 48 votes. The winner was James Newell. Two of the assemblymen were Democrats and one a Whig. Samuel Prior of Salem was this year named as clerk of the assembly. In 1843 the Democrats won again, electing Robert Newell sheriff and the entire legislative ticket.

For a long time there had been controversy in New Jersey over a new constitution. There had been too many lawyers to suit the people. The chancellor and the governor were combined in one office and the governor was not elected by the people but by a joint session of the legislature. There were many other reasons why a new constitution was advisable. The agitation came to a head in 1844 when the people voted on the question of electing delegates and submitting the new draft of organic law to the people.

The election for delegates proceeded harmoniously enough in Salem. Party lines were forgotten and a union slate agreed upon. Two were Democrats, Richard P. Thompson and John H. Lambert. The third was a Whig, Alexander Cattell, later a Republican United States senator. All were young men. Cattell was but 29, Thompson 39 and Lambert 45. The work of the convention was later approved by the county, the vote being 648 for adoption against 331. Majorities against it carried in Elsinboro, Lower Creek, Lower Neck and Pilesgrove; the others favored the new constitution.

The first election for governor by the people saw a Gloucester county man elected to the executive chair. This was Charles Stratton of Swedesboro whose beautiful early American home still stands on the banks of Raccoon Creek. Incidentally, the Standard raised a rumpus because Stratton gave Salem county no patronage. The Whigs carried Salem county, although their hero, Henry Clay, running with Theodore Frelinghuysen of New Jersey, went down in defeat before Polk, the Democrat. The Whigs were largely successful in this decade. They won again in 1845, electing Benjamin Acton to the senate, although two Democrats, Bilderback and Remster, slipped in with one Whig assemblyman, Ephraim Carll.

The Whig party had several leaders at the time. Ben Acton, Thomas Jones Yorke and Charles Perrine Smith were three of the leaders. Smith devoted his National Standard to the Whig cause and at this time (1847) had not split with the other Whig leaders. This he did some years later, leaving two of his old allies in his memory book as being "Mr. X. nearly everything." He meant Acton and Yorke, who had run for practically every office in the county.

Of 1847, Smith wrote in his memoirs, "This year I engaged in the Post Office War." It really was an acrimonious affair but even at that, not as bitter as the Jeffers-Brooks controversy of twenty years previously.

Solomon Merritt was then the Democrat postmaster of Salem. A "renegade" Whig president, Tyler, had named him and another man as postmaster on the same day but as Merritt's commission was dated first, he was allowed to keep it. The fact of his appointment by a Whig president incensed the Whigs and they had been "after" Merritt for some time. The storm broke over which newspaper should receive the advertising for unclaimed letters. It was supposed, theoretically, that the postmaster should give it to the paper with the largest circulation. Smith's paper had the largest circulation but the new Democratic paper, the Sunbeam, got the job from Merritt.

For weeks Smith used a column or more of print in "riding" Merritt. Joseph Kille, Democratic leader, cancelled his subscription to the Standard and said Smith abused him. Smith then turned on Kille and said that he had written the various articles of defense published by Merritt. Smith added that

Merritt "was known to be totally incompetent to write even a line of the rejoinder to which his name was signed." After much abuse, the controversy became funny. Someone lost a letter and claimed the post office brown mouse ate it. Someone else alleged that Merritt waited in a hurry on only the pretty girls. A middle-aged female, not answering the above classification, received a letter, thrown at her by the postmaster, which hit the floor. She promptly threw it back and hit him in the face with it. Smith demanded that postmasters be elected instead of appointed but no one paid much attention to him. But he did chortle with glee when President Taylor, a Whig, removed Merritt on May 13, 1849 and put Thomas Ware Cattel in his place.

This year Henry Ellet, once of Salem, was a Democratic member of Congress from Mississippi. 1847 and 1848 saw more Whig triumphs in the county with but two exceptions. In the senate battle of 1848, John Summerill of Helms Cove defeated Clawson of Woodstown by 120 votes and in the same year Charles Perrine Smith, fresh from his postmaster war, lost his fight for surrogate to Isaac Hackett. When he was Republican state chairman he blamed his defeat on leaders of his own party who he said had double crossed him. He tells names in this frank political history.

Upper Pittsgrove was formed as a separate township in March of 1846. "It elected two Whig freeholders at once," chortled Smith in the Standard. Again there was agitation to place old or lower Pittsgrove in Cumberland county.

The last year of the decade showed victory divided between the forces. Copner, a Democratic assemblyman, Newell, Githens and Remster were sent to Trenton. Blackwood, a Whig, won a scant sheriff victory by 50 votes over John Lambert. Two Democratic and one Whig coroners were elected.

In 1843 someone brought a live alligator to Salem and exhibited it. They named it John Tyler in "honor" of the Whig president who was fast disappointing the Whigs and pleasing the Democrats.

* * * *

The first news of Sutter's discovery and the following rush for gold trickled into Salem in December of 1848. The report that twenty-five million dollars of gold had been gathered in that short time must have had an electric effect upon the citizens of this little country town. Individuals began to leave for the great Eldorado and as early as January 20, 1849 the California Joint Stock Association was formed at a meeting at the home of

Lot F. Miller in Salem. Some of the prime movers in this company proposing to go west were Isaac Z. Peterson, Samuel Sherron, Minor Henry, Jeremiah Tracey, Israel Wells, Eugene F. Bennett and Richard C. Ballinger. The company raised capital of about $30,000 and elected a captain and a supercargo. A vessel was to be chartered and ostensibly the Cape Horn route was to be followed. Each man who had contributed a thousand dollars was allowed to go or to select a delegate to go in his place. But the odd thing is that here the organized Salem effort began and likewise ended, for no further mention is made of the scheme in the press.

In February, 1849, gold dust made its first appearance in Salem and despite the incredulity of some citizens who called it mica, the return of the assayist proved it to be gold. With anything of this nature it is not long before humor begins to creep into the situation and we soon find the breathless news that gold had been discovered at Rahway, N. J. and of more local interest, in Pittsgrove township. A Salem paper sardonically remarked that it hoped the citizens of this county would not become overextended by the news and concluded that the home product of marl was a much surer financial return than gold anyhow.

Some bright young journalist of Chester, thinking it was funny to call the budding town of Penns Grove "California", remarked that he was taking a river trip to California. The Salem Standard caustically stated that while California was connected with visionary speculation, the village of Penns Grove was associated with the home of thrifty, honest industry. If that local writer rising in righteous defense of his home county lived sixty-six years longer, I wonder what he would have thought of the little village of Penns Grove from 1915 to 1918. The demand of the allies for powder, raised it from obscurity to national prominence and to it flocked the same sort of people that emigrated to California. The Bret Harte of the powder boom has yet to rise and to proclaim himself, but when he does appear he will find material that will rival boom days of Sacramento.

The merchants of that time in Salem and in Philadelphia saw their opportunity. Stoughten and Belden, local merchants. advertised California gold washers and doubtless sold a large number. A Philadelphia wine merchant offered choice French brandy, cherry brandy, champagne and absinthe for the California trade. One wonders if some of the pioneers thought of that ad in the Mohave desert, or on the Nebraska plains. The papers carried a beautiful engraving of the bark *Warwick* under full sail, all set to go to California on the sixteenth of April, 1849, offering special inducement to Salem countians to transport themselves to the golden west.

Captain Robert C. Johnson and David McDaniel of Salem are mentioned as having sailed to California. These seem to be two of the earliest pioneers to leave home. It may be recalled here that Charles Edward Pancoast had gone to St. Louis before the gold rush and was consequently half way west.

Another story is told of a young man who missed his California boat in Philadelphia and chased it down the river in the Salem packet *Clifton*. His goods and chattels were on the western boat, so he hurried off at Delaware City to get a small boat to take him to the ship, but the chase was fruitless and the young man's goods went west, while he remained in the east, for the time being at least.

A Salemite, John Denn, wrote of very exciting times in crossing Mexico and of frequent encounters with the Gil Blas Indians. The postage to California at the time was forty cents. The articles of Bayard Taylor begin to appear in the local papers and effort was made to have regular correspondents write from the gold country. One of these letters took eight months in arriving at Salem. A reason for the delay was that the captain of the whaler who obtained these letters in the Pacific had merrily gone off on a whaling expedition with them in his pockets.

By July, 1849, the news from California had abated a bit, and in its place came fearful news of the spread of cholera. This disease, while heaviest in the middle west, cost some lives in Salem before it was checked.

William Bassett, Jr., of Salem wrote a very interesting letter back home. As a sample of the spirit of that day, a brief extract is printed here. Bassett made fifty dollars a week furnishing a small skiff to be used in transportation and notes that mule team drivers were getting a thousand dollars a month. His letter concluded:"Hurrah, despondency, I am raised to the pinnacle of joy and hope—joy at the deliverance of ourselves from the horrid death of famishing—hope by the prospects before me—they are very bright. If I fail to accumulate wealth in California, its fine climate, rich fields, blooming forests, green meadows and glowing qualities, I cannot describe, will render it a paradise to live in. I feel that I have stepped into the land of my future home and unless it be to visit my friends in the East, I shall never dwell there more."

William and Elijah Morris, of Salem returned worth a half million dollars having gleaned that huge fortune from conducting a clothing store near the gold fields.

One Salemite admitting he had lots of money, bemoaned the lack of eligible wives in the west country and pleaded for some "nice girls" to come out as soon as possible.

There was lots of poetry spilled in Salem over this epic migration. One of the choicest of these is as follows:

> The fever is abating—Dig-Dig-Dig
> Till you sweat at every pore—Dig-Dig-Dig
> To rot in the deep black sand
> And this is to be a citizen of a free and Christian land.
>
> And its, oh, to be a slave to the heathen and the Turk,
> To rid the hands of a Christian man,
> From such dirty toilsome work.

And in conclusion, the most famous song of them all, to the tune of "Oh Susanna," slightly paraphrased:

> I come from Salem City,
> With my wash bowl on my knee,
> I'm goin' to California,
> The gold dust for to see.

CHAPTER XXIII

SALEM IN THE 1850's

The principal event in this decade was a celebrated murder case known as the Treadway affair. For years afterward, and even at the present time, this case still attracts attention. The principal reason for this notoriety comes from the story in connection with it, told on one of Salem's prominent politicians of that day, the honorable Samuel Plummer, one-time sheriff of this county and a United States marshall for the district of New Jersey.

A stout gentleman leaned impressively against the office rail of one of Philadelphia's best hotels. "I want a room," said the portly gentleman. "Sorry," said the young clerk, "but there is a convention going on in town and we are filled up." He turned away. "Young man,"called the newcomer, "I am the high sheriff of Salem county, I hung Treadway, and I want a room in this hotel." "Sir," said the clerk, "if you were sheriff of hell and hung the devil it wouldn't make any difference to me;there are no rooms in this hotel." He didn't get a room but the story is one of Salem's best yarns and is frequently related.

Who was Treadway and why was he hanged?

At seven o'clock on the evening of November 11th, 1852, in the kitchen of the farmhouse of Edward Bilderback, near Halltown in Mannington township, two women were washing dishes. One was a colored woman named Felicia Heison, destined to be the state's star witness in the subsequent case, and the other was the estranged wife of Samuel T. Treadway, a farm hand in Elsinboro. Without notice, a shot rang out, the broken window glass tinkled, a couple of candles went out and Mrs. Treadway fell to the floor.

The Bilderback family gathered, first aid was given to the wounded woman and a fruitless search made for the assailant. In twenty minutes, before the doctor arrived, the woman was dead. Nothing more seems to have been done that night although before her death Mrs. Treadway gasped out to the maid that she was sure her husband had shot her.

In the morning a small wad of paper was found on the rain

soaked ground. It had evidently been used as wadding for the gun. At nine o'clock Saturday morning the constable arrested Samuel Treadway in his farmhouse in Elsinboro. In his gun, standing in the corner of the room, was another piece of paper wadding, matching that found on the Bilderback farm. On his way to Salem the officer informed him that his wife was dead whereupon he nearly collapsed but maintained a resolute silence. At the hearing he pleaded not guilty and was held without bail. The evidence against Treadway was not direct but as excellent a case of circumstantial evidence as could be assembled. No one saw him fire the shot but threats against his wife were proved, the gun wadding was very damaging evidence and several people had seen him at sunset near the Bilderback farm carrying a gun.

He lingered in jail until the thirty-first of December when his trial started in the Salem County Court of Oyer and Terminer before Mr. Justice Elmer of Bridgeton, the same man who gave his name to old Pittstown, now the modern borough of Elmer. The lay judges were T. Jones Yorke, J. Kille, James Newell, T. Lawrie, and Eph .Carll. The members of the jury who made Sheriff Plummer famous were: Foreman, Amos Harris; David Sparks, Charles Loudenslager, George Peterson, William Titus, Charles H. Chew, Henry Miller, Elmer Reeves, Wallace Taylor, John P. McCune, John Wallace and Edward Cox.

The defendant was without funds, so Francis L. McCulloch, in later years a Salem county prosecutor, was assigned by Justice Elmer to defend him. For the state appeared the attorney general of New Jersey, Richard P. Thompson of Salem, the only attorney general ever to come from Salem county. It is needless to say that the court room was filled. Public opinion in the case ran high, the newspapers printed nothing else and the fair sex demanded and received reserved seats in the courtroom.

The colored maid, Felicia Heison, testified and although she did not see the murderer, her testimony as to Mrs. Treadway's dying declaration that her husband had shot her, went far to damage the defense at the start. Her testimony and that of one John Conover were the high-lights of the case. Some short time prior to the murder, Mrs. Treadway had complained of her husband's threats and had him locked up for safe keeping, his release from that charge only occurring a week before the crime. Conover had been his roommate in jail and testified that Treadway had told him he would kill his wife when he got out of jail and furthermore would ascertain the identity of his wife's boy friend.

THE TREADWAY MURDER

Several different witnesses traced the defendant's movements during the day when he was seen wandering around with gun in hand. The purchase of powder, caps and small shot by him was likewise established. Mr. Gwynne, editor of the Sunbeam, testified as to the paper wadding and showed it to be part of the Philadelphia Sunday Globe, the untorn portion of the paper being found in Treadway's room. The prisoner did not take the stand and his counsel confined himself to pointing out to the jury the danger of convicting on circumstantial evidence. The home-town attorney general made an impassioned plea for conviction and the justice gave a long and elaborate charge to the jury which was a careful exposition of the law of murder but which seems today to have been unduly tedious. Justice Elmer must have been fond of long speeches because his speech to the grand jury was likewise lengthy and his sentence was a sermon.

The jury returned with a verdict of guilty after staying out two hours and fifteen minutes. The verdict was hardly a surprise but another huge crowd gathered the next day, New Year's Day, 1853, and heard Justice Elmer sentence the convicted man to the gallows.

On January 11th, in the presence of six ministers and his counsel, Treadway confessed that he had murdered his wife. The confession was substantially the same as the testimony with the added fact that he did not intend to kill his wife until he saw her in the kitchen. He seemed to have made no effort to escape but went quietly home and waited until the arrest. From that time until the execution on March 1st, there seems to have been an organized effort to save him from the gallows and to have his sentence commuted to life imprisonment. Several columns of the local papers were devoted to the pros and cons of capital punishment and a Philadelphia orator named Burleigh came to Salem and made a speech condemning executions as a means of stopping crime. Apparently no appeal was made to Governor Fort but it is evident that there was some effort made to save his life.

The press of 1853 devoted just as much space and perhaps more to the execution than the papers of today commonly do. On March 1st at noon in the rear of the old jail the affair took place. Three sheriffs were present, those of Cumberland, Gloucester and Salem, four doctors and three preachers. Over a hundred invited "guests" saw the execution and afterwards the entire populace was allowed to view the swinging remains. Treadway seems to have been very composed; he prayed, sang hymns, smiled, and left a dollar legacy to his niece.

He also left to posterity a long letter of advice to young men, enjoining them to mind their parents and to avoid liquor. In this letter he denied the charge that he had cruelly burned his only child to death by placing it on a red hot stove. Evidently this accusation had been hurled at him previously but in the old records no other mention is made of the child.

* * * *

The 1850's began with the final wiping out of an epidemic of cholera that had swept this county the preceding summer and fall. It was with a great deal of relief that the doctors of Salem county early in 1850 announced that this virulent disease was finally exterminated. One of the first news notes of this decade was the obituary notice of Nicholas Harris, a Salem countian who had served the infant nation at the battle of Quinton and at Red Bank. He was a member of the family which produced many veterans of the Revolutionary War. He was a deacon in the Baptist Church at Salem.

Coincident with his death came the intelligence that the Second Baptist Church of Salem had purchased a lot of ground on Penny Hill, East Broadway, Salem. This church was built in 1851. It was doomed to a short existence. By 1865 the congregation had collapsed under the burden of carrying the debt and the church was torn down and the bricks sold for building material. It stood just east of what is known as the bake shop property now owned by John Harris on the south side of East Broadway.

The port of Salem, one of the oldest ports of entry in the United States, was in these years still doing a rushing business. In addition to the two steamboats which competed for this business there were a large number of other ships which entered and left the port, so many, in fact, that the newspapers of that day printed the arrivals and departures as regularly and faithfully as the New York Times does now. The shipping business was not without its hazards and dangers. On March 2nd, 1850, the *Clifton* had an explosion in its boiler, killing a fireman, a man by the name of Foster, while the boat touched at New Castle, Delaware. Several other people were injured.

Another soldier of the Revolution, Daniel Nelson, died at Sharptown, aged 92 years. This decade saw the passing of the last of the men who had aided in the birth of the new republic. William N. Jeffers, one of the foremost citizens of Salem thirty years before, died in this same year. He died in the harness of the politics in which he had been engaged for almost half a century. He was prosecutor of Camden county when he passed away. He had been prosecutor of Salem county, he had organized a bank, he had been minister to South America under President Jackson, and he had been one of the leading lawyers and politicians of his time. In the 1830's he had come within a hair of being governor of New Jersey. The home he built in Salem on the corner of Griffith and Market streets stood until 1935.

Prosperity was coming back to Salem in the early years of the decade. All the newspapers reported building booms, especially in Woodstown. At that time in the borough of Woodstown there were two flourishing hotels known as Park's Hotel and Keen's Hotel. The section of Salem known as Oak street was first beginning to be developed. In this decade a large number of houses were built on this street. The Nelson House was completed in 1850. Prosperity, however, was not so kind to the infant congregation of the Roman Catholic Church because their building lay idle for three years during this period, for want of funds to finish it.

A long controversy started in 1852 concerning the possessor of the oldest published book. An Alloway man, his name unknown, was the first to claim the honor by saying that he possessed a book known as "Perkins on The Catholics" published in 1609 in Cambridge, England. The claim was soon disposed of by Josiah Harrison, a venerable lawyer of Salem, who produced a dictionary printed in 1590. A Salem preacher named Helm offered to show that he had a book known as the "Sermons of Capelleus," printed in 1560. The contest waged merrily until Harrison came back with proof that he owned a book containing the comments of Martin Luther on the first twenty Psalms of David, printed in 1521 at Nuremburg in Germany. This last announcement of Harrison's ended the contest and he was adjudged the winner.

It was a period of restless activity. The politicians were seeking to break the hold of the Camden and Amboy railroad. In this connection they proposed the Southern Central railroad to run from Key Port to Hancock's Bridge, but this dream never became a reality. The railroad in time did receive its charter and did run from Key Port to Bayside, as a part of the Central Railroad of New Jersey.

The agitation over railroads was comparable to the agitation over bigger and better camp meetings. The spirit of that age demanded an outlet. There were several meetings organized in this county, the principal one being near Penns Grove on what is now known as the Harding Highway. These camp meetings with their concessions did a big business and there was keen competition for these privileges. The steamboats offered special rates as cheap as a quarter for a round trip to attend the camp meeting near Penns Grove. The colored folks had their camp meetings also. One of them at Baileytown, near Woodstown, was suppressed because it was too noisy.

In January of 1854, the first telegraph wires to enter this county were constructed as a part of the Camden and Cape May system. Benjamin Acton, the first agent and operator of this company, had his office on Market street. In this connection it is interesting to recall that the road which leads from Alloway to Bridgeton was known and still is known as the Telegraph road because the wires were strung along that road.

Building was still the order of the day. The National Standard proudly announced that the Navy Yard at Philadelphia had bought oak wood from Hall's Woods in Elsinboro to be used in the construction of the last few wooden ships that were to be built for the United States Navy. It is interesting to note that the resort known today as Oakwood Beach got its name from the fact that there were many oak trees there. The Brown Building, the first skyscraper in Salem, rearing itself to the impressive height of four stories, was erected in 1855. It is better known today as the Wheeler Building. In this same year through the efforts of Messrs. Acton, Harbert, Tyler, Otis and Garrison, the first gas works was constructed in Salem and for the first time the streets of the city were illuminated by something other than oil. At the same time an iron foundry was started in this city. The Second Baptist Church, which was being built at this time, received a sixty-nine-foot steeple which marked it from a long distance outside of Salem.

The decade had startling events as well. In 1854 a great rumbling was heard which the inhabitants of the city believed to be an earthquake, but it was only another explosion in the du Pont plant at Wilmington. Since that time the inhabitants of the county have become used to false earthquakes.

Tragedy reared its head in August, 1855, when the widow of Reverend Mr. Prescott, Margaret Smith Prescott of Salem, was killed in a railroad wreck at Burlington. Mr. Prescott had died at sea a decade before. He was the rector of St. John's Episcopal Church at Salem and a brother of the famous historian, William H. Prescott. His wife had been visiting Bishop Doane at Burlington and was on her way home when she was killed. Her death, on August 29, 1855, cast a shadow of gloom over this locality.

THE 1850's

Engaged in a drunken brawl, a man by the name of Brown, was thrown overboard from the steamboat *Miantomi* in Salem creek. Two brothers by the name of Somers were arrested for the crime but at the trial no one could prove their guilt and the murder went unsolved.

Isabel Parrott, poetess of parts, a lady known for her humanity and a member of one of the oldest families of Salem, died in 1855 in her seventy-fourth year.

The decade had its lighter side as well. One very amusing incident occurred in 1858 which reminds one of the modern term of "sucker". Ezekiel H. B. Doolittle, the celebrated Yankee clock maker and self-made man, announced himself as a lecturer in a Salem hall. His advertisement on a hand bill passed around Salem advertised not only his fame but also his rather mysterious slogan that "I will make myself visible and invisible and no one knows from whence I came or whence I go". The admission was twenty-five cents and ladies would occupy the front seats. On the night in question Mr. Doolittle appeared at the crowded hall. After having taken the admission fee himself he mounted the platform, said that he had left his manuscript at the hotel and begged the indulgence of th audience until he could go and get it. He disappeared and the audience waited the better part of an hour. Finally a small boy appeared with a note which some kind soul in the audience read to the others. The note read: "I will make myself visible and invisible and no one knows from whence I came or whence I go. Ezekiel H. B. Doolittle." While the note was being read Mr. Doolittle was on his way behind the fastest team the local livery stable possessed.

Photographers were coming into their own in this decade, in fact so much so that two of the local artists had a lively war through the columns of the newspaper over who was the better photographer and ambrotyper. One of these gentlemen insisted that the other's pictures made the client look like a "louse" instead of a real person and argued seriously that his pictures could make the person look as he was. The two artists exhausted much advertising, money and several weeks of violent scrapping before one of them finally left town. The writer's great-grandfather was, in 1854, at a town meeting, called upon to preside over a delegation which sought to muzzle dogs. In 1851, the children of Salem had probably their longest and best day. In the summer of that year a complete circus was stranded in Salem for four weeks while an attachment suit was being litigated. It is needless to add that the kids of eighty years ago enjoyed to the fullest extent this free exhibition.

Speaking of lecturers, an astronomer had a bad evening at Hancock's Bridge in July of 1851. He had advertised that he would lecture on the starry heavens. He did, or rather tried to, but in the middle of his discourse, the Lower Creekers, caring nothing about the heavens and more about their aim, disposed of the speaker with a number of rotten eggs. Even the staid National Standard admitted that it was a good use for bad eggs.

The pride of the farmers over their tall corn and fast horses filled the newspapers of the day. A gang of hoodlums, known as the "killers" got loose on Star Corner for a few Saturday nights until the local constabulary effectively disposed of them. A shark was seen in Salem creek. Lecturers who were not "rotten-egged," were frequent in Salem as a part of the lyceum course. In December of 1850, George Lippard, whose novels, rather terrible now to read, were then the rage of the day, lectured in Salem on his pet project, "The Brotherhood of Man". In 1859 Horace Greeley, later destined to become the worst defeated man who ever ran for president, lectured in Salem. The Salem newspaper wasn't particularly enthusiastic over Mr. Greeley's lecture. It said: "Truth compels us to state that the efforts of Mr. Greeley on the said occasion were anything but satisfactory. His awkward gestures and indistinct enunciation of words ruined what might have been a good lecture."

A new-comer to the field of education was the boarding school at Eldridge's Hill which ran between 1855 and 1861 and was conducted by a worthy Quaker, Allen Flitcraft. To this school came boys from all over the eastern part of the United States. Here was educated John Rutter Brooke, who distinguished himself on the field of Gettysburg and became a major general in the army of the United States.

On the religious side of the decade it is interesting to note that the Salem newspapers printed in 1857 a comparison between the number of churches in this county fifty years before and at that time. The comparison shows very clearly great growth in churches in that half century. In 1857 the Episcopalians had two churches, St. John's in Salem with a pastor, and St. George's at Churchtown with no pastor. The Presbyterians had three churches, one at Salem, one at Daretown and one in Woodstown, which was then the township of Pilesgrove. At the latter church there was no regular pastor. The Friends, pioneers in the religious settlement, at that time had six meetings, two in Salem, two in Woodstown, one at Pedricktown in Upper Penns Neck, and one at Hancock's Bridge in Lower Alloway's Creek. The Lutherans still maintained their church at Friesburg in Alloway township, still one of the oldest churches in the county. The Seventh Day Baptists had in 1811 built the church at Marlboro which by a few yards is in Salem county. The Roman Catholics had finished their church at Salem and had a resident priest, Father Cannon. The Baptists had two congregations in Salem, the present First Church and the now extinct Second Baptist Church. There were Baptist churches at Woodstown, Daretown, Alloway and Canton.

The Methodists had the largest number of churches at the time of this census. In Salem they had the old First Church behind whose walls Benjamin Abbott is buried. They had a parsonage for their minister and the census gave it a total valuation of $8,000. In Lower Penns Neck they had a church at Pennsville and even a home for the sexton. In Upper Penns Neck there were three churches, two brick and one frame. In Mannington there was the church at Haines Neck, a frame building valued at $500, in which, the census declared, there was regular preaching. Pilesgrove had the largest number of Methodist churches, five in all. Upper Alloway's Creek had churches at Alloway, Aldine and Quinton with one parsonage and one pastor. Pittsgrove had three churches with two pastors on circuit.

In addition to the white churches there were at this time in Salem county, six African Methodist churches. There was one in Lower Penns Neck, one in Mannington, two in Salem and two in Pilesgrove township.

This very interesting census shows the marked increase in religious buildings and interest in the fifty years since 1807. The Methodists in 1807 had but six churches; fifty years later they had seventeen. In July of 1850 the Methodists added a new church to their number with the dedication of the Broadway Methodist Church in Salem. It was formed by members from the old First Church on Walnut street.

* * * *

It was true in the 1850's as it has been true in every decade since political parties were first organized that politics were both interesting and, at times, acrimonious. It is true also that the interest of the people and the newspapers of that period lay largely with politics. The campaigns would start in the middle of the summer. They would fill the columns of the papers for almost five months to the exclusion of everything else. For this reason, it becomes necessary in properly dealing with the history of Salem county that space should be given to these campaigns which held so much attention.

It must be remembered that these were the last ten years of existence for the Whig Party; in the decade from 1850 to 1860, the Whigs and the Democrats contested for the last time. By 1860 the Whig Party had gone into the merciful shades of oblivion and the Republican party had been born to take up the battle where the Whigs had left off.

The year 1850 opened auspiciously for the Democrats. In that year this party had a candidate for governor in the person of John Summerrill, who the year before had been elected to the state Senate. Summerrill has the distinction of being one of the few Salem county men who ever came close to a nomination for governor. In the convention of 1850, he ran second to Dr. Fort who that fall was elected governor. There have been other candidates or aspirants for the honor from this county but Summerrill came the nearest to the prize. Democrats swept the election of 1850. Dr. Fort carried the county by 350 votes over his Whig opponent. The Democratic congressman, Stratton, one of the few Democrat Congressmen in the last hundred years, also carried the county by three hundred votes. Three Democrats, Bilderback, Benner and Richman, were elected assemblymen and to cap the victory, three Democratic coroners were elected. Nor did the Democratic tide diminish the following year. In the election of 1851 Allen Wallace, a Democrat, was elected state senator to succeed Summerrill by a margin of 150 votes over his Whig opponent, Mr. Rusling. By the census of 1850, the Salem County representation had been cut to two assemblymen. However, the Democrats elected both of these, John C. Lummis and Jacob Hitchner, who defeated their Whig opponents by over a hundred votes. Three Democratic coroners were also elected.

The next year, 1852, provides as good a picture of politics as may be obtained. That was a presidential year in which the Democrats sought to regain the presidency which they had lost four years before. It is worth digressing to show in some detail this campaign of 1852. Turn back the pages of history to this year, and you will find as pretty a picture of mud slinging and abuse as may be found in any presidential election. In 1852 Millard Fillmore was president by the act of God which had taken away old Zachary Taylor, doughty hero of the Mexican War. The Whigs were in power but the Democrats meant to be there. Mindful of the vote-drawing power of an old soldier, the Whigs had selected as their candidate another hero of the

CAMPAIGN OF 1852

Mexican War, the bluff old veteran of the war of 1812 and the hero of Cherubusco, Winfield Scott.

The Democrats, after a hard convention fight in Baltimore, named a comparatively unknown statesman, Franklin Pierce, whose status was somewhat akin to that of the late Warren G. Harding in 1920. In other words, he was safe but mediocre.

As early as June of '52 the Salem papers prepared their broadsides and girded their editorial loins for the battle. There are two main frameworks to follow through this old campaign, one of which was the attempt to prove or discredit the war record of Franklin Pierce and the other a purely personal tilt of petty recriminations between the editors of the Sunbeam and the National Standard. If today the editor of one paper mildly calls the political stories of the other "hot air" think nothing of it; read what one said about the other in the opening days of the fight of 1852. The Democratic Sunbeam knew that Pierce's war record was above reproach and wanted the Standard to think so too, but when that paper continued its charges of cowardice against the Democratic nominee, the local Jeffersonian sheet declared: "This puerile attempt on the part of the editor of the Standard to blacken the character of a great man is disgraceful and beneath our notice. If our statements are not enough refutation to confound the minions of this sheet and to damn forever the miserable attempts of this paper's stool pigeon to commit both slander and libel, we have more evidence yet to prove our case."

Beneath their notice or not, the Standard continued its barrage of vitriol for six long months in never ending flow and the Sunbeam replied in like vein until at last the argument grows tiresome and hackneyed.

The battle centered over the charge that Pierce, a brigadier general in the American army, had become so terrified at the battle of Cherubusco that he had fainted and had later resigned to seek the safer territory of New Hampshire. It was this charge that the one paper constantly pressed and the other just as constantly refuted.

The Sunbeam was horror stricken at the Standard calling Pierce "a skulker in epaulettes" but it did not hesitate to classify the Whig nominee as "a nauseous dose of superannuated pottage."

Nor did the newspapers confine their attacks to editorial abuse. Songs—hundreds of them—appeared in the local press, the majority written by local songsters for local consumption. What the editorials missed in this feverish campaign the songs included. Here is a specimen of the friendly way in which

Pierce was regarded by the Standard:

> "Franklin Pierce, Franklin Pierce,
>   Never saw a tent;
> Polk dressed him in uniform
>   And a-soldiering he went.
> A sword he had and epaulettes,
>   A plume and a chapeau;
> Accoutred thus he started off
>   To Scott in Mexico.

Another ditty shows again what the good Whigs in Salem county thought of General Pierce:

> "All to his saddle tightly tied
>   To Cherubusco Frank did ride;
> He fainted when he saw blood flow
>   'Cause war was rough in Mexico."

> "Chapultepec was the last fight;
>   He gave up as the tale is right.
> He got the gripes and this we know,
>   He killed no one in Mexico."

And so the controversy raged, very seriously we want you to know, over whether or not the general from New Hampshire had played the coward or not. Column after column appeared in the Sunbeam to prove that Pierce was wounded and had an excuse for fainting and the rebuttal crammed the National Standard to prove that he was a quitter and that brave old General Scott was much better fitted to fill the White House than his opponent.

The songs then were sung and the local editors went pleasantly on with their task of tossing buckets of mud in the other's face. Said the Sunbeam editor of the Standard editor, "We consider him incapable of uttering one single original thought in decent grammatical language," and the editor of the Standard roared concerning the tactics of the former editor, "Oh, what consummate hypocrisy, what fiendish maneuvers."

Despite the fact that the local Democrats had a split in their county party due to a factional fight between Judge Kille and Attorney General Richard P. Thompson, the campaign progressed nicely and along in late October we find the Jacksonian boys marching down the streets of Salem singing:

> "Hurrah the old Democracy
>   Are in the field once more
> No factions in their steady ranks
>   To break them as of yore
> With hands and hearts united all
>   Fling out the banner high
> And Pierce and King and Victory
>   Shall be our battle cry."

POLITICS OF THE 1850's

The lusty boys who shouted their battle cry through the streets of Salem were correct and victory did perch upon the shoulders of the gentleman from New Hampshire, but the fight referred to cost the Democrats in this county the sheriff's position, and returns favoring Samuel Plummer, Republican, over Thomas Flannigan, Democrat, by a margin of 150 votes. The Democrats retained one assembly seat by Swing's victory, but lost the other to Blackwood, a Whig. Franklin Pierce carried the county by 50 votes and the jubilant Democrats burst into song again with one entitled "Way Down, Way Down By The Old Salt River."

> Far, Far away.
> That's where the Whigs are fixed forever,
> That's where they're doomed to stay.
> All up and down its whole existence
> Sadly they roam,
> Still groaning that the late convention
> Set them from the White House at home.
> All the Whigs are sad and dreary,
> Everywhere they roam,
> Singing, Brothers, how my heart grows
>   weary
> Far from the White House at home.

The election of the following year saw a divided victory between the two forces. Rodman N. Price was elected governor of New Jersey but lost this county by a hundred votes. Benjamin M. Smith, a Whig, was elected county surrogate over Bilderback, Democrat, by an unusual majority. The Democrats elected one assemblyman but lost the other and were successful in obtaining three coroners. The next year the Whigs elected their congressman, Isaiah D. Clawson, of Woodstown, by an ample majority. True, the Democrats elected both their assemblymen, J. Thompson and John Harris, but they lost the state senator and the county clerk. In the Senate contest Allen Wallace was defeated for election by the scant majority of 40 votes. The gentleman who defeated him, Charles Perrine Smith, had been editor of the National Standard. He had been defeated a few years previously for Surrogate but this victory in the year 1854 started him on a path of political glory. He was destined to be clerk of the Supreme Court and eventually chairman of the Republican State Committee. More attention will be given to Smith later on, but at this juncture it must be said that he left behind him a memoir of his political career which is one of the frankest expositions of politics that is on record. His book, written in long-hand, is still obtainable by permission in the State Library at Trenton. It tells the truth about his political opponents and his political friends. He wrote as he felt and he did not spare the truth. Smith willed that his political dynamite should not be given to the world until after his daughter's death. When she died some years later it was given to the State Library and has proved a most valuable reference book for students of political science.

The new clerk of Salem county elected in that year was Maskel Ware, who defeated Samuel Copner, the incumbent. Around the defeat of Copner there occurred a political tragedy. Copner had been a pioneer in obtaining the free public school system for this state. He had perpetuated his name in the school which is known today in Salem as the Grant Street School. But on the political side he had broken with the powerful Democratic boss of that day, Joseph Kille, and Kille had given him the "works" in the election of 1854. Copner also had financial reverses and, as a result of his political defeat, he became enfeebled in mind and health and soon died.

With the defeat of Copner for county clerk came a repercussion the following year in what was a most interesting election. The actions of Joseph Kille towards Copner for a few years, at least, split the Democratic Party. And yet Kille, the man who caused it, defeated in the nomination for the assembly, ran as an independent Democrat and won. In this election Richard C. Ballinger, Whig, was elected sheriff over Newell, Democrat, and the Temperance candidate, Garrison only ran 100 back of the defeated Democrat, showing the strength of the dry forces in the county at that time. The other assemblyman elected was Samuel Plummer.

This was the beginning of the end of the power of Joseph Kille but at the climax of his career he deserves more than passing notice. As previously stated, he had been a congressman, he had been a judge, he had been a sheriff, he had been a county clerk. In fact, he had held practically every office within the gift of the people of Salem county. When he successfully broke through his own party to win his last job, the assembly seat of 1856, he began at once to aim for higher things. He announced his candidacy for governor and by doing that drew upon himself the fire of the other section of the Democratic Party and the undiluted scorn of the Salem Sunbeam. Throughout the year 1856 in this newspaper he became the object of ridicule and political hatred. He had been so unfortunate as to make a speech saying that he could carry Salem county at any time he wished for $500.00. He was like some of the other chieftains of his time who believed with Horace Walpole that every man had his price. To further his campaign, he gave a free dinner at Allowaystown, the guests receiving an additional dollar for attending. In connection with this dinner, one of Kille's political enemies named Ezra Anderson wrote a diatribe in the Salem Sunbeam entitled "Joseph in the Sanhedrin," and marked it "Tadmore in the Wilderness," thus giving the origin to the well known nickname of Allowaystown.

Kille beat them in the election of 1855, but the next year he was not so successful. Under blasts from Editor Gwynne of the Sunbeam, who Kille called "that damned Irish editor," the would-be governor went down to defeat in the election of 1856 by over 400 votes. His victorious opponent was Thomas W. Jones, a Whig. This was the end of Kille politically although there is still mention of him in the remaining years of the decade as having either helped or hindered the Democrats of that period. About 1860 Kille moved from Salem to Kille's Island near Billingsport in Gloucester county. At this place, in 1861, on his seventy-first birthday, the Democrats of this section flocked to give him a testimonial dinner. He died at the ripe old age of 75 in March of 1865.

James Buchanan carried Salem county in the presidential election of 1856. The Whig candidate for governor, Newell, who claimed relationship to the Salem Newells, swept Salem county by 200 votes over Alexander. One Democrat, William Beckett, gained an assembly seat but Kille, whose name was left off the "masthead" of the Sunbeam, was overwhelmingly defeated in the other district. It is interesting to note that at this date the citizens of Mannington in their township elections still used the ancient English custom of "viva voce" voting, using the open announcement instead of a secret ballot.

The following year the Democrats elected their last state senator for thirty years, Joseph K. Riley being the successful candidate. William Plummer, whose son was for twenty-five years surrogate of Salem county, was in this year elected on the Democratic ticket for a five-year term. The lower part of the ticket was not so happy for the Democrats, for they lost the three coroners and the two assemblymen.

In 1858 two more Republican or Whig assemblymen were elected and Samuel W. Miller, Republican, of Allowaystown, was elected sheriff of Salem county. This year marked the incorporation of the city of Salem. In that year, too, Robert Carney Johnson, son of Robert Gibbon Johnson, the historian, was elected the first mayor of the city of Salem.

The last year of the decade witnessed the election of a Democratic county clerk, Robert Newell, by the close majority of nine votes over John C. Belden. The Whigs or Republicans yelled "fraud" with all their might because Newell put in his office as deputy a Republican named Rusling, who was alleged to have sold out his party to gain this position. A Democrat, Samuel Habermayer, was elected to the assembly with a Republican colleague, Joshua Lippincott. Thus ended a stormy decade of Salem county politics.

CHAPTER XXIV

Salem in the Civil War

"There can be no question of vacillation now. Every citizen is bound to sustain his government. It is no longer a party question; not a Republican, not a Democrat question, it is a question of government and law and country.

"The Government must be sustained and the laws must be obeyed."

Years ago, the above quotation flew at the masthead of the Salem Sunbeam, calling upon Salem's loyal citizens, Democratic and Republican alike, to support a war that at the time of writing, was only two days old. The marvelous new invention, the telegraph, had flashed news even to remote Salem, of the fall of Fort Sumter and the start of a four years war which, at the time of beginning, was confidently predicted to last only three months.

Tremendously engrossing is this story of Salem and the Civil War, and tremendously interesting is the sociological study of its people during that trying era. The best material available for the study are the files of the newspapers, the Standard and the Sunbeam, both loyally supporting the war. In those files are revealed all the glory of war, all its horror, all the bitter hates the struggle caused, all the pride it engendered at the start and all the disgust and antipathy it aroused in its last years. The complete story would fill a good sized volume with relation to Salem alone. Failing in that some few cross sections of the influence of the war upon this community should be preserved.

Salem moved with swiftness and celerity to do her share in preserving the fast dividing Union of the United States. Mass meetings were held in Washington Hall, Salem, funds were raised, the water mains coming into Salem guarded and as early as the 25th of April, the Johnson Guards marched away to Trenton.

At seven o'clock on that spring morning, the little troop of Salem's first volunteers marched down the tree-lined avenue of West Broadway to embark upon the steamer Cohansey at the wharf, said goodbye to their friends and relatives and were off down the winding creek to Beverly where they were to camp. The enlistment period was for three months, a significant tragic fact in itself, showing the utter inability to foresee a death struggle between two portions of the country which would take years and not months. True, the Johnson Guards came home again, only to enlist for the duration of the war and their second departure would be far more tragic than the first.

The first concern of the residents of Salem was the river and its one fort, Delaware, on Pea Patch Island. Colonel Johnson, son of the historian, and Dr. J. H. Thompson went over to the fort to offer volunteers to the commandant but they had a merry time in rousing the commanding officer who was very indignant at the suggestion he needed any help in this modern fortress whose walls were considered superior to Sumter. He told them that twenty men, which was all he had, could hold Delaware against a thousand. But the worried Salemites were not so sure about it and through Charles Perrine Smith and the mayor of Philadelphia asked protection against the possible invasion of the Confederates. The aid was finally granted and in a couple of weeks additional troops were sent to the fort.

Flag raisings, that popular war pastime in all patriotic communities, were held in practically every village and township of the county. Salem furnished by the 4th of July, three companies, one the Johnson Guards, who had been sent to the Virginia battlefields by that time, the Fenwick rifles, and the Home Guards. An artillery company was soon to be organized also. A Salem farmer introduced a cotton grower from the South who declared that Salem's sandy soil could support that much-needed commodity.

Characteristic of the surcharged feeling of that time is an excerpt from an editorial from the Salem Sunbeam which tries to reason for more sanity. Its editor says, about the first of July, "the public mind has been so excited for months past that the daily report to inquiries 'No fighting yet' has produced disappointment. Occasionally a refrain such as 'Thank God for that,' would issue from human lips, but this has been the exception rather than the rule."

They had not long to wait. Less than a week after this publication, the telegraph brought the news to Salem of the overwhelming defeat of the Union army at Bull Run; of the disgraceful retreat that was more than a rout, of the startling intelligence that the national capital lay open to Confederate attack and instead of being able to wipe the Rebels off the map at the first encounter the Northerners had been wiped out themselves. Bull Run brought not only sorrow but consternation in its wake. Said another county paper, "Those who imagined that the rebellion would be overthrown by the magic of General Scott's name and a few troops are doomed to disappointment. So also are those who concluded the Johnson Guards would not have even to serve their three month apprenticeship at war. This struggle is far more colossal than the humblest citizen imagines."

With the defeat of the Union army, intense bitterness creeps into the story. It was bad enough to have rebellion and sedition break out in Virginia, three hundred miles or less to the South, It was hard enough to have the town's native sons slaughtered upon the field of Bull Run. It was far from encouraging to realize that a prospective three months' war might go on indefinitely. But when the actual reality of treason broke out at Salem's back door, here was trouble indeed and a situation which might, if allowed to go on, bring fratricidal strife to the peaceful fields of Salem county.

The story has never been properly told. The survivors of that era of seventy years ago who could shed light upon that vast eruption are few and far between. Those who are alive and who can remember, tell, and the papers bear them out, that all was not serene with the war, even in South Jersey. There were still slave owners here and there who were outright Southern sympathizers who felt that the Federal government had no right to coerce an unwilling state. Take a map of the United States and you will see that South West Jersey is not so far north of the Mason Dixon line to escape the category of the border state. The commandant at Fort Delaware had been warned to watch Southern sympathizers.

It was necessary to keep an eye on Salem also, for although fortunately no open warfare ever resulted, several Salem countians were jailed for their seditious beliefs.

At Alloway on Saturday evening, July 27th, in Mulford's Hotel, now known as the Hotel Alloway, the first sign of trouble showed itself. That evening there was announced a Union Democratic meeting for the announced purpose of opposing the present "unnecessary war and the methods of the Administration."

There was no mistaking the tendencies of those who called and addressed the Alloway meeting. The principal speaker was Dr. John R. Sickler of Gloucester county who the Sunbeam referred to as an "ultra and notorious pot house politician" and who gave "a sore throat as an excuse for a short speech" but that speech uttered strong denunciations of Lincoln and his course. He denounced the war as unnecessary and left but little doubt in the mind of his auditors that here was treason no further off than Alloway.

Sensing the idea, the Unionists present took over the meeting with fervent speeches urging the support of the president and the conduct of the war. Sergeant Edward A. Acton (grandfather of the present Mayor of Salem), who had just returned on furlough from the battlefield of Bull Run, indignantly denounced the speaker and the resolutions which the meeting had passed condemning the war.

The meeting grew warmer and warmer. Dr. Sickler slipped out the back door of the hotel and whisked himself away to Gloucester in his carriage which, probably fortunately for him, was awaiting outside. The chairman of the meeting, Ezra Anderson, was escorted home by two Union soldiers to save him from possible attack and the secretary of the meeting, a local man referred to by the Standard as a "whiskey loving Breckinridger", was followed home by hoots and jeers.

Both Salem papers broke into indignant protest. "Traitors in council," said the Standard, "and in our own camp." Proceeding they declared, "The cheek mantles with indignation that such a meeting should be held at such place and in such a time of national crises," and ended its editorial comment with the significant lines:

> "Those that are betrayed,
> Do feel the treason sharply, yet the
> Traitor stands in worse case far."

The copperhead reaction did not subside very quietly. Taking no warning from the Alloway affair, the Union Democrats held a secret meeting at Quinton's Bridge the following Saturday night and the news leaked out and caused more editorial castigation.

The struggle between brother and brother seems intensified when one reads in the Standard the following letter:
To Major Samuel G. French of Mississippi,

Knowing the National Standard is subscribed for and read by many of your relatives I wish to tell you through its columns of the contempt in which you are held by them and by your former friends.

You will not forget that you were born at Mullica Hill of poor but respected parents, that by the agency of kind friends you were sent to the Military Academy at West Point where you graduated with high honors.

At the time of the breaking out of the Mexican War you were a lieutenant in the United States army and at the battle of Monterey were wounded which occasioned deep grief to your friends and invoked fervent prayers for your recovery, but where are you now?

In open rebellion to the generous power which took you from your rural and humble home and made you what you are today. Should hostilities cease between the government and the traitors with which you are leagued, and the Stars and Stripes thrown to the breeze again, will you dare to return to that home against which you have taken up arms?

Will you be received as before with the marks of respect which saluted you when you returned from Mexico? No, you will be received as a traitor and the owner of a treacherous and defamed heart.

Adieu,

A RELATIVE

"All's quiet along the Potomac tonight" meant opportunity for the men in the field to write letters home. A letter taken at random indicates that one soldier's mind was troubled by the thought that there were some men back home who might just as well be stalking the picket post, as to be softly settled upon some one's sofa in the act of making love to the soldier's former sweetheart. "There are those who would rather play carpet knight with their lady loves than come to the rescue of their country. If the ladies will follow my advice they will abandon these cowardly fellows altogether, unless they come to the rescue of their lost rights, then after they have regained them, they can with more consistency and hope of success, renew the attentions of the fair ones whom they now adore."

The soldier who wrote the above in 1861 probably little realized that within a year the first draft of conscripted men would go into uniform to replenish the Union army with much-needed fresh material. The first draft passed Salem by because she had supplied her quota of volunteers. But there were more drafts to come when the country would be forced to send men to war whether they wished to go or not. However, the business comes more properly during the latter part of the war and will be given more attention.

The tone of the papers, at last sensing a long and bitter struggle, became intensely bitter. Everything that bore the name of Democrat was open to suspicion. The Sunbeam wholeheartedly defended the Administration and the war but was subject to several bitter attacks by the Standard for imaginary non-support of the war. This called forth caustic comment by the former paper as to whether it was a Republican war or a national one.

"The grapes of wrath" as evidenced by the bitter tone of the press, shows itself in the following quotations, the first from the Standard, the second from the Sunbeam.

"Traitor Samuel French, (of Mullica Hill referred to previously), has been made a general by the rebels, we suppose his estates in Gloucester county will suffer confiscation. This is the man who went South some years ago and married a plantation and a lot of negroes belonging to a white woman who has since died."

"John Tyler, (President from 1841 to 1844), is dead. He died a traitor and the Congress of Traitors have resolved to erect a monument to his infamous memory."

Before the first year of war was over Fort Delaware, so far safe from attack, became a prison camp for captured Confederates and starts an interesting history which is a volume of human misery in itself. The first prisoners, caught in West Virginia on a raid, sang on their arrival at the Fort, "All we do is sign the payroll, but we never get a ———— cent." The local papers made much of their dejected attitude and filthy condition, predicting revolt in the ranks of the Rebels from the "cruel tyrants who molested them." But still the war kept on and more prisoners came to the island fortress which was soon to be a death house for hundreds of them.

When the first large detachment of Rebels arrived containing a lieutenant colonel, the captured officer became a stickler for etiquette and demanded rights as befitted his rank. To this the commanding officer of the Fort replied, "that if they had their just rights they should all be hanged immediately," which somewhat put the quietus upon the prisoner, so the Standard assures us.

Worthy of Victor Hugo was the incident of a soap salesman, who, being in Salem when a batch of prisoners arrived from North Carolina and hearing that they were mostly boys from certain Carolina counties, went to the Fort and discovered his seventeen-year-old-son who had been impressed in the Confederate army. The Standard pictured a heart-rendering reunion and cheered its readers with the intelligence that plans had been made for the boy's release.

In the early days of the war, several wild stories emanated from the Fort. One was that the prisoners had mutinied and captured the Fort; which upon investigation proved to have been a solitary Confederate officer who became intoxicated and had carved up a negro employed on the Island. The other was that the entire garrison of the Fort had deserted; which simmered down to the fact that a handful of Union soldiers had gone to Finn's Point to spend a summer afternoon and had partaken of too much grog to safely navigate back to the Fort that same evening.

* * * *

The Trent affair on November 8th, 1861, gave rise to a fresh concern to local citizens. On that date, Captain Wilkes of the

Union gunboat San Jacinto stopped the English ship Trent, bound from Havana, and removed Mason and Slidell, two agents of the Confederate Government from under the British flag, despite a very strenuous protest from the British captain.

Opinion in the North greatly favored the act and the Salem papers like all the rest vociferously applauded the Union sea captain—only to accept with more or less good grace the decision of Lincoln and Seward to return the prisoners and to apologize to the British government. The Salem folks, seeing like every one else the imminent danger of a rupture with England, pleaded for more forts to guard the Delaware. They feared a British naval attack, which might have been far more serious than a Confederate one, and suggested another coast defense at Elsinboro Point and one on the Delaware side to supplant the island fort in the middle of the river. It is to be noted that some years later the War Department did construct the additional forts asked for, although in rather different locations than those mentioned at this time.

The Salem papers, after unanimously arguing that the seizure of the envoys was perfectly legal, quickly reversed themselves when the government decided they were wrong in seizing them from a neutral power's ship. When restitution was made to England the same papers agreed that Lincoln and Seward had done a "wise and prudent act."

In the last issue of 1861 appears this editorial in the Sunbeam characteristic of the stormy year which was closing: "The curtain is falling upon the most eventful year in the history of the United States. Commencing in gloom the clouds of distrust, doubt and dismay hung over us for six months before the nation awoke to a full appreciation of its perilous condition.

"The bold bad men who opened the flood gates of ruin are feeling most heavily the fatal consequences of their own unblushing and unequalled infamy."

Local state pride crept into the papers with the news of the first Union successes in the operations of Burnsides (he of the famous whiskers) around Newbern, North Carolina. New York papers claimed that the glory for winning a fight at Roanoke Island belonged to New York troops and ignored the New Jersey regiments who claimed the honor of winning the battle. Contention over what states won a particular battle shows itself several times during the course of the war and called forth a large amount of editorial comment as to "who was who" in various engagements.

In 1861 efforts were made in the state by ministers and church workers to organize a regiment composed solely of church members. The published announcements called for volunteers who would pledge themselves to abstain from the use of intoxicating liquors, profanity, gambling, cards, to avoid useless desecration of the Lord's Day and to obtain for the regiment a high moral and religious character. Beyond the first announcement of the call for the church regiment no further attention seems to have been given to it.

Vast shipments of cigarettes and tobacco to the soldiers in the World War recall the Ladies' Aid Societies of the Rebellion days when a sample shipment to the men in the field consisted for example of the following: 78 pairs of stockings, 37 pairs of mittens, 5 pillows, 42 pillow cases, 47 pairs of drawers, 9 arm pillows, 7 wash towels, 14 papers of corn starch and farina, 8 pounds of crackers and 9 comfortables.

August 29th, 1862, witnessed the second battle of Bull Run and the first fatality of one of Salem's sons although several of them had died of disease in the previous months of the war. Unscathed at the first battle of Bull Run, but wounded at Williamsburg a few months later, Captain Edward A. Acton was killed on the historic Manassas field while leading his company in a charge against the enemy. His men rallied around his body and kept it from possession of the enemy and had it buried under the Union flag on the field. The body was later brought to Salem and interred in the Friends Burying Ground. Acton left several half grown children, one of whom, Jonathan W. Acton, later became mayor and prosecutor of the city and county. It was Edward A. Acton who broke up the secessionist meeting at Alloway and who had also had charge of the recruiting service in this county before going back to active service. In the same battle fell some other Salem men among whom was a man named Sovereign whose father was a former Salem minister.

Salem and other New Jersey troops suffered heavily in the battle of Fredericksburg. At first disguised in the papers as a drawn battle, it soon was revealed as a disastrous Union defeat. It was in this battle that New Jersey's Twenty-fourth Regiment, under Col. William Robertson, received its baptism of fire, with terrible results.

The gloom prevailing in the North after the disastrous defeat at Fredericksburg in 1862 was accentuated six months later when on May 3rd at Chancellorsville, Virginia, the Confederates under Lee and "Stonewall" Jackson decisively whipped the new Union general Hooker and threw the Northern army into retreat and rout.

This was probably the darkest hour for the North. Indicative of the anguish experienced in Salem alone, is the following editorial from the Standard: "General Hooker's manoeuvers of last Thursday raised to a high extent the hope of capturing Lee's army and the speedy overthrow of the rebellion. Such was the state of the public feeling when on Thursday night came news of the defeat of Hooker and of his retreat across the Rappahannock with his army badly beaten and demoralized. No pall ever spread a more sudden or deeper gloom over the solemnities of death than did this intelligence over the entire community.

"None had ever dreamed of any such contingency. In that army were most of the sons, husbands and sires who had enlisted in the war from this county. In its success were bound up the hopes and fears of hundreds of happy households and patriotic hearts." The loss to Salem county alone at Chancellorsville covered a half column of print in the casualty list.

But the fates of war were beginning to change, for on the heels of the news of the Southern victory came the intelligence that "Stonewall" Jackson, the able Southern leader, had been killed at Chancellorsville.

Commenting upon the death of Jackson, the Standard said:

"He was a man of most indomitable energy, perseverance and unflinching courage. He has given our troops some of the hardest blows they have received during the war and in his death the rebels have met with a loss greater than all the threats of their mongrel soldiery."

Despite the prevalent gloom over Lee's invasion of Pennsylvania, the appointment of Meade to succed Hooker raised some hopes in Union hearts. Read this lament from the Standard over the state of mind in New Jersey as Lee's army swept up the Cumberland Valley into Pennsylvania:

"There is only a feeble response from the city of Philadelphia. Business goes on as usual and thousands of able bodied citizens capable of destroying Lee's entire army, walk the streets, occupied only with the pursuits of pleasure and wealth and with a great deal of unconcern, view the bulletins giving the latest news of the traitors advance into their own community. Perhaps their unconcern may change when Lee captures Harrisburg. The Delaware river and Jersey pluck we believe, will save our own soil from the invader's desecration, but we cannot be any too well prepared for such an emergency."

Governor Joel Parker summoned the New Jersey militia to Trenton but the need was gone as about ten o'clock on Sunday night, July 5th, came the news that Meade had done the seemingly impossible and had turned Lee back at Gettysburg for the greatest Union victory of the war.

The victory caused great rejoicing in Salem. A cannon was

dragged around the streets in a parade to inform sleepy citizens of the great news and the enthusiasm manifested itself throughout the night.

Several Salem people traveled to the battlefield and gave to the papers graphic accounts of the various scenes of horror which two weeks or more later, still were to be seen. Someone in the Standard advised prospective tourists "to take their own provisions, to be prepared to sleep in a chicken roost and not to mind the awful stench which permeated the battlefield."

Following Gettysburg came this editorial blast from the Sunbeam, showing that even victory could not lessen the burdens and the torture of war: "May this be the beginning of the end and may the end come speedily. Everybody is tired and sick of this cruel war. Everybody wants peace."

The fact that this war between the states was a struggle between brother and brother and cousin and cousin is portrayed by the fact that two members of a Salem family fought against each other and rendered distinguished service for their respective causes. Henry Ellet, son of Mrs. Sarah Ellet of Salem, who had moved to Mississippi a few years before the war started, was appointed postmaster general of the Confederacy. A member of the same family, General Alfred W. Ellet, who at that time came from Illinois, but whose son lived in Salem, was prominent in the reduction of the state of Mississippi by the Union forces.

In this city political feud broke out between two prominent Salem families, the Johnsons and the Chews. Colonel Robert Johnson had been appointed provost marshall of the draft by President Lincoln. He was later removed, and immediately dashed into print and charged Sinnickson Chew with a "sneaky conspiracy." Johnson, in his article in Chew's newspaper, accused these men, who he claimed had had him "fired," as being "cormorants and leeches joining with the rebels." He further accused Chew of having cheated the government on printing.

Before the war ended, there came the fearful fighting in the wilderness district of Virginia and the list of casualties included several more Salem countians. Among these was a much respected young man from Woodstown, John M. Fogg, who was killed by a sharpshooter near Chancellorsville. Fogg was a second lieutenant of Company H, the Twelfth New Jersey Regiment which suffered severely during the war. A long letter from a comrade to the Standard at this date, May 13th, 1864, gives a full account of his death and the scenes at his burial under fire. H. A. Mattison, a captain of this regiment, was reported killed, but was in reality a prisoner; he later escaped and got within Sherman's lines months afterwards. At the

THE LAST DRAFT 283

Battle of the Wilderness, the Twelfth Regiment was cut from 448 active men to 175. The loss to this community was so great that the editor of the Sunbeam, over the list of those who died for their nation at this terrible battle, put these words:

> And love will faithful tend her vestal lamp
> And keep their garlands green with constant tears,
> While o'er their ashes with historic tramp
> Looms up the grandeur of the passing years.

In the summer of 1864 appeared the first notice of Salem's volunteer war nurse, Miss Cornelia Hancock of Lower Creek, contained in a long but exceedingly laudatory account by a war correspondent for the New York Tribune. Miss Hancock's work from the battle of Gettysburg on to the end, was of a most benevolent and meritorious nature and to her goes the added honor of being one of the very first of the volunteer war nurses whose services in that war and other wars have made life a bit easier for the sick and wounded.

In February, 1865, occurred the last draft to swell the Union armies. It was no secret that in Salem county as well as in other sections of the North, the draft was decidedly unpopular. There were several ways around it, the most famous loophole being to engage a substitute which is what a great many Salem countians did. Countless cases appear in the press of substitutes who obtained several hundred dollars from conscripted citizens, enlisted, deserted and appeared again in some distant locality to offer their services again. Bounty jumpers vied with this other form of gentry and added greatly to the perplexities of the officials in charge of the conscription. Several localities, this included, offered bounties to volunteers so that the draft might pass by them when it came. If a particular township had a quota of thirty men to raise, this quota might be filled by volunteers who, tempted by bounties for joining, would relieve the locality of furnishing that many men to the draft.

The exemption list was not carefully made out and classified as was the case in the World War and we read instances of ministers being drafted and their congregations being compelled to buy them off by hiring substitutes. In this last draft, all the townships of Salem county filled their quota except Pilesgrove, Upper Penns Neck and Upper Alloways Creek. It was in this last named township that the famous "secess" meetings had been held four years previously. A late Salem county official, whose parents were rank copperheads, once told of an instance when, as a boy of six, he hurrahed at the news of the death of President Lincoln.

The fall of Richmond brought realization to Salem that the days of the war were numbered and with peace at last in sight, we find the Standard a forerunner of the conquered province theory of treatment of the South.

Said the Standard, "We are utterly opposed to the President's issuing more proclamations of mercy to the rebel chiefs and their deluded white followers. If they will not trust in Mr. Lincoln's forbearing and merciful disposition after all that he has done they are beyond human redemption. The only sure and effective means of restoring peace to our country, a peace that will not forfeit our nation as a nation, lies in our judgment, in the relentless and vigorous prosecution of the war until the rebel armies everywhere either surrender or disperse and the rebel simulated government is annihilated."

Following the fall of Richmond and the surrender of Lee at Appomattox came the black bordered editions of both papers announcing the shooting of Lincoln by Booth in Fords Theatre, Washington, April 14th, 1865.

"Slavery murders President" said the Standard. The assassination loosed again the floodgates of wrath and rage and it is not surprising to see the papers clamoring for the gibbeting of that "incarnate fiend Davis" and the imprisonment of that "arch traitor and prisoner starver, Robert E. Lee." Editorially and actually it seemed very evident that the period of reconstruction engendered more hatred and animosity than the war itself.

A very celebrated contemporary book "The Tragic Era" by Claude Bowers tells only too vividly of the political assassination of President Johnson and the subsequent events both North and South which led to more strife after the war was safely over.

In this same book occurs a reference to Salem and riots which took place here in those hectic days of reconstruction. This reference is a clipping from the New York World repeating the Standard for June 24th, 1865.

Substantially the facts were these, although it seems a far call from the riotous condition of the country as alleged by Bowers to this isolated instance in Salem which seems to have been more of a free-for-all fight than anything else. On the night of Saturday, June 17th, a number of whites and blacks started to fight on Star Hall Corner over what was alleged to have been insulting remarks from a colored woman to a white woman. The whites gathered in force and ran the blacks down Broadway, pursuing them with bricks, vegetables and similar articles. One brickbat grazed the head of the mayor of Salem.

Several of the pursued colored citizens took refuge in various friendly stores and homes, probably fearing a repetition of the New York anti-colored demonstration two years before.

The police got the upper hand and the riot seems to have been over in two hours. But the next morning at Kent's Corner on the Salem-Elsinboro line, hostilities broke out again when a gang of colored men attacked two Irishmen, brothers named John and Patrick Roosney, who were on their way home from church. Various remarks prefaced the actual hostilities which ended when one of the negroes drew a gun and shot John Roosney in the shoulder. The negroes ran off after the shooting but were rounded up and arrested. The wounds of John Roosney were not serious and Father Cannon, the Catholic priest, who was summoned, dispersed the angry crowd bent on retaliating against the negroes.

The majority of the Salem men in the various New Jersey regiments were returned home in June and July of 1865 and the excitement over the war died down to leave room for the many political controversies carried on in the current press.

* * * *

In Finn's Point National Cemetery, Lower Penns Neck township, there is a huge granite monument lifting its shaft into the air far above the graves of 2436 Confederate soldiers who died while prisoners of war at Fort Delaware. It is ironic to contemplate that a massive stone marker was erected by the federal government to designate the last resting place of men who had died under that same government's custody seventy years before.

Few people realize the true significance of Fort Delaware. It meant to the Southland exactly what Andersonville and Libby meant to the North and while there is no attempt to prove that cruelties such as were perpetrated by Wirz at Andersonville went on at Fort Delaware, there is a decided move to demonstrate just how unhealthy and unsanitary that prison camp was to the soldiers of the Confederacy. As one of the few Salem survivors of that day said to the writer, "Fort Delaware was poison to the Confeds," just so plain will be the effort to show how bad it was and how, long after the war was over, the Southern states made representations of terrible conditions afforded their prisoners on the island in answer to the Northern claims for ill treatment in the prison camps of the South. It must be recalled also that the Union executed Wirz, the warden of Andersonville, for his barbaric treatment of Northern prisoners.

One of the most noted blasts against the prison camp at Fort Delaware comes from no less an authority than Dr. S. Wier Mitchell, celebrated Philadelphia doctor. During the war Dr. Mitchell was a Federal inspector of prisons and in his memoirs, recently published, has this startling revelation to give of the Fort.

In a letter to his sister, Elizabeth Mitchell, the doctor says, "Tomorrow, (July 26th, 1863) I go to Fort Delaware to inspect that inferno of detained rebels. A thousand men ill, twelve thousand on an island which should only hold four, the general level three feet below low water mark, 20 deaths a day from dysentery and the living having more life on them than in them, occasional lack of water and thus a Christian nation treats the captives of its sword! Two weeks ago the rebel officers plotted to take the fort but were betrayed and carried off to Sandusky."

In another portion of his book, Mitchell tells of his first trip to the Fort and says, "I was employed as an inspector of hospitals and prison hospitals, a very serious business in those days. A most interesting opportunity of this kind was a visit made by order of the Department to Fort Delaware which is on an island ten miles below New Castle. There were some 9000 persons on the island including the garrison—a number of surgeons were confined in the casemates of the fort (these were the bomb-proof chambers of the fort). I thought their lot a hard one.

"In retaliation we held all the surgeons captured at Gettysburg. I knew some of these gentlemen and later by gifts of books, money and tobacco, tried to assist them."

Fort Delaware had considerable history long before the Civil War gave it additional prestige. The island on which it was situated was said to have been caused by the sinking of a schooner loaded with peas enroute from Philadelphia to Boston, thus giving the island its name of Pea Patch. It was about 1784 when the island appeared in the river according to old men who were living in 1847 when a suit was heard to determine whether it belonged to Salem county or to the state of Delaware. The government had purchased it from the state of Delaware and had erected a fort upon it but suspended operations pending the determination of the suit. The litigation went against James Humphreys, the New Jersey citizen claiming title to it, and the government finished in 1859 the fort which had previously been burned and inundated by a high tide.

Three times since the completion of the fort it has been heavily garrisoned and its men's anxious eyes turned south down the river to watch for hostile fleets which might try to force their way up the Delaware. The first was the Civil War, the others the Spanish-American and World Wars.

As soon as the break occurred with the South and about the time Fort Sumter capitulated, Fort Delaware was garrisoned to some extent of its strength but not as much as the citizens of this section and of Philadelphia and Chester thought desirable. Consequently, protests were made to the War Department that insufficient protection was being given this territory and demands for additional forts on either side were made. Forts Mott and DuPont came at a later date but after a few days of fighting, the additional troops asked for were sent to the fort and the inhabitants breathed easier.

It was late in 1861 that the government, probably feeling safe from the enemy, began to use it as a prison camp for captured Confederates. Up to a year later comparatively few were imprisoned there although two of Salem's leading citizens and others from various Eastern cities were detained for copperhead tendencies. Boston Gosling and Dr. E. S. Sharpe, both outspoken Southern sympathizers, were put there for short periods until they were willing to take the oath of allegiance to the United States.

It was 1862 when the fort began to fill up with prisoners and grew from an internment camp of about 1000 to a young city of almost 12,000 in the latter days of 1863. This rapid growth of population compelled the government to construct additional housing facilities in the shape of a huge stockade surrounded by barbed wire, on the north end of the island. Here went the great mass of the captives while the officers, surgeons and political prisoners were largely confined in the casemates and dungeons of the fort itself. Refractory prisoners were placed in solitary confinement in dungeons built into the masonry of the fort. These dungeons, which may still be viewed by visitors to the island, are entirely without light now, but in those days were illuminated by a huge oil lantern suspended from the ceiling. Ventilation to these underground fastnesses were secured by air passages, too small for escape, which ran from the dungeon to the top of the fortifications. At various times the commandants of Fort Delaware were Major H. S. Burton, Colonel Herman Segebarth and during the latter years of the war, a major general by the name of Schoepf. Schoepf was a Hungarian political refugee who obtained a commission in the Federal army.

The peninsular campaign netted the North its first substantial batch of prisoners and with those captured at Seven Pines, Va., on May 31st, 1862, came General James Johnston Pettigrew, who was exchanged some weeks later. Among the political captives was a speaker of the House of Representatives, Mr. Crisp, of Georgia. Rumor has it that no less a celebrated personage than Henry Stanley, who a decade later found Livingston in Africa, was also confined here, until he took the oath of allegiance to the Union cause.

There were many, many attempts to escape from the Fort, most of them being unsuccessful. Quite a few were shot down in the water while trying to swim away but those who did get away made good their escape by the underground railroad which existed for that purpose throughout Salem county and Southern Delaware.

One day the *Major Reybold*, on her regular trip from Philadelphia to Salem, landed a group of prisoners at the fort and having discharged them proceeded down the river and was about in the entrance of the creek when a "hissing noise convinced the captain something was amiss." An instant later, a cannon ball whistled over the bow of the steamer and gave another hiss when it landed in the water. The captain kept on his way into the mouth of the creek when a third shot again narrowly missed the boat. Convinced that either the fort, or one of the gunboats off the fort, wanted him to come back, the *Major* was turned around and half-way back met the Union gunboat which had fired upon them.

When the fort had checked the prisoners the *Major* brought, they found they were one colonel short and thinking he was a stowaway on the boat, heading for Salem, had ordered the gunboat to fire upon the Salem steamer. Investigation later showed that the officer was not on the boat but had effected his escape in Philadelphia.

The gunboat captain was kind enough to tell the *Major's* captain, when the excitement had died away, that the last shot was meant to hit them, and that he was annoyed at the poor marksmanship of his gunner. The *Reybold's* crew however, were rather glad that the gunner was not an expert, because there was a large number of women and children on the boat. Both Salem papers bristled with righteous indignation at the unnecessary use of cannon balls. Said the Standard, "The consequences might have been disastrous as there were a large number of people on board returning from camp meeting."

Following Gettysburg came the largest influx of prisoners that the fort had yet sheltered with the population of the island up to almost 12,000 including the Federal garrison. This is the period of which Dr. Mitchell speaks, and these summer months of 1863 witnessed the outbreak of the fearful epidemic of cholera morbus which played havoc with the captured Confederates.

The first intimation of epidemic on the island come from the Sunbeam of June, 1863, which says, "There is a great mortality on the island. Lack of water, exhaustion, etc., are daily causing the death of large numbers of the confined rebels, and we are informed that there are daily burial parties on the Jersey shore at Finn's Point."

One other account in the Standard for about the same date, states that there were forty deaths a day from an outbreak of diarrhoea. Outside of these comments, and an appeal for funds for relief of the garrison and sick prisoners, the Salem press was silent on the situation across the river where over two thousand Confederates died the death of pestilence and disease.

The late Charles W. Dunn, whose farm was close to the Finn's Point Cemetery, remembers vividly seeing the trenches used for the burial of the dead at that place and recalls also being in the cemetery when the steamer from Fort Delaware brought over its daily consignment of dead. The story is told that the Unionists were contemptuous enough of their stricken foe to have brought them over to the Jersey side in flat bottomed scows and to have thrown them feet first in the common grave, like so many dead horses. This story Mr. Dunn contradicts and adds that the bodies were all placed in wooden boxes and were laid, with some reverence, row by row in the large trench on the north side of the cemetery.

Although Northern writers and some military men have pointed out that the amount of mortalities on the island were not excessive considering the conditions, yet in view of Dr. Mitchell's opinion and others, it must be seen that the Union forces should have known that crowding 9000 prisoners on an island only large enough to hold 2000 would mean disease and pestilence. The death of 2436 prisoners is enough to give one pause to think when the mortality of an average engagement in the war, on both sides, was not equal to that number.

* * * *

While the Civil War was raging on the battlefields of Virginia, one of the great leaders of Quakerism, Lucretia Mott, spoke in Salem on the subject of "Peace". A startling event which attracted much public attention was the sinking of the *Major Reybold* on the rocks at the mouth of Salem creek. There was no loss of life but the passengers were in danger until rowboats from the shore broke through the ice and rescued them.

The lovers of sport in this county will be interested in

knowing that the first baseball game played within the confines of this county took place in the summer of 1865 following the close of the war. The baseball team which first represented the city of Salem was known as the Mosacsa, named after a tribe of Indians in this locality. Oddly enough, the team they played in this opening game was known as the Lenape team from New Castle, Delaware. The Lenape Indians had been the foremost tribe in this section of South Jersey. The Mosacsas defeated the Lenaps by the overwhelming score of 37 to 11. The lineup of this first Salem team was: Stretch c, Eakin p, York 1b, Ingham ss, Grey 2b, Stratton 3b, Sinnickson lf, Billop rf, Homer cf. This club was organized in May of 1865. The grounds were on South street, now Walnut, opposite the Walnut Street Methodist Church.

At the conclusion of the war, the Salem and Bridgeton Turnpike Company was organized. The business men of Salem who formed this company to build a good gravel road between the two towns were George M. Ward, Robert English, George Hires, Johnson Hitchner, William Shimp, Job Ayres and John Lambert. This road, with its three toll gates, remained a private highway until 1915.

This decade also saw the completion of the first railroad into the county. On July 1st, 1863, the first railroad train puffed placidly into Claysville to inaugurate rail service between Salem and Camden.

The story of the Salem Railroad, to give it its original name, reads like a romance. The courageous, far-sighted men who made it possible deserve all the credit a community may give them and although their handiwork was doomed to comparatively short popularity, yet nevertheless they were builders and producers of their time. With divided public opinion as to routes and grave financial troubles in a very turbulent national period, it is a wonder that any railroad ever came to Salem, but the pioneer spirit of the Salemites, undaunted by the heavy task, made it possible.

Its history is largely a history of routes and money. The first idea of a railroad seems to have appeared about 1848 in the shape of a suggestion by Richard P. Thompson, Attorney General of New Jersey, who proposed to build a railroad from Salem to Pennsville, establish a ferry and connect with the present Delaware Division of the Pennsylvania Railroad at New Castle, Delaware. A part of the present division was in operation at that early date. Acting on this advice and largely through Mr. Thompson's efforts a charter was obtained from the New Jersey Legislature in 1850 for such a road. It was called the Salem and

THE RAILROAD ARRIVES

Delaware River Railroad and Transportation Company and its incorporators were the following prominent citizens of Salem: James H. Hannah, Thomas Jones Yorke, James Brown, Lewis S. Yorke, Joseph H. Thompson, Jacob W. Mulford, Jonathan Ingham, John Wistar, Andrew Sinnickson, Thomas J. Casper, Joseph Bassett, George M. Ward, Thomas D. Bradway, Benjamin Holme and William Powell. The capital stock was fixed at $100,000 which could be increased to $150,000. Despite the obtaining of the charter, the idea did not take strongly with the business men. Most of them felt that it was only a temporary expedient and that if possible a direct line should be made to Camden. Realizing this, no strong attempt was made to sell stock and the idea was soon abandoned.

Mule teams and bathing beaches were two reasons why the South Jersey railroads were eventually constructed and this had a direct connection with the construction of the Salem line. From their flourishing glassworks at Glassboro the Whitneys were obliged to use mule teams to haul the completed ware as well as their supplies and they were anxious to have rail connections with the outside world. Cape Island or Cape May in the middle of the nineteenth century was the leading seashore resort of the nation and to keep their trade they were equally anxious to have a railroad. As far as Salem was concerned, the impossibility of keeping the river open in the winter coupled with the long and arduous stage journey made it imperative that the town have some kind of rail outlet. In 1852, a meeting of representative South Jerseymen was held to consider the road direct from Camden. A committee obtained a survey and an estimate of the cost. The route decided upon was through Millville and Glassboro to Cape Island with a branch to Salem. The estimate of the cost was a million dollars for the main line and $275,000 for the branch to Salem. Another charter was obtained from the legislature of 1852 and the West Jersey and Seashore Railroad Company was formed.

But is was one thing to get a charter and another to raise the required amount of money. There had been a small road built from Camden to Woodbury which had been a failure and local citizens were wary of sinking their money in something which looked so doubtful. T. Jones Yorke of Salem deserves a great amount of credit for his untiring efforts in obtaining the necessary funds.

By 1857 enough money had been raised to construct some of the road and in 1861 it was opened to Bridgeton. The lack of money had caused Cape Island to fade out of the picture until later, and it was likewise quite apparent to Salem people that if a branch was to be had with the main line at Elmer or Glassboro that they would have to rely largely upon their own efforts. Bridgeton had the road and was satisfied but unless Salem could raise in the neighborhood of $275,000 to connect with it, they would be left out in the cold entirely. Another charter was obtained from the willing legislature, this time for the Salem Railroad Company, in 1856.

The public spirited men who began to see "railroad daylight" coming were: Richard P. Thompson, Charles P. Smith, Joseph Bassett, William Reeve, Richard M. Acton, Richard Greer, Samuel Abbott, Isaac Johnson, Abram Richman, David Pettitt, Joseph Jessup, Samuel C. Harbart, James Brown, Lewis C. Yorke and others. Again it became a question of opening the subscription books and soliciting stock sales. This time the area for solicitations was restricted and it was indeed a man sized job to get the required amount. The county was thoroughly canvassed by D. W. C. Clement whose indefatigable exertions finally resulted in the assurance of the branch road. Mr. Clement was treasurer of the company and remained in this position until his death in 1882. William R. Reeve was the first president; he was the owner of a flourishing ship yard at Allowaystown. Mr. Reeve died in 1878 and was succeeded as president by Benjamin Acton, Samuel Abbott and Richard M. Acton. When General Sewell became president, the Salem Railroad Company had been merged with the West Jersey Railroad Company.

The money question being settled, the question of a route then agitated the promoters. Woodstown was the principal stumbling block as the backers of the road felt that much good might accrue to Woodstown by having the road come that way but the Pilesgrove citizens seemed apathetic and took little interest in raising the money or in wanting the road, so it was finally decided to go via the Alloway woods and Daretown to Pittstown, the modern Elmer. Actual work was started in 1861 but it progressed slowly, with the nation in the grip of a Civil War. In January, 1863, the road was completed as far as Yorktown and trains ran that far and were met by stages from Salem. On the first day of the battle of Gettysburg, trains ran for the first time into Claysville. Hampered by lack of money it had been decided to stop work at Claysville and use stages into Salem. The estimate of the cost of a bridge across the creek seemed high and there was some difficulty over the right of way so the road terminated at Claysville until 1882 when the creek was bridged and entrance made into Salem. In 1868, the citizens of Swedesboro backed the extension of the road to that place and with revived interest, through to Pilesgrove and in 1882 connected with the old road at Riddletown Junction.

The stations on the road were: Acton Road, Middletown Road, Abbottsford, Alloway, Oakland, Yorketown, Paulding, Daretown, Newkirk, Pittstown (Elmer).

* * * *

There was a building boom and likewise an increase in industrial effort in Salem following the Civil War. The Salem Glass Works, today one of the largest glass factories of the United States, was organized in 1863. Three years later a new glass factory managed by the firm of Holtz, Taylor and Clark, started in this city. This firm has gone out of business but in the period of the 1870's the plant was sold to a young English immigrant by the name of Gayner and since that time has been continued as Gayner Glass Works. Thus, Salem with its two large factories of the Craven or Salem Glass and the Gayner Glass carry on at this day the honorable tradition of Casper Wistar and Wistarburg. In March of 1866, a local boy who had made good, Dr. David Jayne, died in Philadelphia worth three million dollars. His father had been a Baptist preacher in Canton. The son had nearly starved to death on a farm. Moving to Philadelphia about 1830, he had gone into the drug business, had picked up the idea of patent medicines and from that idea had made this money. For years his palatial home stood at Nineteenth and Chestnut streets in Philadelphia.

An oil cloth factory was organized and started to manufacture floor covering in 1866; 250 colored soldiers, veterans of the Civil War, paraded through the streets of Salem; the first night school was established; the Meridian Houses, used by surveyors to establish bounds, were erected on the school house grounds on Grant street; and in Alloway a three masted schooner with a keel of 110 feet was launched.

The 1860's were noted in this locality for their very solemn and impressive funerals. They were noted also for maudlin obituary notices. A sample one reads:

> Sweet Little Willie, thou was't not given
> Long here to dwell,
> From earth's rude blasts thou art safe in Heaven,
> Farewell, oh farewell.

In one week of 1865, five men who had been pioneers in the life of this county died. They were Josiah Harrison a prominent lawyer and the author of "Harrison's Reports," who died at the age of 90; Elisha Bassett, a prominent Quaker; William H.

Nelson, the builder of the hotel which bears his name and an eminent political leader of his period; Josiah M. Reeve, ship builder of Allowaystown; and Judge Joseph Kille, the stormy petrel of Democratic politics for forty years.

The famous Thunderbolt race track on the Hancock's Bridge road was completed in 1868. The citizens of this county at that time were proud of their horses and the newspapers of that day are full of the exciting races at this old track. The artistic side of life also received attention. There was a lyceum course and under its auspices there were frequent entertainments and lecturers. There were two performances by the Swiss Bell Ringers, there was a drama company which played in reckless profusion, "Hamlet", "The Octoroon," "East Lynne" and others, and there came again to Salem Horace Greeley, who articulated better than he had fifteen years before. There came also a company which played the reigning favorite of that day "Ten Nights in a Barroom". John B. Gough, a temperance orator, spoke from the lyceum stage. De Witt Talmadge, a celebrated minister, also was a speaker. A Salem boy, George W. Pettit, who was an artist of ability, exhibited in Philadelphia his portrait of Hamlet and Ophelia. He likewise painted the assembled solons of the Philadelphia City Council.

The end of the decade saw a great increase in religious feeling. It was in that year and in the spring of 1870 that one of the largest religious revivals occurred in this county. The First Baptist Church under the leadership of Pastor Murphy had so many converts that it was necessary to form a new church which was called the Memorial Baptist Church in memory of the great revival of 1869. This church took the place of the Second Baptist Church which had failed of support four years before. In this same year there was a new Methodist Church dedicated at Quinton. There was one dedicated at Watson's Corner, near Aldine, known as the Nazareth Church, and there was one completed at Elmer. An eminent Presbyterian minister, the Reverend Daniel Stratton, died at this time. There was a religious revival at Canton in Lower Alloways Creek which accounted for a large increase in membership of the Canton Baptist Church. One of the great members of the Episcopalian ministry, Phillip Brooks, spoke in St. John's Church in October of this same year. A Y. M. C. A. was established in the Ingham Building over the post office. It successfully held forth here and in the Patterson Building, now the Lummis Building, until the present Y. M. C. A. building was erected in 1894.

General U. S. Grant was the hero of the day; his fame had reached to Salem, because a livery stable owner, purchasing a new omnibus or hack, had painted on the side in gaudy green and purple a beautiful portrait of General Grant.

The Rumsey Building, now known as the Erhardt Building, was built in the 1860's, primarily as a boarding school. In this building the Reverend J. W. Smiley on September 9, 1867, opened the Salem Collegiate Institute, a finishing school for young ladies. This was a combined boarding and day school. Reverend Smiley ran it until 1869, when John H. Bechtell assumed charge. After three years, H. P. Davidson became the head master and for ten or twelve years had a very successful educational institute. Davidson had ideas of his own on advanced education and in connection with his school, printed a newspaper called "The Alert." In the preparation of this publication, the students took an active part, setting the type and printing the paper. When Bechtell took charge of the school it was made co-educational and conducted so until the school ended in the early 1880's.

The old jail which had stood since 1775 in front of the court house was torn down at this time. The wreckers found underneath the floor a secret cellar of which the oldest inhabitant had never heard. The story circulated around Salem that there was a large amount of gold and silver hidden in the cellar but the anxious treasure seekers found nothing but dirt for their efforts.

* * * *

On the political side, the '60s were largely Republican triumphs. The Whig party had died and the Republican party in its second election, that of 1860, had by virtue of the split in the Democratic party elected their president, Abraham Lincoln. In this county, save for one or two upsets, the Republican party maintained its supremacy during the Civil War and more especially during the reconstruction days which followed.

In the first year of the war, the Republicans entered the campaign with a pledge not to buy votes. They elected their two assemblymen and the sheriff in the person of Owen L. Jones, one of the outstanding political figures of his day. The next year saw one of the few complete Democratic triumphs of this era because Joel Parker, Democratic candidate for governor, carried Salem county by 300 votes. Former Congressman Stratton won the county by the same majority. Richard Greer, Democrat, was elected surrogate. Two Assembly seats went to the Democrats, Joseph W. Cooper and Joseph Waddington. They also won three coroners in this, their last great victory for some time to come. In 1863 James W. Mecum, Democrat, lost to Richard M. Acton, he whose name is perpetuated in the name of a Salem school. William M. Hancock, Republican, and war veteran of Lower Alloway's Creek, won one of the Assembly seats and Mr. Cooper was re-elected to the other.

With the soldiers voting in the field in the fall of 1864, George B. McClellan lost the county by 40 votes although he carried New Jersey over Abraham Lincoln. The election was close throughout. I. V. Dickinson lost by 17 votes to his Republican opponent, Congressman Starr; 70 votes gave victory to Jonathan L. Brown, Republican, over William Wood, Democrat leader of Upper Pittsgrove, for the position of surrogate. Two Republican assemblymen were elected and the lowest one of the Republican coroners held his job by a one-vote margin over the highest Democrat.

"No time to dilate upon this glorious event," said the Standard following the election of 1865. Again they swept the field electing Ward, Republican governor, who carried the county by 200 votes, two assemblymen and three coroners. One of the men who won the Assembly seat this year had the distinction of having more initials to his name than any other Salem countian in public life. His full name was Auxendrico M. P. V. H. Dickinson. Some people were so much disappointed after the election of 1865 that they were poor sports enough to throw printer's ink all over the front of the National Standard Building.

Following the election of 1866 came a practical application of a gerrymander. Pittsgrove township, in the extreme eastern end of Salem county, was full of Democrats and their two-hundred vote plurality was very comforting to the Salem county Jeffersonian leaders. The Republican total hardly ever exceeded sixty. At that time also the colored man had not been given the franchise and the Grand Old Party thought of Elbridge Gerry and got to work.

Prior to 1857 there had been an attempt made in the New Jersey Legislature to swing Pittsgrove township over to Cumberland county where its Democratic pluralities would do no damage, but Senator Richard M. Acton put his foot down on the idea. He was a Republican and saw the party benefits, but steadfastedly refused to "play ball." In the election of 1866, Samuel Plummer was elected state senator over his Democratic opponent by a margin of 105 votes. At that time Salem had two assemblymen in the house. One district comprised Salem, Elsinboro, Mannington, Alloway and Lower Creek. The other district took in Pittsgrove, Pilesgrove, Upper Penns Neck, Upper Pittsgrove and Lower Penns Neck. In the first district in that momentous election of 1866 the Democrats elected John S. Newell, and in the other district the Republicans elected Samuel Garrison of Pittsgrove to the Assembly. In the entire legislature the Republicans had 46 seats to the Democrats' 35. They also had the governor, Marcus L. Ward. So the stage was completely set for the idea of divorcing Pittsgrove township from Salem county.

During the election of 1866, the Democrats were suspicious of this new "Polish partition" and turned their guns on candidate Plummer, declaring he had signed a petition to Senator Acton urging this division. Mr. Plummer was quite indignant and signed an affidavit that he had not signed any such petition and was backed by Senator Acton in the statement. However, becoming senator, this gentleman promptly began the work in Trenton for this very thing and as he had not sufficient Democratic opposition to stop him the bill passed its successive readings in the Senate and was well on its way to enactment. The Democratic Sunbeam, sensing trouble, yelled thief with all its might. The first plan was to make a separate county of Millville, Vineland, Landis Township and Pittsgrove, but this plan was soon abandoned by the managers, who contented themselves with the amputation of Pittsgrove. The bill passed the Senate and went to the Assembly, with the Sunbeam still shouting murder.

Meanwhile the Republican Standard, outside of the mere mention of its passage, maintained a resolute silence. When the bill passed the Assembly in April, 1867 and became a law the indignation of the Sunbeam knew no bounds; in blazing headlines, Editor Gwynne referred to the "deep damnation of their taking off", and said: "The last and greatest political outrage has taken place. We cannot express our contempt for the men who have done this thing. Let the finger of scorn be pointed at every man who has been accessory to thus despoiling Salem County of her domain and of forcing the entire population of a township to cut loose from the ties they had formed among us and cast them off, not only unwilling but indignant and protesting to the uncongenial embrace of a stranger. And more especially let the public indignation fall upon those in official position who have basely betrayed the county that has fostered and the people that have elevated them.

> "Oh for a whip in every honest hand,
> To lash the rascals naked through the world."

So Pittsgrove passed to the embrace of Cumberland county and the lamentations of the disconsolate Democrats knew no bounds.

In July of 1867 a small riot broke out at Pittstown in which some unruly blacks from Gouldtown and disreputable whites from Vineland got mixed up with some home town boys in which the results were a bit bloody. "Surely," said the Sunbeam, "this is proof positive. As a part of Salem county this township was a decent law abiding community and look at it now. Surely something must be done to relieve old Pittsgrove from its bondage which it has been thrust by bold bad men who care nothing for the ruin they accomplish if they can advance their party by so doing."

A tabled resolution in the Salem Board of Freeholders condemned Senator Plummer's action and lauded Ex-Senator Acton for his part in refusing to go along with this measure. From then until election the Sunbeam sounded the tocsin loud and often, always ending its fervid editorial appeals with the cry, "Remember Sam Garrison," "Remember Pittsgrove." The election of 1867 drew on and even the Trenton True American took up the cudgel for the lost township and pleaded for its restoration. In Salem the election for the Assembly went against the Democrats and two Republicans were elected, Andrew Smith Reeve and Henry M. Wright. But in the state the Democrats ran wild, getting control of the Senate and the House with a majority on a joint ballot of 33 votes. Even Cape May county returned a Democratic senator. "Now," thundered the Sunbeam, "is the time to recover the lost province," and until February 20th, 1868, the paper kept tirelessly and strenuously after the redemption of Pittsgrove. On the above date, the overwhelming Democratic balance in the legislature returned the lost lamb to the fold.

At Trenton, the limelight turned for a brief instant upon the embattled senator from Salem who had cast aside his own people and the gentleman had a bad day explaining his vote on the matter. He arose in a hostile senate to make a speech on the retention of Pittsgrove. He argued that Bridgeton as a county seat was nearer by ten miles than Salem, that he was acquainted with these people, that he had known them all his life and that he loved them and wanted to do what was best. "Ah," interrupted the Democratic senator from Hudson, Mr. Winfield, "does the gentleman from Salem love them enough to take them to his bosom again?" Heckled and jeered the Salem senator gave up the ghost and retired from the field. Three of his own party left the Senate, refusing to vote on the measure which was passed by a vote of 11 to 7.

In Salem, the local Democrats were jubliant over the return of the "native." The Standard broke a stony silence to comment that "geographically the township belongs to Cumberland and there were other reasons why it should remain where it was."

POLITICS IN THE 1860's

Exulting, Editor Gwynne burst into poetry and sang: "Time at last brings all things even."

* * * *

In 1867 the City Council of Salem organized three wards, the east, west and middle. This arrangement only lasted four years when it was changed back to the present arrangement of the east and west wards. Under the 1867 division the east ward ran from Parrott (now Seventh) street east to Keasbey creek. The west ward ran from Oak street to Salem creek. The middle ward took what was left over in the middle of the town.

The reconstruction days brought woe to the Republicans of Salem for a time, because late in the fall of 1867 Colonel William B. Robertson, who had rendered distinguished service in the Union Army at Fredricksburg and elsewhere, was removed as postmaster by President Johnson as a part of his fight against a hostile, radical Congress and a Salem storekeeper named Nehimiah Dunn was put in his place. The Republicans were bitter over Robertson's removal. They called Dunn a know-nothing who did not even know which party he belonged to. They brought much pressure in Washington, for five months later Dunn was removed and Robertson put back as postmaster in which office he remained until 1875. Except for the one victory of John S. Newell in 1866, the Democrats lost everything in the two years of '66 and '67, nor was 1868 any better for them. Although Randolph, Democrat, was elected governor of New Jersey over Blair, Republican, he lost this county by a large majority and his ticket shared the same fate. It was not until 1869 that the Republicans lost a county office in a general election. In that year, John C. Belden was elected state senator over Joseph Waddington. Two Republican assemblymen won, but for county clerk, Jacob M. Lippincott, the lyric poet of Salem, defeated by a margin of 55 votes his Republican opponent, Owen L. Jones, who was called, and rightly so, one of the outstanding Republicans of his day. Samuel Plummer, former sheriff, senator and assemblyman, was this year appointed by President Grant as the United States marshall for the district of New Jersey, being the only Salem county man who has ever held this high federal position.

It was in this period that Salem county had one of its sons, and its only one, elevated to the purple of the United States Senate. This was Alexander Gilmore Cattell, who on September 3, 1866, took his seat as a United States Senator, having been elected by the legislature of New Jersey to fill the unexpired term of William Wright. Cattell was a native son of Salem. His grandfather, Elisha Cattell, according to tradition, had rowed a boat across the Delaware river to join Washington's army when he heard the guns of the Battle of the Brandywine. His father, Thomas Ware Cattell, who was named after a famous Methodist evangelist, was an upright and honest citizen of Salem, having been for a four-year period postmaster of the city. Alexander Cattell had entered politics at an early age. He was elected to the Assembly of New Jersey for the session of 1840 whence he wrote to the home folks interesting episodes of his legislative career. He wrote among other things and with sorrow, "that I occupy the desk of Joseph Hancock who only a year ago sat in this place and who is now gathered to his fathers." Hancock had died suddenly and Cattell had taken his seat. In the Constitutional Convention of 1844 Cattell, then 28 years of age, was one of the three delegates from Salem county. By a few votes he had been defeated for the state senate and by 1850 had moved to Philadelphia, where he became a successful banker. At the close of the Civil War he again picked up his New Jersey interests and is credited with being one of the founders of the modern town of Merchantville. But for nearly two decades he had been entirely out of politics and out of the state. His election, therefore, by the legislature of 1866 occasioned a great deal of surprise and his enemies were quick to say that the large means which he had gathered as a banker were responsible for his election. He served almost a full term in the Senate, retiring on March 3, 1871. It fell to Cattell's lot to be one of the few Senators in this nation who ever voted in the impeachment trial of a president of the United States. Cattell, being strictly a Republican organization man, voted guilty in the famous trial of Andrew Johnson in 1868.

CHAPTER XXV

SALEM IN THE 1870's

The 1870's opened with a visit to Salem by the world's greatest showman, "The Mighty Barnum," otherwise Phineas T. He did not come to Salem with his circus but as a private lecturer under the auspices of the local lyceum course. The title of his lecture was "Monstrosities and Humbugs" and no one in this wide world was better qualified to talk upon that subject. To the same lyceum stage in this period came Anna Dickinson and Petroleum V. Nasby.

Salem organized a Board of Trade in 1871 under the presidency of Richard M. Acton. This organization was the predecessor of the present Chamber of Commerce. In this era, business was picking up. A new oil cloth plant had been started. The Salem Glass Works were in operation and doing a good business.

Many of the factories which started about this time are still in operation. Following the success of the Salem Glass Works another glass plant at the foot of Broadway was begun by Messrs. Holtz, Taylor and Clark, which for them was not successful and the plant was leased to a New York firm who sent here as manager a Mr. John Gayner, the man who would buy the plant and make this factory the modern Gayner Glass Works. Its neighbor, the oil cloth plant, was started in 1868 by Messrs. Hall, Dunn and Hunt. Eventually, William Morris and a company known as the American Oil Cloth Company took it over and continued it for many years. It is now the Salem plant of the Congoleum Company.

Following the Civil War, the canning business received much attention and several local citizens entered this line. One of the most successful of these was the Patterson and Jones Canning Factory which started in 1864 and was first erected on Church street. Later, when Owen L. Jones and Patterson bought out the company it was moved to Fifth street in the building now occupied by the Salem Coal, Ice and Storage Company. In 1875, the Fenwick Canning Works operated by Starr and Mecum, and later by the Starr Brothers. The frame building used by this plant has burned down but it stood at the foot of Broadway between the Congoleum plant and Major's Wharf. The Patterson and Jones Canning Company proudly pointed to their output of six hundred thousand cans of tomatoes a season while the Starr Company produced five hundred thousand cans a season.

John P. Bruna and J. Q. Davis were manufacturing ice cream in Salem at this period and were very successful. The old papers spoke of the blue tubs of Davis and brown tubs of Bruna and suggested that the contents of either were "most delectable and pleasing to the palate." Bruna had started his milk and ice cream business by selling ice cream on the *Major Reybold*. Later he shipped considerable to Cape May for the summer trade and then entered the business on a large scale in Salem. His residence and place of business still stand on East Broadway, now occupied by Samuel Klein's store.

It was also in the 70's that an enterprising young Quaker named George Abbott shipped to Philadelphia by train several cans of milk, cooled in pans of ice, for the consumption of the Philadelphia trade. This infant business is today the Abbott's Dairies, one of the largest firms of its kind in the United States.

The Quinton Glass Company, organized in 1863, was flourishing. They made window glass in contrast to the bottle business of the two Salem firms. The company was organized by George Hires, Jr., a Quinton storekeeper; S. P. Smith, John Lambert, Charles Hires and William Plummer. They shipped glass all over the world and were especially proud of the fact that they made considerable glass for windows at the Centennial Exposition at Philadelphia in 1876. This factory was later abandoned and there are now few traces of it. Most of the ground is occupied by the Smick Lumber Yard on the banks of Alloway's Creek at Quinton.

Another Salem enterprise still in existence is the Salem Sash Factory, built in 1825 by a man named Hastings, the first location being on Griffith street. This building as it now stands was built in 1866. It passed through many hands, finally going at a sheriff's sale to A. M. Bell and Richard Woodnutt. In 1916 the Bells and Woodnutts sold the mill to Norris Trullender.

It was in 1872 that a century-old dream came to fulfillment with the completion of the Penns Neck Canal. The agitation for it started in the closing years of the eighteenth century. The tortuous windings of Salem creek made it necessary for the farmers of Upper Penns Neck township to cover a considerably longer distance in negotiating the comparatively few miles to the Delaware river. In 1800 a stock company was organized under an enactment of the Legislature to allow the building of a canal across the narrow stretch of Upper Penns Neck to Deepwater Point in order to allow goods of that region a quicker means of egress. After spending $6,000 on a futile attempt to connect Salem creek and the Delaware, it was abandoned. But the demand for a canal still continued. The sons of the organizers of the first company tried again in 1832 and in 1852, each time losing $10,000 more in their futile attempts. In 1868 the Salem Creek Consolidated Meadow Company was formed for the same purpose and four years later, on February 2, 1872 the work was again started by a construction company which agreed to dig and excavate for $20 a lineal foot. This time the canal was completed and in the same year farmers were enabled to save many miles of transportation for their produce. With the increase in automobile travel, the old canal became obsolete after fifty years of faithful service and is today blocked off by a railroad bridge at Deepwater.

There was a terrific hail storm in May of 1870 which shattered practically every window in both the Walnut Street Church and the Court House. There were many churches dedicated in the early years of the 70's, the Elmer Methodist Church being dedicated in May of 1870, the new Catholic Church at Woodstown in 1871, and the re-modeled Alloway Methodist Church in 1870. The Salem Memorial Baptist Church was dedicated in the summer with the temperature at 101 in the shade. This latter church had the misfortune to pick one of the hottest spells on record when for seventeen days in the summer of 1870 the average temperature was 94. An innovation in preaching took place this same summer when the Reverend Mr. Mason of this church preached several Saturday nights on Star Hall Corner.

It was a flourishing period for schools and the schools of Salem were many and in good condition. The Salem Collegiate Institute, located in the modern Erhardt Building, was doing a good business under the supervision of J. H. Bechtell. The Salem Academy, the oldest school in Salem, where the Grammar School now stands on Market street, had for its principal J. W. Bradin. The Friend's School, which still stands at the corner of Walnut Street and East Broadway, was under the tutelage of Miss Pauline Waddington. The public schools, fighting for their own, and with no high school as yet organized, were in charge of L. C. Force. It was not until 1875 that the first high school class graduated. Prior to that time a student desiring to attend high school was forced to pay tuition at one of the three private schools.

Richard Stockton Field died in 1870. At the time of his death he was a Federal Court judge and one of the most prominent lawyers in the state. Fifty years before, as a young man, he came to Salem from his North Jersey home. He remained for about seven years, working as a newspaperman and later studying law. Field caused a commotion in 1824 when he attacked certain Salem county officials. About 1831 he moved back to North Jersey and for a brief time, one month to be exact, was a United States Senator filling an unexpired term.

The ship yards were still launching vessels. A boat with the high sounding name of *May Montayne* was launched at Captain Townsend's Ship Yard near Major's Wharf at Salem. The Summerill Ship Yard, at Penns Grove, was building smaller craft.

Excursions to Cape May were popular and were conducted by Mr. John Bruna, of the ice cream firm.

On September 1, 1870, the Dick family held a celebration in the family homestead on East Broadway near Walnut street. Besides having a social gathering they exhibited the various antiques gathered throughout the years. One antique which attracted attention was an old mahogany clock made in Salem county by Joshua Hollinshed, in the days of the Revolution.

Horace Greeley, who had yet to take a beating from Grant in 1872, entered into a controversy with David Pettit of Mannington over the proper depth of farming. Pettit was a dirt farmer, Greeley imagined himself an expert. The controversy did not continue long before notice was served upon the famous editor of the Tribune that while he might know a good deal about newspaper publishing and possibly politics, he knew nothing about farming.

The Salem Collegiate Institute held a social which was given a column of space in a local paper, the editor declaring that he thought ten o'clock was entirely too late an hour of the night for young people to stay out of bed.

There were still entertainments and lectures galore. One account taken at random shows that the local citizens wanted something for their money. We find this very sententious account of the performance of one J. P. Eldridge, who brought to Salem a so-called opera troupe: "But we could stand that if he did not see fit to trot out a Madamoiselle who in operatic screeching excelled anything we ever heard and a would-be comic singer, who was unintelligible either as an Irishman or a Dutchman."

The newspapers of that day were not above using sarcasm and satire to bring home their points. The Sunbeam, speaking of the possible nomination of a certain man for Congress, said: "He will not get it for of course it goes to the highest bidder."

The papers could be sarcastic in other matters, too. One editor had a run-in with a prominent Salem man who was accused of usurious practices. The argument came up over the question of taxation for the free public schools. This gentleman, being very penurious, expostulated over the heavy taxes. Whereupon the Sunbeam let go with this blast: "He growls at paying taxes to educate our children while we cheerfully pay to educate other people's children and would even so to educate James' if the Lord had thought proper to curse this land with such progeny." Nor was that all; the editor cheerfully composed some "poetry" for this same man. It read:

> Here lies old 35%,
> The more he got the more he lent,
> The more he got the more he craved,
> The more he made the more he shaved,
> Great God—can such a soul be saved?

The editor suggested that these lines should be this man's epitaph.

The aftermath of the gerrymander of Pittsgrove township came up in 1871 when Landis, the founder of Vineland, attempted to pass a bill through the New Jersey Legislature forming a new county with Vineland as the county seat. Pittsgrove, once taken away and only restored four years before, was to be a part of this new county. The citizens waxed indignant and held several meetings of protest. The new county was to be called "Fruitland," although there were some stories that Landis wanted it named after himself and still others that it would be called "Lincoln" county. The attempt failed and the bill died in the Legislature.

However, the Republicans in the Legislature did succeed in carving a new township out of Upper Alloway's Creek, which they named Quinton. It was, of course, another gerrymander by which the township was so divided that the new municipality would be Republican. This plan was successful and outside of one or two upsets throughout sixty years, the township has never changed its allegiance to the G. O. P. The Democratic newspapers said the new township could be taken out of Lower Alloway's Creek as well but the original plan went through.

In 1872 occurred what was known as the "fish war." It was the same old quarrel between Delaware and New Jersey as to who controlled the river between New Castle and Pennsville. In this case twenty New Jersey fishermen, fishing off Pennsville, were arrested, taken to New Castle and fined $25.00 apiece. It looked for a time as if there might be serious trouble since some of the men from Delaware were armed, but the Governor of New Jersey, Joel Parker, issued a proclamation asking the citizens of this state to keep their heads until the matter was adjusted by the Supreme Court. There was no blood shed, but the patient citizens had to follow the advice of Governor Parker for almost sixty years until the Supreme Court of the United States finally decided against them in 1934. As it stand now, Delaware owns to the low water mark on the New Jersey side, which makes the piers at Pennsville and Penns Grove the territory of the state of Delaware. New Jersey now owns half the river below the 12 mile mark, but at the time there was a great deal of agitation and a great many reprisals in various forms over this fisherman's war.

The sportsmen of Salem were happy because their new race track was completed on Walnut street, taking the place of the old Thunderbolt track on the Hancock's Bridge road. This track was abandoned some years later when the last one in Salem was built on Johnson street.

Fortifications on the New Jersey side of the river at Finn's Point were started in 1872. At that time they were known as the Battery. It is today Fort Mott.

The citizens of the early 70's were stirred to read of the default of the Internal Revenue Collector of this district, W. S. Sharp. Sharp, a politician holding office under President Grant, had gone "in the red" to the tune of twenty-five thousand dollars. The newspaper which he owned at that time, the National Standard, was sold at a sheriff's sale and Sharp moved to Trenton. Some two or three years later, the Sunbeam was moved to high scorn on reading that Sharp, who was in the printing business in Trenton, was lecturing up and down the state on "Political Morality."

Jesse Bond, age 91, one of the first school masters of this county, died in 1873. As early as 1805, Bond came from Burlington county and taught private school in Mannington. Although noted for his severity with the birch rod, his students nevertheless loved him and as a token to his memory named after him the road which leads from Compromise School House; it is still known as the Jesse Bond road. He owned the old colonial house near Compromise School built by Richard Brick in 1751. Another death in this same year was that of Lewis

CENTENNIAL YEAR

Eugene Yorke, son of Congressman Thomas Jones Yorke, who died in Cincinnati at the age of 41. He was one of the first surveyers of the Pennsylvania Railroad. He entered the Civil War as a private, fought at Bull Run and Vicksburg and marched with Sherman to the sea. He arose from a private to a general in the course of four years.

Before the days of the Historical Society, the ladies of Salem held a Centennial Tea Party to celebrate the one hundredth anniversary of the Boston Tea Party. This celebration was to have been held at the Grant House on Market street but the house was too small to hold the crowd and the celebration was held in Rumsey's Hall. The ladies displayed old costumes and antiques. Chief among the exhibits was a ring containing a lock of George Washington's hair which is now preserved by the Salem County Historical Society.

For amusements, the people of the 70's held strawberry festivals and there were many excursions to Cape Island and on the *Major Reybold*. Horse racing was extremely popular and baseball games were frequent. In 1873, there was a grand balloon ascension in the West Jersey Park on Walnut street, Professor Justin Buisley ascending into the heavens in his mammoth balloon "Meteor."

The Fourth of July celebrations were a thing of joy to young and old alike. Frequently visiting fire companies, such as the Shackamaxon Company of Philadelphia, would come to Salem in their costumes, parade and have a good time. The biggest celebration of this time, however, was the Centennial Harvest Home held in Johnson's orchard in July of 1875. Johnson's orchard is now Johnson Park on Market street, Salem. This was one of the greatest affairs of its kind ever held in Salem. President Grant was invited, did not attend, but many thousands did. There were exhibits of all kinds—booths with tempting foods displayed, exhibitions of patchwork quilts and handiwork and all the things that go to make up a modern fair.

The Philadelphia Centennial drew many people from Salem. There are still souvenirs of the exhibit in many Salem homes. At times the town was well nigh deserted as the people flocked to Philadelphia.

The newspaper business was very flourishing during the '70's, although some of the attempts to establish permanent newspapers were failures. However, the two old stand-bys of the county, the Sunbeam and the National Standard, were still in existence. The National Standard had a bankruptcy sale, but under the management of Samuel W. Miller and later Sinnickson

Chew, the paper was at this time in prosperous condition. Robert Gwynne, Sr., had completed twenty-five of the fifty years he spent as editor of the Sunbeam. A new paper was started in Penns Grove in November of 1878 by J. W. Loughlin and was named the Penns Grove Record. For a brief time, Joseph D. Whitaker assumed charge of the paper but since 1884 the present owner and editor, William A. Summerill, has been in charge. Mr. Summerill has thus eclipsed the record of Editor Gwynne. Thus the third of the present Salem county newspapers came into existence.

Woodstown had had a combination of newspapers for twenty years before this period. The first news sheet, issued in 1853, was called the Woodstown Register. In rapid succession there came the American Eagle and Jersey Blue and then the Eagle alone, later The Monitor. Finally, in 1892, the Woodstown Monitor-Register came out of these earlier papers with Benjamin Patterson as editor and owner. The Elmer Times, the fifth newspaper in the county in point of seniority, was not established until 1886, by Samuel P. Foster. The paper is now owned by his son, Preston Foster.

In 1881, the South Jerseyman was started by D. Harris Smith and C. N. Bell. This paper in 1904 consolidated with the National Standard. The newest paper in the field is the Penns Grove Press, established in 1934.

There were other papers that did not long exist, nor were they ever consolidated with others. For instance, in 1878, a paper called the Salem Light made its appearance in Salem for a short time. Then there was a monthly paper devoted to literature called The Salem Record which had a short existence in the 70's. In 1871 there appeared a very mysterious journal called The Moonly Voice, edited by Robert Sinnickson; this also lasted but a very short time.

A still unsolved murder was committed in February, 1874. Abigail Dilks, a housekeeper for John Lloyd, a farmer in Lower Penns Neck township, was found dead in the yard of Lloyd's home with her throat cut. William Sadler, a colored man, was arrested and tried for murder. There was no concrete evidence against Sadler and he was speedily acquitted. The jury included one colored man, Reubin Pierce, the first of his race to serve on a jury in Salem county. Suspicion rested on other people in the neighborhood but no one else was ever brought to trial for the crime.

On July 8, 1874, Professor King dropped out of the clouds to earth in Quinton township with his mammoth balloon, terminating a flight from Buffalo, New York. He had come from Buffalo to Salem in 13 hours and in an interview with the local newspapers, minutely described his travels across the mountains. He landed just in time to escape one of the worst summer storms that ever swept this neighborhood, a storm which did a great deal of damage to Salem crops in July of '74.

Excitement ran high in Salem that summer over the activities of a gang of young toughs who called themselves the "Modocs," after a tribe of unruly Indians in the west. These young thugs broke up the Broadway Methodist Sunday School picnic at Oakwood Beach and badly beat up a young man named Bilderback, who nearly died from their assault. Several of the "Modocs" were arrested by Sheriff Hires and given jail sentences.

A Salem boy, E. S. Wood returned from Texas a millionaire.

Samuel Lord, an officer of the *Major Reybold*, was crushed to death by a rope in December of 1874.

A Salem man named Dilks who had been listed as killed in the Battle of the Wilderness ten years before, suddenly appeared from Nevada to visit his relatives in Salem.

The Fourth of July of the Centennial year was a marked success. Practically every town and county had its holiday celebration. Alloway, however, took the prize. Said the Sunbeam, "Under the superintendence of Mr. Coutch, there was a magnificent display of fireworks which bespangled the cerulean vaults of heaven with their fiery tentacles until an early hour."

On September 17, 1876 occurred the worst storm Salem county had since 1846. The heavy rain storm, aided by a high wind, caused $500,000 worth of damage.

The stage line to Bridgeton boasted an old hollow-backed horse named "Bill" which had traveled, it was estimated, eighty-seven thousand miles.

Alloway was complaining about the large number of tramps which infested that town and the natives used a little direct force to make their homes unpopular to the wandering gentry.

A Salem man, John C. Belden, was made a special Post Office Inspector as a reward for his political work.

The famous and valuable book of Thomas Shourds, entitled "The History of Fenwick's Colony," was published in 1876. The book has been commented on many times but it is needless to say that in publishing this vast genealogical history of the families of this county, Shourds performed a most worthy and creditable serivce. He saved for posterity the records of the families of Salem county.

A celebration was held at the Finn's Point Cemetery in 1877, in which the dead of both the Confederate and the Union

Armies were honored in the first Memorial Day services held there.

But by far the most startling events of the 70's occurred in this same Centennial year of 1876. With two prize fights, one resulting in a death, and a descent upon Salem by river pirates, this year provided many thrills for the local citizens.

Pennsville, in the century of its existence, has recorded many stirring events; however, the use of its terrain sixty years ago as a prize ring occasioned probably the most intense excitement of all. A group of Philadelphia fight promoters, outlawed in their own city, contrived to use what is now Brandriff Beach, Pennsville, as their arena.

To the vast delight of the local fight fans and to the intense disgust of the church folks, the late evening of July 28th, 1876, witnessed the landing of a boat containing two hundred pugilistic adherents and the principals. They repaired to the field at the south end of Brandriff's Beach where, under a huge pine tree since destroyed, they marked off the ring. Apparently there was no admission fee; the Pennsville residents saw ninety-four rounds of gory scrapping for nothing.

The contestants were John Kennan and James Collins, both of Philadelphia. Kennan was 18 years old, weighed 118 pounds and was five feet four inches tall. His opponent, Collins, weighed 116 pounds and was 20 years old, and an inch taller. Attired for the ring, Kennan wore light blue knee pants and a white silken cord hanging by his side, white socks and, as the local reports go, had a beautiful scarf tied around him. Collins wore white flannel knee pants, white socks and a blue scarf. There is no mention as to the beauty of the Collins scarf. Neither did he wear a cord.

In the ninety-fourth round, Kennan pushed Collins to his corner and he fell without a blow. Then his seconds threw up the sponge. Thus ended the longest fight in New Jersey ring history. The police made no attempt to stop the fight although it was openly in defiance of the statutes at that time. The press of the day openly admitted that the police at Pennsville were afraid of the blood-thirsty crowd and probably they had good reason to be. The newspaper expressed the hope that if any more gamblers, prize fighters and cut-throats assembled at Pennsville again, they would receive a dose of Jersey justice that would convince them that they could not break the laws with impunity.

Kennan, for all his services rendered in drubbing Collins, received the princely sum of one hundred and fifty dollars.

Collins received the aforementioned beating. One gambler who won $500 on the fight took the precaution not to join the fraternity in its boat trip back to Philadelphia, but stayed over in Salem and returned on the *Perry* the next day.

The reaction to the fight was positive in two different ways. Those fans of Lower Neck who saw the historic fight marathon sixty years ago, still refer to it with interest and call it an event of momentous excitement, while on the other hand, a member of the Pennsville Methodist Church wrote this letter to a county paper:

"A most disgraceful and beastly affair took place near this village a few days ago in the shape of a prize fight. Two human beings stripped to the waist dealing blows at each other's eyes, head and ribs until they appeared more like demons than anything else and all this to the delight of a multitude who stood and countenanced the cowardly act. It is brave to do right."

Despite the warnings of press and pulpit, the fight promoters of Philadelphia staged another scrap in the same locality in the early morning of August 31.

That fight passed into history as the Walker-Weeden bout, lasted seventy-five rounds and ended in the death of Walker and a subsequent trial for manslaughter. On August 30, five tugs left Philadelphia at 11 P. M., carrying 600 fight fans from Philadelphia and New York. About five the next morning they landed at Pennsville and walking about a half mile to the scene of the fight, staked out the ring, enclosed it with ropes and proceeded to the affray. Beneath a white oak, now destroyed, on the present boundary line between William Acton's park property and the Brandriff tract, and a few rods in from the oyster shell road, the historic bout was staged.

A man by the name of Gormley was selected as referee and stripped to the waist, the two fighters faced each other. Before any blows were struck Walker approached Weeden and offered to bet $50 on the result which offer was accepted, and the fight was on. The size and weights are not apparently preserved and we are indebted to Grant Gibbon, Esq., of Pennsville, an eyewitness to the fight, for this detail and subsequent other data concerning the match. Mr. Gibbon states that the fighters were both thick set men weighing in the neighborhood of 160 pounds, that Walker was a trifle thicker and heavier than Weeden. The first eight or ten rounds of this encounter seemed to comprise a lot of fancy footwork and dancing by both pugilistic artists. About the tenth round, the first decisive blows were struck in which Walker severely hammered Weeden about the eyes. In the eleventh round, the fight became bloody. Gone was the side-stepping and the fancy dancing and gone also was any semblance of fighting rules. The two would apparently clinch, wrestle, throw one another to the ground and hit. From here on to the end Walker's ponderous fists fell hard on the body and head of Weeden, whose powers of resistance to these sledge hammer blows was remarkable. He took his punishment and in return battered away round after round at Walker's eyes.

In the seventieth round of this exceedingly gory struggle, Weeden's greater strength bore fruit, because Walker's face was almost battered to a pulp and his eyes were closed. It is said that in the last three rounds, Walker was led out blind by his seconds, his arms supported by them, so that he could reach out and blindly flail his adversary. This is denied by Mr. Gibbon, but at any rate in the seventy-sixth round, with his eyes closed and arms flashing harmlessly in the air, Weeden clinched with Walker, struck him savagely and according to one account, kneed him in the stomach. This was the end. Walker lay senseless in the squared circle and every effort to arouse him failed. Dr. Morgan, of Pennsville, stepped into the ring and giving a quick examination quietly remarked that he was dead. The doctor's assertion apparently convinced the crowd and they quickly melted away leaving Colyer, Walker's second, to arrange for the removal of the body.

Thus in the somberness of death ended the second and last prize fight battle of Pennsville. All the crude methods of the middle ages were here in evidence. A hard-drinking, gambling, bloodthirsty crowd were the witnesses of a fight with bare hands, barren of any humane regulations, which went beyond the bounds of human endurance and ended with the macabre picture of a stark and bloated body lying inert in the Pennsville corn field.

Very few Pennsville citizens saw the encounter and those who did formed no part of the threatening crowd that the sheriff was called upon to disperse. Mr. Gibbon tells how in the early morning he saw the crowd disembarking from the boats and followed them to the field of combat, where he witnessed the fight from the very front row. There was no gate charge and little if any notice, so that the attendance of native sons was limited.

While the battle raged in the early hours, Sheriff Hires was hurrying from Salem to Pennsville to uphold the majesty of the law. Reaching the fight alone, he demanded its cessation. The appeal being fruitless, he went to the Philadelphia navy at the wharf and collecting a small posse, waited the return of the crowd. Following the collapse of Walker, the fight fans hurried to the wharf to find the sheriff on the gangplank of one of the boats. Ordering them to disperse, the answer of one of the multitude was to hurl a bologna sausage at the sheriff and to follow that shot with a well directed beer bottle. The sausage hit him in the eye and the beer bottle narrowly missed his head. He was shoved down off the gangplank and then, apparently losing his head, fired at the crowd. The boats shoved off and some shots were fired in return but no one was injured. One account states that the sheriff became frightened and hid behind a board fence.

Losing his quarry at the Pennsville ferry the sheriff telegraphed ahead to the chief of police of Philadelphia. The water police of that city cooperated with celerity and apprehended the largest of the boats. All the principals at that time escaped. Weeden, badly battered, alighted at Chester. Later that day and on the following day, all the principals were rounded up and arrested. Governor Bedle, of New Jersey, at once requested their extradition and in about a week's time Sheriff Hires had them all in the local jail. Meanwhile, the dead body of Walker, alias Koster, was unceremoniously dumped on the salt wharf at Greenwich Point and some time later was taken to his home on Second street in Philadelphia.

The arrival of the prisoners at Salem occasioned a great deal of interest. Weeden is reported to have had a plain honest face, appeared dejected in spirit, and could not look one straight in the eye. He said he was "egged on" by the sporting gentlemen of the big city and expressed the desire of having some of them share his present lot. Locked up with him were Clark, Weeden's trainer; Sam Colyer, trainer of Koster; Richard Goodwin or Spring Dick, and Fiddler Neary.

On November 7, 1876, the five were tried. The presiding law judge was Justice Reed and the associated lay judges were Messrs. Ware, Cook and Summerill. In the absence of Attorney-General Vannata, Prosecutor A. L. Slape conducted the case for the state. Counsel for the defense included James Scovel, of Camden; John H. Fort, J. K. Hewitt, H. L. Slape and Colonel Valentine. Counsel fought hard to maintain that Weeden's blows did not cause Walker's death, saying that he might have died from his head hitting the boat when he was carried from Pennsville. There was little doubt, however, that Walker was actually hammered to death and the Philadelphia coroner's testimony bore out the contention. The jury came in and found all five defendants guilty of manslaughter. Members of the jury were: H. Crispin, foreman; John S. Newell, W. B. Willis, John D.

Jackson, William Kelty, Lorenzo Nichols, Charles Barber, J. Wilmer Barber, Smith Bilderback, Daniel Counsellor, Clement Sparks and O. P. Hitchner.

Mr. Justice Reed at once sentenced Weeden, Colyer and Goodwin to six years in prison and Clark and Neary to two years in the same place. On November 6 of the next year Weeden died in prison, largely as a result of his weakened condition.

* * * *

This same year of 1876 saw a descent upon Salem by a gang of Philadelphia river pirates. Without apparent casualities, this episode presents today all the comic opera requirements of a South American revolution.

Seven inoffensive oyster boats were the cause of this raid upon Salem and the subsequent melee which passed into history as the Battle of North Bend or the naval engagement of Salem creek. The oyster boats were the property of John McCabe of Philadelphia, who owed the shipbuilding firm of Carter & Day of Camden, the sum of $3500 for repairs to the boats. Not obtaining the money the owners secured an attachment, and the boats were tied up at Townsend shipyard on Salem creek in the custody of Sheriff Hires. On the night of August 5, 1876, two tugs carrying twenty-five armed men, entered the creek and in the most approved pirate fashion proceeded to haul away the boats. McCabe seems to have been the ringleader, in company with his son and one Washington Whalen. One tug fastened on to four of the boats and without any trouble, carried them out of the creek into the figurative arms of the owner. In getting the other three, the second tug got one of the anchor chains fastened around the blades and shafts of the propellor, preventing it from moving and causing it to drift ashore. A yawl from the tug carried one more oyster boat out to the mouth of the creek. The sheriff had had one encounter with similar Philadelphia thugs, so he had placed a watchman to guard the crafts. The watchman summoned the sheriff but too late to prevent the first tug from getting away with four ships. But the sheriff captured the second tug and lodged its crew in jail. The two remaining boats were removed to a place of safety above the Penn's Neck Bridge. The ringleaders in this first episode seem to have escaped. The crew was given a hearing, the bail set, and the tug and the crew released.

This was far from being the end of the matter. Mr. McCabe yearned lustily for his two missing oyster schooners. He sent two of his henchmen to Salem to spy out the location of the two remaining boats. At midnight, on the twenty-first of

August, 1876, a tug entered the creek and dispatched some of its crew in yawls to secure the remaining boats. These ships were lying some distance up Fenwick creek, just above the modern Heinz factory. The pirates took the precaution to open the Penn's Neck Bridge draw in readiness for the escape. But they reckoned without the night watchman, J. Fleming. Fleming heard the boats rowing up the creek and called upon them to stop. Receiving no answer he fired, and although the shot was not heard around the world, it went far enough and loud enough to wake up Salem and call the sheriff from his bed. Fleming referred proudly to his gun as an "old residenter" and probably no fire siren would have been more effective. It was a duck gun with a very large bore and filled with buck shot made a noise like a young cannon. The pirates had returned his first fire and kept steadily up Fenwick creek when he fired a second time and changed their minds. They reversed their course and sought to retreat. One of them called out to Fleming and implored him "not to fire that thing again." The pirates managed to get through the open draw and reach the tug in comparative safety but apparently enraged at their failure to secure the boats, stayed in position and returned fire for fire. They volleyed for almost an hour and then finally retreated out the creek. Not since the Dutch and the Swedes fought with blunderbus and ancient cannon off Fort Elfsburg two hundred and more years before, had the peaceful shores of Salem listened to such a leaden uproar. Warned by the first fire a considerable posse of Salem citizens gathered to have a hand in the artillery practice and to speed the parting guests. With all this cannonade there seem to have been no casualities, although the minutemen on the bank were quite sure some of their shots were effective.

The chief hero seems to have been Fleming, whose duck gun turned the tide of battle. Fleetwood, Madara and Hill were three of the posse who were first on the scene and aided the venerable Horatius in defending the sacred soil of Salem from the invader. The next day Fleming found in the reeds on the other side of Little creek, a small boat which contained an army rifle, two sledge hammers, cold chisels, lanterns and muffled oars, apparently having contained some of the attacking party who finding their retreat shut off, pulled into shore and leaving the boat hustled across Mannington to catch the early morning train home at a safe distance up the line. Another army rifle and a coil of rope were found on the bridge.

Following the conflict of North Bend, the local citizens were considerably aroused. They even debated the advisability of asking Secretary of Navy Robeson for a United States gunboat to greet the pirates should they make a third descent upon Salem. The Democratic Sunbeam, in attacking this proposition, advanced the belief that had this battle taken place in the conquered provinces of the South the Republican administration would have been only too glad to have dispatched a cruiser to stir up more strife and bloodshed upon any pretext.

But no gunboat and no bluejackets were necessary. McCabe, evidently safe from arrest as a buccaneer, meekly came to Salem and paid the attachment and costs. The oyster boats were released and quiet settled down upon North Bend and the adjoining creeks.

More excitement came to Salem on January 2, 1878 for that was the date of the worst fire which Salem has ever seen. An entire block was burned and outside help from Camden and other points had to be summoned. This fire broke out at 7:15 P. M. on the night of January 2, in a building behind the First Baptist Church on West Broadway and the store of Clinton Bowen. It razed a number of barns in the rear of the block bounded by West Broadway, Market street and Griffith street, then turned by a sudden switch of wind, right into the heart of the business section between Bowen's store and Star Hall Corner, playing havoc with the row of frame structures in between. By heroic efforts, the firemen kept the flames from crossing Broadway.

At 3 A. M. on the morning of the third of January, a special train arrived from Camden with additional fire apparatus, but by this time, due to the heroic efforts of the Salem firemen, the conflagation had been well checked. Seventeen property owners suffered losses totaling $85,000. The fire companies did their work in a manner that brought editorial praise from both local papers, but the vials of wrath fell around those able-bodied men, not firemen, who, in their interest in watching the fire, continually got in the way of the fire fighters. In the same decade, seven years earlier, there had been a fire in the rear of the present Green's Hotel which destroyed several barns and kept the firemen fighting all night, but this earlier fire was slight compared to the awful conflagation of 1878. This latter fire was so bad that it looked for a while as if the town might go with it, but the local firemen were successful in keeping it on the north side of West Broadway.

Longevity records for residents of Salem county were broken in the 70's when Henry Van Meter, a former slave, died in Bangor, Maine, aged 116. Van Meter, not having any name in the old days of slavery, adopted as did many of the slaves of

THE TELEPHONE COMES

Salem county, the name of his master. The master in this case was I. W. Van Meter, of Pittsgrove township. Another death in the same period was that of Jacob Hitchner who died at the age of 95 and who proudly remembered up to the time of his death that he had for seventy consecutive years attended the Democratic conventions of Salem county.

1878 saw two more very bad storms. One of these was a tornado which hit Pittsgrove township heavier than the rest of the county and which in its violence, unroofed many houses and tore out numerous trees by the roots. On October 23, 1878, two months after the storm in Pittsgrove, another bad wind storm struck the city of Salem, breeching the banks along the creek, flooding Hancock's Bridge and unroofing the Presbyterian Church in Salem.

In September of that year, John W. Acton, a Salem boy whose father had died for the Union on the battlefield of Bull Run, was appointed to the United States Military Academy at West Point. Mr. Acton did not finish his military course but instead studied law and later in life became prosecutor of Salem county and mayor of Salem. About the same time there died in Salem a most respectable citizen of this place, Henry B. Ware. Mr. Ware, years before, had had an appointment to West Point where he was a classmate of such prominent military figures as McClellan and Burnside. Mr. Ware also had relinquished a military career, had become prominent in the Salem National Bank and for a short time had been postmaster of Salem.

James G. Blaine, the "plumed knight," who six years later was destined to lose the presidency of the United States, spoke in Salem on the Academy grounds on Market street, October 19, 1878 on the subject of finance.

The citizens of Woodstown, anxious to have their own government aside from Pilesgrove township, held a vote to determine whether they should become a separate municipality or not. This election was lost by 35 votes but a few years later, another election was held and the proposition was successful.

1854 had seen the telegraph come into Salem and 1879 witnessed the establishment of the first telephone, which was erected between the Salem National Bank and the telegraph office on Market street in July of this year. The manager of the telephone company, J. J. Burleigh, personally solicited subscribers to the telephone service and on the date of the installation, held a public reception in Salem at which many prominent citizens were allowed the pleasure of talking for the first time over the telephone to someone in Camden.

Religious revivals still continued. A large one was reported from Penns Grove in the last years of the 1870's. The Walnut Street church, dating from the days of John Firth and Benjamin Abbott, had become obselete for the congregation and a new church was decided upon in 1879. In the same year, a ministerial union was formed with Reverend Dr. Bannard of the Presbyterian Church as the first president.

That the citizens of this town took their commencement addresses seriously is evident by the fact that the Standard said, commenting on the commencement of Salem High School in 1878: "The young ladies' effusion caused many eyes to fill with tears."

Salem people flocked to see General Grant at a public reception in Philadelphia in December of 1879. One unfortunate citizen reported that due to the great crowds, he "saw General Grant at a distance, but came home minus a gold watch."

* * * *

Salem county in the year 1870 was emerging from the throes of a Civil War which left deep and indelible stains on the body politic. The Republican party with the war behind them had triumphed time and again and were strong in this county. The Democrats were trying hard to overcome the division of the late rebellion.

In the Republican Congressional Convention of 1870 (all these elections were before the days of the primaries) held at Vineland, John W. Hazelton, grandfather of the present president of the Salem National Bank, was nominated for Congress. His opponent was Benjamin Lee of Cape May, an old guard Democrat warrior. In their county convention, the Republicans selected former sheriff John Hunt as their candidate; for the same honors the Democrats named William A. Casper, well known auctioneer. The campaign was unusually warm. Mr. Casper especially worked hard. His candidacy was regarded as little more than a joke by the Republicans, but great was the consternation the morning after election, when it was learned that he had defeated Hunt by 300 votes. It was a real upset as Casper was the first Democratic sheriff in twenty-four years.

At this period Salem had two assemblymen. Previously they had had three, but in 1870 there were two districts in the county. This continued until 1882 when the redistricting under the census of 1880 gave this county but one assemblyman.

In the '70 election, the Democrats made a clean sweep, their first since long before the Civil War. Lee carried the county for Congress by 200 votes over Hazelton but the latter won the election elsewhere. The two Democratic assemblymen, Dickinson and Hitchner, were elected and the three coroners also won.

Now we come to a curious feature of elections in those times. The sheriffs were elected for one year only but once a man was successful like Casper, both parties re-nominated him by courtesy for the next two years. This continued until the 80's when a three-years term was established by new amendments to the constitution.

The Republicans were wiped out in the surprise of 1870. This was a gubernatorial year and they have proved as acrimonious sometimes as presidential years. In the state Cornelius Walsh was named by the Republicans for governor and the Democrats put up the doughty old war governor, Joel Parker, for another term. In the county the two Democratic assemblymen were re-named and the G. O. P. selected Smith Hewitt and Daniel P. Dorrell to run against them. The Standard blasted loud and long, especially at Parker, and among other things said they "refused to be hoodwinked by the shallow subterfuges of Joel Parker."

The former governor won the state election. The Demoratic party did not fare as well in Salem county. Walsh won the county by 13 votes and the two Republican assemblymen were winners. Hewitt beat Dickinson by the narrow margin of 7 votes and Dorrell was returned victor with a safer margin of 88 votes. The narrowest margin of all came when the lowest Republican coroner defeated the highest of the three Democrats by one vote.

The Republicans thus reinstated to power, made plans for the first presidential of the decade. This was the year when Horace Greeley took a terrible beating from President Grant and was the beginning of the modern landslide. The campaign was peppy enough, for the Standard alleged that the Democrats were trading everything for Mr. Morrison, their candidate for surrogate. Local option first reared its head and temperance began to figure.

"Amen," said the Standard, in the first issue after election. "Greeleyism is but an echo now." And they were right, because the landslide cleaned house. The Republican congressman, Mr. Hazelton, was re-elected with a handsome majority and Isaac Newkirk became senator from Salem county by a margin of 500 votes, an exceedingly high majority for those days. The two Republican assemblymen were elected and Samuel P. Allen won the surrogate fight.

So the Democrats soothed their sorrow and waited for the next year but it helped them little. It was another smaller landslide. John Hires became sheriff by 150 votes; William Carpenter, Republican, won a House seat by 220; and Dr. Izard in the second district was cut to 40 votes by his opponent, Charles P. Swing.

But in 1874, with the Democrats' favorite contest, the governorship, coming apace, the lines were tightened and the Jeffersonian party again had a look-in. Temperance was now figuring largely and the Standard argued strenuously for the temperance people to join hands with the Republicans and not divide their strength.

"Don't split your ticket," cried the Standard. "It is too much to ask a personal favor like that."

"Vote as your conscience dictates," pleaded the Sunbeam, "but make that conscience be Democratic."

Alloway with its traditional Democracy figured large that autumn and the Republican editor said: "If Alloway should ever see the light we should be the first to cry Hallelujah."

But the hallelujahs were well divided when the votes were counted. Bedle, the Democrat, defeated George A. Halsey for governor. For Congress, Salem's own Clement Sinnickson won his first term at Washington. Hires was re-named as sheriff and Carpenter won the Assembly by six votes over Dunham. Dunham's run was all the more gallant when it was remembered that Carpenter had enjoyed 200 pluralities formerly. In the other Assembly contest Swing beat Dr. Izard by 200 votes in a grand upset. The Democrats won all the coroners and re-elected Jacob Lippincott county clerk by 200 votes.

The next year came a mild sensation in politics, for according to the Republicans, the Democrats violated the golden rule in regard to the sheriff's office and ran a candidate against Sheriff Hires who still had an unopposed year to run. Both papers went into clinches on the issue but the Republicans were victorious once more throughout the county. Hires won his third year by 200 votes. Charles S. Plummer became senator for Salem and the two assemblymen were elected. Coles, the Republican candidate in the second district, won by only three votes over William Lawrence. Robert Gwynne, the editor of the Sunbeam, was a defeated candidate for Assembly this year.

Now we are plunged into the most argumentive year of American politics, the year when Hayes and Tilden ran and the year from which still comes the argument as to who was the winner. It was one of the hottest elections ever witnessed in

Salem county. Tilden was a swindler and a perjurer according to the Standard, and Hayes a perjurer and a defrauder if the Sunbeam is to be believed.

Songs always played a prominent part in politics and space is taken for one stirring stanza the Republican boys sang about the Democrats:

> Give us men of God's creation,
> Not the feeble spawn
> Bred for Honor's desecration
> Give us brain and brawn.
> Give us men who seized the musket.
> Men with nerve to fight
> And we'll grant you four years leisure
> Sammy T. Good Night.

This was supposed to settle Tilden and the local Democracy. But it had little effect. Tilden carried the state, losing the county by 100 votes, and the Democrats elected John S. Elwell of Yorketown, a sturdy Democrat figure for years, to the Assembly. In the other district, Quinton Keasbey, Republican, was elected and the Republicans won the Congress seat with Clement Sinnickson again. So the honors were divided.

By the next spring the high commission by a strict party vote had decided that Louisiana had voted for Hayes and that the Ohio man was president. The Union bayonets were taken out of South Carolina and New Jersey settled down to the election of another Democratic governor.

This time there flashed across the political sky the dashing figure of George B. McClellan, erstwhile candidate for president against Lincoln in 1864 and who now was leading the Democracy against the Republicans in the campaign for governor. The Standard, sensing the tide, let loose this barrage: "He is a genteel carpet bagger who speaks in a gust of meaningless enthusiasm. He never had a home in this state; he is a rank outsider." The Sunbeam retaliated against a certain local candidate saying that "he sold cider on Sunday".

The day after election there was great rejoicing in the ranks of the local Democracy because McClellan carried the county and state. George Morrison, defeated in 1872, won the surrogacy by 320 plurality and Kates, a Democrat, won one Assembly seat, Quinton Keasbey, a Republican retaining the other with a handsome vote in the teeth of the landslide.

"Too much money," said the Republican papers. "We all expected defeat anyhow."

But there was always another year and this time after the result of 1878 it was the Sunbeam which said "too much money," for the Republicans, working harder than ever, had elected a congressman again and had sent Quinton Keasbey, three times assemblyman, to the Senate by a majority of 318 votes. John Elwell, the Democrat nominee for sheriff, went down to defeat before George W. Barton by 29 votes. This was the first election for a three-year term of a sheriff in this county. The Democrats elected one assemblyman, Henry Barber, of Upper Neck, while the Republicans elected John T. Garwood for the other.

In the last year of the decade, which closed as it had opened, with a Democratic victory, the Republicans swept the state elections and controlled the legislature. Jacob Lippincott was elected county clerk for the third term and Henry Barber went back to the Assembly in the second district with his Republican mate, John T. Garwood.

The decade closed on a hectic era of American politics. It saw the banner of victory perch first on one side, then on the other, and it witnessed the greatest controversy of American politics. Those were the days of the torch light processions and the first votes of the American freedman. They were flamboyant days of vile abuse and hard cider, of strenuous canvasses and of close returns.

CHAPTER XXVI

Salem in the 1880's

No less a personage than Susan B. Anthony opened the lecture season of the 80's by an appearance in January at which time she spoke on the subject of "Suffrage." The admission for the "cause" was twenty-five cents and the hall was crowded. In the same hall, which was then the public forum of the city, a bad boy dressed up as a Sioux warrior, ruined a perfectly good juvenile performance of "Pinafore."

"Think of it," said the South Jerseyman, "General Sewell eats Daretown butter." Proudly, the same paper declared that Salem's output of cigars (segars in those days) exceeded 540,000 during the past year. The Salem Soap Works on Second street was flourishing and the old pottery plant on Ward street was still in existence. A new county newspaper and one with a short career was the Enterprise, published at Sharptown by J. H. Gardiner. Robert Sinnickson of Moonley Voice fame, then living in Trenton, wrote "Excelsior Songs and Poems" which retailed for ten cents. Commodore W. N. Jeffers, kinsman of the Salem man of same name, was for a brief time acting Secretary of the Navy under President Hayes. Marshalltown, better known as Frogtown, had a brand new post office with Benjamin Abbott as the first postmaster.

The winter of '80-'81 was cold. At times that winter the temperature fell to 12 or 14 below zero. Trains on the old road stalled in drifts. Horses and sleighs raced on the ice over the river. An engine on the Penns Grove branch ran away from the round house at that place and complacently snorted its way to Oldmans station where a farmer "caught" it and brought it home in reverse. A new physician in Salem, Dr. A. T. Beckett, moved here from Mullica Hill in early 1881. He is still active in Salem. In March of '81 died Robert Carney Johnson, a colonel in the Civil War, the organizer of the Johnson Guards and the son of Robert Gibbon Johnson. At the same time died Amy Reckless, a former slave, in the household of Robert Gibbon Johnson aged 90.

Church building persisted. The Baptists built their new

chapel in Salem, the same building which was used as an influenza hospital in 1918. In the same year the new Elmer Presbyterian Church was dedicated.

Industry was picking up, according to the South Jerseyman. There was a new brick and tile works established near Yorketown and a spindle factory started at Miller's sawmill in Allowaystown. George M. Ward of Salem started a pickle factory.

The first Salem Waterworks were established at Quinton pond during the administration of Mayor Charles S. Lawson.

In 1882 there arrived in Pittsgrove township the first settlers from Russia. They were all Russian Jews who came here under a colonization plan to better themselves in the new world. Their towns, now flourishing, are Alliance, Brotmanville and Norma. Norma was formerly Bradway Station and the man after whom it was named was a friend in need to these pioneers. Some of these men who came here as children with their parents are still living in this locality. They are Joseph Zeager, Myer Salinsky, Isreal Oppenschinsky, William Cohen and William Levine. The community's cultural effect upon this county has been marked. Several of their sons have become distinguished men in law, medicine and the arts.

For ten years there had been much agitation for the extension of the Salem railroad direct to Camden instead of via Elmer. Most of this agitation came from the inhabitants of Swedesboro and Woodstown and it was finally decided to build a branch line through Woodbury and Swedesboro and Woodstown meeting the old road at Riddletown Junction. This road was completed in 1882 and at the same time the line which terminated at Claysville was extended across Fenwick creek into Salem. The pride of the 1880's in the new station built at this time is demonstrated by the newspaper account which described the building as a handsome Gothic structure presenting a neat and commendable appearance. One looks at the forlorn old building on Grant street today and is inclined to laugh at any one who ever thought it handsome.

One of the great events of the early 80's was the realization of a dream of many years. This was the erection of the new lecture hall, later the Grand Opera House, which in the thirty-one years of its existence, from 1881 until it was burned in 1912, provided a community center for the citizens of Salem. For many decades before this there had been speakers, shows and musical entertainment but in this period of our history, it was a sign of retrogession for a town not to have its own theatre, no matter how unpretentious it might be.

LECTURE HALL 325

Local citizens financed the Hall and local artisans constructed it, therefore it was with pardonable local pride that the handsome structure was dedicated on December 27th, 1881.

Lest we underdo the stir that surrounded this grand opening, the reader is referred to the files of the Sunbeam for December 28th: "We think the Company deserves the hearty thanks of our citizens for their liberality and enterprise. Mr. Wall, the artist, is at work now upon the ceiling and walls and his work must receive the highest praise. The dome is painted to represent the sky at night with stars shining, and is said to light up beautifully. On the ceiling leading to the dome are banners on which are painted musical instruments. The walls are covered with paper of a very beautiful design and the balcony and woodwork around are very tastefully painted and gilded. The stage is a very roomy one and is fitted with every appliance for quickly moving the various scenes. The scene shifter is stationed on a balcony on the right above the stage and has a myriad of ropes at his command. The seats are very comfortable and are arranged so that every person has a clear view of the stage. All the doors are made to swing either in or out and this, with very wide exits, makes danger to persons from fire very little indeed. All together it is the neatest, prettiest and most convenient public hall in South Jersey."

The opening attraction was the McGibney family who possessed "not only a national but a transatlantic reputation." The reputation and features of this talented family have unfortunately not survived the years but in this first season of its opening glory the Lecture Hall did house one speaker whose fame was world wide in more ways than one.

On January 30th, 1882, the celebrated pastor of Plymouth Church, Henry Ward Beecher, spoke in this new gilded palace dedicated to Thespian arts.

But Salem was a long way from Brooklyn and the new urge of modernistic religion, so the silver tongued orator left bad tastes in the mouths of his auditors when he essayed to give a modern interpretation to the Bible. Fosdick and John Haynes Holmes could not have caused more heart burnings than the worthy Beecher caused in this town of Salem.

The outraged editor of the Sunbeam can tell better than we the flurry Beecher started. He said: "Thus far in his speech everybody could say Amen to all that Mr. Beecher said but when he undertook to say what certain passages of the Scripture did not mean and when he ridiculed texts sacred to the human mind and heart for centuries past, and which are among the principal lessons of the church of every denomination of Christians at the present time, he failed to carry his audience with him and sadly blemished an otherwise grand and instructive discourse. If Mr. Beecher has essayed to explain what the passages quoted did mean he might have mollified the ruffled feelings of a large portion of his audience but he did not do so and left the audience with the assertion that it did not mean so and so without saying just what it did mean in his opinion. This mixing up of scripture with worldly matter and worldly opinions never has been a success and never will be."

Bob Burdette soon followed and almost emulated Beecher when he said that Robert Ingersoll was "sound" but soon got back on solid orthodox ground by saying "sound" as a "noisy bass drum." The joke greatly pleased the audience.

The first year of this new institution saw a galaxy of performances, some good, some very bad. In the case of a certain company's rendition of "Humpty-Dumpty" we find an outraged editor saying that this show proved "a greater farce than the most wanton imagination could conjure up in the line of the ridiculous."

A. K. McClure, gifted editor of the Philadelphia Times, spoke one night on the "Personal Recollection of Abraham Lincoln" and no one could deny his authority to speak, for a better political mentor and friend the war President never possessed.

Soon also came the inevitable "Uncle Tom's Cabin" played by a splendidly equipped company which wiped out memories of a miserable performance of the same masterpiece the year before in Rumsey's Hall. As a contemporary note on the theatre the New York Times of January 4th, 1931, carried the intelligence that there was no longer a company of "Uncle Tom's Cabin" on the American stage.

Fire, apparently started by an incendiary, wiped out much of the interior of the Lecture Hall on May 25th, 1882. But the fire did not dim the ardor of Salem's theatrical promoters and with repairs the fall of 1882 saw the Lecture Hall well under way again although the complaint arose from the friends of legitimate productions that good attractions were not well patronized and that only minstrels could fill the house.

The subsequent years proved the truth of that prediction. For many years, with an occasional lapse, the Hall catered to cheaper and more popular shows and we find it at last advertising "James Ryan who will appear in an Athletic entertainment in a grand passage of Arms with Jack Fogarty." The passage at arms however did not meet with much more favor than had some of the high brow lectures, as that class of amusement was rather unpopular since the Pennsville affairs.

But in the next ten years a vast variety of entertainments poured into the Opera House at divers times. A few of them were the tasteful home romance "Muggs Landing", "Blind Tom", "Fun in a Grocery," the Rev. Madison Peters on the topic, "The Ideal Wife," "Monte Christo," "Lights of London," "Josh Billings", "Esmeralda", with its scenes laid in Paris and North Carolina; Governor Leon Abbott, "Field of the Cloth of the Gold", stereopticon lectures, Bob Burdette, "Rip Van Winkle", without the immortal Jefferson; "Dr. Jekyl", Female Minstrels, "Camille", "The Battle of Gettysburg", "Ten Nights in a Bar Room", innumerable "Uncle Tom's Cabins." and the same McGibney Family who had so delightfully entertained at the opening a decade before.

Came also the paragon show of the universe, Daniel Boone with real, genuine Siberian bloodhounds, and a farce ostensibly made for home consumption called "The Star Corner Dummy Policeman." In the realm of better things we find Kellar, certainly one of the great magicians of all time; "Erminie," "The Mikado" and Johan Strauss' famous "Queen's Lace Handkerchief."

The audiences were not always appreciative and the actors were forcibly reminded of their frailties. One badly acted play caused a need for police interference and several young men left the balcony under police protection. The Sunbeam stated that they could hardly see the need for possessing fire-arms on the part of young men in the gallery.

In 1882 a swindler worked a subscription racket with a "blind" woman as an accomplice; they were caught in Woodstown and sentenced to jail. Three prisoners left the Salem jail without permission. "What is the matter with it?" screamed the Sunbeam. The Democrats held a flag raising at Penns Grove but the orator was constantly annoyed by a drunken schoolmaster who, according to the Sunbeam, "was in his sober moments a Republican".

Charles Perrine Smith died on January 27, 1883. His old friendly enemy Robert Gwynne wrote for him a well deserved and handsome eulogy in the Sunbeam. On February 1, 1883 the first railroad train to enter Salem steamed into the new Gothic station. At the same time members of Lafayette Post Number 68, Grand Army of the Republic, held a reunion at Rumsey Hall for eight days. They exhibited their own battle flags as well as a Confederate flag captured by their comrade

Ramsey at Centerville. The veterans pointed with pride to the fact that J. S. Kiger, then the state assistant adjutant-general, was a Salem boy. Another Salem boy who made good on the scholastic side was Dr. W. C. Cattell, president of Lafayette College, Easton, Pa. In the hunt for notables came also the revelation that Jonathan Ingham, the son of the Secretary of the Treasury under Andrew Jackson, married Harriet Sinnickson of Salem and was a member of the Republican convention of 1860 which had nominated Abraham Lincoln. In the 80's a boy born at Quinton many years before, became the Attorney General of the United States; his name was Benjamin Harris Brewster.

Bob Burdette was popular in Salem. He made many speeches here and in one of them uttered the well known words concerning the Salem Oak. He said, "It is the greatest tree on the continent and is four years older than the Atlantic Ocean."

Old-timers, especially politicians, mourned the passing of the Nelson House balcony. From 1849, when it was built, it had served as a stump for politicians to lean across its railings and exhort the "dear people" in the street below. Here Joel Parker Leon Abbott, Jim Scovel, and the great McClellan had spoken. When the new balcony was erected a pint of apple-jack was placed in the open pillar and it remained there until 1931 when the present owner of the Nelson House, Captain J. D. Summerlin, discovered it in tearing down this balcony.

The principal event in the year of 1884 was a most horrible and ferocious crime. This was the murder of Ella Watson on August 18, 1884 and is very familiar to old Salem residents. It was probably the worst example of murder ever committed in this county. Without going into the case too minutely, the main details were these: Ella Watson lived near Oakland station, Alloway township, and on the afternoon of August 18th, 1884, walked to Yorketown to sell some eggs and produce. A short distance from home she passed a farmer, Charles Sickler and his wife, the last people to see her alive. Not coming home at the expected time the family became alarmed and near midnight a search was instituted and the body of the girl was found in a clump of bushes along the railroad track.

The case was solved in a novel and interesting manner. Near the young girl's body was found a stick evidently freshly cut from a tree. A reward was offered for knowledge of the origin and location of the club. Present during this investigation nearly two weeks after the murder, was a negro boy named Howard Sullivan, of Yorketown. Hearing of the reward he led the sheriff directly to a tree not far from the scene and pointed out a newly severed branch.

The speed with which Sullivan designated the tree was sufficient to arouse the suspicions of the police. Sullivan was immediately arrested and taken to Salem. Later a small colored boy produced a knife sold to him by Sullivan with which he had cut the branch. Money in his possession also cast more suspicion towards Sullivan as Miss Watson had been robbed of a few dollars.

Sullivan's inability to refrain from the $10 reward for the club sent him to the gallows before the year was out. A short time after his arrest Sullivan confessed. An interesting aspect of the case was the planting of a Pinkerton detective in the Salem jail under guise of a murder suspect. He talked with Sullivan and obtained his first confessions. Later Sullivan made several confessions in which he altered his story but finally pleaded guilty.

Justice Reed heard the case and decided there were no mitigating circumstances to save the confessed murderer from the gallows. He accordingly sentenced him to be hung at Salem on December 2nd, 1884.

Following his conviction and sentence Sullivan was placed in the hospital room of the jail. The convicted prisoner was anchored with a ball and chain, but when a short time before the execution the sheriff set the death watch and attempted to unlock the fetters, he found the lock so broken and twisted that the key would not work.

The authorities also had noted the absolute indifference of the convict and had judged that something was wrong. Upon close examination they found that Sullivan had broken the chain around his ankles and had temporarily bound it with wire, which enabled him to dispense with his shackles at his pleasure.

All of this was noticed three days before the date set for the hanging. Finally, under pressure from police officers, Sullivan told a story that sounded like a tale from the Arabian Nights.

The story is best told in Sullivan's own words, copied from the files of the Salem Sunbeam for December 5th, 1884:

"I pried off the ventilator with a bed screw after piling several boxes on top of each other. The light was out and people from the street could not see me. I got on top of the boxes and picked at the laths with a knife. That is all I did that night. The next night, I broke the lath in two, the nails came out of the slates with the laths; I pushed the slates to one side and got up on the roof; I could have jumped down on the cedar tree in the yard but I was afraid I would fall and kill myself and go to hell and I would rather be hanged than that. For several nights I would come out on the roof and look at the town lights. I was out on Wednesday, the night of the parade and saw the torchlight procession all over town below me. It was very pretty. I thought Officer Fleming saw me as he looked up but I guess he didn't. Then next night it was three o'clock when I got up to the roof and as I was afraid that it would be daylight before I got to Yorketown, so I put it off for that night. On Friday morning about 6 o'clock I was out on the roof again. I expected to go down the lightning rod but found it broken. That night, Friday the 28th, the guards were put in my room. I have had the ball and chain off for two weeks. A girl in the room below gave me the knife which she passed up through a crack in the floor. I lowered a string and she tied the knife on it, I drew it up."

The parade he referred to was that of the Democrats on the 26th of November, celebrating the election of Grover Cleveland to the presidency.

Elected that fall, Sheriff Clinton Kelty had the task of executing Sullivan. The plans were better carried out than they were at the Treadway case and the morbidly curious were excluded. The new jail had been built by this time and the hanging took place at the rear of the surrogate's office at 11:30 A. M. on December 2nd. It was the last execution in Salem county.

* * * *

The first railroad car lighted by gas made its appearance in Salem in April, 1884. The Salem Library building on West Broadway was erected in this same year. It is now a free library.

The history of a library in Salem goes back to 1804 when a circulating library was started in an old house on West Broadway. It was incorporated in 1872 and housed for a time in the Ingham and Brown Buildings until the present structure was built.

Another important event in 1884 was the founding of the Historical Society which has rendered incalculable and invaluable service in preserving for future times the priceless records of Fenwick's Colony. The Society now owns the Alexander Grant House (built in 1714) and has the finest collection of museum pieces in the state of New Jersey.

The afternoon of August 3, 1885 saw disaster strike the *Major Reybold* in the form of a tornado which hit the Salem steamer in the Delaware river opposite Gloucester City. The boat had, just some few minutes before, left Arch Street Wharf at 3 P. M. with sixty passengers on board. The tornado appeared almost without warning, lifting the upper deck and the pilot house into the river. Emory Townsend, pilot, was swept from the pilot house and his body recovered two days later at Gloucester Point. Captain Eugene Reybold escaped injury as did the other passengers. The upper framework of the boat was completely ruined but the crew and passengers were safely taken off shortly after the accident.

One of Salem's needs in the 80's was a new cemetery. The graveyards of the various faiths were overcrowded. Several public spirited men discussed the problem, offered stock for sale and purchased a tract known as the Quinton Keasbey farm on the outskirts of Salem for this use. It was named East View. It is today one of the most beautiful and well kept burial grounds in this section. The company kindly offered free ground in the cemetery on which to erect a monument to the founder, John Fenwick, but unfortunately the plans never came to fruition.

To add to the antiquity of the new cemetery, Superintendent John Lawson secured four old tombstones and set them anew. They may be seen today immediately back of the keepers lodge. Three are of marble and one is of sandstone and the inscriptions are perfectly legible. They formerly marked tombs in a family graveyard of the Van Meters on Alloways Creek.

Churches were still being erected. There was a new Methodist Chapel at Canton, and a new one at Pennsville, in which was placed a bell weighing 800 pounds, given by an anonymous donor. At Penton, in Alloway's Township a non-denominational chapel was built in 1882. Services have been held in this church continuously ever since.

Industrial notes predominated in the news for 1887. Craven Brothers shipped the first load of glass direct from their works and in addition built a new tank. The Elmer Shoe Manufacturing Company was organized with a capital of $10,000. Fogg and Hires at Quinton illuminated their canning factory with gas and arranged to cap cans by the same means. The factory of the Fitzhugh Manufacturing Company at Centreton burned to the ground with a loss of over $10,000 but within three weeks was being rebuilt. A new creamery with the latest machinery started at Richmantown and another one at Monroeville. Benjamin Borton started a butter factory in Woodstown. Borton is better remembered as a writer than as a butter manufacturer because it was he who wrote and published "Awhile with the Blue," his personal recollections of service at Fredericksburg and Chancellorsville in the Civil War. This splendid story of the Twenty-fourth New Jersey Regiment is well worth reading.

Most people recall 1888 as the year of the great snow. The blizzard was just as severe in Salem county as it was elsewhere. The railroads were blocked for days and the county roads were impassable. For nearly a week Salem was cut off from the rest of the world.

Echoes of the "Mutiny on the Bounty" and of lonely South Sea islands came in a letter published in the South Jerseyman. The letter, written by Captain George Davies of the British bark *Queens' Island* to J. C. Parker of Wilmington, Del., described a visit to a distant and lonely isle in the South Pacific ocean, known as Palmerston Island. Upon this exclusive territory Captain Davies said that one William Marston, who claimed to have formerly lived near Salem, New Jersey, reigned like a veritable Monte Cristo, lord and master of all he surveyed.

The letter continued: "When the bark was off Palmerston Island, Captain Davies was surprised to see a boat's crew put off from the shore and signal that they wished to be taken on board. The craft was loaded with cocoanuts and tropical fruits. Islanders were out on a trading expedition and appraised Captain Davies of their desire to exchange their cargo for wearing apparel and other products of civilization not to be obtained on their lonely island. The crew welcomed the strangers and sat around watching William Marston spin his yarn. He spoke with feeling of his old New Jersey home and claimed his parents are still living in that state. Twenty-five years ago, he shipped as seaman on the bark Rifleman at San Francisco bound for Tahiti, one of the group of Society Islands. He deserted the vessel and remained on the island for three years. He then migrated to Palmerston Island where he planted and grew cocoanut trees, selling copra to traders who visited the Island about once a year in the interest of San Francisco merchants. The population of Palmerston Island is 35 souls, all of whom but Marston are natives."

In 1888 the Salem post office was robbed to the extent of seven hundred dollars. The new East Avenue Hotel was opened in Woodstown. The Haines Neck Methodist Church cornerstone was laid in September.

There was a destructive cyclone early in August, 1888. Coming across the river it hit first in Lower Penns Neck and demolished the Smith Sickler brick works at Supawna. The employees saved their lives by laying flat on the ground outside. It caused the Chew and Bilderback canning factory to bulge out into Salem creek, resulting in the loss of many thousand cans of goods. It upset many barns and ruined countless orchards.

The county of Salem voted "dry" by a majority of a thousand in the local option election, but the next year the legislature rejected the act and the sale of liquor continued.

St. Mary's Roman Catholic Cemetery on Walnut street road

THE CANNON DISPUTE 333

was consecrated. The third and present Walnut Street Methodist Church was completed. The Methodist Conference met here in 1889.

The last year of the 80's saw the unusual spectacle of a base ball game played on Christmas Day between teams from Penns Grove and Pedricktown. The score was more suggestive of football, being 25 to 21 in favor of Pedricktown.

A fox hunting club was organized in Mannington, reminiscient of earlier days when Gloucester county sportsmen pursued the fox into the main street of Salem.

A gang of White Caps terrorized Berry's Chapel, breaking up religious meetings. It developed that the White Caps were really another color underneath the disguise. But a Woodstown physician, Dr. Pierpont, really had trouble with White Caps who were another color and upon being threatened by them in person, used his buggy whip to good advantage and dispersed them.

A new Salem street came into existence. This was Chestnut street, made possible by the grant of Thomas J. Yorke to the city. The first families to build on this new street were the Bowens, Diaments, Smiths and Hireses. At the intersection of Chestnut and Broadway, stood a house, since moved back on the street, which was erected by Thomas Sinnickson, a member of the First Congress. It is now number nine Chestnut street and is an excellent example of Jacobin style woodwork, having been built in 1798.

Princeton and Rutgers once fought over a cannon. So in 1889 and for many years to come, did Salem county and one Isaac Nichols of Bridgeton embroil themselves in an argument over the cannon at Pole Tavern. In 1814 the Americans had captured a cannon from the British at the Battle of Plattsburg. Some of these were bought by the state of New Jersey and sent to the various counties. One was sent to that post of the Salem Brigade stationed at Pole Tavern some time in the 1820's. From there it was taken by Nichols and his men from Cumberland county acting, they said, under the authority of the Quartermaster General, Lewis Perrine. At any rate, the gun was taken from Pole Tavern and the Salem papers roared, "Bring back that cannon." In addition, the ordnance kidnappers took away many rifles from the old barracks and gave them to all and sundry on the road from Pittsgrove to Bridgeton. General Perrine was quite indifferent when appealed to and said Salem county did not own the cannon. Salem said it did and furthermore, had possession thereof for over 60 years. The cannon was taken to Trenton where Perrine said it was "unfit for use." It was not until 1913 that Salem representatives in the legislature at Trenton regained the cannon and brought it back to the old square at Pole Tavern where it now is.

Salem had electric street lights in 1889 which worked one week but not the next. The new Salem National Bank, now the Salem Municipal Building, was finished and ready for occupancy in October.

The town was scandalized in July when serenaders so annoyed a newly married couple that they were forced to move west. Calithumpians had been active in Salem for many years but on this occasion disapproved of the match and raised so much tumult that the saluted pair left town. The woman, a much respected citizen of Salem and one who had rendered Red Cross service in the Civil War, had married a much younger man, who was a foreigner, so the mob made haste to register their disapproval.

* * * *

Salem politics in the 80's were no less warm than they had been in the 70's. Three presidential elections held the stage with their great heroes flitting across it, Blaine and Conkling, Garfield and Harrison, Cleveland and Hill.

The decade opened with the famous campaign in which Garfield secured the nomination over Grant on the thirty-sixth ballot and swept to victory over General Hancock, the Democratic candidate who was so unfortunate as to say that "the tariff is a local issue."

It was the campaign of the "bloody shirt," when the Civil War was re-fought and the Confederate flag was alternately cheered and hooted, depending upon the locality. The shirt continued to wave on behalf of the Republicans until the 1900's but this was its peak and the contest was bitter. In this county the Standard, Republican paper, hailed the victory with enormous headlines.

The Democrats, even in the teeth of the landslide, had something to crow about for they saved Henry Barber, assemblyman from the second district, by twenty-two votes. Incidentally, this was the last election in which two assemblymen were chosen.

In addition to Barber the Democrats elected Ludlow governor by a few hundred votes, upsetting the tradition of Republican governors in presidential years and keeping their slate of successive governors since the Civil War unbroken. The rest was all Republican. John T. Garwood went back to the Assembly for the third straight time and the Republicans carried the county for president and governor.

Nor in 1881 did the Republican wave diminish; in fact, it increased. For state senate William A. Casper, ex-sheriff and auctioneer, lost to George Hires by 600 votes and the Assembly candidate went down before Henry Coombs of Upper Pittsgrove by a like margin. It was a doleful two years for the Democrats.

In 1882 the Democrats experienced an epic. They elected a congressman, Thomas Ferrell, of Glassboro. It had been thirty years since one had represented this district at Washington. And what is more significant it has been over fifty years since they have elected another.

George M. Robeson was the man he defeated. A former member of Grant's cabinet and a Republican statesman of renown, Robeson had stirred up things in his district by certain votes in Congress, one of which, an appropriation on the rivers and harbors, had raised considerable criticism. In vain did Robeson beseech the voters of the first district to forget everything and send him back to Congress.

The people spoke with more than accustomed force. Ferrell swept Salem county by 150 and carried Gloucester and Camden as well. In the county George Morrison was returned to the office of surrogate by 225 votes over Collins Allen, but Henry Coombs, Republican assemblyman, won again over his Democratic opponent by the comfortable majority of 211.

This was in 1882 and the Hayes-Tilden controversy was six years back but to illustrate the political bitterness which still existed, this item is gleaned from the Sunbeam of 1882: "Rutherford B. Hayes has at last, been honestly elected president of the National Prison Association."

The election of 1883 saw a new and popular state figure emerge in the person of Leon Abbott, who was elected governor for his first term by a very flattering vote over Jonathan Dixon, Republican. But in Salem county the tide was against the Democrats and Dixon carried the county as did Henry Coombs, the assemblyman, who won his third term by defeating Henry Barber, Democrat seeking his fourth term, by 120 votes.

"Which will you choose?" cried the Sunbeam in 1884. "Tell the truth by Grover Cleveland or burn this letter by James G. Blaine?" For this was the presidential in which a Democratic president took his seat in the White House, the first since Buchanan in 1856.

The county Democrats did not all have the luck of Cleveland. Clinton Kelty, of Quinton, nosed out Smith Reeves by 53 votes for sheriff and one Democratic coroner went through but the rest were defeated. Particularly tough was the defeat of John Elwell, of Yorketown, for senator. Elwell had been an assemblyman and was defeated for sheriff in 1878 by seven votes. This year he again lost, after a recount, by seven votes to Wyatt Miller, who became senator.

Clinton Coles, Republican, took the office of clerk away from the Democrats by defeating William Shimp by 156 votes. The Republican assemblyman, Whitaker, followed Henry Coombs to the legislature by defeating Samuel Lecroy. Even the doughty Tom Ferrell, congressman, failed to regain his seat, going down to defeat before George Hires of Salem.

1885 was a quiet year, perhaps the quietest of this turbulent decade. Only one office was to be filled, that of the General Assembly, for which the Republicans nominated Joseph D. Whitaker, their successful candidate the year before. The Democrats named Jacob Lippincott who had served three terms as county clerk, but the ex-clerk went down before Whitaker by 280 votes. The temperance question was by this time assuming huge proportions and Pemberton Pierce, the prohibition candidate for Assembly, polled over 400 votes.

"Things look very green for the Democracy but it is the green of decay and not the green of new life," said the Standard in the fall of 1886 as the new campaign opened, but after election the same paper said, "Providence smiled on the weather but not on the Republicans," for the Democrats elected another governor and the veteran Whitaker lost out by eight votes to a new star on the Democratic horizon, William Newell. George Hires of Salem was re-elected congressman giving the G. O. P. some comfort.

Whitaker applied for a recount, loath to lose his Assembly seat without an effort, but the court upheld Newell and gave him a majority of 17 votes. No less a famous politician than the late Alan McDermott, of Hudson, appeared as counsel for Newell.

1887 will always be remembered as a red letter election for the party of Jefferson and Jackson for in this year the local Democracy for the first time since 1870 effectively and completely cleaned house. Proudly the Standard said before election, "The Dutch took Holland and the Democrats hold the fort in Baltimore but we'll bounce them in Salem county," but afterwards remarked, "Well, we met the enemy and didn't get 'em."

James Butcher, undisputed leader of the Democracy of Salem for this period, arose to great heights when he was elected sheriff by nearly 400 votes over William Carney and by his victory paved his way towards a state senatorship three years later. Assemblyman William Newell defeated Samuel Lippincott for the senatorship by 177 votes and became Salem's first Democratic senator since the beginning of the Civil War.

George Morrison won his third term as surrogate by defeating his opponent by 353 votes. The closest was that of the Assembly where both parties claimed the victory. The first returns showed the Hon. Millard F. Riley elected by five votes over John C. Ward, his Republican opponent. Then because of an error in the count from Quinton the Republicans claimed victory by seven votes. When the loyal Democrats finally aroused the election officers of Quinton that hectic after-election morning, they found that the Republican return was wrong in the matter of Ward's majority for that district and that Riley was the winner by fifteen votes.

Mr. Riley is now a resident of Elmer where he has enjoyed a long and honorable career in civic and political affairs. He is the sole survivor of the legislators who represented Salem county in the 1880's. He is also the sole survivor of the execution jury at the hanging of Howard Sullivan in 1884.

The next year was the third and last presidential struggle of the decade. Like most of its kind it was good to the Republicans in Salem county. Harrison was swept into office by a large vote and carried the county easily over Cleveland. C. A. Bergen of Camden, Republican, followed George Hires to Congress and carried Salem county by over 200 votes. In the only county contest John C. Ward of Pittsgrove defeated Assemblyman Riley, a candidate for re-election, by the same majority as the congressional candidate.

1889 closed another hectic decade on American politics. It found the Democrats with another governor, Leon Abbott, who went into office over General Grubb. Grubb carried Salem county and Ward was re-elected over Strang, Democrat, but former sheriff Clinton Kelty nosed out Clerk Charles D. Coles for the clerkship by 17 votes, giving the Democrats plenty of solace for their other defeats.

In the last issue of 1889 the Republican South Jerseyman said, perhaps a fitting epitaph to the dying decade: "Goodbye 1889, you brought us wet weather, poor crops and Democratic majorities."

CHAPTER XXVII

SALEM IN THE 1890's

The gay nineties were about the same in Salem as they were in any other part of the land. It was an era of amusements, of fast horses, of fancy clothing, of many social events and all the other things that went to make up this much discussed period of our history. It was a period of repression. Young men were extremely careful as to what words they used and when. It was still undignified to speak of a person's leg; it was then called a limb. For the past ten years Salem had had a Lecture Hall; in reality it was a theatre, but folks were still afraid to use that term and the nineties opened with the more dignified term of "Lecture Hall" in use. Late in the nineties, yielding to public demand, it became the Salem Opera House but the adjective "Grand" was yet to come. This Lecture Hall or Opera House, call it what you will, was the center of attraction for the City of Salem.

Visiting stock companies and travelling lecturers had no monopoly on the Opera House. Home talent quite frequently held forth here and presented the current favorites of the age such as "The District School" and "What Happened to Jones". Once in the 90's they held a minstrel show, in which the present editor of the Standard and Jerseyman danced as Carmencita and the late Robert Gwynne, Jr. sang in costume "When Mamma Was a Little Girl Like Me". The home talent entertainments packed the house, which was more than could be said of the visiting professionals. A great deal of the time the Opera House was dark because of poor patronage.

The nineteenth century ended with few local theatrical attraction to mark its departure. Here and there through the turn of the century we find "Uncle Sam in Cuba", "Richelieu", "Peck's Bad Boy", and the "James Boys in Missouri".

These were the days of Bellman, the famed race horse owned by Clark Pettit of Hedgefield in Mannington. Bellman, with all the glories of the nineties on his equine shoulders, lived to a ripe old age and did not die until two decades later. Some years ago in building a house on Morrison avenue in Salem workmen found his bones, which had been buried in the center of the race track park.

On the 27th of October, 1891, passed one of Salem county's most distinguished citizens, Thomas Shourds, the author of "Fenwick's Colony" and a historian and genealogist of more than passing fame. It was recalled at his death that in 1856, having joined the Whig Party, he rose in the Philadelphia convention to nominate William Dayton of New Jersey for Vice President of the United States.

Commencements with all the attendant tear shedding were very much in vogue. The High School commencement called forth columns of print. In the stifling heat of June days each graduate, whether he or she could talk or not, was supposed to speak a piece. The first colored school commencement was held at Mt. Pisgah Church in 1891.

Not only the city schools, but the country schools as well, were doing their best to educate the youth of their respective communities. For example Beasley Neck School, now extinct, in Lower Alloway Creek Township boasted and not in vain, that from its halls had gone forth three sheriffs and two assemblymen of Salem county and in addition the member of Congress from the first congressional district, George Hires.

In this decade a new grade school was put in use. This building is still in use and is now known as the R. M. Acton School. The cornerstone was laid in 1890. At the dedication Doctor Edward F. Sharp, probably one of the most prominent men Salem ever produced, gave a long but interesting address in which he outlined the history of the Salem school system. Dr. Sharp made very clear the feeling expressed by many Salem citizens upon the fact that Samuel Copner had not received enough recognition as the pioneer of the Salem free school system. Dr. Sharp said: "Samuel Copner worked and battled for free schools. He went to Massachusetts at his own expense to see and talk to Horace Mann . . . Let him who won it wear the palm. . . Lamentable it is, but there is no stone to mark his grave next door." Yet with all the interest in education no Salem boy took the examination for the Rutgers Agricultural College at this time.

The great Frances Willard, founder of the W. C. T. U., spoke in the Broadway Methodist Church in 1890. Anna Howard Shaw, foremost woman suffrogette also spoke in Salem in 1890. in 1890.

The Quinton Baptist Church was dedicated on May 12, 1890

and the present building soon after completed. The Alloway Baptist Church held an anniversary service in this year which was largely attended.

Lower Alloway Creek fancied that some of their inhabitants would soon be the possessors of countless treasure because a farmer digging in his field found several Spanish coins. It must be remembered that Spanish-milled dollars were quite customary in colonial days. Hancock's Bridge also put forth a story to the effect that on the site of the present post office stood an old oak tree called the Revolutionary Oak. The tree was there—there is no question about that. The story comes down that four Tories were hanged from its limbs and also that because the trunk of this tree was hollowed it was a favorite place for inebriates to sleep off their potions.

Another story of the past came to life when Captain John Smith caught two cannon balls in his net while fishing in Alloway creek. This gave rise to other stories of a big naval battle and of the capture of an American gunboat in the War of 1812. It gave rise also to a story that during this war one Sheppard Ferren, a native of Hancock's Bridge, displayed such a liberty of speech favoring England that he was almost hung.

The railroad was flourishing and the South Jerseyman related the building of the new station, Acton, three miles from Salem. There is no station there today. The new branch line from Alloway to Quinton was completed on December 21, 1891. The citizens flocked to see the first engine enter town and it is said that the railroad gave free rides to all who wished to go to Quinton on the first trip.

Other industries were in good shape as well. Blessings Iron Foundry was in flourishing condition at Fourth and Griffith streets, Salem. Sturgeon fishing was at its peak in the spring of 1890. Heavy catches marked the shad season and Charles Bright of Pennsville had the record catch of 763 shad.

Salem had a brand new hotel in the spring of 1891. It was built by Charles Ford and was known as Ford's Hotel until 1919 when it became the Salem County Memorial Hospital in honor of the soldiers and sailors of Salem county who served in the World War. This establishment was the last word in modern hotels; it contained not only palatial rooms but had a bowling alley and a mosaic floored bar room.

The year of the World's Fair in Chicago saw many interested Salem folk entrain for the west to behold this magnificent spectacle. Salem county was well represented in antiques sent to the fair. The ladies of Salem interested in these things prepared a pamphlet, which is still available, giving in detail the history of each of the articles.

Lovers of sport will be interested in this item from the South Jerseyman of October 3, 1893: "Salem is to have this year what it has long been in need of—a football team. We have had our baseball and tennis days, but a good football team has never been developed in Salem before. Eleven of Salem's most sturdy young men have been selected and are to be trained by D. Stewart Craven and other college students. W. H. Lawson will uniform the boys, and we hope by Thanksgiving Day to give Salem people a chance to see a good game."

The first game seems to have been played in 1895 between Salem and Quinton but the victor and the score have not survived.

About two years later a high school team, in which former Judge Henry Burt Ware was the moving spirit, was organized but the team did not do much outside of having its picture taken. In the early 1900's a town team was organized under George Hires, Jr., and Walter P. Ballinger. This team did play several games on the race track field on Johnson street. It was not until 1911 that the first Salem High School team which met other schools was organized. Since that time the local high school has never been without a football squad.

In 1898 the sport of basketball made its appearance in Salem. The first game was played on the stage of the Grand Opera House with potato baskets for goals. This game soon became popular and the Y. M. C. A. gymnasium became the arena for this sport.

In the early 90's the hand of Mars was resting heavily on the shoulders of Salem county. At neighboring Fort Delaware modern fortifications were installed and many stone masons and carpenters from Salem were employed on this work. The battery at Finns' Point was being remodeled and the modern emplacements for the guns erected. Two Salem men, William Ryan and John Taylor, were killed in one of the tunnels when a car used to haul powder became unmanageable and ran over them.

But by far the most important event which told of war was the news item in the South Jerseyman of October 3, 1893 which said, "Du Ponts at Carney's Point are making extensive preparations for the manufacture of their smokeless powder. There are five new buildings under course of construction." The Spanish-American War later in the decade gave impetus to this factory but Penns Grove residents who worked there in the 90's could scarcely have envisioned the gigantic plant that this was to be from 1914 on. The starting of this powder plant in 1893 was probably the most important industrial event in the history of the county because it paved the way for the huge works to follow.

The Salem Knitting Mills under J. P. Sheppard received an order for 50,000 dozen hosiery. This plant, along with the Jaquette Marble Works, passed into oblivion in the great fire of 1912.

Mariners along the Delaware river and Salem creek were gratified, through the efforts of Congressman H. C. Loudenslager, in securing a lighthouse to be erected at Finns' Point.

Another baseball season was anticipated when the Salem Baseball Club was organized with B. Frank Wood as manager and Charles N. Westcott as secretary-treasurer. The committee reported that they had found a remarkable left-handed pitcher. Later on in the season the lineup of this team of 1894 was given as follows: pitcher, J. Parks; catcher, James Wildermuth; first base, Howard Stepler; second base, Schuyler Hoffman; third base, Raymond Brandiff; shortstop, James Boogar; left field, Horace Wildermuth; center field, Gus Opel; right field, Harry Mickel; reserves, T. Frank Lawson and Chalkley Willitt.

October 19th of this year brought excitement to Salem in the form of a visit by a portion of the celebrated Coxeys Army. A detachment from this famous caravan, consisting of fifty people and three horses with wagons, visited for a day.

That the musicians were active is evinced by the fact that at the Tri-State Band Tournament held at Neshaminy Falls, Pa., the Salem City Band received third prize, $50.00 in cash, plus a silver bowl.

In this year was laid the cornerstone of the Y. M. C. A. building on West Broadway. Civic and religious men and women in this city had long advocated a community building where young boys could be trained physically and mentally and at the same time be taken off the streets. In the forty or more years of its existence this building has more than justified its erection. One of the foremost men in the Y. M. C. A. movement in 1894 was Edward J. Gayner, who retained his interest in this organization until his death in 1937. On March 3, 1896 the building was formally opened. The "Y" opened with a membership of 139.

January, 1895, witnessed the heaviest fog on the river and in the creeks ever experienced in the memory of the oldest citizen. The next month the river was full of ice and for several days navigation was at a standstill. The third of the winter blasts following the fog and the ice was a terrible blizzard in the middle of February. It was the worst since 1888; railroad travel was at a standstill and snow drifts blocked the roads. There was still ice on the river and there were countless frozen ears, hands and cheeks.

A Salem citizen received well deserved honors when the Board of New Jersey Training School for Feeble Minded Children at Vineland named the hospital, then being erected, "The Josiah Wistar Hospital" in honor of Josiah Wistar of this city. He had been president of the board for the first five years of the school's history.

The subject of music was introduced into the schools of Salem with Charles Glaspey as instructor. Mr. Glaspey taught this subject for over 25 years.

Salem's first Board of Health was organized March 12, 1896 with the following officials: L. Hoelzel, president; C. Bowen, secretary of registration and vital statistics; William Carney, sanitary inspector; J. F. Sinnickson, Esq., solicitor; and C. M. S. Sherron, M. D., physician.

Salem county fishermen protested against the dumping of mud in the Hog Neck Channel of the Delaware river. They said that their nets were four fathoms deep and the middle drift of the channel was so filled with mud that it left only one fathom of water which badly interfered with their shad fishing. Other shad fishermen had a holiday when they chased a large seal down the river; after a race of two or three miles the men conceded the victory to the seal. Bacon Brothers, while drifting for shad off Round Island, caught a devil fish which was five feet long. The average net reported from Penns Grove for one week was from 1000 to 1500. And then, showing that fish stories were still popular, Philadelphia papers reported the capture of a monster fish off Alloway's creek but the South Jerseyman said the story was "without foundation" and that "the person who invented this fish story must have been a direct descendant of the originator of old time sea serpent stories".

These were the days of bicycles. The first bicycle appeared in Salem in 1871, 25 years previous. It was made at a carriage factory in Salem by an apprentice in that shop. The wheels were both of one size, built like carriage wheels but smaller; it was called a velocipede. On exhibition in the Salem County Historical Society quarters is a vehicle which answers the description of this wonder of 1871.

The citizens of this and Cumberland counties were shocked to read in their newspapers in August of 1896 of a horrible railroad wreck in the meadows near Atlantic City. The part which affected the Salem county people so sadly was that this excursion was made up of folks from Alloway, Friesburg, Hancock's Bridge and other points in this section. It was a Sunday School excursion and the loss of life in the wooden coaches on that day was terrific. Many others were injured.

In September of 1896 the Supreme Court of New Jersey declared constitutional the act which legislated out of office the "flower pot" judges of this and the other counties of the State. From the earliest days of the republic and even before, lay judges had adorned the bench of Salem county with their more skilled brothers, the law judges, and had earned themselves the sobriquet of "flower pot judges" because they were largely ornamental. The last judges who were not learned in the law to sit on this bench were William Plummer, William A. Wood, and William Newell.

Seventy or eighty years before, the combined judges of this county were accustomed to ride out to the Salem county boundary line where the King's Highway crosses Oldman's creek into Salem from Gloucester county and meet the Supreme Court Justice who was coming to conduct the trials at Salem and escort him with high honors into the county seat.

In 1897 a small hurricane visited this town and county with the result that chimneys were blown down, roofs blown off and countless window lights broken. In June of the same year another bad wind storm unroofed houses in Mannington, Alloway and Quinton. A heavy electrical storm which did much damage over the entire county occurred in August. In October, the wharves were under water and the banks broken when a northeaster made its appearance.

Possibly the storms of 1897 were a prelude to a greater storm in 1898. The annual celebration conducted by the Salem Veterans of the Spanish-American War on the anniversary of the destruction of the "Maine" calls attention to Salem's part in the brief struggle.

It is quite true that the war lasted so short a time that very little active participation was rendered by those who went from here. But to both a sociologist and a historian there is much of significance in those crowded months of 1898. A modern South Jersey historian saw fit to write that the war caused hardly a ripple in Salem and that aside from a reception to some soldiers from Fort Mott, the war went past unnoticed. That may be partially true, but all the little incidents, seemingly trivial in themselves, reflect a cross-section of the vast panorama of American history, localized in one community.

The fear of the Spanish fleet in the Delaware is only one story worthy of repetition. Patriotic flag raisings is another incident interesting to the localities in which they occurred. The literary output and the music engendered by the war are still other examples worthy of an American historian's attention.

The explosion of the "Maine" in Havana Harbor February 15th, 1898, called forth only mild editorials from the Salem editors. There was need for actual proof of the cause of the explosion before placing the blame directly upon the Spanish government.

But with the war clouds gathering and fear penetrating up and down the Atlantic coast, the residents of the Delaware marshes probably breathed a bit easier when the government began to strengthen the forts on the river. Before war was declared, the federal government changed the name of the battery on the Jersey side near Salem to Fort Mott in honor of Major Gersham Mott.

Orders came at almost the same time barring civilians from Fort Delaware and Fort Mott. Regardless of secrecy, the papers published a brief note, perhaps to reassure the populace, that Fort Mott mounted six ten-inch disappearing guns behind a breastwork of sand, earth and concrete forty feet thick, and that its guns could fire half-ton projectiles many miles.

When war was actually declared in April, no time was lost by the government in bringing the coast defenses of this section up to full strength. Submarine mines were planted in the river south of Fort Delaware on April 24th. Navigation was immediately curtailed, and completely shut off after nightfall. During the day it was necessary to have confidential naval pilots to take legitimate shipping up the river. At once there arose a vigorous protest from the shad fishermen, who claimed that their livelihood was gone with the curtailment of river shipping. The mines and the stopping of the navigation at nights proved in the end to be a boon to the fishermen. They soon found that they could fish all night and lay nets across their ranges without any fear of disturbance since no vessels could pass Fort Delaware.

Salem's first volunteers were B. C. Currie, who enlisted in the Pennsylvania Volunteers, and John C. Price, who entered the navy.

The du Pont Powder Works at Carney's Point, guarded by

thousands in 1917, was watched by a patrol of regular army men, although a Pennsylvania regiment was afterwards dispatched there. Patriotism began to demonstrate itself in various ways. Flag raisings became popular; the first of these seems to have been at Harrisonville, known locally as "Pig's Eye," where after appropriate ceremonies Old Glory flew from a flagpole over the blacksmith shop. The Salem Glass Works, not to be outdone by the Harrisonville smith, raised a pole and a flag thereon under the leadership of the manager, the late Isaac Bacon.

A searchlight which played incessantly over the river and surrounding country, was put into operation at Fort Mott. Everybody within a radius of fifteen miles claimed that they could hear the sunset gun there.

On June 11th, with arrival of the Fourteen Pennsylvania volunteer regiment came the first sombre note of the unpreparedness that long after the war continued to shake America. The Fourteenth arrived at Forts Delaware and Mott on a Sunday night with no water or food and went without meals until noon on Monday, all because the government had forgotten to notify Fort Delaware and Fort Mott that they were coming. It was only one of the instances which brought down upon the head of Russell Alexander Alger, Secretary of War, the well deserved criticism of a nation whose boys had been fed upon embalmed beef or none at all.

In July the guns at the fort roared approval of the great news of the defeat of Cervera's fleet off the coast of Santiago, and Fort Delaware once more prepared to be a military prison for the captured Spanish soldiers and sailors. The middle of July saw the first mass enlistment of Salem men when nineteen of them joined Company E, Sixth Regiment of New Jersey Volunteers. They were: W. B. Jackson, Robert M. Bartlett, Preston P. Merrion, Rev. George C. Hillman, Lin Hogate, George L. Butler, Harry Snitcher, Harry Parsons, Lemuel Harvey, Jr., E. A. Morris, W. B. Furber, Arthur Horner, Elias Griner, Charles F. Stoms, Harry B. Hutchinson, Harry Ashton, Frank Youker, Joel W. Vanneman and Daniel W. Fries, Jr. There were of course others who went from Salem and saw service not only in Cuba but later in the Phillippines and China.

Before the May Day battle of Manilla, when spirit was at its height, the reaction of war feelings had its marked influence upon literary output as well. A trace of the bitter hatred against Spain is evident in the following verse:

> We, as free men take this oath
> That shall it be proven true,
> That Spanish malice caused this ruth
> We will make them deeply rue.
>
> We'll shed the last drop of our blood
> We'll freely give our lives.
> To wipe her ships from off the flood
> In offering to our hero's wives.
>
> We'll pluck her bloody banner down
> We'll trail it in the dust;
> For she beneath the nation's frown
> Our vengeance will be just.

One could hardly call it poetry, but it at least is expressive.

In lighter literary vein the Sunbeam remarked: "The girl I left behind me is very numerous in these days of war and good-bye. But never mind, she's all right. She'll soon be riding along the dusky lanes in the soft moonlight on her bike with the fellow who couldn't pass the examination.

> "My fellow says he'll go to war.
> And kill those Spanish critters
> And blend his rich Missouri gore
> With Cubanesque mosquitters.
>
> But one consoling soothing thought,
> My grief somewhatly smothers,
> If he should fatally be shot,
> Thank heaven there are others."

Salem's most active participation was its reception on July 20th to the Fourteenth Regiment stationed at Fort Mott. The celebration was held in connection with another flag raising, this time at the West Jersey railroad station on Grant street. Unfortunately, the committee picked the hottest day of the summer and the troops were forced to march to Salem under a sweltering sun to witness the flag raising and later to participate in a reception in the Ingham orchard. The regiment almost had some casualties on account of heat prostrations but at least it did not march back to the Fort until after sunset.

But regardless of all that, this was one of Salem's gala days and the gentlemen and ladies did themselves proud in entertaining the soldier boys. There was quite a celebration at the railroad station, and much more fun under the shade afforded by the apple trees of the Ingham orchard. Here lunch was served by the ladies of Salem and the soldiers had a chance to sit down once more.

By mid-August, the mines were taken up in the river and the range lights at Hamburg Cove near New Castle were relighted and the blasts for typhoid deaths, poor sanitation and bad food began to pour in upon the head of the luckless Secretary of War. The spirit of disaffection, now that the war was safely over and won, manifested itself with the same Pennsylvania regiment which marched to Salem when the soldiers, fretful at their delayed discharge, made a demonstration and openly shouted to their officers, "We want to go home." The New Jersey national guard were mustered out but the volunteer regiments remained in service for some time.

From the other side of the globe a Woodstown man, Daniel Wright, wrote of participation in the storming of Manilla City with the Astor Battery, and H. B. Mulford of Salem wrote from the same place one of the first accounts of Dewey's friction with the unfriendly German fleet in Manilla Bay.

Among previously unsung heroines of the war was the late Abba Harris of Lower Creek, who served as a Red Cross nurse in the fever stricken camps and battlefields of Cuba. This courageous woman's work deserves to be better remembered than it has been and it is refreshing to find that the Salem camp of the Spanish-American veterans have decorated her grave in grateful memory of the succor she rendered their comrades.

With a sham battle at Fort Mott, to which flocked the populace of the town of Salem, the Spanish war about ended its influence in this region. All credit to the men and women of the United States who risked their lives not only in battle, but in what was far worse, the fever stricken camps of the South and Cuba.

* * * *

Salem was gay in February of 1899 when a brilliant Hostess Ball was held in the new Mecum Building. That was only one of many such affairs in this decade. Two weeks later came a blizzard which the local papers declared was the worst in the county's history. Some said it surpassed the blizzard of 1888. Roads were blocked and railroad service was at a standstill.

In March of this year Editor Robert Gwynne of the Salem Sunbeam passed away. Had he lived twelve days longer he would have celebrated fifty years of service as editor. In 1849 he had come to Salem a stranger and associated with Nathan Hales in running the then five-year-old newspaper.

In the same month the Blessing Iron Foundry in Salem burned. It was one of the very bad fires of this period.

EVENTS OF THE 90's   349

In May, eight new phones were put in by the telephone company and they announced that only two more phones were necessary to be installed to establish all-night service; the additional ones were soon secured.

On December 27th, 1898, Mason M. Bennett, a prominent Salem liveryman, was found dead in his barn off Walnut street. Prior to the discovery of the body he had been seen on the streets in a very tottering condition aided by a colored man by the name of George Willett, who announced that he was taking him home. No one paid any attention to Willett until after Bennett's body was found, then he was arrested and searched and on his person was found Bennett's watch and some money. He protested he was innocent of the killing, but he was tried in October, 1899 and convicted for second-degree murder and sentenced to State prison for ten years. He became insane and was confined in the Criminal Insane Division at the State Hospital in Trenton, where he died a few years ago.

* * * *

The gay 90's in Salem politics saw the Democrats dominate the first half of the decade and the Republicans the latter half. This was the era of race track agitation, of free silver, of the boy orator of the Platte, of Mark Hanna and his money bags.

The 1890's opened with a sweeping Democratic victory under the leadership of Senator James Butcher, who developed the Democratic organization to its highest peak in years. Senator William Newell, running for Congress, carried Salem county by 200 over Congressman Bergen and although he lost outside of Salem, gave the congressman something to think about. Sheriff Butcher became senator from Salem county by defeating Richard T. Starr by an overwhelming plurality. Another Newell came into the limelight when James Newell was elected sheriff by a big majority over Shute, Republican. James Strimple became assemblyman by defeating George Stanton, Republican.

One Republican elected was Charles W. Denn, who won out as coroner by the margin of fifteen votes. Said the South Jerseyman:

> "Bugler, proclaim the news
> To native bower and foreigner;
> We got licked, it is true,
> But we scooped a coroner."

The campaign was enlivened by a dispute between the editors of the two Republican papers over the patronage of state printing and merrily the bout waged with the editor of the South

Jerseyman paying his respects to the editor of the Standard as a "political lunk-head" and being called a traitor in return.

Nor was 1891 much more profitable to the Republicans. Secure in their stronghold the Democrats re-elected Strimple to the Assembly by 379 votes over Hunt, Republican.

1892 saw the Democrats win again. Cleveland went back into the White House, carrying Salem county by 84 votes. Werts, the Democratic candidate for governor, continued the string of successive Democratic governors since the Civil War by defeating John Kean. Werts also carried the county. Congressman Loudenslager, always very popular in Salem, carried it by five votes. He was the lone Republican elected. William Diver succeeded James Strimple as the Democratic assemblyman, defeating Allen, Republican, by 220 votes. George Morrison, surrogate, won his fourth term by a handsome plurality of 400 over Richman Coles, Republican.

But 1893 saw a check in the Democratic wins. The Republicans carried the banner of race track reform high in the air as they campaigned against the Democrats on that issue. By the close margin of 90 votes John C. Ward became senator of Salem county by defeating Robert Gwynne, Jr., editor of the Sunbeam, and four times mayor of Salem, in a close and exciting contest.

The Republican sheriff candidate was also successful, Wriggins winning by 115 votes over his Democratic adversary. Assemblyman Diver, who had voted against the race track bill, was the only Democrat returned victorious. Diver won by 40 votes over Charles W. Powers, Republican.

"It didn't snow this year, but the Republican votes fell like snowflakes," proudly exclaimed the Jerseyman after the election of 1894. Powers, defeated for Assembly the year before, retired Diver to private life by a 350 plurality. Luther Richmond became county clerk by defeating Clerk Clinton Kelty by 105 votes and Loudenslager swept the county again in his Congress campaign.

The next year the Jerseyman used the same snowflakes story and they were right, for the votes fell again and John W. Griggs became the first Republican governor of New Jersey in thirty years. No wonder the loyal G. O. P. rooters of Salem flocked into Trenton bearing banners "Salem County for Griggs by 524". Powers was re-elected to the lower house by 350 votes over Joseph Bell, Democrat.

1896 deserves special mention of the details of that famous campaign when William Jennings Bryan leaped into fame with one speech and convulsed the electorate as no campaign since that time has done.

Those who were faithful to Bryan had ample cause to mourn in Salem county. McKinley carried it by 996 and every Republican candidate with him had at least 700 majority. It was a bad day for the local Democracy. Richard C. Miller was re-elected senator. Benjamin Westcott became sheriff and Joseph B. Crispin, assemblyman. It was really a Republican tidal wave, the greatest in history up to that time.

But the Democracy had a quick recovery. Tradition seemed to hold that no matter how strong the Republicans might be in a given era, the job of surrogate belonged to the Democrats. Surrogate Morrison, who had held the office for twenty years, died in 1896 and Governor Griggs appointed Henry Coombs as the ad interim surrogate. In the election of 1897 Loren P. Plummer, who was destined to hold that office for a quarter of a century, decisively defeated Coombs. Crispin, the Republican assemblyman, was forced to extend himself by Joel Langley, the Democrat and Crispin only won by 186 after an 800 plurality the year before.

1898 saw the Democrats score an Assembly victory in a marked upset. Frank Wright, a young and popular Woodstown business man, defeated Gray, Republican, by 174 votes. Wright carried Woodstown and held Gray to four votes in Pilesgrove, a truly remarkable run in those stalwart Republican districts.

Samuel Iredell, of Cumberland county, carried this county by 45 votes over Loudenslager for Congress but as was customary, lost elsewhere by heavy totals. The Republicans elected another governor, Foster M. Voorhees, who won Salem by 196 votes over Crane, his opponent.

The last year of the decade saw a hectic and turbulent election. In iron-bound Mannington the Democrats elected a freeholder, former sheriff James Newell, and with him the rest of the ticket. Robert N. Vanneman became sheriff of Salem county, carrying Mannington by one vote and the county by forty. This was the extent of the Democratic triumph. Miller was re-elected senator, nosing out the formidable James Strimple by 64 votes. Henry Blohm was elected assemblyman, defeating Jacob Edwards, Democrat, and Clerk Richmond retained his office by a heavy plurality over attorney Edward M. Sickler.

CHAPTER XXVIII

OF SALEM SINCE THE TURN OF THE CENTURY

It is exceedingly difficult to write of one's own times. Possibly the scribe feels the Kleig light of criticism and the danger of offense too deeply to be properly daring in his treatment of men and things of his own day. Sufficient then, that the last thirty-seven years of the narrative must necessarily be not only sketchy, but retrospective along the lines of one's own memory.

The reader may discover many omissions which must be pardoned, for to describe adequately three decades so filled with events would require a volume in itself.

The two great points of transition and change come in these years: first, with the advent of the automobile, and secondly, with the World War and the powder boom, followed by the development of the dye and chemicals industries. But before those topics are disposed of allow the historian to tell what he himself recalls from the time when he was old enough to survey the mundane scene for himself, about 1903. For about thirty-four years, the chronicle deals with personal recollections, many of which accentuate the fact that many of these things are no more. Since 1640, the writer has dealt with records only and has placed in black and white the things other people remembered in their own time. Refreshing it is, therefore, to boldly stalk forth from the jungle of old newspapers, old deeds and old "I-told-you-so's" to say for himself regarding Salem, "I remember this."

It is a long call from the pre-historic days, from the Swedes at Elsinboro Point and the New Haven Colony to Henry Frisby's ice cream and hokey-pokey wagon, but nevertheless it is the first scene of the Salem act that the narrator recalls. Frisby, a colored man, sold delicious hokey-pokeys and had a mournful trumpet which awakened a sleeping boy on hot summer afternoons. Then in the same class were the trips to Bobby Jacquett's candy shop on Fifth street where the best candies ever feasted upon were found.

About 1905 came the moving picture. The first was exhibited in the defunct Grand Opera House but a year or so later came

THE MOVIES

the first strictly movie houses, the Bijou Dream and the Dreamland. The first held forth at 141 West Broadway, the present offices of W. O. Schalick and H. C. Berry. The second, at 153 West Broadway, is now occupied by Dwyer's Store.

Then there was the Salem Amusement Park, operated in the open air by Benjamin Bee at the site of the Post Office. It was surrounded by a high board fence and in summer time was a mecca for those who enjoyed the silent flickers and vaudeville. To enjoy it meant silent suffering on the part of the devotees of Thespian art, because all and sundry were victims of the ubiquitous New Jersey mosquito.

Later came La Ray Theatre on Walnut street and the old Palace on the North side of West Broadway; now gone into oblivion. Today two theatres grind out the talkies, both built within the past twenty-five years, the Palace and the Fenwick. Back of the Bijou Dream, where a Gramophone blared the wares of this palace of thrills, was Jobie's. Jobie Denn made and sold ice cream and here on warm nights gathered colored and white alike to cool themselves. Another cooling place was the old Andrews pharmacy, once John Ballinger's store at the head of Market Street, where now runs the extension of that street.

One of the first youthful remembrances are two orchards, once beautiful things with rows of box bush and flowers, long before the infants of 1905 played in their ruins. These were the Ingham orchard, through which New Market street now passes, and the Dick Garden on the west side of Walnut street. Back of the Dick Garden were the Jacquette Marble Works, the Grand Opera House and the Salem Knitting Mills, all three of which were destroyed in the great fire of 1912.

Across Walnut street stood the Friends School, now an apartment house. Its spacious lawn, on which strawberry festivals were held, is now covered by modern store buildings.

There were several base ball parks in these decades. The first recalled was where North Union street extends north of Broadway. The next was on the prairies opposite the old Ingham orchard on Wesley street. Then came the park on Johnson street with its high board fence. This also has yielded to residences. After an unsuccessful attempt to place a field in the marshes at the end of Chestnut street, the City Athletic Ground is now on Walnut street in the location popularly known as Sicklerville. Football was played on some of those fields and on the huge oval in the center of the Race Track. After the new high school was built on New Market street the grounds at the rear were used as a football field for several years.

The Race Track was not only impressive to the juvenile

mind because of its huge size and layout but also, because one was told that bad people sat in the grandstand at nights when they should have been home. The bogey of nightfall dispensed with, it was a lovely place in daytime with fences to hurdle, a track to run on, a starter's bell to blare and a grandstand to romp over. Then there was the lonely outbuilding, covered by the proverbial honeysuckle, and marked "Ladies Only."

The Driving Park Association, the last follower of Thunderbolt and the Fair Grounds, lasted from about 1902 to 1918. The land occupied by it makes up present home sites on Johnson street, Allen, Craven, Morrison and Fenwick avenues.

Most of Salem's swimming holes in these early years of the Twentieth century have also passed into history. There was the Sand Hole at the foot of Van Meter Terrace, long since filled in. Keasbeys Creek, Pioneer's Pond, First Oak and Lucky Bridge were also favorites with the boys. Most of these ditches are impassible with muddy vegetation today but Salem Creek and Oakwood Beach have not lost their appeal. Two bridges from which the youth of 1907 dove to splash in the waters below have gone likewise, into the rubble heap of time. They were the Red bridge on Quaker Neck road and the Covered bridge at the foot of Market street. The Covered bridge was such a venerable Salem institution that when the State Highway Department purposed to remove it, some years ago, several citizens of Salem remonstrated, but to no avail.

The youthful mind remembers only too well, (it scared him once) the wooden Indian which stood in front of Garwood's Cigar Store on the North side of East Broadway. Both the store and the Indian have vanished. Where Lummis's Jewelry Store now stands, 209 East Broadway, was the undertaking parlor of John McDonnel. Mrs. Passwaters' Notion Store, 180 East Broadway with it's sunken glass cases has yielded to the radio store of Russell S. Morton. Newkirk's Oyster Saloon, on Market street, selling their slab-sided ham sandwiches will long be remembered. The site were it stood is covered by an annex of the City National Bank. The dry goods store, once Thompson's, later Stiles & Freas, and finally Butcher & Harris, 195 East Broadway, has given up to a chain store. Here one gloried in the little change trolleys which skipped about on their wires over the store. Here also, in the waiting room countless young maidens waited for their papas and mamas to finish Saturday night shopping so that they might all clamber into the wagon for the ride home. Gone now are all the livery stables with their own inimitable odors. Vanished are the stout railings which stood around Colonel Johnson's house and the high boarded fence which kept the pupils of the Grant Street School from trespassing on what is now the Johnson Park. The last of the meridian houses on the school grounds was removed in 1912 and across the street, although the railroad still operates two trains a day, the sheds and the long platform through which many youthful Salem citizens played have disappeared. With them has gone also one of Salem's most celebrated events, that of meeting the trains.

Then there was Sam Wright's Store, Union street and Broadway, which contained the most expert exponents of the art of expectoration. Here the writer watched with admiration the all-American spitters load, aim and fire at the barrel stove without a single miss. There were many patent medicine shows as well as that most popular pastime, the circus. Not forgotten is the raucous voice of the barker declaring, "see Minnie HaHa, half man, half woman."

Another dead and gone institution is the old Stone Mill at the Griffith street bridge. There was also Elkinton's Mill near Alloway, the Tannery in Fifth street where the Episcopal Parish House now stands, the old Starr Canning Factory, the Major's Wharf nearby, and last but not least which delighted the frolicsome boys, because it was always cool, was the Pickle Plant in the Pioneer's meadow, south of Broadway and west of Third street. This was once the Alva Glass Works. The site today is occupied by the Congoleum factory.

At the Fort Elfsborg beach were Oakwood with it's once gaudy pavilion and plenty of nails and sand-bars to trouble bare feet and the old Salem Country Club (at the site of the present Fort Elfsborg Country Club) with it's iron steps running down the bluff to the beach, the raft, the yellow bath house, the six hole golf course with it's distance flags flying bravely in the breeze; the kind and worthy Dave Fox bringing back the horses across the golf links to carry the visitors back to Salem.

All of these things have gone with Thebes the Golden but the memory is imperishable in the mind of the historian and to him they are as much history as any recorded documents.

* * * *

It was in 1900 that Horace VanLeer of Alloway chugged over Salem county roads with a new-fangled contraption known as an automobile. For some years to follow, few were the souls who were brave enough to purchase a horseless carriage. The few of them in Salem in the first ten years of the new century were rare enough to excite the awe, admiration and scrutiny of a crowd. People boasted widely of their first ride. After

1910, the automobile gradually evolved from an expensive novelty to a basic necessity. In the next decade, one by one the livery stables disappeared. With the standardization of parts, and with the great increase in wages during the World War, the automobile crowded the railroad trains from the local picture in the third decade of the century almost to the same extent as they had the horse in the second decade.

The historian may not overlook the tremendous significance of the automobile. Eighty years before VanLeer introduced the automobile into Salem county, there had been a move to move the county seat to Woodstown on grounds that it was more central and because traveling was extremely difficult. There is no such protest today. The automobile has consolidated the county into one large unit. Any part may now be reached in less than forty minutes. Just as the steam boat and the railroad opened up certain parts of the county to trade in the interchange of goods, the automobile unified every part of the county. It made it possible for every farmer and dealer to find an outlet for his goods and to come into full contact with his town neighbors.

The roads of thirty years ago were mainly of run-of-field dirt with a few improved with oyster shells or gravel. Shell Road, running through Carney's Point, derives its name from oysters and not from shrapnel. With the coming of the automobile the roads were revolutionized. The oyster shells and the dirt disappeared and the State Highway Department and County Board of Freeholders extended miles of concrete throughout the County. Many of the city streets were paved with a hard surface of stone and asphalt. The gasoline tax provided millions to finance the network of commerce and communication. With the main arteries paved, the next step was the farm-to-market drive, enabling the farmer to get out of the mud.

As the automobile ruthlessly destroyed horse and rail transportation, so in Salem county, it also turned back another rival, the trolley. From the 80's on, when traction companies filled the cities of America with their tracks, there had been a demand for a trolley line in Salem county. The most popular one on paper was the route connecting Bridgeton and Salem but it never came to pass. Finally in the war years of 1917 and 1918 the trolley did enter Salem county. By that time the automobile was a healthy infant but the rail competition was still strong. In order to facilitate the movement of workers in Penns Grove, Carney's Point and Salem to the Powder Works, the DuPont Company, with local backing, was largely instrumental in having the first and only trolley built in the confines of this county. It was finally finished in 1917 after many delays. The line extended from the end of East Broadway to the wharf at Penns Grove.

But it's life was not long. As automobiles and highways continued towards perfection the trolley business dwindled and the end came in 1933. The tracks have either been removed or covered over and an auto bus now holds the franchise between Salem and Penns Grove.

* * * *

The brightest star in the literary firmament after the turn of the century was Albert Elmer Hancock. He was born and raised on Fifth street, Salem. Graduating from Wesleyan he became a professor of English literature at Haverford. Under him in the classroom sat a young man who has since carved out his own niche in American letters. His name was Christopher Morley.

Hancock, while a member of the faculty of Haverford, wrote a splendid treatise on the life of John Keats. Furthermore, he penned two novels of American life, one entitled "Henry Bourland" and the other, "Bronson of the Rabble."

About Henry Bourland there should be more than passing notice. It is extremely doubtful that Margaret Mitchell in far away Atlanta ever heard of either Hancock or his novel Henry Bourland, but compare it with her "Gone with the Wind" and one finds the same epic theme of the decayed and stricken South. Because Hancock penned such a powerful description of the post-war South in this particular book, it now becomes in the light of subsequent books such as "Gone with the Wind", a forgotten novel to be re-read and remembered.

Hancock's life ended tragically by his own hands at the Delaware Water Gap, Pa., in December of 1915. He was 44 years of age.

Alfred M. Heston, the author of the celebrated "Jersey Wagon Jaunts," was for a short time a resident of Salem being editor of the National Standard in 1884. In recent years, Salem county has had an addition to its literary circles by the acquisition of George Agnew Chamberlain, a popular fiction writer. He came from Bridgeton to reside on the old Lloyd Landing farm on Alloways creek in Quinton township. Chamberlain wrote a master line in his "Lantern on the Plow" when he referred to Salem as "the city of the red brick houses where the decades are but as a single day."

On the artistic side this county had Connarroe and Pettit in the past century. Now two great modern artists who may call this their home are Everett Shinn of Woodstown and Morris Hall Pancoast, of Salem. Shinn is celebrated for his murals, especially the one in the Belasco Theatre, New York, while Morris Pancoast is favorably known for his sea and landscapes.

For the footlights of the stage this county has produced Wallace Ray of Alloway who played successfully for several years in both the theatre and in silent moving pictures.

* * * *

The past three and a half decades have not been without turbulence and violence in the history of Fenwick's Colony. It is unfortunate that so many murders have to be recorded in so short a space of time. At that, there is not enough space to tell them all. Murder is a sorry business and while there has been plenty of it in this county, some of them must be related even with scant detail. The most notorious of the crimes were first, the murder of guard Joseph Westcott, on Christmas Eve 1916. Westcott was a Virginian working at the Du Pont Plant. Three Italians named Pettito, Constanttino and Nichols got him drunk, loaded him in a wagon, went out into the Bevis Tract, near Penns Grove and murdered him in cold blood. That the crime was atrocious is revealed by the fact that when his body was found, a stake was driven through his eye. The three Italians were arrested, tried for murder and two of them, Pettito and Nichols were convicted of murder in the first degree. Constantino missed the chair with a thirty-year sentence. The two were executed on March 27, 1917. They were the first criminals from Salem county executed by electricity and this was the first capital case since the execution of Sullivan in 1884.

The next brutal murder was the shooting of Paymaster J. W. MacCausland of the Salem Glass Works in the early morning of October 24, 1930. The paymaster, a resident of Salem, was on his way from the office to the Works, carrying a tray of money when suddenly some men jumped out of an automobile and shot him in the back without warning. The bandits scooped up some of the money and made their escape. Two numbers of the car license were noted down by a bystander, which eventually led to the arrest of Charles Fithian and Peter Giordano. In their confessions of guilt they named an accomplice, Henry Green, missing at the time. The trials of the two were held separately and both were convicted and sentenced to die in the electric chair. On the night of his conviction, Fithian posing as asleep and having a dummy in his cell to fool the guard, escaped through a ventilator to the roof. From here he jumped to the roof of the Surrogate's office and disappeared into the darkness of the December night. All trace of him was lost until a week later when he was captured in Troy, New York. He was executed at Trenton, December 28, 1931.

Henry Green, the alleged accomplice, was not apprehended until 1936, when he was captured in Los Angeles, California. He was tried in December of that year and, after a highly sensational trial, was acquitted.

In March, 1932, occurred a dastardly murder affair which is as yet unsolved. A colored woodchopper, Irvin Hite and his wife were enroute to the woods on Burden's Hill in Quinton township. Suddenly, a stranger in an auto stopped in the road in front of them and without warning, produced a gun and shot Hite. His wife escaped. Upon investigation it was found that the stranger had "dumped" a corpse out of his coupe and thinking the Hites had seen the act, killed Hite to conceal the crime. Neither the stranger who murdered the woodchopper nor the corpse found in the woods nearby, have ever been identified.

On August 2, 1935, a prominent Mannington farmer Harry Dolbow came home with his wife and young daughter from a fair in Delaware. Dolbow took the car to the garage and was never seen alive afterwards. His body was found with the skull crushed, in the barn early the next morning. After a few days of questioning and investigation the wife of the deceased, Marguerite Fox Dolbow and her alleged lover, Norman Driscoll, a neighbor, were arrested for the murder. Mrs. Dolbow confessed the crime, implicating Driscoll and a colored farm hand named Drummond. The confession showed that Driscoll had done the killing by means of a harrow axle and that Mrs. Dolbow had tipped him off to the right time of their arrival home. The trial of the case started in October, 1935, but ended in a mistrial when the wife of one of the jurors passed him a note. The case was started again on January 28, 1936 before Judge Frank T. Neutze of Camden and after lasting two weeks, the jury returned a death verdict against Mrs. Dolbow and Driscoll. Drummond, the accessory pleaded guilty and was given life imprisonment. The appeal of Mrs. Dolbow and Driscoll is at this time before the New Jersey Court of Pardons. If they should be executed they will be the third pair of murderers electrocuted at Trenton from this county.

The most destructive fire in the city of Salem during this period was that which laid waste the business section of Walnut street in 1912. The Jacquette Marble Works, the Grand Opera House and the Salem Knitting Mills was destroyed. However, the worst fire in the history of the county was that in Penns Grove on March 1, 1932 when several blocks of stores and residences along the Delaware river were wiped out. Valiant efforts of firemen from Wilmington and all of South Jersey saved the rest of the borough from almost certain destruction.

* * * *

Politics since the turn of the century has been largely one-sided since most of the years from 1900, have been marked by Republican triumphs. In fact, the Democratic victories until recently, have been so few and far between that it is much easier to recount the exceptions than the rule.

Early in the first decade while Senator Butcher still held the reins of the Democratic party they were successful in a sweep for all the offices. This was in 1902 when James Strimple was elected Senator over John Tyler, William Johnson, Sheriff over B. B. Westcott and Ephraim Harris was named assemblyman. During this period, also the Democrats held the Board of Freeholders. In 1902, Loren P. Plummer, Democrat, received his second term as Surrogate. He won in 1907 by a 98-vote majority over Howard B. Keasbey. In 1912, the year of Wilson's victory, he swamped his Republican opponent by a 2 to 1 vote. Finally in 1917, he was elected to his fifth and last term over W. F. Miller by 120 votes. Mr. Plummer retired in 1922 and his successor is T. B. Reed Pancoast, a young Republican, wounded in the World War, who is now serving his third consecutive term. There were no more Democratic victories in the county, save for Plummer's in 1907, until 1908 and that was a gift to the Jeffersonian party. In that year of Taft's election to the Presidency, the Republicans got into a factional split over the stand of their candidate for Assembly, Mr. Crispin, concerning local option. Most of the Republicans bolted Crispin and backed Samuel Ridgeway, of Woodstown, on what was called a Loyal Temperance Legion ticket. The split which ensued elected John D. Schade, a Democrat, of Pole Tavern, to the Lower House of the Legislature.

In 1911, the Democrats began the push which kept them in power for three years. John F. Ayres of Alloway was elected Sheriff; Isaac Smick, Assemblyman, and John Warren Davis, a Baptist minister of Pedricktown, was elected State Senator over the then incumbent, William Plummer, of Quinton. Davis' rise to power by this election was meteoric. He had been for some years the minister of the Baptist Church at Pedricktown and had studied law on the side. In 1910, his critics alleged, he had desired to join the Republican ranks but was not successful. The following year, he did join the Democratic party and surprised the entire county by winning over Senator Plummer.

Davis then became "solid" with Governor Woodrow Wilson. Upon Wilson's elevation to the Presidency, Davis swept forward rapidly. Even though he had only been a lawyer for a few years, he was named by President Wilson, in rapid fire succession, District Attorney of New Jersey, Federal Court Judge, and last, a judge of the Circuit Court of Appeals, the highest U. S. bench, except for the Supreme Court.

In 1912, taking advantage of the Wilson landslide, the Democrats swept Salem county merrily. Plummer was re-elected as surrogate and Isaac Smick, Democrat, for the second time became the assemblyman. The next year, 1913, Smick became state senator for the unexpired one-year term of Senator Davis, who by that time was named as U. S. District Attorney. William M. Wheatley was elected to the assembly. This closed the brief Democratic era. In 1914 former Sheriff Collins B. Allen, Republican, retired Senator Smick. Allen held the job for three terms and in the last one was President of the Senate while Edward I. Edwards was governor.

During the years 1910 to 1913 two presidents of the United States and one aspirant for the presidency came to Salem. William Jennings Bryan, three times defeated for this high office, spoke as a part of the Democratic Campaign of 1913 in the Bee Amusement Park, now the site of the Post Office. He was then Secretary of State and came on a special train. In 1912, seeking re-election, came William Howard Taft whose special train backed into Salem yards affording the President a chance to speak on the rear platform. A small boy released from school for the great occasion, pressed through the crowd to enable himself to reach up on the platform and touch the presidential shoe. In fact, the writer got more than he bargained for, because the President spluttered very much in his address and in addition to the great honor of touching his shoe, the boy received a shower of presidential saliva.

In the campaigns of 1910 and 1911, on the stage of the old grand opera house, Woodrow Wilson, destined to be president of the United States, made two addresses. The second was one of his masterpieces and was most prophetic. In this speech of October 4, 1911, he said in conclusion, "I believe that there exists in America that indomitable spirit of independence which takes zest with such changes of affairs as have occurred in our home state of New Jersey. I believe that in the rest of the country there still resides that political sagacity, that political capacity, that political foresight which makes us institutions—makes as well as institution administrators, and that Americans stand ready, when the way is pointed out, to stand by those who lead them in the paths of public purity and of public integrity."

From 1914 with Davis removed to Trenton and former Senator James Butcher retired from politics and active life, the Democratic party lapsed into a hopeless and ineffective minority. In all the years from 1914 to 1928 only two Democrats were successful in the county. They were Loren P. Plummer for surrogate in 1917 and Robert W. Kidd for sheriff in 1923. The last election was most interesting and closely fought. At the primaries that year, William T. Mifflin who had been the Republican sheriff from 1917 to 1920, won the nomination of that party over George W. Brown. Hundreds of Republicans dissatisfied with the result, backed Brown who ran as an independent. The Democrats had nominatd Mayor Robert W. Kidd of Penns Grove. In a three-cornered contest, Kidd won by 16 votes over Brown, his nearest contender. The total vote was Brown 3796, Mifflin 3092, and Kidd 3812. Friends of Brown asked for a recount in view of the fact that Brown was a "written in" or "sticker" candidate; and that the intent of the majority of the voters was for Brown though the election boards had failed to count them. Despite the contention, Justice C. C. Black of the Supreme Court ruled against Brown and his backers, and actually increased Kidd's majority to a 107 votes.

The year 1928 saw the peak of the Republican strength in Salem county. In a G. O. P. landslide Hoover carried this county by 9,000 votes. All the other Republican candidates shared his victory, most of them winning by pluralities of over 7,000. From that year on, the Republican majorities have waned and at times in the last few years have been not majorities at all, but losses. In 1927, a young attorney from Pittsgrove Township, W. Orvyl Schalick, settled in Salem and proceeded to re-organize the nearly defunct Democrats. In 1929, young Mr. Schalick elected his candidate for sheriff, the late George P. Dixon, by a 98-vote majority.

In 1930, the Republicans with the popular candidate Dwight Morrow easily carried this county for all the offices including Mr. Morrow for United States Senator. But in 1931, Mr. Schalick's new leadership struck again and in a surprise victory which the Republicans did not in the least anticipate, carried the county by 1400 votes for Governor A. Harry Moore and elected Joseph S. Sickler as a member of the Lower House of the Legislature. The writer was thus the first Democrat Assemblyman in eighteen years which was the longest interval of time since the formation of the Democrat party that it had been without a representative at Trenton. Since 1910, the Board of Freeholders had been in Republican hands. In this year of 1931 the Democrats tied the vote at seven apiece.

1932 being a presidential year, the Republicans got out their full strength and carried their entire ticket by majorities ranging from 250 to 5,000. However, the Democrats, although they lost the county, carried the Townships of Lower Alloways Creek and Upper Penns Neck in the freeholder contests, giving them undisputed control of the Board. The next year in another close assembly fight, Erwin S. Cunard, Republican, won his seat again by another 200-vote margin. 1934 saw another Republican triumph in the county although A. Harry Moore, running for United States Senator, burst into the Republican score and carried the county for the United States Senatorship. It was in this year that the Democrats captured two more Republican seats in the Board of Freeholders, Oldmans and Upper Pittsgrove, thus making the Board stand eleven Democrats and three Republicans. This was a record in that no political party had ever been reduced to such a small representation before. The 1937 Board stands ten Democrats and four Republicans.

1935 witnessed the most complete Democratic victory since 1913. The party swept the boards in the November election. Colonel D. Stewart Craven who for twenty-five years had been a member of the State Board of Education, defeated Senator S. Rusling Leap, of Woodstown, by a margin of 38 votes. Norman P. Featherer of Penns Grove won over Assemblyman Cunard by an 800-vote margin, becoming the second Democratic Assemblyman in four years. The most smashing victory however, came with the success of the late Hildreth S. Reeves for Sheriff, young World War veteran, who decisively triumphed over his opponent William H. Morris, by a majority of 2800 votes. James E. Hitchner became Coroner by a huge margin over Dr. J. Horace Loscalzo.

The death of Sheriff Reeves exactly one year after he took office, cast a deep gloom over the county. Few men in public life ever enjoyed the "dear love of friends" as he did.

The election of 1936, marked an epic in Salem's political history. Four years previously the rock ribbed Republican county of Salem had refused to be swept away in the landslide which removed Herbert Hoover from office. This time, the position was reversed. Whereas President Roosevelt had lost the county in '32 by 2700 votes, he carried it in '36 by 4000. The reason for the upheaval was the natural result of a trend manifested for years, but never coming to such full fruition before. The main reason was the colored voter. Time and time again since the War between the States, the Republican party had carried Salem county on the strength of the colored vote. About four thousand numerically, it frequently meant triumph for the G. O. P. In close elections it was always their salvation.

Still another trend demonstrating itself was in the vote of the laboring man. The election of 1936 proved that the labor vote of the county organized or unorganized, voted for President Roosevelt.

With the colored and labor vote weaned from the Republican side, it is easy to see that the local ticket would follow the national to victory. The Assemblyman, Mr. Featherer and two Coroners were elected by large majorities, giving the Democratic party two successive years of clean sweeps.

* * * *

The World War, the Powder boom and the large influx of population into the Penns Grove area of Salem county necessitated the organization and building of several new churches. Among these newcomers were the Presbyterian Church in Carney's Point, the Episcopal Church of the Merciful Saviour and the Roman Catholic St. James Church in Penns Grove, all of which were built during the World War period. Likewise in Penns Grove a new church edifice was built by the Congregation of the Bethel-Mariners Methodist Protestant Church to replace the one destroyed by the fire of 1932. All of these buildings are a credit to the community in which they stand and their congregations are large and flourishing. New Methodist Chapels were built at Carney's Point and Deep Water in the same period.

Throughout these years most of the churches maintained their position. Some of them however, have become extinct. An example is the Orthodox Meeting on West Broadway in Salem. The Twentieth Century in religious circles, unlike the eighteenth and nineteenth, has not been in order for religious revivals. The one exception to this rule since the turn of the century was the brief revival experienced in Salem during the winter of 1915 when the Reverend Billy Sunday held forth in Philadelphia. At this time, a large number of people joined respective churches throughout the county. Reflections of this revival occurred in Salem county in the building of large wooden tabernacles in Penns Grove and Salem, and the engagement by union church effort of visiting evangelists.

* * * *

It has been stated that the two most important events of these years was the introduction of the automobile and the World War. At the outbreak of this struggle in 1914 the

DuPont Company which had operated a small smokeless powder plant at Carney's Point since 1893, was appealed to by the Allied Forces for powder. Responding to this demand they set to work to build two more units of their smokeless powder plant at Carney's Point. In less than a year this huge manufacturing concern had extended from a tip of land on Carney's Point several miles southward to the canal at Deep Water point. The demand for carpenters, masons and workmen generally far exceeded the supply. Farmers of Salem county dropped their plows in the field to become carpenters, mechanics and operators at fabulous wages. The skilled labor of this county and of neighboring Wilmington was drained to the last drop. From all parts of the United States, knowing that a job awaited them in far distant Penns Grove, came skilled workmen and laborers in droves.

The little borough of Penns Grove whose population in 1910 was less than 2,000 jumped to 10,000. There were not accomodations in Penns Grove for one-tenth of the eager multitude. Many hundred rubberoid and frame houses were hastily erected in Carney's Point and Deep Water to shelter the workmen. A large portion of the overflow came to Pennsville, Woodstown and Salem. At one time it was estimated that 20,000 men were employed here. This increase of population led to the building of the Salem and Penns Grove trolley line in 1917.

Many worth while people came to Penns Grove and to Salem county in the years from 1914 to 1918. Many of them are still here and are among our most useful citizens. As was the case in the gold rush, in the rush to the Klondike and other sudden booms, with the better class came a flock of adventurers. The crime proportion of Salem county jumped to a staggering figure and the court dockets of the Salem county criminal courts were loaded. In 1916, a band of thugs attempted to blow the safe in the Penns Grove post office. They were surprised and captured. Other crimes of violence were numerous and finally the Du Pont Company helped the local authorities to keep order by employing a corps of plant policemen.

It is a pity that no Bret Harte was here with a story like "The Luck of Roaring Camp" to perpetuate the epic of the powder boom. Fires, explosions, murders, hold-ups, swindlers, confidence men, picturesque adventurers, alike were crowded into this pulsating drama of four and one-half years duration. One riding past the plants at night either by boat on the river or by car on the road had an ample picture of Dante's "Inferno."

The effects of the powder boom cannot easily be estimated. They touched every part of Salem county life, from the industrial center at Penns Grove to the farms in remote Pittsgrove. In a word, the boom changed Salem county from a purely agricultural community into an industrial community. True there were other going industries before Du Ponts enlarged in 1914 but at one fell swoop, this gigantic plant transformed the county almost over night. The fruits of that enterprise are still with us and have been the greatest single source of change and growth in all the county's history.

While the world war was raging and the Du Pont Company was busily engaged in supplying powder to the warring forces of the allies in Europe, there was started at Deep Water Point a small plant which has since grown to mammoth proportions. This was the dye works. Here on a gigantic scale the magic of the chemist was to "beat our swords into plowshares" and lay the foundation for a permanently greater Salem county. The chemist chiefly responsible for this development was Charles L. Reese. Due to his farsightedness comes the dye works of today. Dr. Reese had seen a fact more clearly than most of his associates who were thinking about munitions at that time and little else. He saw that the war had totally cut off the importation of German dyes and that even when the war was over the United States would suffer thereby. He proposed, therefore to experiment and perfect processes which would enable this nation to engage in an industry which up to that period was monopolized by Germany.

The nucleus was at hand for his efforts. Picric acid is used in high explosives and was being made for that purpose in Deep Water during the years of 1914 to 1918, but it also is used in the making of sulphur black, a fundamental dye. The price of dyes were then prohibitive. The field was wide open for American manufacture. Such dyes as were then on the market were sold at the exorbitant prices (up to $150 a pound where ordinarily the cost was about $1.50.) The British government was forced to go into the manufacture of dyes to sustain its own related industries. The American government had not acted.

So, in this corner of New Jersey, Dr. Reese seeing clearly this need for American dyes in the reconstruction days to come, labored long and faithfully to establish, over night as it were, an American industry. He had help of course and had gathered around him all the chemists he could lay hands on to aid him. Fundamentally the dye and munition business are tasks for organic chemists and it was the presence of these organic chemists which made and preserved the plant at Deep Water. Years after the war was over and the smokeless powder plants of Number 2 and 3 had gone into the rubble heap of time, the chemists at Deep Water were busy laying the foundations for new industries based on the original conception of the American dye trade. Save for one setback in the fall of 1920, when the German dyes threatened to break the American market, the dye plant has gone steadily on its way in the work of establishing the Du Pont Company as the leading makers of dyes in America.

But the upward trend of business which has so materially increased the prosperity of Salem county did not stop with the perfection of dye manufacture. The presence of the organic chemists at Deep Water drew other industries to that locality. Furthermore the great school of chemistry set up here, devised, formulated and patented other chemical inventions which led directly or indirectly to entirely new products.

Following the success of the dye plant about 1922, came the first of newcomers, lead ethyl. Turning from dye and munition bases these men perfected the process for making a new and valuable adjunct to the gasoline field, discovered by General Motors. In 1922, the Du Pont chemists, experimenting with lead ethyl produced a gallon. Fifteen years later the production of Deep Water in lead ethyl is around fifteen million pounds a month. The perfection of this permits the oil maker to turn out a standard gasoline. In other words, a product that will give a standard performance.

The next Du Pont innovation from the Salem county workshop was rubber accelerators. An accelerator is a chemical agent used in rubber manufacture to cause the process of vulcanization to be completed very quickly. Since the heat of vulcanization weakens the finished product, the use of an accelerator means a much stronger finished product. Thus, in 1920, one bought for about $45 an auto tire which the manufacturer boasted would last for 3,000 to 5,000 miles. Today, a tire costing $10 will run from 20,000 to 30,000 miles. This was an important factor in removing one of the great inconveniences of motoring. It reduced the expense to the point where the poor man could afford a car; and it opened the way for high speed commercial transportation by buses and trucks at prices below railway freight. Thus Salem county's chemists made a great contribution toward "putting the nation on wheels."

Branching off in the rubber field, Deep Water chemists of Du Pont invented neoprene, a rubber-like compound and partial substitute for it. Rubber, as is known, is an expensive commodity. It can be made more so by the actions of the various foreign governments which control its supply. Neoprene has aided the rubber industry of the United States in that it has held down the price of rubber by its appearance on the market. In certain respects it is superior to natural rubber and for specialized uses it finds a market at a higher price. Neoprene is an exclusive product of Du Pont and is made nowhere else.

From the laboratories at Deep Water also comes constructive competition with another nation and another natural product, camphor. In the past five years the chemists of Du Pont have by their inventions, broken the camphor monopoly of Japan. This commodity, like neoprene, is an exclusive Du Pont and Salem county product.

It is common knowledge that since 1930, theatres, Pullman and railroad cars, office buildings and so forth have been air conditioned against the heat of summer. It is also known that most of the gases first used in such refrigeration were dangerous. To illustrate, if a railroad train should have been derailed, none of the passengers would have been able to escape since the poisonous gases such as ammonia would have quickly asphyxiated them. Now, due to the kinetic refrigerants such a catastrophe will not result. The chemists have perfected harmless refrigerants for use in air-conditioning. Thus, danger has been removed along with discomfort. This product is known as "Freon," and also is made exclusively at Deep Water. Added to the safety feature, it has made air-conditioning practicable on a large scale.

The list is still long and not yet completed. Carbon ice or dry ice is made here at Deep Water also. It is a by-product and was come by automatically in the manufacture of other products.

Then, soapless soap, a synthetic product widely used in the textile industry. Despite the name which sounds contradictory to most of us, who always thought soap was soap and let it go at that, it has all the useful properties of that valuable material, without some of its deleterious characteristics. The Du Pont soapless soap has very diversified commercial uses.

The alcohol plant existing at Deep Water, dates from shortly after the war when the Du Pont Company was forced to stop buying alcohol for their multifarious needs and set up their own plant.

Most recently the chemical school at Deep Water has produced, and again as a natural result of other studies, a drug used in killing the dreaded germ of streptococci infection. This by-product, not intended at the time for such a purpose, is called sulphanilamid. This is not manufactured at Deep Water, it is simply a by-product used in pharmaceutical pursuits.

It is interesting to know that all these various inventions used for preserving the span of man's life as well as in peaceful pursuits of commercial enterprise emanate from two research laboratories at the Deep Water plant. These two are the Jackson and Technical Laboratories. In differentation, the Jackson is the research or formulative workshop while the Technical is concerned mainly with adapting the discoveries of the Jackson laboratory research in the sales field. The name of the Technical laboratory speaks for itself. The name of the Jackson laboratory is derived from a chemist, Oscar R. Jackson, whose bravery and tenacity won him a famous name and the undying gratitude of his employers. Back in the last century, a terrific explosion wrecked the plant of the Du Pont Company at Repauno in the neighboring county of Gloucester. One of the Du Pont family was killed by the blast as well as other high ranking officials. In fact, the entire set of officials were wiped out. A private in the ranks, Dr. Jackson, calmly and on his own initiative set about to reorganize the stricken plant and to carry on with no orders from Wilmington. He thus managed Repauno just as if nothing had happened.

Therefore the name of the great chemical power house is in the best traditions of the company, honoring a man who "carried on".

The brain power at Deep Water consists of about 130 chemists, who with their various helpers and assistants make up a total of 400. The entire personnel of the Dye and Powder works is in the neighborhood of 5500 men.

From Dr. Reese's foresight twenty years ago, has come the present plant at Deep Water, a typical American industrial pioneer which has taken nothing for granted and has never admitted defeat. No individual names come out of Jackson Lab. The splendid team work of the Du Pont chemists, bound in a common enterprise, have eradicated individual hopes for glory. This teamwork over a period of two decades has enabled large sections of American industry to profit by their determination, back in Deep Water, that no longer should this nation be dependent on imported materials. The dye situation was only the beginning but it taught American chemists that we could, with study and research depend upon our own efforts. This, in a broad general sense is the great Contribution of Deep Water to American history.

If the effects of the Du Pont industries in the United States as a whole have been noteworthy, in Salem county they have been tremendous. The great bi-weekly payroll is the basis of a sound and lasting prosperity. With the war boom past and permanent peace-time industries established, the influx of transients and trouble makers has disappeared and in their place has come a solid and growing population of worthwhile people. With this injection of new blood and with the automobile and the radio Salem county's rural isolation and provincialism has been broken. Residents of all parts of the county, as well as of neighboring counties, travel quickly over improved roads to their daily work at Deep Water. There they are thrown into contact with men and women from Delaware and Pennsylvania; and into contact with the very vortex of the spirit of industrial pioneering and progress.

In addition to the private corporations situated on the east bank of the Delaware is the large Ordnance depot of the United States government outside of Pedricktown in Oldmans township.

The Atlantic City Electric Company, together with affiliated companies, completed in 1929 a huge generating plant on the south side of the canal in Lower Penns Neck township. It stands on the site where the Swedes settled in 1638 and not far from their original New Jersey house of worship, St. Georges in Churchtown.

This huge electric station sends forth current over the entire southern and western part of the state and it is coupled with the power systems of Delaware, Maryland and Pennsylvania. Its carrier antenna stretch on iron poles across Salem county from west to east terminating in Atlantic City.

The Salem Glass Works, the oldest industrial plant in the county is in a most flourishing condition and recently has joined forces with the Anchor Cap and Closure Corporation. Its plant is likewise a huge one and during the late depression this factory was a large factor in carrying Salem reasonably well throughout the economic hardships of the years between 1929 and 1933. The Gayner Glass Works in Salem is likewise flourishing. It is one of the nation's principal manufacturers of large ware and hand-made specialties.

There are two floor covering concerns in the city. One is a branch of the Congoleum Company which occupies the site of the original American Oil Cloth Company, first founded by Salem men; the other is the Mannington Mills, also a Salem Company. About 1911 the H. J. Heinz Company of Pittsburg, established a branch plant here which manufactures from Salem county tomatoes many thousand bottles of catsup annually. It is interesting to remember that less than a hundred years before the Heinz plant came to Salem tomatoes were considered poisonous. Col. Robert Gibbon Johnson, the sponsor of the tomato, had hard work in convincing the natives that it was an edible vegetable.

Likewise, the utilities have increased in this county. The number of customers of the Atlantic City Electric Company

PROFESSIONAL LEADERS 371

which serves electric current to all Salem county, the Bell Telephone Company and the various gas companies have all during the last forty years trebled and quadrupled their services. Back in the 1850's the first of the so-called utilities, the telegraph made its appearance in Salem. It has survived all these years in the Western Union Telegraph Company which still maintains an office on Market street in Salem.

In the professional fields, the number of lawyers has increased many times since John Jones, an Englishman, hung out his sign in 1732. Undoubtedly, his old law office erected in 1735 and still standing behind the Salem National Bank is one of the oldest in the United States.

The members of the bar of this county are all men of high standing and character. In a quiet way they have been an honor to their profession. In 1846 to 1850, Thomas Sinnickson of Salem was a judge of the Court of Errors and Appeals. The late Martin P. Gray was a vice-chancellor of the Equity Court from 1896 to 1906. J. Warren Davis, previously referred to, is at present a justice of the United States Circuit Court of Appeals. W. Orvyl Schalick of Salem is an assistant United States District Attorney for New Jersey. The late Anthony Q. Keasbey, originally of Salem, but in later life a resident of Newark, held the position of United States District Attorney from 1861 to 1886.

The township of Pittsgrove claims the honor of being the birth place of two justices of the State Supreme Court. Thomas W. Trenchard, who presided over the case of State versus Hauptman at Flemington in 1935, was born at Centreton, December 13, 1863. Justice Joseph Perskie was born at Alliance in the same township on July 20, 1885. Mr. Perskie is the son of Russian immigrants who settled at Alliance in one of the first Jewish colonization plans in the early eighties.

The medical profession has also increased. For a great many years there were never more than six or seven doctors in the entire county, now there are over thirty. In 1919 at the close of the World War, through the efforts of the physicians and interested laymen of Salem, a movement was started which resulted in the formation of the Salem County Memorial Hospital which was dedicated, aptly enough, to the soldiers and sailors of the World War. It is housed in Ford's Hotel on Market street in Salem and with its modern equipment and efficient staff does a great deal of humane and good work in the community.

It was in the 1840's that the first of the Salem dentists, Dr. Samuel C. Harbert, established himself in Salem as a doctor of dental surgery. Prior to that, tooth pulling had been done by the blacksmith, the cabinet maker or whosoever was handy. Dr. Harbert was not only the pioneer dentist in this section but he was an authority as well, having written a text book on dentistry. This profession also has increased its membership in Salem county.

The great impetus given to education by the World War must not go passed unnoticed. Before the World War, the number of students who went forth from Salem High School to colleges were few and far between. Since that time the number has been legion. The University of Pennsylvania, Dickinson, Temple, Bucknell, Swarthmore, Wilson, Rutgers and Delaware have all claimed a given portion of Salem's youth bent on higher education. Recently our students have gone south to colleges such as the University of North Carolina, Duke, and the University of Alabama. The encouraging feature is that more go every year. In addition a large number of high school graduates enter the nearby business colleges and the several Normal schools of the State. In 1900 the Salem Academy, relic of the century before, was still functioning. In 1905, the present Grammar School was built as a high school. In eight years it was outgrown and in 1913 the Salem Board of Education built the new high school in the Ingham Orchard on New Market street. This building has been enlarged in the past five years. Woodstown which used the old Bacon Academy up to twenty years ago, has erected a large high school building with new additions. In 1936, the magnificent and imposing Regional High School in Penns Grove, built with Public Works Administration funds, was opened for scholastic use. In the rural districts the little red school houses, except in one or two townships like Mannington and Elsinboro, have disappeared and in their place central township grade schools have been erected. To these modern structures the student comes by auto bus instead of on foot. The State Department of Education has provided helping teachers for the various grade schools and maintain a county superintendent for their oversight. In the past three decades art, manual training, music, physical training for boys and girls, have been introduced to all the high schools of the county.

* * * *

In 1915 a high school boy in Salem wondered upon reading the newspaper accounts of impending war, whether or not his home would be shelled by the Germans when they came up the Delaware river to attack Fort Delaware and Fort Mott. This speculation followed the war scares precipatated by the sinking of the **Lusitania.**

WORLD WAR

He stood out on Broadway on the early morning of July 27, 1917, and watched the home town boys of Company F, 3rd Regiment, National Guard of New Jersey form in line preparatory to their entrainment for Sea Girt, New Jersey. The war had come.

Another two years and most of the lads returned. Some did not. One of them, Harry P. Morrison, who was killed in France is remembered by the American Legion Post which bears his name. A Salem street is also marked in his memory.

The 147 officers and men which formed Company F were only the first offerings of this county to the World War. The records show that 63 more men volunteered and 1205 were drafted. 183 of the drafted men were colored. In addition, Salem county furnished ten trained nurses, two Y. M. C. A. workers and two chaplains.

The casualty list was fortunately much lighter than in the War between the States. Even at that, thirty besides Harry Morrison paid the supreme sacrifice in the war for democracy, twenty-four died of disease and thirty-one were wounded. Eight Salem men were decorated for valor and one of them, John Crowe of Salem, is the proud wearer of the croix de guerre and the American distinguished service cross.

Company F, after being at Sea Girt, was returned to Salem for a brief holiday and fete in 1917. After this they were sent to Camp McClellan at Anniston, Alabama where following the regimentation plan of this war, their state units were broken up and the men assigned to different army divisions. Some few of the men were returned home as skilled workmen, to labor in the various industrial plants. The majority of the Salem troops were finally assigned to units in the 29th or Blue and Gray Division.

As such they were sent across the seas in 1918 and formed a part of the offensive in the Argonne forest. It was during the bitter fighting in this sector, October 11th and 12th, 1918 that the heaviest casualties were suffered.

As a matter of bibliography the very best material on the participation of Company F is to be found in the story of Edward Crowe entitled "The Reminiscence of Company F." This accurate and painstaking work which depicts to the fullest extent, the bravery and heroism of the men from Salem is to be found in the files of the Salem Sunbeam from July 22 to October 28, 1931.

Besides Company F other men and women from this county likewise served their nation with honor and distinction both on foreign battlefields and at home. As in the war between the

States, a unit of home guards was organized to protect this territory.

Parades, orations, liberty bond drives, sock knitting, sweater knitting, letter writing, all these things and more besides were the occupation of the citizens who were left at home. On the financial side alone, the figures for this county's contribution are available and impressive. The total, contributed by the citizens of Salem county was $6,965,779.39. By way of contrast, it was $6,000.00 in the War of 1812.

* * * *

The lyric poet of Salem, Jacob M. Lippincott died before the turn of the century. In one of his poems he had written a master line, "The still back water of our country life." It was the still back water which had engrossed the historian for 250 years.

But the years since the turn of the century have removed this category. With science dominant, with epic inventions like the automobile, the telephone, the radio, power and light plants, and the marvels of chemistry, Salem has emerged from the rusticity of a rural countryside into the full light of a new industrial day.

THE END

INDEX

Abbott, Abdon: 139, 172
Abbott, Benjamin: 115-121, 192, 193, 226.
Abbott, Benjamin: 323.
Abbott, George: 302.
Abbott, Samuel: 160, 292.
Abbott, Thomas: 68.
Abbott, William: 160.
Abbotsford: 293.
Abercrombie, Lt. Col.: 143-145.
Acton, Benjamin: 252, 262, 265, 292, 318.
Acton, Clement: 180, 189, 227.
Acton, Edward A.: 237, 276, 280.
Acton, John W.: 317.
Acton, Richard M.: 292, 295-298, 301.
Acton Road: 293.
Acton Station: 340.
Adams, Eli: 240.
Adams, Elizabeth: 25, 50.
Adams, Fenwick: 25.
Adams, John: 25.
Adams, Mary: 25.
Adams, Philip: 172.
Aldine: 265.
Allen, Capt. J.: 132.
Allen, Collins B.: 361, 335.
Allen, Samuel P.: 319.
Allen, Samuel A.: ("My Own Home and Fireside") 244, 245, 248-250.
Alloway: 55, 68, 80, 92, 183, 184, 196, 204, 209, 213, 220-222, 229, 230, 234, 235, 242, 265, 271, 275, 276, 292, 293, 296, 303, 309, 320, 324, 340.
Alloway, Ghost of: 174-176.
Alloway, Indian: 2, 26, 55.
Alloway, Sedition Meeting at: 275, 276.
Alloway, Ship building at: 229.
Alloway Creek: 53, 55, 67, 93, 103, 124, 128, 153, 156, 208, 229-231, 344.
Alliance: 324, 371.
Alva Glass Works: 355.
American Eagle: 308
American Oil Cloth Co.: 301, 370.
Amwellbury: 54, 55.
Anderson, Ezra: 271-276.
Andross, Sir Edmund: 33-39, 101.
Angelos, Charles: 57.
Angelos' Landing: 54.
Andrews, Thomas: 207.
Anthony, Susan B.: 223.
Applegate, Samuel: 184.
Asbury, Bishop Francis: 192
Ashton, Harry: 346.
Assamhocking: 2, 21.
Atkinson, Samuel: 203.
Atlantic City Electric Co.: 370.
Atwood, Anthony: 192.
Austin, David: 178.
Austin, Cornelius: 205.
Axford, Eliza: 91.
Ayres, John F.: 360.
Ayers, Job: 290.

Back Marsh: 128.
Bacon Academy: 372.
Bacon's Adventure: 54.
Bacon, Andrew: 151, 152, 173, 227.
Bacon, Isaac: 346.
Bacon, Jeremiah: 57.
Bacon, John: 61.
Bacon, Mary: 57.
Bacon: 67.
Bailey Town: 262.
Baker's Tavern: 223.
Ballinger, Enoch: 178.
Ballinger, Jonathan: 172.
Ballinger, Richard C.: 254, 270.
Ballinger's Store: 353.
Ballinger, Walter P.: 341.
Baptist: 68-70, 103, 113, 114, 193, 202, 204, 206, 221, 231, 294, 303, 323, 339, 340, 354.
Baptist, Second Church: 260, 262.
Baptist, Seventh Day: 69, 70, 265.
Barber, Charles: 314.
Barber: 67.
Barber, Henry: 322, 334.
Barber, Wilmer: 314.
Barnum, Phineas T.: 301.
Barrett: 69.
Barry, Captain John: 143.
Bartlett, Robert M.: 346.
Barton, George W.: 322.
Baseball: 290, 333, 342, 353.
Basketball: 341.
Basse, Mr.: 57.
Bassett: 68.
Bassett, Elisha: 293.
Bassett, Joseph: 291, 292.
Bassett, Samuel: 89.
Bassett, William, Jr.: 255.
Bassett's Tavern: 196.
Baton, Michael (Barrowne): 39.
Battle, Delaware River: 194.
Bear Point: 128.
Beatty, Rev. Charles: 111.
Beatty, Elizabeth: 133.
Bechtell, John H.: 295, 303.
Beckett, Dr. A. T.: 323.
Beckett, Wm.: 271.
Beecher, Henry Ward: 325.
Beery, Jonathan: 57, 61.
Beasley's Neck: 62, 157, 159, 339.
Beesley, W. G.: 199, 221.
Beesley, Walker: 162.
Belden, John C.: 299.
Bell, C. N.: 308.
Bell, Captain: 229, 230.
Bell, Joseph: 350.
Bellman: 338.
Ben, negro boy: 77, 78.
Bennett, Eugene F.: 254.
Bennett, Mason M.: 349.
Bergen, C. A.: 337, 349.

INDEX

Beriton Fields: 54.
Berkeley, Lord John: 17-19, 28, 33, 44, 46.
Berkeley River: 21.
Berry's Chapel: 333.
Berry, H. C.: 353.
Bijou Dream: 353.
Bilderback, Peter: 60, 181, 189.
Bilderback, Smith: 314.
Billingsport: 141, 144, 146, 181.
Binfield: 21.
Blackburn, James: 153.
Blackwood, Kerrenhappuch: 69.
Black, C. C.: 362.
Black, Rachel: 114.
Black, William: 185.
Blaine, James G.: 317.
Blessings Iron Foundry: 340, 348.
Blessing Town: 54.
Blohm, Henry: 351.
Blue, Priscilla: 114.
Boogar, James: 342.
Boon, Robert: 220, 240-242.
Borton, Benj.: 331.
Bowen: 68-69.
Bowen, C.: 343.
Bowen, Clinton: 316.
Bowen, Jonathan: 169.
Bowen, Samuel: 130.
Bowen, Thomas: 190.
Bradfield: 54.
Bradford, William: 57, 73.
Bradin, John C.: 303.
Braithwaite Hall: 54.
Bradstreet Ship Yard: 230.
Bradway: 67-68, 188.
Bradway, Edward: 39.
Bradway House: 64.
Bradway Station: 324.
Bradway, Thomas D.: 291.
Brainard, John: 111.
Brainard, David: 111.
Brewster, Benj.: 328.
Brick: 67.
Brick, John: 77.
Brick, Samuel: 130.
Bridgeman, Capt.: 26.
Bridge Street: 27.
Bright, Charles: 340.
Brooks: 68.
Brooks, Elijah: 199, 205-210, 215-221.
Brooks, Rev. Phillips: 294.
Brooks, Timothy: 69.
Brown, David P. (David of York): 237-239.
Brown, George W.: 362.
Brown, James: 291-292.
Brown, John M.: 244.
Brown, Jonathan: 296.
Bruna, John P.: 302, 304.
Brundage's Tavern: 203.
Bryan, William Jennings: 361.
Bryant, Jacob: 240.
Buck, Henry: 245.
Buckshutem: 113.
Budd, John: 130.
Burden Hill: 248, 359.
Burdett, Edward: 40.
Burdett, Mary: 40.
Burdett, Robert: 326, 328.
Burdett, William: 84.

Burke, John: 85.
Burleigh, J. J.: 317.
Burrows, Mrs.: 171.
Burt, Rev. John: 211-212.
Burton, H. S.: 287.
Bush, George: 221, 244.
Butcher & Harris: 354.
Butcher, James: 336, 349, 369.
Butler, G. L.: 346.
Button, William: 68.
Buzby: 68.
Byllynge, Edward: 18-24.
Bywater, Gervas: 25.

Cadle, Rev. R. F.: 199.
Caesar, slave: 134-137.
Cain, Noah: 245.
Cain, Sarah: 245.
Cain, William: 244-248.
California Gold Rush: 253-256.
Campbell: 189.
Canady, James: 128.
Cannon, Father: 285.
Canton: 118, 193, 209, 265, 331.
Cantwell, Capt. Edmund: 34, 35.
Cape May (Cape Island): 291, 304.
Carey, John: 138.
Carll, Ephraim: 252, 258.
Carlls: 189.
Carney, Thomas: 177.
Carney, William: 336, 343.
Carpenter: 191.
Carpenter, Powell: 163.
Carpenter, William: 320.
Carrary, Roger: 58.
Carter: 203.
Carteret, Sir. George: 17.
Casper, Thomas J.: 226.
Casper, Tobias: 245.
Casper, William A.: 318, 335.
Casperson: 106.
Catholic Church: 108-110, 231-233, 25, 265, 303, 332, 364.
Cato, Sutey: 210.
Cattell, Alexander G.: 193, 251, 299, 300.
Cattell, Dr. W. C.: 338.
Cattell, Nancy: 157.
Cattell, Thomas Ware: 253, 300.
Cattells: 188.
Centreton, (Dayton's Bridge, Centerville): 201, 331.
Challis: 188.
Chambless: 89.
Chamberlin, George Agnew: 358.
Chammeys, Edward: 25.
Chammeys, John: 25.
Chammeys, May: 25.
Charles I: 6.
Charles II: 5.
Checkenshaw: 27.
Cheesemans: 113.
Chew and Bilderback: 332.
Chew, Charles: 258.
Chew, Sinnickson: 282, 308.
Church of England (St. Johns): 101-108.
Cincinnati, Ohio: 189, 191.
Clark, John: 59.
Clawson, Isiah D.: 269.
Claysville: 53, 79, 213, 292, 324.
Clement: 191.

INDEX

Clement, D. W. C.: 292, **293**.
Clement, Samuel: 221.
Clows, William: 57.
Coggeshall: 9.
Cohansey: 68-70.
Cohansey Creek: 2.
Cohen, William: 324.
Collier, Captain John: 35.
Coles: 188.
Coles, Bartholomew: 245.
Coles, Charles D.: 337.
Coles, Quinton: 336.
Coles, Richman: 350.
Colleges: 372.
Collins, James: 310.
Collin, Rev. Nicholas: 107, 108.
Colson, David: 177.
Colyer, Samuel: 313.
Committee of Observation, list of: 133.
Company F, 3rd Reg. N. G. N. J.: 372, 373.
Cohanzick: 27-29.
Conahockink: 2.
Congleton: 112.
Congoleum Company: 301, 302, 310, 355.
Conover, John: 258.
Connarroe, George W.: 220.
Coombs, Henry: 335, 336, 351.
Coombs: 111.
Cook, Joseph: 205.
Coopers Creek: 62.
Coopers Ferry: 125, 128.
Cooper, Furman: 198.
Cooper, Joseph: 207, 295.
Copner, Samuel: 270, 339.
Copner: 113.
Cornbury, Lord: 71.
Cornwallis, Lord: 108.
Cotting, Elias: 123.
Counsellor, Daniel: 314.
Court, Long: 171-172.
Coutch, John: 183.
Covert, Elizabeth (1st Mrs. John Fenwick): 40.
Covered Bridge: 354.
Covert, Sir Walter: 40.
Cowman, John: 172.
Cox, Edward: 258.
Cox, Daniel, 73-75.
Crawkerne, Wood: 54.
Craven, D. Stewart: 341, 363.
Craven, Richard: 30, 215, 217.
Cravens Ferry: 183, 200, 205, 206, 209, 211.
Cripps, Whitten: 166, 176, 177.
Crisp, Mr.: 288.
Crispin, H.: 313.
Crispin, Joseph: 351, 360.
Croes, Bishop: 200.
Crook, Eliza: 90.
Crowe, Edward: 373.
Crowe, John: 373.
Culin, Peter: 178.
Cumberland, Duke of: 122.
Cunard, Erwin S.: 363.
Currie, B. C.: 345.

Dailey, Dennis: 161, 163.
Dallas: 68.
Dancer, Luke: 245.
Daniels: 67.

Daniels, Elmer: 258.
Daniels, Joel: 172.
Dare, Bennomi: 130.
Dare, Smith: 245.
Daretown: 200, 265, 293, 323, 373.
Darkin: 61.
Darkin, Richard: 11.
Davidson, H. P.: 294.
Davis: 67, 191.
Davis, Benjamin: 82.
Davis, German: 172.
Davis, John Q.: 302.
Davis, John Warren: 360-362, 371.
Dayton, Aaron Ogden: 206.
Deacon, George: 49, 58.
Dean, James: 172.
Deepwater: 366-370.
DeHaes: 35.
Delaware City, Del.: 221.
Delaware River, Battle of: 194.
Denn: 67.
Denn, Charles W.: 339.
Denn, Job: 353.
Denn, John: 255.
Dennis: 67.
Denn's Canal Meadow Co.: 196.
De Vries: 13.
Diamond, William J.: 224.
Dick, Dr. Samuel: 147, 166, 176-178.
Dick Mrs.: 174.
Dickeson, Auxencico Mari Pena Venezuela Hildreth: 296.
Dickinson, Anna: 301.
Dickinson, I. V.: 296.
Dickinson, John: 182, 199, 203.
Dickison, William: 171.
Dilks, Abigail: 308.
Dilmore, Sinnickson: 198.
Diver, William: 350.
Dix, Dorothea: 233, 234.
Dixon, George P.: 362.
Doane, Rev. G. W.: 226.
Dolbow, Harry: 359.
Dolbow, Marguerite: **359**.
Doolittle, Ezekiel H. B.: 263.
Dorrell, Daniel P.: 319.
Dreamland: 353.
Driscoll, Norman: 359.
Dubois, David: 206.
Dubois, Jed: 179, 181.
Dubois, Jerry: 179.
Ducloss, Francis: (Decoe): 151, 152.
Dunham, John W.: 320.
Dunlap, Captain: 157, 158.
Dunlap, Elizabeth: 84.
Dunlap, James: 84.
Dunn: 67.
Dunn, Charles W.: 289.
Dunn, Nehemiah: 237, 299.
Dunkirk, New York: 188.
DuPont Company: 341, 345, 356, 364-370.
Dwyer's Store: 353.

Eagle Island: 128.
Eakin, Alfonso: 209, 244.
Eakin, Rev. Samuel: 112.
East Fenwick: 55.
East Jersey: 71.
East View Cemetery: 331.
Eaton, Michael: 25.

INDEX

Edminson, Elisha: 103.
Edwards, Edward I.: 361.
Edwards, Jacob: 351.
Eldridges Hill: 196, 264.
Eldridge, John: 23, 29-32.
Elkinton: 68.
Elkinton Mill: 355.
Ellet, Alfred W.: 282.
Ellet, Henry: 187, 253, 282.
Elliott, William: 31.
Ellis, Colonel: 143.
Ellis, Wiliam: 67.
Elmer, Daniel: 244, 246.
Elmer, Ebenezer: 132.
Elmer, Jonathan: 169.
Elmer, L. Q. C.: 258, 259.
Elmer Shoe Co.: 331.
Elmer Times: 308.
Elmer, Timothy: 132.
Elmer, borough of: 292-293.
Elsinboro: 2, 7-9, 11, 13, 15, 26, 39, 55, 87, 139, 140, 160, 165, 202, 231, 257, 258, 262, 296.
Elsinboro Point: 12, 278, 352.
Elwell: 113.
Elwell, Henry H.: 217-219.
Elwell, Israel: 172.
Elwell, John: 129, 321, 322, 336.
Elwell, Mary: 212.
Elwell, Susanna: 114.
English, David: 212, 215.
English, Isaiah: 200.
English, Robert: 290.
Erickson, John 39.
Evans, Rev. David: 111.
Ewing: 70.
Ewing, James: 132.
Ewing, Dr. Thomas: 132, 169.

Fairfield: 56, 70.
Farley, Captain: 208.
Farney, George: 141.
Featherer, Norman P.: 363-364.
Fenwick, Anna: 20.
Fenwick Canning Works: 307.
Fenwick Creek: 315, 324.
Fenwick East: 55.
Fenwick, Elizabeth (Burdett): 40-42.
Fenwick's Ivy: 46.
Fenwick, John: buys West Jersey: 18, Career of, 18-19; disputes with Penn, 19-21; plea of, 22-23; gives mortgage 23-24; first order of, 28-29; oath of office, 34; Sent to New York, 35-37; returns to Salem, 37; second trial in New York, 37-38; letters from wife, 41-43; remonstrance of, 43-46; Conveys to Penn, 47; writes will, 50; death of, 51; marker to, 51.
Fenwick, Priscilla: 25.
Fenwick Rifles: 274.
Fenwick Theatre: 353.
Ferrell, Thomas: 335, 336.
Ferren, Sheppard: 340.
Ferris: 13.
Field, Richard Stockton: 206, 213, 219, 303.
Finley, James: 163.
Finley, William: 163.
Finns Point: 278, 285, 289, 309, 341, 342.
Finnstown Point: 52.

First Oak: 354.
Firth, John: 178, 318.
Fishers Hotel: 213.
Fisher, James: 246.
Fisher, Maria: 246.
Fithian: 70.
Fithian, Charles: 358.
Fithian, Joel: 132, 169.
Fithian, Rev. Phillip Vickers: 132, 133.
Fithian, Sara: 91.
Fitzhugh Co.: 331.
Flannagan, Thomas: 269.
Fleming, J.: 314, 315.
Flemington: 371.
Flitcraft, Allen: 264.
Fogg: 67, 189.
Fogg, Charles: 162.
Fogg & Hires: 331.
Fogg, John M.: 282.
Fogg, Wm.: 245.
Football: 345, 353.
Foray of Fort Delaware: 207, 208.
Force, L. C.: 303.
Forcus Creek: 26.
Ford, Charles: 340.
Ford's Hotel: 371.
Fort Casimer: 13.
Fort Christiana: 13.
Fort Delaware: 204, 207, 220, 274, 275, 278, 285-287, 289, 341, 345, 346, 372.
Fort DuPont: 287.
Fort Elfsborg: 11-14, 355.
Fort Mott: 287, 306, 344-346, 348, 372.
Fort Nassau: 8, 10, 11.
Foster, Preston: 308.
Foster, Samuel P.: 308.
Fourteenth Pennsylvania Regiment: 346-348.
Fox, David: 355.
Fox, George: 48.
Freas, Henry: 214, 219, 222, 244.
Freeman's Banner: 220, 235.
Freeman, Henry: 250.
Freeman, Oliver: 199.
Freeman, Rev.: 200.
French, Gen. Samuel: 243, 276, 277.
French's Hotel: 220.
Friends of Peace, in War of 1812: 181.
Friends, Society of: 19, 48, 66-68, 222, 223, 264, 364.
Friesburg: 110, 265.
Frisby, Henry: 352.
Fries, Daniel J.: 346.
Furber, W. D.: 346.

Gallachrone, John: 85, 86.
Gallows Hill: 53, 79.
Galveston, Texas: 191.
Gandy, Daniel: 163.
Gardiner, Lieut.: 207, 208.
Gardner, J. H.: 323.
Garrison, Amos: 243.
Garrison, Daniel: 171, 206, 211.
Garrison, Isaac: 178.
Garrison, Samuel: 296-298.
Garwood's Cigar Store: 354.
Garwood, John T.: 332, 334.
Gayner, Edward J.: 342.
Gayner Glass Works: 293, 370.
Gayner, John: 301.
Geere, Eleanor: 25.

INDEX

Geere, Ruth: 25.
Geere, Zachariah: 25.
Gibbon, A. K.: 188.
Gibbon, Edward K.: 188.
Gibbon, Grant: 131, 132, 311, 312.
Gibbon, Leonard: 242.
Gibbon, Dr. Quinton: 245.
Giordano, Peter: 357.
Githens, Dr. Samuel: 220.
Glaspey, Charles: 343.
Glassboro: 291.
Glass Works (See Wistarburg, Salem, Gayner, Quinton, Alva).
Gloucester County: 54, 141, 344.
Godbolt, Francis: 74.
Godfrey, Dr. C. E.: 56.
Goodwin, Benjamin: 190.
Goodwin, Mr.: 226.
Goodwin, Susanna: 91.
Gosling, Boston: 286.
Gosling, Samuel: 157, 158, 160.
Gouldtown: 50, 297.
Graham, Dr.: 129.
Grant, Alexander: 77, 330.
Grant, Anna: 91.
Gravelly Hill: 54.
Gray, Martin P.: 371.
Greely, Horace: 264, 304, 319.
Green, Rev. Ashbel: 200.
Green's Hotel: 193.
Green, Henry: 358, 359.
Greenwich: 27, 52, 70, 130, 132.
Gregory, Joseph: 77.
Greismeyer, Simon: 93.
Grey, Mary: 91.
Grier, Richard: 292, 295.
Griffith, Captain: 24.
Griffith, Elijah: 240.
Griffith, William: 77.
Griner, Elias: 346.
Griscom: 191.
Griscom, John: 191, 210.
Griscom, Mary: 191.
Grundel Hill: 54.
Guilford Manor: 64.
Guy, Richard: 30, 31.
Gwin, William: 129.
Gwynne, Robt. Jr.: 338, 350.
Gwynne, Robt. Sr.: 259, 271, 297, 299, 308, 320, 327, 348.

Habermayer, Samuel: 262.
Hackett, Isaiah: 253.
Hackett, Joseph: 3.
Hackett's Tavern: 201.
Hager: 77.
Haines Neck: 195, 265, 332.
Hales, Nathan: 348.
Hall, Dunn & Hunt: 301.
Hall, Edward: 166, 169.
Hall, Joseph: 188.
Hall, John: 180, 216.
Hall Margaret: 144.
Hall, Mary: 194.
Hall, Morris: 215.
Hall's Mills: 54.
Hall, William: 61, 71-76.
Halltown: 257.
Hampton, William: 62.
Hancock: 67.
Hancock, Albert Elmer: 357.

Hancock's Bridge: 148, 156, 157, 264, 265, 317, 340, 344.
Hancock's Bridge, meeting at: 65, 164.
Hancock, Cornelia: 283.
Hancock House: 156-160, 163.
Hancock's Hurst: 54.
Hancock, Joseph: 215, 221, 300.
Hancock, Morris: 179, 199.
Hancock, Richard: 32, 89.
Hancock, William: 67, 159, 162.
Hanks: 162.
Hannah, James M.: 220, 291.
Hannah, Dr. Charles: 195.
Harbert, Dr. Samuel C.: 292, 371.
Harmer: 67.
Harmersville: 67, 161.
Hartshorne, Richard: 30, 31.
Harris: 188, 191.
Harris, Abba: 348.
Harris, Amos: 258.
Harris, Eleazer: 245.
Harris, Ephraim: 360.
Harris, Isaac: 171.
Harris, John: 269.
Harris, Nicholas: 260.
Harrison, Josiah: 181, 250, 261, 293.
Harrisonville (Pigs Eye): 346.
Hatton, John: 138, 140, 166-168.
Haynes, Edward: 195.
Hazleton, John W.: 318, 319.
Hedge, Anna: 25.
Hedge, Samuel: 25, 59.
Hedgefield: 54, 55, 338.
Heinz Company: 370.
Heison, Felicia: 257-259.
Hell Neck: 118.
Helm's Cove (Penns Grove): 209.
Henaminky, Indian: 26.
Henderson, Jacob: 76.
Hendrickson, Lawes: 60.
Henry, Minor: 253.
Heritage, Joseph: 222.
Hewitt, John: 77.
Hewitt, Smith: 319.
Hopewell: 56.
Horner, Jacob: 239.
Hill, Thomas: 1.
Hillman, Rev. Geo. C.: 346.
Hilton, Joseph: 172.
Hires, Charles: 302.
Hires, George: 335-339.
Hires, John: 312, 314, 320.
Hitchner, Jacob: 266, 317.
Hitchner, James E.: 363.
Hitchner, Johnson: 290.
Hitchner's Tavern: 183, 184.
Hite, Irvin: 359.
Hoelzel, Lewis: 343.
Hoffman, Schuyler: 342.
Hogate, Lin: 346.
Holbrook, Rev. John: 101-105.
Hollinshed, clockmaker: 199, 304.
Hollyborne: 54.
Holme, Abigail: 169.
Holme, Col. Benj.: 138, 140-144, 150-154, 158, 165-169, 291.
Holme, John: 69, 169-171, 213.
Holmes, Obadiah: 66-68.
Holtz, Taylor and Clark: 293, 301.
Home Guards: 274.
Home Island: 128.

INDEX

Hopewell: 56.
Hopkins, Rev. M. M.: 204.
Hopkinson, Francis: 123.
Hopman, Andrew: 77.
Horner, Arthur: 346.
Horner, Jacob: 239.
Horwood, Nathaniel: 105.
Hospital, Salem County Memorial: 371.
Howard, William: 245.
Howell, Dr. Ebenezer: 166, 169.
Howell, Lewis: 132.
Howell, Richard: 132.
Howe, Henry: 242.
Huddy, Hugh: 73.
Huddy, Joshua: 129.
Huffman, William: 141.
Hufty, Jacob: 166, 179, 180.
Hull, Caroline T.: 244-248.
Humphreys, James: 286.
Humphreys, John: 243.
Hunloke: 57.
Hunt, James: 132.
Hunt, John: 243.
Hunt, Mrs.: 235.
Hunter, Rev. Andrew: 132.
Hunter, Richard: 196.
Hunter, Robert: 72-75.
Hurley, David: 214, 217, 219.
Hutchins, Harry B.: 346.
Hutchins, Sarah: 25.
Hutchins, Stephin: 194.
Hyde, Edward (Lord Cornbury): 71.

Indians, Tribes of: 36.
Ingham, Jonathan: 291, 328.
Ingham Orchard: 347, 353, 372.
Ingham, Samuel D.: 214.
Iredell, Samuel: 351.
Irving, Washington: 12.
Izard, Dr. John: 320.

Jackson, Haliday: 227.
Jackson, Dr. Oscar R.: 369.
Jackson, W. B.: 346.
Jacquette: 65.
Jacquette Marble Works: 342, 353, 359.
Jacquette, Robert: 352.
James, James: 178.
James, Patience: 69.
Jamestown, Virginia: 92.
Janson, Catherine: 92, 93.
Janvier, Rev. George W.: 200, 212.
Jayne, Dr. David: 193.
Jeffers, John E.: 216, 240.
Jeffers, William N.: 203, 205, 207, 208, 211-213, 215-217, 260, 261, 323.
Jenkins, Rev. Nathaniel: 113.
Jericho: 52, 54.
Johnson: 65.
Johnson Guards: 273-275.
Johnson, Isaac: 213, 219.
Johnson, Reyneer: 82.
Johnson, Richard: 64, 66.
Johnson, Richard, House of: 64.
Johnson, Robert Carney: 255, 271, 282, 323.
Johnson, Robert Gibbon, historian: 8, 16, 32, 64, 66, 155, 161, 162, 196, 198, 200, 202, 205, 206, 208, 210, 227, 242, 250.
Johnson Street: 644.
Johnson, William: 360.
Jones: 68.
Jones, John: 84, 90, 371.
Jones, Owen L.: 299, 301.
Jones, Samuel: 188.
Jones, Thomas: 193.

Kalm, Prof. Peter: 107.
Keasbey, Anthony: 177, 371.
Keasbey's Creek: 299, 354.
Keasbey, Delzil: 199.
Keasbey, Dr. Edw.: 69, 138, 166, 171.
Keasbey, Howard B.: 360.
Keasbey Meadow Co.: 196.
Keasbey, Prudence: 69.
Keasbey, Dr. Quinton: 245, 321, 331.
Keith, Geo.: 68.
Keller (Magician): 327.
Kelly, Mary: 91.
Kelsey: 190.
Kelty, Clinton: 330, 337, 350.
Kelty, William: 314.
Kendall, Joseph: 172.
Keen's Hotel: 261.
Keen, Jonas: 178.
Keen, Mounce: 129.
Keen, Nicholas: 166.
Kenney, Stephen: 85.
Kent's Corner: 61, 285.
Kent Street: 54.
Kidd, Robert W.: 362.
Kieff, William: 8, 9.
Kiger, Adam: 109.
Kiger, J. S.: 328.
Kiger House: 110.
Kiger (Geiger) Mathew: 109.
Kille, Joseph: 203, 206, 211, 221, 251-252, 258, 268, 270-271, 294.
Kile, slave: 134-137.
Killingsworth, Thomas: 61, 68, 69.
King's Highway: 45, 53.
Kinseyville: 62.
Kirby: 68.
Kizar: 78.
Kline, Samuel: 302.
Knights of New Albion: 6,7,8.
Kollock, Isaac: 185.
Konigsford, Conrad: 97.

Lambert, John H.: 227, 228, 251, 253, 290, 302.
Lamberton: 41.
Lambson: 106.
Lambson, Thomas: 211.
Langhorne, Richard: 44-46.
Langley, Joel: 351.
Langley, Reuben: 139.
Laughlin, J. W.: 308.
La Ray Theatre: 353.
Latrobe, Benj. H.: 213.
Lawrence, Horatio: 206.
Lawrence, William: 320.
Lawrie, Gawen: 19-21, 30-32, 43-45.
Lawrie, Thomas: 258.
Lawson, Charles: 324.
Lawson, Edward: 199.
Lawson, Frank: 342.
Lawson, W. H.: 331.

INDEX

Leake, Samuel: 34, 169.
Leap, S. Rusling: 363.
Lecroy, Dorothy: 86.
Lecroy, Samuel: 336.
Lee, Michael: 130.
Leeds, George W.: 243.
Lefever, Hippolite: 25.
Lefevre, Mrs.: 41.
Lefevres, Chase: 54-55.
Levine, William: 324.
Lewes, Delaware: 13.
Lidenius, Rev. Abraham: 106.
Lippard, George: 264.
Lippincott: 67.
Lippincott, Jacob M.: 4, 237, 320, 322, 336, 374.
Lippincott, Joshua: 272.
Lippincott, Samuel: 337.
Lippincott, William: 202.
Little Creek: 315.
Livingston, Governor William: 168, 171-174.
Lloyd, Bateman: 174, 178.
Lloyd, Stacy: 182, 205.
Locke, Ismael: 230-231, 251.
Logansport, Indiana: 189.
Logtown: 112.
Longbaugh, Henry: 172.
Long, Edward: 194.
Long Lane, Battle of: 155.
Lord, Samuel: 309.
Loscalzo, Dr. Horace: 363.
Loudenslager, Charles: 258.
Loudenslager, H. C.: 342, 350.
Lowden, Anthony: 163.
Lower Alloways Creek: 55, 160, 164-165, 191-193, 240, 296, 339, 340, 363.
Lower Penns Neck: 112, 113, 146, 155, 198-199, 206, 211, 285, 296, 308, 332.
Lovell, William: 243-245.
Lucas, Nicholas: 19-21, 30-32, 43-45.
Lucky Bridge: 354.
Lumies Sawlay: 54.
Lummis, John C.: 266.
Lummis Store: 354.
Lupton, 67.
Lutheran Church: 70, 110, 265.
Lutherland, Thomas: 57-60.

MacCausland, J. W.: 358.
Mackassen: 94.
Mackinippuck: 2.
Mahawsky: 27.
Mahoppany Creek: 2, 26.
Major's Wharf: 302-304, 355.
Malander, Rev. Olaf: 107.
Malster, William: 25, 29, 39.
Mammo, Catherine: 97.
Maneto: 2, 55.
Manimuska: 2.
Mannington: 2, 55, 62, 76, 183-184, 195-196, 211, 257, 271, 296, 315, 333, 344, 351, 359.
Mannington Creek: 53.
Mannington Mills: 220, 370.
Mannington, W. Va.: 188.
Margarets Lane: 119.
Marshall, James: 92.
Marshalltown (Frogtown): 323.
Marston, William: 332.
Maskell: 70.
Maskell, Daniel: 169, 270.

Mason, Rev. Henry M.: 214.
Masons, Lodge of: 210, 220.
Mason, John: 64.
Mason, John G.: 199, 208, 215.
Mastodon: 2.
Mattson, H. A.: 282.
Mawhood, Col. Charles: 146-149, 150, 155-156, 165-167, 176.
Maul, Eliza: 195.
Maurice River: 56, 242.
Mayhew: 113.
Mayhew, John: 171.
Mayhew, Tabitha: 114.
Mayhew, Mrs.: 174.
Mayhew, Anna W.: 223.
McCabe, John: 314-316.
McCalla, James: 217.
McClellan, George B.: 296, 321.
M'Clure, A. K.: 326.
McCullough, F. L.: 211, 244, 258.
McCune, John P.: 258.
McDonnell, John: 354.
McDaniel, David: 255.
McDaniel, James: 255.
McKay, Lt.: 150.
McKim, Mr.: 226.
Mechanicsburg, Ohio: 189.
Mecum Building: 348.
Mecum, James W.: 295.
Mecum, William: 171.
Menantico: 2.
Meridian House: 293, 355.
Merrion, Preston P.: 346.
Merritt, Solomon: 252-253.
Methodist Church: 115-121, 179, 193, 203, 222, 226, 232, 265, 294, 303, 311, 331, 333, 364.
Meyer: 94.
Mickle, Harry: 342.
Mickleton: 146.
Middleton, Hugh: 61, 75.
Middletown Road (Penton): 293.
Mifflin, William T.: 362.
Militia, List of: 138-139.
Miles, Francis:113.
Mill Hollow: 149-151.
Miller: 67.
Millerites: 232.
Miller, Henry: 258.
Miller, John: 243.
Miller, Joseph: 202.
Miller Lot: 254.
Miller, Mark: 208.
Miller, Michael: 172.
Miller, Richard C.: 351.
Miller, Samuel W.: 271, 307.
Miller, William: 171.
Miller, William Finlaw: 360.
Miller, Wyatt: 336.
Mills, Ephraim: 169.
Mills, Isaiah: 129.
Milltown: 89.
Mitchell, Colonel: 160.
Mitchell, Elizabeth: 286.
Mitchell, Dr. S. Weir: 286-289.
Mahut: 27.
Moonly Voice: 308, 323.
Moore: 70.
Moore, A. Harry: 362.
Moore, Richard: 113.
Moore, Alexander: 132.
Moore, Patrick: 163.

INDEX

Monmouth: 55, 56.
Monroeville: 331.
Moravians: 107-144.
Morrison, Harry P.: 373.
Morrison, George: 319, 321, 335, 337, 350.
Morgan, Dr.: 312.
Morristown: 142.
Morphey, Edmund: 90.
Mormons: 232.
Morris, Elijah: 255.
Morris, E. O.: 346.
Morris, Robert: 346.
Morris, Redroe: 64.
Morris, W. H.: 363.
Morris William: 301.
Morris William: 255.
Morrow, Dwight: 362.
Morton, Russell S.: 354.
Mosacka: 2, 26.
Moseleys Shield: 54.
Moss: 67.
Mott, Lucretia: 289.
Mt. Holly: 144.
Mt. Pisgah A. M. E. Church: 339.
Muddy Run: 242.
Muhlenburg: 110.
Mulford, H. B.: 348.
Mulford's Hotel: 274.
Mulford, Jacob W.: 291.
Mullica Hill: 276, 277.
Murphy, John: 116.
Murphy, Thomas: 179.
Muskingum, Ohio: 190.
Muttontown Woods: 176.
Myggenborg: 13.

Nasby, Petroleum V.: 301.
Nashville, Tenn.: 191.
National Standard: 235, 306, 307.
Neary, Fiddler: 313.
Nelson, Daniel: 260.
Nelson House: 260.
Nelson, Joseph: 218.
Nelson, William H.: 294.
Neutze, Frank F.: 359.
Nevills: 112.
Neville, James: 25, 48-50.
Newcomb, Capt. John: 26.
Newcomb, Gen. Silas: 141-169.
Newby, Mark: 26.
Newell, James: 179, 222, 251, 258, 349.
Newell, John S.: 296, 299, 313.
Newell, Robert: 271.
Newell, William: 337, 344.
New Amsterdam: 8-13.
New Bethel: 203.
Newhall, John B.: 190.
New Castle, Del.: 13, 87-88, 194, 196, 200, 290, 306, 348.
New Haven Colony: 8-15.
New Jersey Farmer and Literary Gazette: 217.
Newkirks: 111.
Newkirk, Isaac: 319.
Newkirk's Oyster Saloon: 354.
Newkirk Station: 293.
Nichols, Lorenzo: 314.
Nicholson: 25.
Nicholson, Abel: 25.
Nicholson, Capt.: 26.
Nicholson, Elizabeth: 25.

Nicholson, Joseph: 25.
Nicholson, Parobal: 25.
Nicholson, Samuel: 25.
Nicholsons Frank: 172.
Nicomis: 226.
Nielsons: 65.
Nixon, Jeremiah: 114.
Noble, Richard: 29-32.
Noble, Thomas: 153.
Norma: 324.
Norris, Thomas: 171.
North: 186.
North Bend, Battle of: 314-315.
North Cohansey: 55.
Northampton County, Virginia: 104.

Oak, Old: 3, 66.
Oak Street: 235.
Oakford: 67.
Oakford House: 174-176.
Oakford, William: 174.
Oakland Station: 89, 293, 328.
Oakland Mills: 223.
Oakwood Beach: 262, 354, 355.
Obisquahassit: 2.
O'Brien, Mary Ann: 126.
Observer, Salem: 185-186.
Ogden, Isaac: 189.
Ogden, Jedidiah: 189.
Ogden, Samuel: 169.
Ogilby: 23.
Ohio Pyle. Pa.: 190.
Oldmans: 119, 363.
Oldmans Creek: 21, 34, 45.
Opera House, Salem: 324-327, 338, 341, 352-353, 359.
Orr, Alexander: 222.
Outhout, Foppe Jansen: 38-39.

Pages Plantation: 54.
Palatine: 192.
Pancoast, Charles Edward: 191, 255.
Pancoast, Josiah: 243.
Pancoast, Morris Hall: 358.
Pancoast, William: 245.
Pancoast, T. B. Reed: 360.
Parks Hotel: 261.
Parks, J.: 342.
Parrott, Isabelle: 263.
Parrott, Street: 299.
Parrott, William: 178, 179.
Parsons, Ann: 25.
Parsons, Harry: 346.
Parsons, Mark: 25.
Passwater, Mrs.: 354.
Patterson, Benj.: 308.
Patterson and Jones: 301, 302.
Patterson, Robert: 169.
Patrick, Anthony: 191.
Paulding Station: 293.
Paullins Hotel: 209, 213.
Payne, Capt. Edward: 26.
Paynes Pytle: 54.
Pea Patch Island: 286.
Peck: 70.
Peck, John: 169.
Pedrick, Rodger: 30.
Penns Grove: 220, 254, 261, 304, 308, 315, 342, 352, 365.
Penns Grove, fire at: 359, 360.
Penns Grove Press: 308.
Penns Grove Record: 308.

INDEX

Penn, William: 19-21, 30-32, 43-45, 48-50.
Penns Neck: 55, 65, 69, 106-108, 112, 113, 165, 192.
Pennsville, fights at: 310-313.
Penny Hill: 242, 260.
Penton: 331.
Penton, William: 39.
Perry, William: 191.
Perskie, Joseph: 371.
Perth Amboy: 80.
Petersfield: 54.
Peterson, George: 258.
Peterson, Isaac C.: 254.
Pettigrew, General James J.: 287.
Pettit, M. Augusta Austin: 5.
Pettit, Clark: 338.
Pettit, David: 292, 304.
Pettit, George W.: 294.
Philpott, N.: 65.
Pickle Plant: 355.
Picturs, Lucas: 39.
Pierce, Reuben: 308.
Piercey, Christian: 186.
Pierpont, Dr.: 333.
Pig's Eye (Harrisonville) 346.
Pilesgrove: 54, 55, 65, 69, 106-108, 112, 113.
Pioneer's Pond: 354.
Pinhorne: 73.
Pittsgrove: 182, 242.
Pittstown: 297.
Plantagenet: 6.
Pledger: 189.
Pledger, John: 25.
Ployden, Lord Edmund: 6-10, 14, 15.
Plummer, Charles S.: 320.
Plummer, Loren P.: 351, 360, 362.
Plummer, William: 271, 302, 344, 360.
Plummer, Samuel: 257, 269, 271, 296, 297, 299.
Port Elizabeth: 68.
Portsmouth, Ohio: 189.
Powell, William: 291.
Powers, Charles W.: 350.
Presbyterian Church: 70, 110-113, 200-202, 264, 324, 364.
Prescott, Institute: 236.
Prescott, Margaret Smith: 262.
Prescott, Edward: 240, 251.
Price, John C.: 345.
Prior, Samuel: 220, 227, 251.
Printz, John: 11.
Proctor, George: 86, 87.
Provoes, Holt: 54.
Pyle, Thomas: 54.

Quaker Neck: 155, 354.
Quakers, underground railroad of: 229-230.
Quarry, Robert: 73.
Queen's Rangers: 148, 156, 159.
Quihawkin Church: 112.
Quinton: 54, 55, 69, 150, 160, 167, 305, 308, 324, 331, 337, 339, 340, 344, 359.
Quinton's Bridge: 130, 148, 152, 154, 173, 230, 244, 245, 276.
Quinton, Edward: 90.
Quinton Glass Co.: 302.
Quinton, John: 90.
Quinton, Temperance: 69.

Race Track: 294, 306, 354, 355.
Ragged Island: 128.
Rains, Isaac: 153.
Ramong, Capt.: 87.
Randolph, Charles: 243.
Ray, Samuel: 179.
Ray, Wallace: 358.
Ray, Zachees: 199-218.
Reedy Island: 128.
Reed: 113.
Reese, Dr. Charles L.: 366-369.
Reeve, Mark: 25.
Reeve, Samuel: 225.
Reeves: 189.
Reeves, Andrew Smith: 298, 335.
Reeves, Elmer: 258.
Reeves, Hildreth: 363.
Reeves, Josiah: 163, 205, 294.
Reeves, Thomas: 204.
Reeves, William: 226, 227, 228, 229, 230, 235, 242, 292.
Reckless, Amy: 323.
Reliance Fire Co.: 209.
Repauno: 369.
Reybold, Capt. Eugene: 330.
Richman, Abraham: 292.
Richman, Moses: 177.
Richmond, Indiana: 191.
Richmond, Luther: 350, 351.
Richmantown: 331.
Ridgeway, Samuel: 360.
Riley, James: 191.
Ridman: 94, 110.
Roadstown: 123, 168, 169, 203.
Roberts, Ned: 245.
Robertson, Archibald: 164, 165.
Robinson, Benjamin: 198.
Robeson, George M.: 335.
Rock, John S.: 250.
Rolph, John: 90.
Roosney, John: 285.
Roosney, Patrick: 285.
Rosenhayn: 123.
Round Island: 344.
Rowan, John: 166, 177, 202.
Rumsey Building: 295, 307, 326.
Rumsey, Daniel: 77.
Rumsey, Elizabeth: 90.
Ryan, William: 341.

Sadler, William: 227.
Salem Academy: 250, 372.
Salem and Bridgeton Turn Pike Co.: 290.
Salem Country Club: 355.
Salem County Historical Society: 330.
Salem County Memorial Hospital: 340, 371.
Salem Collegiate Institute: 303, 304.
Salem, fire at: 316.
Salem Glass Works: 293, 301, 346, 370.
Salem, Indiana: 187, 190.
Salem, Iowa: 187, 190.
Salem Library: 330.
Salem Light: 308.
Salem Knitting Mills: 342, 353, 359.
Salem, Massachusetts: 209.
Salem Messenger: 199.
Steam Mill: 207, 212, 215-218; (See also Salem National Bank).

INDEX

Salem National Bank: 323, 334, 370. (See also Steam Mill).
Salem National Bank: 215, 235.
Salem, Ohio: 187, 188, 190.
Salem, Oregon: 187, 190, 192.
Salem-Penns Grove Traction Co.: 357, 365.
Salem Railroad: 291, 292, 324, 330-340.
Salem Record: 308.
Salem Soap Works: 323.
Salem Statesman: 217, 220.
Salem Sunbeam: 235, 307.
Salem, Telepraph in: 317.
Salem Union: 220.
Salinsky, Myer: 324.
Satterthwaite, Phoebe: 91.
Sand Hole: 354.
Sandy Burr, Wood: 54.
Sandy Point: 58.
Sandin, Rev. John: 107.
Sandwich, Mass.: 92.
Saunders, Captain: 157.
Saunders, Thomas: 227.
Sayre, Abbott: 163.
Sayre, Ananias: 123, 168.
Sayre, James: 70, 163.
Sayre, John: 162.
Sayre, Joseph: 163.
Sayre, Leonard: 190.
Sayre, Reuben: 162.
Sayre, Reuel: 161, 190.
Sayre, Thomas: 161, 171.
Schacanum, Indian: 26.
Schade, John D.: 360.
Schalick, W. Orvyl: 353, 362, 371.
Schenk, Rev. William: 112.
Schmidt, Rev. Frederick: 144.
Schnider, Father: 109.
Schoepf, General: 287.
Scroggins, Jacob: 127.
Scultown (Now Auburn): 140, 198, 209.
Seagraves, Artis: 177.
Seeley: 70, 123.
Seeley, Enos: 169.
Seeley, Josiah: 132.
Sefreit, Joseph: 232.
Segebarth, Colonel Herman: 387.
Seven Stars Tavern: 54.
Sewell, William J.: 292, 323.
Shakers: 232.
Sharp, Edward: 287, 339.
Sharp, Isaac: 78.
Sharp, Thomas: 178.
Sharp, W. S.: 306.
Sharptown: 53, 109, 144, 191, 202, 222, 261.
Sharptown M. E. Church: 268.
Shaw, Anna Howard: 339.
Shell Road: 356.
Sheppard: 67, 265.
Sheppard, Catherine: 69.
Sheppard, Charlton: 161.
Sheppard, David: 129, 190.
Sheppard, Furman: 163.
Sheppard, Hope: 190.
Sheppard, J. P.: 342.
Sheppard, Reuben: 191.
Sherron, Dr. Clifford: 343.
Sherron Hotel: 201, 213, 221, 284, 291.
Sherron, James 76-78, 185, 187, 202, 294.
Sherron, Samuel H.: 193, 222, 237, 254.
Sherry, Recompense: 134.
Sherry, Boston: 134.
Shiloh: 70.
Shimp, William: 290, 336.
Shinn, Everett: 358.
Shinn, Isaiah: 185.
Shinn, Joseph: 194.
Shinn, Wm. J.: 210, 215, 306.
Ships: Aetna, 196; Beginning, 81; Belle of Mt. Holly, 229; Charles, 227; Clifton, 222, 240, 241; Cohansey, 273; Dolphin, 81; Dorothea, 26; Dragon, 81; Essex, 150, 211-221; Exeter, 81; Express, 235; Flushing, 222; Gale, 81; Greyhound, 132; Griffin, 25, 26, 308; Henry and Ann, 26; Hornet, 140; Jersey, 173; Kent, 26, 37; Lafayette, 207; La Fortune, 85, 87, 88, 194; Le Tigre, 198, 276; Liverpool, 139; Livingston, 241; Lexington, 139, 140; Marianna, 206; May Montayne, 304; Major Reybold, 288, 289, 302, 307, 330; Mary, 26; Miantomi, 263; Morning Star, 81; New Adventure, 26; New Jersey, 241;Ohio, 222; Perkins, 81; Perry, 311; Pioneer, 226, 240, 330; Pons, 229-230; Raccoon, 229; Reprisal, 140; Roebuck, 139, 146; Robt. Morris, 222; Salem, 222, 229; Shield, Stockton, 26; Stephen, Baldwin, 229; Success, 81; Towanda, 229; Tyrall, 81; Warwick, 254; Yorketown, 315.
Shoemaker, David: 245.
Shourds: 265.
Shourds, Thomas: 11, 114, 257, 258, 261, 309.
Shreve, Colonel Israel: 169-171.
Shreve, William: 235-237.
Shuccotery, Indian: 26.
Shute, William: 166.
Sickler, Adam: 206.
Sickler, Charles: 328.
Sickler, Edward M.: 351.
Sickler, Dr. John R.: 275, 276.
Sickler, Joseph S.: 362.
Sickler, Smith: 332.
Sickler, William B.: 99.
Sicklerville: 353.
Sikes, Esther: 89.
Silver: 67.
Silver, Aaron: 130.
Simpkins, Job: 214.
Sims, Abner: 100.
Sims, Samuel: 100.
Sims, Sarah: 100.
Sinnickson: 106, 191.
Sinnickson, Andrew: 155, 166, 171, 194.
Sinnickson, Clement: 320, 321.
Sinnickson, Harriet: 328.
Sinnickson, J. Forman: 343.
Sinnickson, Dr. John Jacob: 225, 226.
Sinnickson, Robert: 308, 323.
Sinnickson, Thomas: 162, 177, 180.
Sixth N. J. Volunteers: 346.
Smart, Isaac: 25, 64-66.
Smick, Isaac: 360-361.
Smiley, J. W.: 295.
Smith: 25.
Smith, Andrew: 245.
Smith, Benj.: 269.

INDEX

Smith, Charles Perrine: 239, 252, 253, 269, 274, 292, 327.
Smith, D. Harris: 308.
Smith, Edward: 208-209.
Smith, Ellen Bradway, M. D.: 163.
Smith, John: 1.
Smith, John: 144.
Smith, John: 177.
Smith, Lydia: 140.
Smith, Phoebe: 69.
Smith, Richard: 89.
Smith, Samuel: 129.
Smith, Sarah: 69.
Smith, Merriam: 184.
Smith, Capt. William: 140, 141, 150-153, 171.
Sneathen, Joseph: 69.
Sneathen, Rachel: 69.
Sneathen, Waitel: 163.
Snitcher, Harry: 346.
Sooy, John: 214.
South Cohansey: 55.
South Jerseyman: 235.
Sowder: 74, 110, 111.
Spanish War, influence on Salem: 344-348.
Sparks: 111.
Sparks, Clement: 314.
Sparks, David: 258.
Sparks, Henry: 168.
Sparks, Simeon: 198.
Spencer: 126.
Sportsman Hotel: 201.
Steam Mill: 215-220.
St. Georges: 106-108.
St. Johns Church: 102-108, 199, 200.
St. Stevens: 104, 105.
Stacks, Henry: 132.
Stanley: 112.
Stanley, Henry M.: 288.
Stanton, George: 349.
Star Hall Corner: 284.
Starr Canning Factory: 301, 302.
Starr, Richard T.: 349.
Stenger, Jacob: 97.
Stewart: 67.
Stewart, Frank H.: 51, 161.
Stewart, Samuel: 191.
Stevens, Rev. Abel: 117.
Stevenson, Capt.; 157, 158.
Stiles and Freas: 354.
Stoughton and Belden: 254.
Stow Creek: 128, 221.
Stratton, Rev. Daniel: 294.
Streets: 188.
Streets, Salem: 228.
Street, Zadock: 188-190.
Stretch: 67, 191.
Stretch, John: 128.
Stretch, Joseph: 200.
Stretch, Peter: 245.
Strimple, James: 349-351, 360.
Stuart, Charles Edward: 85.
Stuarts, Insurrection of: 86.
Stubbins: 67.
Stump, John: 144, 153.
Stuyvesant, Peter: 13, 14.
Swedes, Settlement of: 11-14, 53, 64, 109, 149, 191, 202.
Swedesboro: 108, 146.
Swinney: 69.

Swinney, Deborah: 69.
Swing, Charles P.: 194, 205, 320.
Sullivan, Howard: 328-330.
Summerlin, Capt. John D.: 328.
Summerill, John: 171, 218, 253, 265.
Summerill, William A.: 308.
Sutton, Jacob: 172.
Sutton, John: 172.
Sutton, Moses: 172.
Sutton, Thomas: 172.

Taft, William H.: 361.
Taggert, Jacob: 171.
Tattletown: 54.
Taylor, Augustus: 217.
Taylor, John: 341.
Taylor, Wallace, 258.
Telegraph: 317.
Telegraph Road: 234, 262.
Test: 67.
Test, Edward: 130.
Test, John: 191.
Test, Samuel: 191.
Test, Sarah: 91.
Temperance Hotel: 234.
Thomas, John M.: 240.
Thompson: 191.
Thompson, Benjamin: 94.
Thompson's Bridge: 93, 148, 158, 175, 229.
Thompson, Dr. J.: 245, 274.
Thompson, Hedge: 179, 202.
Thompson, John: 83, 269.
Thompson, Joseph: 162, 291.
Thompson, Joshua: 194.
Thompson, Missionary: 105.
Thompson, Richard P.: 240, 246, 258, 290, 294.
Thompson's Store: 354.
Thompson, Thomas: 166.
Thunderbolt Race Track: 294, 306.
Titus, William: 258.
Tide Mill Meadow Co.: 196.
Tindall, Richard: 32, 50.
Tobel: 94, 110.
Torucho, Indian: 27.
Tospaninkey, Indian: 26.
Townsend: 68.
Townsend, Emory: 331.
Tracy, Jeremiah: 254.
Treadway, Mary: 257-260.
Treadway, Samuel: 257-260.
Trollenger: 94, 110.
Tuft, John: 177.
Tranberg, Swedish Minister: 106, 107.
Trap, Tavern: 209, 210.
Trenchard, Curtis: 177.
Trenchard, Thomas: 371.
Troy, New York: 359.
Turner, Robert: 25.
Turner, Capt. Nathaniel: 9.
Twelfth New Jersey Regiment: 282.
Twenty-fourth New Jersey Regiment: 280, 331.
Tyler: 67.
Tyler, Catherine: 189.
Tyler, Job: 204.
Tyler, John: 360.
Tyler, Richard: 194.
Tyler, Tannery: 196, 355.
Tyndales Bowery: 54.

INDEX

Underground Railroad, of Quakers: 230-231.
Union Fire Company: 201.
Upper Alloways Creek: 134, 139, 183, 283, 305.
Upper Penns Neck: 119, 139, 283, 296, 363.
Upper Pittsgrove: 128, 138, 255, 296.

Valley Forge: 142, 143, 145, 168.
Vanneman: 106.
Vanneman, Joel: 346.
Vanneman, Robert N.: 351.
Van Meter: 112.
Van Meter, Henry: 316.
Van Meter, Dr. James: 112, 209.
Van Meter, Robert: 112, 195.
Varkens Kill: 7-10.
Van Thirst, Raynier: 38, 61.
Vickers: 70.
Vining, Capt.: 102.
Von Helfenstein, Edward C.: 5.

Waddington: 67.
Waddington, Joseph: 295, 299.
Waddington, Pauline: 303.
Wade, Edward: 25.
Wade, Rev. John: 108.
Wade, Robert: 25.
Wade, Samuel: 25.
Walker-Weeden, fight of: 311-314.
Wallace: 113, 204.
Wallace, Allan: 363.
Wallace, John: 258.
War, World, influence on Salem: 373, 374.
Ward, John C.: 337, 350.
Ward, George M.: 227, 231, 290.
Ware: 67.
Ware, Henry B.: 317.
Ware, Henry Burt: 341.
Ware, Jacob: 189.
Ware, Maskell: 313.
Ware, Thomas: 193, 222.
Warner, Edmund: 23-32, 41-44.
Warner, Simon: 150.
Wasse, James: 30, 44.
Watson, Ella: 328-330.
Watson, John Fanning: 57.
Watsons Ranthorpe: 54.
Wayman, William: 188.
Wayne, Gen. Anthony: 142-145.
Weatherby: 149.
Weatherby, Edmond: 137.
Webbs Arladon: 54.
Webb, Edward: 25.
Weedon-Walker, fight of: 311-314.
Weekly Visitor: 220.
Wells, Isreal: 235, 254.
Wentzell, John: 93, 94.
Wertenbaker, T. J.: 88.
Westcott, Benj.: 351, 360.
Westcott, Joseph: 358.
West Fenwick: 55.
West Jersey: 29, 30, 32, 34, 37.
West Jersey Gazette: 185.
Western Union: 371.
Whalen, Washington: 314.
Wheatley, William M.: 361.
Wheeler's: 235.
Wheeler, Caleb: 237.

Whittaker: 189-190.
Whittaker, Richard: 25, 172.
Whittaker, Summerill: 189.
Whites: 67.
White, Christopher: 189.
White, John Moore: 112.
White, Joseph: 189.
White, Josiah: 189.
Whites Dene: 54.
Whitefield, George: 111, 112, 117.
White's Vineyard: 54.
Whiteworth, Abraham: 116, 117.
Wick, Jacob: 214-217.
Wildermuth, Horace, 342.
Wildermuth, James: 342.
Wilkinson, William: 25.
Willett, Chalkley: 342.
Willett, George: 348.
Williams, Josiah: 163.
Williams, Mary: 78.
Williard, Francis: 339.
Willis, W. B.: 313.
Wilson, Ward: 205, 206.
Wilson, Woodrow: 361, 362.
Windham: 11.
Windrufea: 107.
Windsor, Eliza: 90.
Windsor, Samuel: 51.
Winters, John: 243.
Wistar: 191.
Wistar, Casper: 92-98.
Wistar, John: 98, 291.
Wistar, Josiah: 343.
Wistar, Richard: 94-98.
Wistar, Sarah: 98.
Wistar, Wyatt: 99.
Wistarburg Glass Works: 92-98.
Wood: 67.
Wood, B. Frank: 342.
Wood, Jechonias: 130.
Wood, Richard:123.
Wood, William: 344.
Woodnutt, Thomas: 188.
Woodnutt, Ann: 91.
Woodnutt, Richard: 89, 302.
Woodruff, Thomas: 60, 61.
Woodside, John: 245, 246.
Woodstown: 54, 67, 193, 196, 198, 202, 213, 222, 264, 265, 282, 292, 308, 317, 331, 332, 348, 356.
Woolson, Woole: 60.
Woolverson: 65.
Wootsessingsung: 2.
Worledge, John: 58.
Worth, Joseph: 25.
Worth, Rev. Wm.: 113.
Wright: 112.
Wright, Daniel: 348.
Wright, Frank: 351.
Wright, Henry M.: 298.
Wright's Store: 355.
Wyatt, Bartholomew: 132.
Wyncoop's Woods: 176.

Yarrow, Dr. Thomas: 195, 245.
Y. M. C. A.: 294, 341, 342.
Yorke, Lewis: 290, 292, 306.
Yorke, Lewis Eugene: 185, 189.
Yorke, Patton: 189.
Yorke, Sarah: 189.
Yorke Street: 69.

INDEX

Yorke, Thomas: 57.
Yorke, Thomas Jones: 227, 252, 258, 290, 291. 306, 333.
Yorketown, New Jersey: 293, 328.
Youker, Frank: 346.

Zager, Joseph: 324.
Zaiser House: 147.
Zanes, Joseph: 205.
Zanes, Robert: 66.
Zanesville, Ohio: 190.
Ziegler: 110.

ERRATA

Page 145, Line 8: read "wrote" for "whote".
Page 160, Line 15: Mitchell, Lieutenant Colonel Mitchell of the 27th regular British regiment.
Page 185, Line 29, should read: "the West Jersey Gazette was the first paper published in."
Page 189, Lines 24 to 29: Jacob Reed Ware is twice named. The secend entry should be "his descendant Enid Ware Foster is now a prominent attorney of Mechanicsburg, Ohio."
Page 251, Line 20: Rev. William Prescott should read Rev. Edward Prescott.
On map: Spot marked "Here High Sheriff of Salem County was murdered by his slaves" should actually be in Mannington Township on the Kings Highway, two and a half miles from Salem, instead of in Pittsgrove Township as shown.

ADDENDA

Page 157: Line 44, Samuel Gosling's family has now dropped the "g" and are known as Goslin. One of his relatives, much renowned, is Leon Goslin, commonly known as "Goose" who has carried the name of his home town, Salem, to fame on the baseball field. Mr. Goslin has terminated seventeen years service (1920-1937) in the major professional baseball leagues having been a member of the Detroit, St. Louis and Washington teams in the American League.
Page 260: Among the deaths of 1850 was that of Robert Gibbon Johnson, first historian of Salem who died at New Haven, Conn., in October of that year.
Page 286: Regarding first four paragraphs, Dr. S. Weir Mitchell uses this same set of facts as part of the plot in his novel "Roland Blake."

BIBLIOGRAPHY

Newspaper Files
Archives of New Jersey: Newspaper Extracts 1704-1783.
Elmer Times: 1883-1937.
Penns Grove Record: 1884-1937.
Salem Freeman's Banner: 1834-1840.
National Standard: 1840-1904.
New Jersey Farmer and Literary Gazette: 1830-1831.
Salem Messenger: 1819-1834.
Salem Observer: May 4, 1799.
South Jerseyman: 1881-1904.
Standard and Jerseyman: 1904-1937.
Salem Sunbeam: 1844-1937.
Salem Union: 1834-1836.
Weekly Visitor: 1834.
West Jersey Gazette: 1816-1819.
Trenton State Gazette: 1794-1810.
Trenton True American: 1801-1820.
Woodstown Monitor-Register: 1892-1937.

Books and Pamphlets
Acton, Richard M.: Paper on old Wistar Glass Works, 1885.
Andrews, Bessie A.: "Old Houses of Greenwich."
Archives, Church of England: London, Sir Edward Colpoys Midwinter, Archivist.
Allen, Samuel A.: "My Own Home and Fireside", London, 1846.
Barber and Howe: Historical Collections of N. J.: Newark, 1860.
Beck, Henry C.: "Forgotten Towns of South Jersey", New York, 1936.
Borton, Benj.: "Awhile With the Blue".
Bowers, Claude G.: "The Tragic Era".
Boyer, Charles S.: "Early Forges and Furnaces of New Jersey", Phila., 1931. "Notes on Old Taverns" (unpublished).

BIBLIOGRAPHY

Asbury, Herbert: Article on Benj. Abbott, "American Mercury", 1926.
Burr, Amelia: Life of S. Weir Mitchell.
Clayton, Mary R. C.: Graveyard Inscriptions of Salem.
Crowe, Edward: "Reminiscenses of Company F.", Salem, 1931.
Elmer, L. Q. C.: "History of Cumberland County", Bridgeton, 1869.
Ferris: "Early Settlements on the Delaware."
First Congressional District: 2 volumes, Phila., 1900.
Firth, John: "Life and Gospel Labors of Benjamin Abbott."
Flynn, John: "History of the Catholic Church in New Jersey."
French, Samuel G.: "Under Two Flags", Nashville, Tenn., 1904.
Friendship Methodist Church, History of
Goggin, Margaret, "Poems."
Green, Ashbel: Autobiography.
Green, Thomas J.: "The Mier Expedition in Mexico."
Heston, Alfred M.: "Jersey Wagon Jaunts."
Hunter, F. W.: "Steigel Glass", 1914.
Johnson, Robert Gibbon: "Historical Account of the First Settlement of Salem", Philadelphia, 1839; "Historical Notes", Salem, 1844.
Jones, Edson Salisbury: "Notes on Salem County", 1907.
Kittle, R. M.: "Early American Glass", New York, 1927.
Lee, F. B.: "New Jersey as a Colony and a State," 1902.
Lippincott, Jacob M.: "Poems". London, 1898.
Maylin, Anna W.: "Poems".
Mecum, Ellen: "The Old Dick Garden."
New Jersey Historical Society; Publication of: 1846-1937.
Parrott, Isabell: "Poems".
Patterson, William: "Steamboats and Other Notes".
Pancoast, Charles Edward: "Quaker 49'er".
Pettit, M. Augusta A.: "Battle of Quinton's Bridge", Salem, 1908. Notes.
Pettit, Clark: "Old Houses of Mannington", Salem Sunbeam, 1907.
Pittsgrove Presbyterian Church, History of: Pamphlet.
Robertson, Archibald: Diary of
Sackett, W. H.: "Modern Battles of Trenton".

Salem County Court Records; Salem Clerk's Office, 1706-1937.
Salem County Hand Book; W. H. Chew, Compiler, Salem, 1924.
Simkins, James: "Account of Revolution in Salem County."
Sharpe, Dr. E. S.: "Schools of Salem, Braithwaite Hall, Old Cannon and other notes."
Sheppard, Charles E., "Cushing's and Sheppard's History of Salem, Cumberland and Gloucester Counties", Philadelphia, 1883.
Shourds, Thomas: "History of Fenwick's Colony", Bridgeton, N. J., 1876.
Sickler, Joseph S.: "Old Houses of Salem"; Salem, 1934.
Sickler, Joseph S.: "History of St. Johns Church", 1937.
Simcoe, John Graves: "Military Journal".
Smith, Ellen B., M. D.: "Massacre at Hancock's House", Salem, 1903.
Smith, Charles Perrine: "Autobiography in Longhand", Trenton State Library.
Sparks, James S.: "Old Salem Trails", Salem, 1932.
Stewart, Frank H.: "Foraging for Valley Forge"; Salem, 1929; "Salem County in the Revolution", Salem, 1932; "Salem Newspaper Extracts", Salem, 1933-1934; "Sharptown", Salem, 1930; Salem Notes in New Jersey Society of Pennsylvania Proceedings: 1930.
Stevens, Rev. Abel: "History of Methodism". 4 vols.
Stevens, Lewis T.: "History of Cape May", Cape May, 1897.
South Jersey, A History: 5 vols. 1923.
Wallace, U. S. Law Reporter: "Pea Patch Island Case".
Ward, Christopher: "Dutch and Swedes on the Delaware."
Watson, John Fanning: Annals of Philadelphia, 2 vols.
First National Bank of Woodstown: Almanacs: 1901-1921.
Van Meter, Annie H.: "History of Presbyterian Church of Salem", Salem, 1924.
Von Helfenstein, E.: "Lecture on Knights of New Albion", delivered in Salem, 1912.
Yorke, Thomas J.: "Photograph Album of old Salem Houses", 1888.

INDEX OF HISTORICAL FEATURE ARTICLES PUBLISHED IN THE SALEM SUNBEAM (1929-1936)

Abbott, Benj., Sketch of: Nov. 21, 1930.
Allen, Samuel: "My Own Home and Fireside": Jan. 2, 1931.
Alloway Ghost: July 6, 1932.
Burning at Stake: Jan. 22, 1936.
Brown, David P., alias David of York, Sketch of: Feb. 4, 1931.
Blue Beard of Burden Hill: March 23, 1932.
California Gold Rush: Oct. 17, 1930.
Elsinboro, Spanish raid upon: June 1, 1932.
Emergency Relief Administration: Aug. 12, 1936.
Fort Delaware: June 10, 1931.
Hall, William, sketch of: July 1, 1931.
Hancock's Bridge Massacre: April 1, 1931; April 8, 1931.
Hayes-Tilden Campaign in Salem: Aug. 17, 1932.
Jersey Devil: Feb. 11, 1931.
Kiger House, History of: May 4, 1932.
King Over the Water: Nov. 25, 1931.
Knights of New Albion: Oct. 7, 1931.
Local Option in 1847 and 1887: Apr. 12, 19, 1933.
Lutherland Murder Case: March 18, 1931.
Mannington Mastodon: Jan. 21, 1931.
Murder, Salem County cases: Dec. 12, 1930.
Murder, Salem County cases: March 23, 1932.
Murder Near the Seven Stars: July 8, 1931.
New Haven Colony: Oct. 14, 1931.
North Bend River Pirates: Sept. 19, 1930.
Old Salem Trails: July 13, 1932.
Pea Patch Island Case: Aug. 15, 1930.
Pennsville Prize Fights: Sept. 5, 12, 1930.
Pittsgrove College: June 17, 1931.
Pittsgrove Separation: Nov. 7, 1930.
Politics in Salem: April 13, Aug. 17, Aug. 31, Sept. 7, 1932.
Race Track, Johnson Street: March 18, 1936.
Railroad, Salem: Oct. 24, 1930.
Robertson, Archibald, Diary: Nov. 18, 1931.
Salem, Civil War History: April 15, May 6, 13, 27, 1931.
Salem Court House Removal Election: March 4, 1931.
Salem, derivation of: Nov. 28, 1930.
Salem County in Revolution: Jan. 2, 1935.
Salem Grand Opera House: Jan. 9, 14, 1931.
Salem Observer: July 22, 1931.
Salem in Spanish War: Feb. 25, 1931.
Salem's Saturday Night: May 25, 1932.
Salem in 1740's: June 8, 1932.
Salem Trolley: Aug. 10, 1932.
Sherron Murder Case: Oct. 10, 1930.
Sherry, Recompense, Murder case: Jan. 28, 1931.
Sketches of 1823; June 21, 1933.
Taverns of Early Salem County: Jan. 10, 1930.
Telephones: May 13, 1936.
Treadway Murder Case: Oct. 3, 1930.
Union Fire Company: June 29, 1932.
Washington's Reported Visit to Pole Tavern: Feb. 18, 1931.
White, Christopher: Dec. 26, 1930.
Wistarburgh Glass Works: Dec. 5, 1930.

www.ingramcontent.com/pod-product-compliance
Lightning Source LLC
Chambersburg PA
CBHW050833230426
43667CB00012B/1985